Critical Regard for
The Revolutionary Ecological Legacy of Herbert Marcuse

Charles Reitz is a major scholar of the work of Herbert Marcuse and an important commentator on the global crises faced by contemporary society. In this new book he continues to apply the critical Marxism of Herbert Marcuse to contemporary problems such as the destructive nature of global capitalism, the politics of neofascism, racism, ecological destruction, etc. This book is a necessary read for anyone who is struggling to understand the social, ecological, political, and economic crisis in which we live. Reitz's careful analysis opens the door for new and creative ways to address our present situation. Indeed, it is a new call for what Marcuse termed the "Great Refusal." —**Arnold L. Farr**, Professor of Philosophy, University of Kentucky, author of *Critical Theory and Democratic Vision: Herbert Marcuse and Recent Liberation Philosophies*.

To the rising fascist threat—brewing since Marcuse's time in Nixon's USA—Reitz counterposes the themes of ecology and humanism, both of these analyzed in a global, multicultural light, from European socialist humanism to African Ubuntu. He brings to life new critical resources from Marcuse's corpus of writings, much of it only recently unearthed. This offers new insights not only into the expected realms of ideology and culture, but also into the underlying economic structures of capitalism, all of it posed in terms of the chances of a genuine human emancipation unseparated from the world of nature. —**Kevin B. Anderson**, author of *Marx at the Margins*

Reitz wields revolutionary Marcusean theory against those who would protect hate speech and promote resurgent fascism in our own day. We really need an EarthCommonwealth Counteroffensive to replace the brutality of capital and patriarchy with global ecosocialism and partnership power! —**Javier Sethness Castro**, author of *Eros and Revolution: The Critical Philosophy of Herbert Marcuse* and *Queer Tolstoy: A Psychobiography*.

What we are against has found *What we are for*! —**Andrew T. Lamas**, University of Pennsylvania, co-editor of *The Great Refusal: Herbert Marcuse and Contemporary Social Movements*.

Things have gotten out of kilter in the United States and within the global capitalist system. The endless search for profit, new markets and resources leads to re-colonization and imperialism, war, death, and destruction. Reitz offers a vision of intercultural solidarity against the resurgent politics of white supremacy and oligarchic wealth idolization. His book is a call to action. —**Ewa Unoke**, Professor and Coordinator of Political Science, Kansas City Kansas Community College, author of *Global Security After Evil* and *Life of Nobody: Reparation to Africa—The Law of Karma is Strong*.

An outstanding contribution to critical social theory that takes account of the intersectional characteristics of global capitalist exploitation including the economies and populations of the Global South in the process of capitalist accumulation as these have led to the ecological catastrophe we are experiencing today. —**Sergio Bedoya Cortés**, Profesor de Filosofía, Facultad de Filosofía y Ciencias Humanas, Universidad Libre de Colombia.

Drawing on immense knowledge of the philosophy of Herbert Marcuse and a wide range of anthropological and other sources, Reitz identifies the promise of happiness contained within a humanist, intercultural ethics grounded in sensuous living labor. In the name of the Earth itself, the time has come for a Great Refusal, and Reitz has provided key insights that can enlightenment and inspire all those involved in the struggle to give birth to a new world. Reitz develops a powerful vision for an ecosocialist alternative to capitalism's mutilation and devastation of our shared environment, EarthCommonWealth. —**Brandon Absher**, Associate Professor of Philosophy and Director of the Honors Program, D'Youville University, author of *The Rise of Neo-Liberal Philosophy*.

Charles Reitz is a leading voice in the resurgence of discussions of Herbert Marcuse, socialist humanism, and ecology. The philosophical views of Marcuse, Karl Marx, and critical educationist Peter McLaren are enriched by African social and ethical philosophy, Indigenous American thought, and radical feminism. Reitz reflects on how the world's wisdom traditions intersect in a richly textured, multi-dimensional vision of intercultural solidarity. He never leaves behind the crucial dimension of political economy. Reitz offers a critique of oligarchic wealth, imperialism, white supremacy/

racism, and the toxic masculinity that is so closely related to authoritarian populism. Reitz's book is a timely theorization of current crises and a clarion call for desperately needed ecosocialist change. —**Terry Maley**, Associate Professor, Department of Politics, York University, Toronto, editor of *One-Dimensional Man 50 Years On: The Struggle Continues.*

For many decades now, Charles Reitz has been working with the critical theoretical approaches of Herbert Marcuse to update a radically ecological theory of society. Reitz's approach is a synthesis between Marcuse's reflections on the affluent society and his critique of capitalism inspired by Marx and Hegel and a critical engagement with the eco-anarchist and social theorist Murray Bookchin. His key new concept, EarthCommonWealth, envisages a new system of common property and management based on a comprehensive vision of an ecosocialist system alternative.
—**Peter-Erwin Jansen**, Koblenz University of Applied Sciences, editor of the literary estates of Herbert Marcuse and Leo Löwenthal.

The Revolutionary Ecological Legacy of Herbert Marcuse

The Revolutionary Ecological Legacy of Herbert Marcuse

The Ecosocialist EarthCommonWealth Project

Charles Reitz

With a postcript by Nnimmo Bassey

Daraja Press

2023

Published by Daraja Press
https://darajapress.com
Cantley, Quebec

© 2023 Charles Reitz
All rights reserved

ISBN: 9781990263811

Cover and book design: Kate McDonnell

Cover photo: Herbert Marcuse Special Collection, Archive Center, Goethe University Library, Frankfurt.
Courtesy of Harold Marcuse with special thanks to Peter-Erwin Jansen.

Library and Archives Canada Cataloguing in Publication

Title: The revolutionary ecological legacy of Herbert Marcuse / Charles Reitz ; with a postscript by Nnimmo Bassey.
Names: Reitz, Charles, author. | Bassey, Nnimmo, writer of postscript.
Description: 2nd edition. | "The Ecosocialist EarthCommonWealth Project." | Includes bibliographical references and index.
Identifiers: Canadiana 20230466486 | ISBN 9781990263811 (softcover)
Subjects: LCSH: Marcuse, Herbert, 1898-1979. | LCSH: Ecosocialism. | LCSH: Environmental economics.
Classification: LCC HX550.E25 R45 2023 | DDC 304.2—dc23

Dedicated to the memory of Philip Lindquist (1943-2020), a U.S.-American opponent of the Vietnam War who emigrated in protest to Montreal, Canada, on May 1, 1967. After graduation from McGill University, he enjoyed a thirty-year career teaching geography and history at Montreal's Chomedey Polyvalent High School and Phoenix Alternative High School.

THE REVOLUTIONARY LEGACY OF HERBERT MARCUSE

The German philosopher Herbert Marcuse fled Hitler's Nazis in 1933 because of his radical socialist politics and Jewish background. In New York City, he developed a remarkable series of books, each published as an English-language original, that represented to the world what would become a potent new perspective, the refugee Frankfurt School's critical social theory: *Reason and Revolution* (1941), *Eros and Civilization* (1955), *One-Dimensional Man* (1964), *An Essay on Liberation* (1969a), and *Counterrevolution and Revolt* (1972). These works challenged corporate capitalism's illusions of democracy characterized by consumerism, cultural anaesthetization, intellectual compliance, environmental degradation, and war as untenable forms of wasted abundance and political unfreedom. Marcuse's critical social theory includes a "green turn" in a militant register, entirely different from that of Horkheimer and Adorno, consistent with the foundations of a dialectical materialist philosophy.

Critical theory for Marcuse was not an Aesopian alternative or substitute for Marxism. He sought to raise the philosophy of Marx to its highest level. His comprehensive critical social theory also stresses the centrality of labor in the economy. It theorizes the origins and outcomes of economic and cultural oppression, and it is engaged politically with the labor force to end abuses. The work of Marx and Marcuse emphasizes that there is a promise of communal well-being and an aesthetic ethos at the core of humanity's material reality. Marx's 1844 Paris Manuscripts poignantly highlighted that human beings could produce in accordance with the laws of beauty. Marcuse's aesthetic ethos was likewise to function as a "gesellschaftliche Produktivkraft," a social and productive force.

Marcuse's work models the path by which we, an international political force of "the 99 percent," can be politically prepared and strengthened. His "utopian" vision calls for a new ecosocialist world system. Even a thoroughly secular philosophy can recognize that organizing for social justice requires respect for others' emancipatory spiritual needs. Critical and creative, this theory builds towards transnational transformation by furnishing new norms for understanding and for justice that enable us imaginatively to construct from within the realities of the present the partnership organizations of the future that will make possible new ways of holding resources and real opportunities for all persons to reclaim the full social power of labor, leadership, and learning. Marcuse's writings contain essential philosophical resources to collectively retake and repossess a common world, creating an *EarthCommonWealth*—characterized by racial equality, women's equality, the liberation of labor, the restoration of nature, leisure, abundance, and peace.

CONTENTS

Acknowledgments	xi
Preface *Our Neofascist Age: Is Humanism Obsolete?*	xiii
1. The Decline of the U.S. World Order and Global Capitalism	1
2. Marcuse Renaissance in the 2020s	15
3. Marcuse on Fascism, Antifascism (Antifa), and the "New Sensibility"	32
4. Nature as Ally: Against Global Catastrophe(s)	65
5. Recovering Our Commonwealth Sense	92
6. Labor Theory of Ethics	110
7. Ecological Materialism	133
8. Critical Political Economy (with Stephen Spartan)	159
9. *Promesse du Bonheur Commun*	184
10. EarthCommonWealth Agenda	194
Postscript by Nnimmo Bassey: *System Change Will Not Be Negotiated*	237
About the author	243
Index	244

ACKNOWLEDGMENTS

With appreciation for encouragement and inspiration: John Abromeit, Brandon Absher, Kevin B. Anderson, Morteza Ardebili, Tamara Agha-Jaffar, Ken Clark, Gene Grabiner, Gail James, Douglas Kellner, David Kingsley, Alfred Kisubi, Ben Kjelshus, Andrew Lamas, James Lawler, Henry Louis, Terry Maley, Peter McLaren, Ulrich Ruschig, John Ryan, Kohei Saito, Frieder Schöpfer, Melanie Jackson-Scott, Michael Simmons, Jr., Curtis Smith, Stephen Spartan, Ewa Unoke, Fred Whitehead, Rainer Winter, and Charles Woolfson. I am solely responsible for mistakes and faults of political analysis and perspective.

Particular thanks to: Roena Lindquist Haynie, 44 years my partner in marriage, for evocative and informed political and literary commentary; Jerome Heckmann, critical historian, for guidance on source materials and comparative interpretive insights; Nnimmo Bassey, Nigerian environmental activist and author for providing this volume's postscript; and Firoze Manji and associates at Daraja Press for superb publications support.

I wish to acknowledge publishers who generously granted permission to reemploy my own passages in an extensively reworked form and to thank also those whose formal permission was not necessary when representing my own work in a fully revised context: Routledge, SUNY Press, Peter Lang Publishing, and Lexington Books. Special thanks to the *Radical Philosophy Review*, the Brazilian journal of aesthetics and politics, *Das Questões*, and the UK's *Theory, Culture & Society*.

PUBLISHER'S NOTE

Daraja Press seeks to build bridges, especially bridges of solidarity between and amongst movements, intellectuals and those engaged in struggles for a just world. The Press is reissuing this volume in connection with our work with social and environmental theorists from the Global South, particularly a set of writings collected in 2023 by Nnimmo Bassey, *Politics of Turbulent Waters: Reflections on Ecological, Environmental and Climate Crises in Africa*.

PREFACE

Our Neofascist Age: Is Humanism Obsolete?

> "... hope **is** given to us."[1]
> – Walter Benjamin (in Herbert Marcuse, *One-Dimensional Man*, 1964)

Cognizant of the prevalence of malevolence and cruelty, conquest, unjust imprisonment, torture and starvation that have continually destroyed and damaged human lives—aware of the current rise of neofascism in the U.S.A. and worldwide—the humanist vision of an egalitarian partnership society to be unfolded here through the work of Herbert Marcuse, Karl Marx, and contemporary critical educationist Peter McLaren may appear to be obsolete. Their vision of ecosocialism and an ethics of commonwealth are defended here against the usual objection that they are impossibly utopian: at best good in theory, but of no practical value. In 1962 Marcuse confronted a core socialist humanist conundrum:

> Today the words "humanity" and "humanism" cause us some perplexity. Clearly something about them has not worked. It seems as though these ideas, these concepts, are of only antiquarian value, that humanism and humanity belong only to history. But what does that mean: that they belong only to history? If something happened just thirty years ago, that is history, and yet it conditions the present and will also affect our future. *What we have learned during these thirty years that we had not earlier known, is this: what human beings can be made to do. They can be made into inhuman beings.* (Marcuse [1962] 2015, emphasis added)

---

1 "It is only for the sake of those without hope that hope is given to us" (1964, 257). Too often misread as sheer pessimism, I emphasize above the dialectical optimism and sense of obligation of Benjamin and Marcuse.

The *Dialectic of Enlightenment* by Max Horkheimer and Theodor W. Adorno ([1944] 1972) profoundly confronted all philosophical and political confidence in the transhistorical truths of high German culture and art. Adorno, as is well known, questioned the very possibility of poetry after Auschwitz. This is quite possibly what led Marcuse to endorse Thomas Mann's call in *Doctor Faustus* (1947) for the revocation of Beethoven's Ninth Symphony, which incorporated Schiller's "Ode to Joy" [*Alle Menschen werden Brüder*— Human beings are brothers all—CR]. For a time, Marcuse found this towering choral and symphonic setting of Schiller's humane vision to be an illusion that justified the "no longer justifiable" (Marcuse [1967] 1973, 66).

Are the values preserved in a humanist ethics at best only abstract criteria of judgment, transhistorically desirable, yet powerless in terms of transformative political praxis? Must the categorical imperative and golden rule also be revoked? Or in some manner can they be considered to retain the *promesse du bonheur commun*, the promise of liberation to the dignified communal well-being inherent in our species essence despite our tragically conflicted material human condition?

My new book on Marcuse's revolutionary legacy points out something seldom taken note of in environmentalist thinking or in Marcuse studies for that matter: In the "Nature and Revolution" chapter of *Counterrevolution and Revolt* (1972) Marcuse propounds the idea that *"nature is an ally"* —

- Nature is a dynamic force, without telos or plan, but Beauty pertains to nature as well as Art.
- Nature can be hostile to humanity, a circumstance against which we must struggle, but the unfriendly aspects of nature subside.
- Human beings uniquely recognize the awe-inspiring, astounding, and humbling qualities (Schiller calls them the "serene or regal" *erhaben* features) of beauty in the natural world, and these prefigure the promise of human freedom, collective happiness and fulfillment.
- Human *senses* and impulses *do* shape our rationality and experience.
- Nature is an educator. It teaches us to think of the ecological system as the unit of critical analysis.
- *By nature* we must reproduce our lives through *social labor* and we can produce "according to the laws of beauty" (Marx).
- In established [corporate capitalist] society natural impulses (aggressiveness and sexuality) are administered, controlled, repressed: early on by the abstemious Protestant-Puritan ethic, now through *repressive*

desublimation, the unrestrained use of sex and violence in commodity culture.
- We comprehend Nature as a liberating force with a vital role in the liberation of society.
- We need a profoundly changed, New Sensibility, a *new socialist rationality* freed from exploitation if social change is to be radical.
- If we recover the life-enhancing forces of nature, we may actualize a socialist humanism—a form of a free nature-protecting society that I call an ecosocialist EarthCommonWealth.

Marcuse argues this perspective constitutes a *modern historical materialism* on the basis of Marx's *Philosophical Notebooks* of 1844, Plato's dialectical idealism, Kant's transcendental humanism, Hegel's historization of conceptual concreteness—and critical consciousness under the impact of the women's movement.

Groups can and do have contradictory material interests. Sometimes these are completely antagonistic, and the context will not allow a resolution of the conflict. Antagonism is certainly not a necessary feature of societies that are internally differentiated. The "99%" indicates a *potential* unity. The notion of *EarthCommonWealth* to be developed here signifies this *unity* in the *fullest, richest, most diverse and intercultural terms*. How to transform society in ways that are just and sustainable is not self-evident; peace has been a transhistorical and critical challenge to human cultures. A central subject matter of this volume is liberation from systems of militarized murder in the service of oligarchic power. An ecosocialist future could serve as a partial redemption of the death and suffering of Wounded Knee, the Ludlow Colorado mine wars, the Tulsa race massacre, the Mỹ Lai genocide, Abu Graib, Ferguson, Minneapolis, etc.

EarthCommonWealth is proposed as a revolutionary alternative to the profitable misuse of limited natural resources, in large measure by negating planned obsolescence and its wasted abundance, negating the capitalist fetish of exchange value. It seeks the liberation of labor from its commodity or wage form. Ending the crisis of the environment is not primarily a proposition involving massive new social costs and investments to cleanse our ecology of the detritus left by an otherwise rampantly polluting corporate capitalism. *Nature is an ally*; it restores us, and its restoration can be a model and inspiration for conservation and social savings by ending costly waste and protecting earth, air, and water as reserves for life.

Immediately after World War II, Herbert Marcuse saw our challenge as a choice between neofascism and "the construction of socialism" ([1947] 1998, 223). "The alternatives (fascism or socialism)" continued to characterize the objective political framework in 1972 (*Counterrevolution and Revolt* 29). In one of his last published pieces, he continued: "The goal of radical change today is the emergence of human beings who are physically and mentally incapable of inventing another Auschwitz" (Marcuse [1979] 2011, 213). Against the misanthropic and cynical conservatism that asserts inborn human aggression, the right of the stronger to economic exploitation, and imperial manifest destiny, etc., Marx and Marcuse saw a philosophical power in humanism. Peter McLaren (1997, 2015) stresses that practical struggles for human dignity, respect, and empowerment led to significant intercultural learning and social progress. He and Marcuse understood that ecological issues have immense volatility and can burst the limits of capitalism. The overarching aim of this volume is to synthesize Marcuse, Marx and McLaren as radical intellectual resources in order to negate neofascism definitively, and to assist in the establishment, through a global ecosocialist rising, of a culture of partnership power. Every reader is encouraged to expand upon efforts of Marcuse, Marx, and McLaren toward human liberation and planetary preservation per your own critical engagement with this *EarthCommonWealth Project*.

Works Cited

Horkheimer, Max and Theodor W. Adorno. [1944] 1972. *Dialectic of Enlightenment*. New York: Herder and Herder.
Marcuse, Herbert. [1947] 1998. "33 Theses" in Herbert Marcuse, *Technology, War, and Fascism* Volume 1, *Collected Papers of Herbert Marcuse*. Douglas Kellner (Ed.). New York: Routledge.
Marcuse, Herbert. [1962] 2015. "Humanism and Humanity" in Charles Reitz (Ed.). *Crisis and Commonwealth: Marcuse, Marx, McLaren*. Lanham, MD: Lexington Books.
Marcuse, Herbert. 1964. *One-Dimensional Man: Studies in the Ideology of Advanced Industrial Society*. Boston, MA: Beacon Press.
Marcuse, Herbert. [1967] 1973. "Art in the One-Dimensional Society," in Lee Baxandall (Ed.). *Radical Perspectives in the Arts*. Baltimore, MD: Penguin.
Marcuse, Herbert. 1972. Counterrevolution and Revolt. Boston, MA: Beacon Press.
Marcuse, Herbert. [1979]. 2011. "Ecology and the Critique of Society" in *Herbert Marcuse, Philosophy, Psychoanalysis and Emancipation*, Volume 5, *Collected Papers of Herbert Marcuse*, Douglas Kellner and Clayton Pierce (Eds.). New York and London: Routledge.
McLaren, Peter. 2015. *Pedagogy of Insurrection*. New York and Bern: Peter Lang Publishing.
McLaren, Peter. 1997. *Revolutionary Multiculturalism: Pedagogies of Dissent for the New Millennium*. Boulder, CO: Westview Press.

1
The Decline of the U.S. World Order and Global Capitalism

Racial animosity, anti-immigrant scapegoating, and a resurgent nationalism/patriotism are being orchestrated today in the troubled system of American/global capitalism. These are neo-populist/neo-fascist instrumentalities of social control and economic stabilization. Critical sociologists Lauren Langman and George Lundskow make a strong case several times over in *God, Guns, Gold, and Glory: American Character and its Discontents* (2016), given our history as a religiously inspired colonial settler society, that U.S.-American culture has become quite instinctively fascistoid: sadistic, aggressive, authoritarian, malicious, and monstrous. Their research, along with that of Roxanne Dunbar-Ortiz (2014), Jill Lepore (2019), Nikole Hannah-Jones, et al (2021), as well as Howard Zinn et al (2008) explicates the underside of the American historical record: genocide against Native people; slavery; property qualifications to vote and govern; predatory adulation of plutocracy and power; religious zealotry; militarism; the denial of science. Langman and Lundskow give a vivid account of the development of a reactionary national character type that is a prevalent pathological model of American manhood: masculinist and aggressive, sadomasochistic, punitive, tough, heroic, and white supremacist and antisemitic. They hold that by means of its WASP racism, antisemitism, and toxic forms of American masculinity, the U.S. has become a self-righteous global power under the delusion that it is free and democratic.

All this is said without mentioning the name of Donald Trump, though it has clear relevance to recent political developments in terms of a resurgence of reactionary rhetoric and racist tendencies on the right. Dunbar-Ortiz with Langman and Lundskow furnish the historical-cultural political backdrop to the conservative cultural-political backlash we are seeing today in, for example, the right wing's attacks on Hannah-Jones and the *New York Times' 1619 Project* (2021) and critical race theory.

Our U.S.-American political delusions of freedom have accompanied the rise of the U.S. as a global power, and *not* just as a *capitalist* society, but as a *complex cultural formation* characterized by its religious conservatism, patriarchy, economic oppression and its racism. Critical economist and historian Douglas Dowd, a key resource to whom I will turn again and again, observes: "This is not to say that, in terms of what is done, America is worse than other societies, Americans worse than other peoples; our evil consists in believing that we are better than others... The gap between what Americans are in practice and what, with our ideals and resources, we should be, is as a Grand Canyon that separates actuality from possibility" (Dowd 1997, 16). Dowd is clear that U.S. capitalism has operated under the imperative to expand geographically in pursuit of access to natural resources and low-cost labor (Dowd 1997, 102).

Of course, millions of immigrants were *not* colonial settlers, though likely restless, ambitious, and even desperate. During the 19th Century in particular many Irish, Italian, Greek, German, Polish, Swedish, Jewish, Lebanese, Serbian, Croatian, and other ethnic immigrants brought essential productive skills like glassmaking, milling, weaving, gun making, pottery, agricultural machinery design and manufacture. Many arrived needy, fleeing poverty, unemployment, and prejudice, and endured much hardship in this country as documented by Jacob Riis and aided by settlement activist Jane Addams. Others also brought progressive political aspirations such as the free-thinking German 48ers and the Socialist Turners of New York City, Cincinnati, and St. Louis (Reitz 2008; 2010). At the same time, Roxanne Dunbar-Ortiz's *Not a Nation of Immigrants* (2021) is essential reading to debunk the self-congratulatory mythology of a land of opportunity built by immigrants.

Up against the "American Pageant" mythology

Donald Trump's advocacy in September 2020 of schooling for American patriotism (Crowley 2020) and against critical race theory reveal the repressive and reactionary political intent of his proposals on education. They extend the culture war begun by Newt Gingrich, Pat Buchanan, Allan Bloom, Lynn Cheney (and criticized by Reitz 2009a, 221; Delores Calderón 2009; Susan Jacoby 2018). Marcuse anticipated back in the 1960s the counterrevolutionary tendencies now raging in the higher education to reduce the liberal arts in American general education to the conservatively filtered monocultural residue of an elitist, Anglocentric curriculum (Kelderman 2020). I have called this the "American Pageant" version of educational philosophy and history (Reitz 2008, 14). Historical writing of this conventional sort has played down immigrant, indigenous, women's, and ethnic minority voices, as well as the resistance of subaltern groups to class, race, and gender-based hierarchies of domination (Reitz 2016a, 217; Loewen 1995; Fitzgerald 1979; Griffen and Marciano 1979).

The American Pageant approach to history writing, like that of Thomas A. Bailey (1961), was consistent with a murderous American patriotism: "The American republic, which is still relatively young, was from the outset singularly favored. It started out from scratch on a vast and virgin continent, which was so sparsely peopled by Indians that they could be eliminated or pushed aside" (Bailey 1961, 4). Even if Bailey did not intend this statement as an explicit endorsement of settler-colonialism or its eliminationist genocide, this embodies the latent racist quality of American historiography that DunbarOrtiz (2014), Lepore (2019), Hannah-Jones, et al (2021), and Zinn et al (2008) have more recently challenged and countered. We must acknowledge that the land upon which we reside to write these lines or to read them was once held in common by Indigenous peoples on every continent and that current property arrangements are the product of colonialism, forced removal, and genocide. This volume builds upon a mindfulness of present participation in this historical context.

Imperial America: Racism and exploitation

Summarizing testimony left by the 15th to 16th Century scholar Ramón Pané and the priest Bartolomé de Las Casas reported early in the New World, critical historian Jill Lepore writes: "[T]he origins of the United States date to 1492... the nation's founding truths were forged in a crucible of violence, the products of staggering cruelty, conquest and slaughter, the assassination of worlds" (Lepore 2019, 10). Among the worlds destroyed were those of the Taíno of Haiti whose lands were appropriated by Columbus by force or arms. Lepore asks a critical question: "[B]y what right can one people take the land of another or their labor or even, their lives" (2019, 16). She relates the written account of the 16th Century priest Antonio de Montesinos who challenged the Spanish crown by denouncing the enslavement of the Taíno (Lepore 2019, 16-22). The British came later to America with Sir Walter Raleigh sending a fleet in 1584 and the arrival in 1619 in Hampton, Virginia, of the first persons enslaved by the English.

David Graeber and David Wengrow (2021) echo Lepore's critique making a similar point from the Native American perspective itself, quoting Kondiaronk, the Wyandot (Huron) philosopher-statesman, as related by the Baron Lahontan, deputy Governor-General of French Canada in 1703:

> *Kondiaronk*: I have spent six years reflecting on the state of European society and still I can't think of a single way they act that's not inhuman, and I genuinely think this can only be the case, as long as you stick to your distinctions of 'mine' and 'thine.' I affirm that what you call money... is the tyrant of the French... and the slaughterhouse of the living. (Graeber and Wengrow 2021, 54-55)

This cultural-political assessment finds resonance in the historical account of Langman and Lundskow as well as that of Oliver Stone and Peter Kuznick's *Untold History of the United States* (2019). Lucidly written at 900 pages this brings back to mind the highlights and the details of this country's militarized and expansionist foreign policy exemplified in its programs and policies that need to be critically remembered today (see also Dunbar-Ortiz 2014; Hannah-Jones, et al 2021; and Grandin 2000).

The beginnings of U.S. overseas empire-building in the late 19th and early 20th centuries are traced to the overseas annexations that the U.S. undertook in its war against Spain (1898): these annexations included taking military control of Cuba, Puerto Rico, Hawaii and the Philippines. Stone and Kuznick emphasize that the U.S. had embarked upon a vision of global supremacy undergirded by fundamentally racist assumptions. Only two years earlier the U.S. Supreme Court had affirmed the constitutionality of racial segregation in *Plessy v. Ferguson* and ushered in the U.S. policy of Jim Crow—America's de jure apartheid to accompany its de facto reality. In the 1898 war against Spain several ex-Confederate officers, who had been pardoned *en masse* after the Civil War, served as generals. Torture through waterboarding was introduced during the effort to take the Philippines from the Spanish. Of course, waterboarding has also been much in the news post 9-11 as used by the CIA at the U.S. prison at Guantánamo and elsewhere (Iraq, Afghanistan, and other black sites).

Stone and Kuznick remind us further that an uprising was orchestrated in Colombia, under the former Rough Rider, then President, Teddy

Roosevelt, to separate the province of Panama from its home country in order to construct the Panama Canal for U.S. shipping interests. In the following decade, the U.S. continued to expand its sphere of trade and investment. It sent its Marines in 1909 to Nicaragua, in 1914 to Mexico, and in 1916 to the Dominican Republic. Major General Smedley Butler, who had participated in each of these interventions, wrote in his famous statement of exasperation and regret, *War is a Racket*, that he had been but "a high-class muscle-man for Big Business, for Wall Street, and for the Bankers... a gangster for capitalism" (Stone and Kuznick, xxxii).

The 20th Century U.S. world order: Counterrevolution

Stone and Kuznick also remind us that media mogul Henry Luce propounded an explicitly hegemonic vision of an "American Century" in 1951. This appellation seemed apt at the time, especially after the U.S. escaped from destruction in World War II and emerged as an atomic superpower. It fit with President Truman's vision of the future as a worldwide conflict between East and West. His program of Cold War militarization and regime change ensued. Winston Churchill was invited by Truman to his home state of Missouri in 1946 to consolidate an Anglo-American anticommunist alliance. Eisenhower concurred with plans for the U.S. and UK jointly to overthrow the democratically elected Iranian president Mossadegh in 1953, given his plans to nationalize Iranian oil, and install the regime of the Shah with what emerged also as his notoriously brutal secret police. Iran was thus secured for British and American oil interests. Similarly, Guatemala's president Arbenz was branded a communist and overthrown in 1954 in a coup engineered by the CIA on behalf of the United Fruit Company.

Vincent Bevins (2020) stresses, as did Stone and Kuznick above, that the U.S. emerged from the close of World War II as the world's most powerful nation. When communists won elections in postwar France and Italy, as in Iran and Guatemala, he recounts that Washington was not pleased and undertook an anti-communist foreign policy that he terms "Global McCarthyism" (Bevins, 19). This included covert anti-communist assassinations and regime change programs in the Congo and Indonesia. Bevins informs us that in 1962 over one thousand Indonesian officers were trained by the U.S. military and at the same time, hundreds of other Indonesians attended an American university. "They were all well-trained, and Americanized, and many of them became anti-communists there in

Kansas [at Ft. Leavenworth and the University of Kansas at Lawrence]" (Bevins 81). Only a few years later (1965-1966), because communism was so widely accepted and prevalent in Indonesia, mass murder of civilians was adopted as a means of achieving U.S. geopolitical goals. The CIA called it the "Jakarta Method" of Washington's counterinsurgency. While the internal political maneuvering was byzantine, "up to a million Indonesians, maybe more, were killed as part of Washington's global anti-communist crusade" (Bevins 157). Bevins notes that the only prominent U.S. politician to speak out against this massacre was Sen. Robert F. Kennedy, soon to be assassinated himself (as Martin Luther King, Jr. also had been, having opposed the Vietnam War, America's poverty, and systemic racism). In the 1970s Nixon's bombing of neutral Cambodia, illegal in U.S. and world law, would kill at least one million Cambodians (Dowd 1997, 198). Even U.S. students protesting the escalation of the war would themselves be killed in shocking law enforcement actions by the National Guard at Kent State and Jackson State (Dowd 1997, 206).

Bevin's account and that of Stone and Kuznick remind us that this history remained largely "untold" because of the impact of the repressive enculturation or socialization processes. In the U.S., establishment media, schooling, churches, and businesses, as well as explicitly political institutions, reinforced the Anglo-conformity that conditioned and reproduced a single-dimensional Americanism in public opinion. For decades via overt and covert McCarthyism this brand of Americanism tended to enforce patriotic compliance with U.S. militarism and opposition to leftist politics in the labor movement, higher education, civil rights, and even Hollywood. We have yet to even mention Korea in the 1950s, Vietnam in the 60s and 70s, Nicaragua and El Salvador in the 80s and 90s, or the more familiar conflicts of the 21st Century, in Iraq and Afghanistan. Critical economist Douglas Dowd argues that the Cold War and McCarthyism were interwoven as the weft and warp of U.S. hegemony (Dowd 1997, 82). The 1947 National Security Act created the National Security Agency, the National Security Council, and the CIA. This is said to have transformed the U.S. into a National Security State, having an "imperial presidency" (Dowd 1997, 275) with the nation's sovereign powers in the shadows (Moyers 1990).

One episode in this sordid history is related by Stone and Kuznick in a section on mass anticommunist murder given the hideous spectacle of "The Reagan Years: Death Squads for Democracy" (2019, 421-462; and by Dowd 1997, 270-277). Staunch anticommunist U.S. President Ronald Reagan oversaw U.S.backed and trained government forces as they executed thousands of civilians in Guatemala and El Salvador who were suspected of harboring guerrilla fighters. U.S.-trained and armed Salvadoran troops known as "death squads" savagely executed regime opponents and those who were suspected of supporting them "in Mỹ Lai fashion" (Dowd 1997, 272), including priests, nuns, and El Salvador's Archbishop Oscar Romero, as well as 700-900 inhabitants of the village of El Mozote. The U.S. was thus testing a post-Vietnam counterrevolutionary doctrine to defeat an insurgency without the large-scale commitment of U.S. forces (Stone and Kuznick 2019, 431). The antiguerrilla campaign in neighboring Guatemala was characterized "between a pogrom or a genocide" even in the mainstream U.S. press (Stone and Kuznick 2019, 429; Grandin 2000). In a third theater of operations, Nicaragua, in 1984 the "contras," whom Reagan called the moral equivalent of the U.S. founding fathers, were financed illegally (rather than through Congress) to overthrow the Sandinista government by the U.S. by selling missiles to its ostensible enemies in Iran (Stone and Kuznick 2019, 431). U.S. policy empowered hardline right-wing anticommunists who had no compunctions about utilizing a reign of terror to suppress popular movements (Stone and Kuznick 2019, 462), and this policy became a counterrevolutionary legacy.

In the late 1970s U.S. covert operations in Afghanistan mobilized and armed Islamic fundamentalists against both the Afghan government and Soviet forces supporting it. "In the battle to defeat Soviet Communism in the Cold War, the U.S. poured billions of dollars into Afghanistan to train 'freedom fighters' that would overthrow the purportedly communist regime" (Kellner 2003, 32). These later became part of the Al Qaeda terror network led by Osama bin Laden. After the 9-11 terror attacks on the U.S., the nation's strategic anti-communist ideological infrastructure morphed into the "War against Terror" which was so open-ended it itself became "A Reign of Terror" (Ackerman 2021) or "Terror War" (Kellner 2003) that destabilized the U.S. domestically through laws and policies legitimating large-scale electronic surveillance, presidential kill lists for extrajudicial drone strikes, and torture, all compatible with an aroused neofascist politics and exemplified by the

January 6, 2021, failed putsch at the U.S. Capitol seeking to overturn the presidential election.

"[W]hat kind of crooks' game are We The People playing with ourselves, or letting be played on us, when we consistently take the wrong side in struggles in the imperialized world . . . ?" (Dowd 1997, 271). Decades before G. H. W. Bush, Clinton, Dubya, Cheney, Obama, and Trump, economic critic Douglas Dowd feared the self-righteous and chauvinistic patriotism that would support the imperial presidency in future years. Likewise, Samuel Moyn has criticized the "humanitarian" pretexts such as the protection against terrorism and for human rights, civil, and gender rights for continuing wars that allow "American war itself to be rehabilitated after Vietnam as legitimate or even progressive" (Moyn 2021, 223).

American empire in decline

Writing about the same time as Marcuse's turn to themes of counterrevolution and political economy (with his 1972 *Counterrevolution and Revolt*), economist Michael Hudson published *SuperImperialism: The Economic Strategy of American Empire* ([1972] 2021). Hudson's work stands out for its comprehensiveness and critical clarity. His account, like others (Greider 1998; Korten [1991] 2001) elaborates the manner in which U.S. foreign investment de-industrialized its domestic economy: U.S. corporations became multinationals, investing capital abroad, hiring lower-cost labor internationally, and disinvesting domestically, shifting production, employment and fixed capital investment largely to Asia. The U.S. thus became trade-dependent for most manufacturers, except, as Hudson emphasizes, for arms-making, still a key source of domestically acquired superprofits.

Hudson centers his critique on the financialization of the economy and what he calls America's financial imperialism—a balance-of-payments analysis of foreign investment and military interventions and expenditures and traces out the related social and political cost implications of disinvestment on what Marcuse and others had called the welfare/warfare economy. "Welfare" here was understood broadly as a range of social needs-oriented programs, not the narrow range of transfer payments to the poor. In terms of international power dynamics, U.S. military spending and foreign investment were creating a new kind of circular flow back to the federal Treasury with other countries' surpluses being siphoned off as the U.S. deepened its deficit. Hudson argues that as the world's major debtor nation today, U.S. Treasury IOUs have been built into the world's money supply.

Hudson's work, like that of Stone and Kuznick, resonates with the larger social history of Imperial America that has been extensively fleshed-out also by Bevins (2020), Immerwahr (2019), Robinson (2020), Vine (2015), Marciano (2015, 2016), Grandin (2000), Dowd (1997), Greene (1970), and Reitz (1976). Hudson describes the U.S. today as a de-industrialized *rentier* economy in a multipolar de-dollarizing world. Global political conflict in his estimation sets the financialized *rentier* U.S. economy against other industrial economies around the world. For their part, industrial countries like "China and Russia [are] creating a de-dollarized system and attracting European and Third World countries out of the confrontational U.S. orbit" (Hudson [1972] 2021, 443). The American empire is losing ground to what he calls "an old-fashioned industrial policy" embodied in a mixed economy keeping basic infrastructure investment in the public domain while taxing rentier income and wealth. While Hudson would also like to see banking and credit creation made into public utilities in the U.S., as well as other public services (like the internet and social media one assumes), he is *not* a radical socialist. Still, his work does pose the right question: "What kind of economy is the world going to have?" (Hudson [1972] 2021, 439, 449).

What monopoly capitalism theorizes as the *cost of reproducing the domestic labor force* was being reduced through several strategies: chiefly the importation of cheapened products from abroad, but also two-tier negotiated agreements lowering wages for younger unionized workers, while increasingly substituting contingent labor in sectors that had previously provided stable employment. It's commonplace today to note the rising precarity that resulted from all of this; working people have increasingly unstable living conditions. Douglas Dowd's 1997 statement that "the real income of four-fifths of the population had ceased to rise in 1973 and has not done so since" (Dowd 1997, 230) is even more true today.[1] This condition is also more harrowing given the intensification of multiple forms of socio-economic and political inequality: the vast and widening differentials in life chances due to the increasing concentration of wealth and income among those at the pinnacle of property ownership,

---

1 Statista.com "Shares of household income of quintiles in the United States from 1970 to 2020" https://www.statista.com/statistics/203247/shares-of-household-income-of-quintiles-in-the-us/

not to mention the heightened race and gender tensions being orchestrated as political and economic weapons. The aforementioned politics of resentment blames immigrants, minorities, "the lesser peoples" or those somewhat higher up on the scale (Listen Boomer!) diverting attention from those *rentier* echelons profiting from the immiseration of the rest of society. The structural power of concentrated ownership of globalized U.S. super corporations and financial institutions is thus protected. Even so, these formerly hegemonic system components are also becoming precarious in their own way. Apropos such systemic precarity, in 2021 Thomas Piketty published a piece called "The Fall of the U.S. Idol." This is the concluding section of his latest book, *Time for Socialism*.

Piketty's much-belated call for socialism is a surprise—even to himself! "If someone had told me in 1990 that I would publish a collection of articles in 2020 called 'Long Live Socialism!' in French, I would have thought it was a bad joke" (Piketty 2021, 1). My work is and has been profoundly critical of Piketty's sleight-of-hand obfuscating the issues of capitalist inequality and distracting from an authentic analysis of its origins (Reitz 2016b). Yet Piketty now wants to stress that a de-mythologizing of U.S. culture is in order. For the last several decades critical educationists in the U.S. have particularly stressed the many ways we are *Up against the American Myth* (Christoffel, Finkelhor, Gilbarg 1970) and how it is necessary to leave the dominant cultural mythology behind (Colombo, Cullen, Lisle [1992] 2018). Piketty belatedly concurs that we need to "go back to history. . . the republic of the United States has been run through by weaknesses, violence, and considerable inequalities" (Piketty 2021, 329). Despite two previous 600 to 1000 page tomes on economic inequality, each having the word "capital" *first* in the title (2014, 2020), neither is grounded in Marx's analysis in *Das Kapital*. "It would be unfair to reduce the question of social justice to the importance of income from labor versus income from inherited wealth" (Piketty 2014, 241). In fact, Piketty separates labor and capital into "Two Worlds," apparently disconnected, and then describes income inequalities *within the world of capital* as being greater than income inequalities *within the world of labor* (Piketty 2014, 244; Reitz 2016). Over more than one hundred pages he describes the inequalities internal to the flow of income to labor that is considered in disjunction from inequalities internal to the flow of income to capital (Piketty 2014, 235ff). There are places where Piketty gets features of 20th Century capitalism right, but these are hidden behind his own mystifications. This allows him to call for a kind of 21st Century socialism falling well short of that theorized within the parameters of critical Marxism. Saying he wants to transcend capitalism, he instead gallantly tries to rescue it by taming its worst excesses in a new global system. "The limited diffusion of wealth implies that the bottom 50 percent have minimal opportunity to participate in economic life by creating and running a business" (Piketty, 2020, 980). He proposes a new and substantially progressive taxation regime for capital, power-sharing in firms, and the diffusion of wealth through a universal capital endowment. This latter feature is a grant suggested as a public inheritance for every young adult reaching about the age of 25. In his example, this amounts to a bequest of 120k euros (60% of the national average for private wealth) in the world's richest countries to be derived from a fund equal to 5% of the national income (Piketty 2020, 981-984). The *system* of capitalism and wage labor, though markedly abated through this and other measures in the direction of social democracy, persists with no change in the relations or forces of production, no expropriation, no decommodification to radically reduce the systemic waste of natural and human resources.

Waste and destruction

Herbert Marcuse emphasized a growing political opposition to U.S. militarism and global capitalism in a series of *seven recently discovered lectures delivered at Vincennes University, Paris, in 1974* (Marcuse 2015). He argued in these lectures that U.S. society represented the "highest stage in the development of monopoly capitalism" (Marcuse 2015, 21) in the following terms:

1. Economic ownership and political power are more highly concentrated in the U.S. than among other advanced capitalist countries.
2. U.S.-dominated multinational corporations have penetrated in a neoimperialist fashion into the developed as well as undeveloped countries. The U.S. is exporting *production itself* from the metropolitan countries to other capitalist and pre-capitalist countries with lower production costs.
3. There is a fusion of *political, economic, and military power* in which the representatives of particular corporate interests have become key leaders in the government and administration.
4. The population, generally managed *without* overt force through

advanced forms of political-economic manipulation, is now increasingly controlled through *the systematic and methodical power of law enforcement*. This enforcement keeps itself within the framework of the patterns of unfreedom that pass for American democracy.

Nonetheless, "You know too well, I suppose, the progress which by virtue of the electronic industry has been made in surveilling an entire population secretly, if desired" (Marcuse 2015, 23).

Marcuse's *Paris Lectures* ([1974] 2015) foresee the possible end of capitalism precisely at a time of its greatest productive capacities and its greatest wealth accumulations. He believed he could discern U.S. societal disintegration on the basis of what was actually happening in the process of production itself: the increasingly destructive waste by those who control the productive forces today (Marcuse [1974] 2015, 32-33). Capitalism's profitable perfection of waste through overproduction and over-accumulation represents a violation of the earth.

Works cited

Ackerman, Spencer. 2021. *Reign of Terror: How the 9/11 Era Destabilized America and Produced Trump*. New York: Viking.

Bailey, Thomas A. 1961. *The American Pageant*. Boston: D. C. Heath.

Bevins, Vincent. 2020. *The Jakarta Method: Washington's Anticommunist Crusade & the Mass Murder Program that Shaped our World*. New York: Public Affairs/ Perseus/ Hachette Book Group.

Calderón, Dolores. 2009. "One-Dimensionality and Whiteness," in Douglas Kellner, Tyson Lewis, Clayton Pierce, K. Daniel Cho (Eds.) *Marcuse's Challenge to Education*. Lanham, MD: Rowman & Littlefield.

Christoffel, Dan, Tom Finkelhor, Dan Gilbarg (eds). 1970. *Up Against the American Myth*. New York: Holt, Rinehart, Winston.

Colombo, Gary, Robert Cullen, Bonnie Lisle. [1992] 2018. *ReReading America: Cultural Contexts for Critical Thinking and Writing*. Boston. MA: Bedford/St. Martin's.

Crowley, Michael. 2020. "Trump Calls for 'Patriotic Education' to Defend American History From the Left," *The New York Times*, September 17.

Dowd, Douglas. 1997. *Blues for America*. New York: Monthly Review Press.

Dunbar-Ortiz, Roxanne. 2014. *An Indigenous Peoples' History of the United States*. Boston, MA: Beacon Press.

Dunbar-Ortiz, Roxanne. 2021. *Not a Nation of Immigrants: Settler Colonialism, White Supremacy, and a History of Erasure and Exclusion*. Boston: Beacon Press.

Fitzgerald, Frances. 1979. *America Revised: History School Books in the Twentieth Century* Boston: Atlantic-Little, Brown.

Graeber, David and David Wengrow. 2021. *The Dawn of Everything: A New History of Humanity*. New York: Farrar, Straus and Giroux.

Grandin, Greg. 2000. *The Blood of Guatemala. A History of Race and Nation*. Durham, NC: Duke University Press.

Greene, Felix. 1970. *The Enemy: What Every American Should Know About Imperialism*. New York: Random House.
Greider, William. 1998. *One World Ready or Not: The Manic Logic of Global Capitalism*. New York Simon & Schuster.
Griffen, William L. and John Marciano. 1979. *Teaching the Vietnam War*. Montclair, NJ: Allanheld, Osman, and Co.
Hannah-Jones, Nikole. et al. (eds) 2021. *The 1619 Project: A New Origin Story*. New York: One World.
Harcourt, Bernard E. 2018. *The Counterrevolution: How Our Government Went to War Against Its Own Citizens*. New York: Basic Books/Hachette Book Group.
Hudson, Michael. 2022. *The Destiny of Civilization: Finance Capitalism, Industrial Capitalism or Socialism*. Dresden: ISLET Verlag.
Hudson, Michael. [1972] 2021. *SUPERImperialism: The Economic Strategy of American Empire*. Dresden: ISLET Verlag.
Immerwahr, Daniel. 2019. *How to Hide an Empire*. New York: Picador.
Jacoby, Susan. 2018. *The Age of American Unreason in a Culture of Lies*. New York: Vintage.
Kelderman, Eric. 2020. "Can 'White Resentment' Help Explain Higher Education Cuts?" *The Chronicle of Higher Education*, January 27. https://bityl.co/CePz
Kellner, Douglas. 2003. *From September 11th to Terror War*. Lanham, MD: Rowman & Littlefield.
Korten, David. [1991] 2001. *When Corporations Rule the World*. Kumarian Press and Barrett-Kohler Publishers.
Langman, Lauren and George Lundskow. 2016. *God, Guns, Gold, and Glory*. Chicago: Haymarket.
Lepore, Jill. 2019. *These Truths: A History of the United States*. New York: W.W. Norton.
Loewen, James. 1995. *Lies My Teacher Told Me*. New York: Touchstone. Marciano, John. 2016. *The American War in Vietnam*. New York: Monthly Review Press.
Marciano, John. 2015. "Empire as a Way of Life: Course Description and Critical Readings," in Charles Reitz, ed. *Crisis and Commonwealth: Marcuse, Marx, McLaren*. Lanham, MD: Lexington Books.
Marcuse, Herbert. [1974] 2015. *Paris Lectures at Vincennes University, 1974*. Edited by Peter-Erwin Jansen and Charles Reitz. Philadelphia, PA: International Herbert Marcuse Society.
Moyers, Bill. 1990. *The Secret Government: Constitution in Crisis*. Newport Beach, CA: Seven Locks Press.
Moyn, Samuel. 2021. *Humane: How the United States Abandoned Peace and Reinvented War*. New York: Ferrar, Straus, and Giroux.
Piketty, Thomas. 2014. *Capital in the Twenty-First Century*. Cambridge, MA: The Belknap Press of Harvard University.
Piketty, Thomas. 2020. *Capital and Ideology*. Cambridge, MA: The Belknap Press of Harvard University.
Piketty, Thomas. 2021. *Time for Socialism: Dispatches from a World on Fire*. New Haven, CT: Yale University Press.
Reitz, Charles. 2016a. *Philosophy & Critical Pedagogy: Insurrection & Commonwealth*. New York: Peter Lang Publishing.

Reitz, Charles. 2016b. "Accounting for Inequality: Questioning Piketty on National Income Accounts and the Capital-Labor Split." *Review of Radical Political Economics*. Volume 48, Number 2, Summer.

Reitz, Charles. 2009a. "Herbert Marcuse and the Humanities: Emancipatory Education and Predatory Culture," in Douglas Kellner, Tyson Lewis, Clayton Pierce, K. Daniel Cho (Eds.). *Marcuse's Challenge to Education*. Lanham, MD: Rowman & Littlefield.

Reitz, Charles. 2009b. "Herbert Marcuse and the New Culture Wars," in Douglas Kellner, Tyson Lewis, Clayton Pierce, K. Daniel Cho (Eds.). *Marcuse's Challenge to Education*. Lanham, MD: Rowman & Littlefield.

Reitz, Charles. 2008. "Horace Greeley, Karl Marx, and German 48ers: AntiRacism in the Kansas Free Sate Struggle," *Marx-Engels Jahrbuch 2008*. Berlin: Akademie Verlag.

Reitz, Charles. 2010. "The Socialist Turners of New York City, 1853" *Yearbook of German-American Studies*. Volume 45.

Reitz, Charles. 2000. *Art, Alienation, and the Humanities: A Critical Engagement with Herbert Marcuse*. Albany, NY: State University of New York Press.

Reitz, Charles. 1976. "Imperialist Rivalry and Industrial Education," *The Insurgent Sociologist* [Critical Sociology] July 1.

Robinson, William I. 2020. *The Global Police State*. London: Pluto Press.

Steel, Ronald. 1971. *Imperialists and Other Heroes: A Chronicle of American Empire*. New York: Random House.

Stone, Oliver and Peter Kuznik. 2019. *The Untold History of the United States*. New York: Simon & Schuster Gallery Books.

Vine, David. 2015. *Base Nation*. New York: Metropolitan Books, Henry Holt & Company.

Zinn, Howard. 2008. *A People's History of American Empire*. New York: Metropolitan Books, Henry Holt.

2
Marcuse Renaissance in the 2020s

Readers of this volume already know the world needs changing and want to help to change it. Who will define the future? The political language of the Republicans and Democrats is patently insufficient. We face the necessity of building the theory and practice *for a new world order today*: one of racial equality, women's equality, the liberation of labor, the restoration of nature, leisure, abundance, and peace.

Marcuse's caustic condemnations over fifty years ago of U.S. capitalism and its systems of economic waste, wealth distortion, neofascist tendencies, racebased police repression, terror war, and environmental degradation are particularly timely and deserve invigorated discussion in cultural and political circles today. As the 2020s have rolled out, racial minorities were hit by the deadliest effects of Covid-19. Police killings of unarmed Black men had become almost routine and continued even after George Floyd's murder ignited a global movement for the equality of Black lives. Neofascist rhetoric of hate and fear emboldened open demonstrations of militarized white supremacy, culminating in Donald Trump's overt and covert mobilization of neofascist American politicians and white power street fighters to discount the Black vote in the 2020 presidential election and physically assault a joint session of the U.S. Congress January 6, 2021. All the while, in the political-philosophical background, something notable has been occurring.

Maroji Visic's 2019 essay, "Renaissance of Herbert Marcuse: A Study on Present Interest in Marcuse's Interdisciplinary Critical Theory," documents Marcuse's re-emergence in today's radical political discourse and his present-day impact. Her research reviews and elaborates the latest scholarly contributions by Marcuse scholars, Arnold Farr (2009), Andrew Feenberg (2014), Sarah Surak and Robert Kirsch (2016), Andrew Lamas, et al. (2017), Terry Maley (2017), and several others including Douglas Kellner, perhaps the foremost Marcuse researcher, who argues that:

> ... in the present conjuncture of global economic crisis, terrorism and a resurgence of U.S. militarism, and growing global movements against corporate capitalism and war, Marcuse's political and activist version of critical theory is highly relevant to the challenges of the contemporary moment. Marcuse is especially useful for developing global perspectives on domination and resistance, radically criticizing the existing system of domination, valorizing movements of resistance, and projecting radical alternatives to the current organization of society and mode of life. (Kellner in Visić 2019, 662)

Marcuse's previously unpublished papers and publications have also proven to be topical, and have recently become available in a six-volume, paperback edition: *The Collected Papers of Herbert Marcuse*, edited by Douglas Kellner and other collaborators (Kellner [1998–] 2014). Peter-Erwin Jansen has edited a similar series published as Herbert Marcuse, *Nachgelassene Schriften* (Jansen 2009). Volumes in these series make important contributions to the analysis of fascism in Germany and disclose Marcuse's suggestions during World War II working with the U.S. government's wartime Office of Strategic Services.

Javier Sethness Castro has written a new monograph, *Eros and Revolution: The Critical Philosophy of Herbert Marcuse* (2018). The volume is comprehensive, nuanced, politically challenging, and rich. Marcuse's works are interpreted anew for the contemporary generation of readers who may have comparatively little familiarity even with the major contours of Marcuse's thinking. They are discussed in a manner sure to resonate with the current critical concerns of younger scholars and activists (i.e. Marcuse's militant environmentalism; his trailblazing encouragement for LBGTQ liberation and alliances; his appreciation for non-reproductive sexuality; his concerns about vegetarianism/veganism; the intricacies of the fraught Israeli-Palestinian relationship). Features of Sethness Castro's analysis that I judge to be especially innovative and illuminating—each with distinctive implications for revolutionary practice today—include: his emphasis on the activist legacy of *One-Dimensional Man;* the current applicability of Marcuse's antifascist analyses written while working for the Office of Strategic Services during World War II; his widened interpretation of the pertinence of Marcuse's "Repressive Tolerance" essay to radical politics today; his discussion of the fruitful Marxist-Anarchist dialogue within Marcuse's writings; and lastly his conception of the ecologically mindful energy of Eros as a philosophical and political force for revolutionary system change.

Ulrich Ruschig has focused attention on Marcuse's call for the liberation of nature as well as the liberation of labor in *Die Befreiung der Natur: Zum Verhältnis von Natur und Freiheit bei Herbert Marcuse* (2020). I will employ several of his insights in chapters 8 and 10 below. Some have questioned the critical, dialectical power of Marcuse's social theory, most recently Marcial González (2018), and I myself have critically engaged aspects of his thought elsewhere quite vigorously (Reitz, 2019; 2000). I stress here on the other hand Marcuse's philosophical and political strengths, especially his revolutionary and antiracist perspectives on the environment and neofascist violence, as well as on the liberation of labor and new forms of property ownership and political-economic relations characteristic of a revolutionary socialist economy (Reitz, 2020; 2019).

On the need for an ecosocialist world system

The importance of ecology to the revolutionary movement and the importance of the revolutionary movement for ecology was evident and vividly elaborated by Marcuse. He is the singular member of the Frankfurt School to occupy himself with wide-ranging ecological issues. Horkheimer and Adorno had eminently addressed humanity's problematic domination of nature as a philosophical theme in *Dialectic of Enlightenment* ([1947] 1972), generally separating nature from civilization and culture, and evaluating nature's at times awesome gravitas and/or radical enchantments as nonetheless beneath the transcendent heights of Great Art.

Marcuse has his own valuable perspective on aesthetics, which I have already discussed elsewhere (Reitz, 2000) and will highlight again in this volume's chapter 9. For now, I wish to emphasize that his critical social theory demonstrates a "Green Turn" in an entirely different register than that of Horkheimer and Adorno, consistent with the foundations of Marcuse's thought in a more thoroughly dialectical materialist philosophy. Marcuse published two notable environmentalist essays rarely appreciated even by readers most familiar with his work in general: "Ecology and Revolution" ([1972] 2005) and "Ecology and the Critique of Modern Society" (Marcuse [1979] 2011). These propose a program of global action against capitalism's wasted abundance and climate change, revolving around what Marcuse considered to be the *radical* rather than minimum goals of socialism. In this chapter, I will emphasize not only Marcuse's revolutionary perspective on ecological issues but also several other dimensions of his work keenly relevant to the present day. Conspicuous among these is the "critique of pure tolerance," developed in his 1965 essay "Repressive Tolerance;" in addition, his views on neofascism, police violence, and his especially illuminating yet rarely examined philosophical understanding of labor as the core of the material human condition (Marcuse [1933] 1973). I will show that Marcuse viewed humanity's creative powers as rooted in our essential capacities of labor and art and intelligence, the key vectors of radical change and liberation.

A militant defense of the earth and its people occupied much of Marcuse's last years of life. His final published essay, "Ecology and the Critique of Modern Society" (Marcuse [1979] 2011), addresses "the destruction of nature in the context of the general destructiveness which characterizes our society."

> Under the conditions of advanced industrial society, satisfaction is always tied to destruction. The domination of nature is tied to the violation of nature. The search for new sources of energy is tied to the poisoning of the life environment. (Marcuse [1979] 2011, 209)

Marcuse's earlier essay "Ecology and Revolution" noted the revival of the women's movement and student anti-war protest in 1972. The ecology movement joined these in protesting against the capitalist "violation of the Earth" (Marcuse [1972] 2005, 174).

> [M]onopoly capitalism is waging a war against nature—human nature as well as external nature. For the demands on ever more intense exploitation come into conflict with nature itself ... and the demands of exploitation progressively reduce and exhaust resources: the more capitalist productivity increases, the more destructive it becomes. This is one sign of the internal contradictions of capitalism. (Marcuse [1972] 2005, 174)

The methodologies of ecology, critical philosophy and sociology take *the system* as the unit of analysis, rather than the individual. They focus on the complex and pivotal underlying structures of economic oppression and exploitation that are too often overlooked (sometimes actively suppressed) by analysts, policymakers, commentators, and educators when examining both the causes and the impacts of imperial corporate globalization. "Authentic ecology flows into a militant struggle for a socialist politics which must attack the system at its roots, both in the process of production and in the mutilated consciousness of individuals" (Marcuse [1972] 2005, 176).

Since the 1970s, the time of Marcuse's initial prominence, the world has become ever more aware and rightfully disturbed about multiple forms of environmental disaster on the horizon. Marcuse advocated a fundamental opposition to global capitalism's predatory and extractive economic order; so too he had a radical respect for our interlocking interdependence with the earth and our need for collective engagement in building an environmentally honorable future.

Capitalism is not effectively concerned with eliminating alienation, exploitation, pollution, waste, poverty, or freeing mankind from the need to toil. It *is* concerned essentially with developing means to maintain a sufficient rate of profit. The tremendous productivity of modern technology does not allow the citizenry of the U.S., or the globe for that matter, to reduce their toil and enjoy abundant leisure. This technology becomes irrational and decadent when it sustains a distorted growth of capital that destroys the ecological base and the humane dimension of our social lives. Nonetheless, the high productivity of modern technology allows tremendous output with a small amount of labor time. Automated technology provides the potential for abundant leisure without the need for excessive toil. Radical philosophy faces the necessity of building the ecologically conscious theory and practice for a new world order. I have discussed a Marcusean approach to ecology and revolution at Reitz (2019) and a Marcusean political economy in greater detail at Reitz and Spartan ([2013] 2015) and Reitz (2016b). Given also the contemporary heightened awareness of the regularity of police killings of unarmed black men in the U.S. after incidents such as Ferguson, Baltimore, Cleveland, New York City, and elsewhere, Marcuse's condemnation in "Repressive Tolerance" (1965) of the violence against minorities demands renewed attention.

Marcuse's critique of the free speech fallacy: No pure tolerance of hate speech

Antiracist progressives today often encounter the conservative backlash that twists the democratic doctrine of free speech into an absolutist or "purist" form—weaponizing it as a warped defense of white supremacy in a way that seems to make racism legally acceptable. Today the New Right or Alt-Right is asserting a putative political need for an ostensibly democratic society to maintain an absolute tolerance of abusive and even assaultive speech—as protected forms of dissent. Marcuse believed that the doctrine of pure tolerance was systematically utilized by reactionary and liberal forces to abuse guarantees against bigotry and discrimination and derail or destroy the possibility of democratic egalitarianism (Marcuse 1965). The free speech fallacy uses the charge that opposition to hate speech imperils free speech (Stanley 2016). Many accept the free speech fallacy and protect fascist speech and white supremacy with little understanding that classical liberalism intended speech protections primarily for powerless minority voices expressing dissent against the prevailing ideology and its power structure, *not* necessarily to protect off-putting establishment voices that are already hegemonic as well as often distasteful.

"This pure tolerance of sense and nonsense . . ." practiced under the conditions prevailing in the United States today ". . . cannot fulfil the civilizing function attributed to it by the liberal protagonists of democracy, namely protection of dissent" (Marcuse 1965, 94, 117). The assertion, often heard today, that racist and sexist views contribute necessary components of cultural diversity and belong within an inclusive pluralism is an utterly perverse example of vicious cultural and political double-speak.

The violence that actually prevails in the ostensibly peaceful centers of civilization today: "is practiced by the police, in the prisons and the mental institutions, in the fight against racial minorities.............This violence indeed breeds violence" (Marcuse 1965, 105). "To treat the great crusades against humanity . . . with the same impartiality as the desperate struggles for humanity means neutralizing their opposite historical function, reconciling the executioners with their victims, distorting the record" (Marcuse 1965, 113). Marcuse's partisanship is clear: "The small and powerless minorities which struggle against the false consciousness and its beneficiaries must be helped: their continued existence is more important than the preservation of abused rights and liberties which grant constitutional powers to those who oppress these minorities" (Marcuse 1965, 110). Marcuse is clear that withdrawing democratic tolerance from the Nazi organizers of genocide would have and should have been a necessary decision, yet even so not lightly made:

> Such extreme suspension of the right of free speech and free assembly is indeed justified only if the whole of society is in extreme danger. ... The conditions under which tolerance can again become a liberating force have still to be created. (Marcuse 1965, 110-111)

Facebook and Twitter, which facilitated a vast expansion of bigotry and hate speech on their platforms, ultimately realized the grave danger and harm it had engendered with no regulation of the racist and neofascist voices of domestic terrorists. After January 6, they banned Donald Trump in what was a clearly effective action against the grave neofascist threat of force and violence against liberal political leaders and any ordinary citizens who get in their way. This *is* a kind of censorship with the purpose of saving the traditional liberal order. Freedom of speech is not absolute, and must be viewed in the context of its real political consequences.

Within the current forms of social unfreedom that are yet called democracies, real crimes by the right (before 9/11, as well as in its aftermath) are systemically tolerated by the state in practice—such as racist police brutality, the deprivation of millions of Americans from comprehensive health care, treating asylum seekers as criminals, implementing the death penalty in a racially biased manner, supplying arms and training to governments and armed groups around the world that commit torture, political killings, and other human rights abuses (Amnesty International, 1998; Bevins, 2020; Harcourt, 2018, Winter 2020). I have explored the nature a Marcusean opposition to racism in the U.S. elsewhere at Reitz (2021; 2016a; 2009).

Imperial America and neofascist counterrevolution

Herbert Marcuse's sharp critique of the counterrevolutionary power of U.S. militarism and cold war empire-building in foreign policy stems in part because Marcuse witnessed Germany's loss of Weimar democracy to a politics of ethnic national identity, an imagined community of blood and soil. Marcuse's "Repressive Tolerance" (1965) essay was a product of his critique of German fascism and right-wing activism, genocide. It expressed his opposition to fascism as well as the liberal doctrines of tolerance that made the Third Reich possible.

By the late Sixties, Marcuse became a proponent of an activist politics against Imperial America's racial and gender-biased capitalism and its concomitant wars and worldwide attempts at regime change. In *Counterrevolution and Revolt* (1972) he warned of the global economic and cultural developments that are now much more obvious given capitalism's crescendo of economic failures since 2008.

> The Western world has reached a new stage of development: now, the defense of the capitalist system requires the organization of counterrevolution at home and abroad. ... Torture has become a normal instrument of "interrogation" around the world ... even Liberals are not safe if they appear as too liberal. (Marcuse 1972, 1)[1]

Political and philosophical tendencies that are often referred to as "neoliberalism" and/or "neoconservatism" in much analytical work today, Marcuse clearly understood by 1972 as organized *counterrevolution* (Marcuse 1972). In historical terms, the U.S. does need to be understood as having originated as a colonial settler society that in spite of or because of its deep Christian religious convictions carried out genocide against Native peoples and exploited a slave economy (Langman and Lundskow 2016; Dunbar-Ortiz 2014). The *interpersonal* force of today's counterrevolution in the U.S. today is largely attributed to angry middle-class white men, Western chauvinists or Christian chauvinists, whose attitudes of superiority over others in religion, culture, and race lead also to behavior mired in the cult of toxic masculinity: tough, hard-nosed, unsparing, fascist, with a willingness to exert deadly force for control and domination. Despite American ideals of democracy and equality, a reactionary national male character type has emerged having a predatory adulation of plutocracy and power but seeing itself as free and democratic. The interpersonal human dynamics in American history are however undergirded by *institutional structures* that have served as covert generative mechanisms for the anger and aggression characteristic also of counterrevolution (Steel 1971, 75, 189-280.

---

[1] Marcuse's perspicacious insight here was articulated almost fifty years before the unmistakably counterrevolutionary attack January 6, 2021, by reactionary loyalists of former President Donald Trump against the joint session of Congress (i.e. liberals) that would certify the election of Democrat Joe Biden as U.S. President.

Today the institutional aspect of the counterrevolution entails a Supreme Court in which "money-is-speech" is protected by the First Amendment, as is a cross burning at a Black family's home. Even though this racist act was construed as repugnant hate speech by Antonin Scalia and the Supreme Court, it was considered protected speech (Scalia 1992). Intensifying inequalities within the U.S. political economy need to be seen as stemming from the financial and monetary policies of the Federal Reserve Bank (Petrou 2021). Then there is the police-state USA Patriot Act and the global "Terror Wars" of the U.S. military, its President and Congress (Kellner 2003). Not long ago the news media brought us disclosures almost daily about the U.S. military's use of torture and prisoner abuse (Abu Ghraib, Guantánamo), civilian massacres and war crimes (Fallujah, Haditha), and the loaded intelligence that the U.S. Defense Department desired as a pretext for the invasion and occupation of Iraq. Such factors are system-derived rather than caused by an individual's personal derelictions. The larger social history of Imperial America has been extensively documented by Domhoff (2022), Bevins (2020), Stone and Kuznik (2019), Robinson (2020), Harcourt (2018), Winter (2020), Vine (2015), and Greene (1970). Marcuse believed that counterrevolutionary forces in the U.S. had gained the initiative and power, making the political alternative of the future the contradiction between fascism and socialism (Marcuse 1972, 29).

> And we should never take comfort in saying, "All right, it may well be that fascism may come, but it will not last and in the long run socialism will triumph." (Marcuse [1974] 2015, 10)

In the U.S. after the civil unrest following the police killing of George Floyd, there was a coordinated deployment of the militarized weaponry of municipal policing (tear gas, smoke bombs) utilizing punitive stratagems by which lawful speech and protest became "unlawful" if they ran counter to law enforcement's arbitrary declaration of "crowd control" measures, such as curfews and special confinement, prior to any even remotely criminal behavior on the part of protesters. In late May, early June, 2020, in U.S. city after U.S. city, the identical scenarios of patently *unwarranted, excessive, and unaccountable* armed force (Bogel-Burroughs, et al., 2021; McCann, et.al. 2020) were implemented by diverse local police departments with most officers looking exactly the same: helmeted for combat, in full body armor, clad with gas masks at the ready and automatic military weapons strapped to their shoulders. Marcuse's *OneDimensional Man* had underscored that "In the contemporary era, the conquest of scarcity is still confined to small areas of advanced industrial society. Their prosperity covers up the Inferno inside and outside their borders" (Marcuse 1964, 241). It also stressed that such circumstances evoked resistance:

> [U]nderneath the conservative popular base is the substratum of the outcasts and outsiders, the exploited and persecuted of other races and other colors . . . . Their opposition hits the system from without . . . it is an elementary force which violates the rules of the game. When they get together and go out into the streets, without arms, without protection, in order to ask for the most primitive civil rights, they know that they face dogs, stones, and bombs, jail, concentration camps, even death. (Marcuse 1964, 257)

The counterrevolution today represents the ongoing conservative counterattack, against the legacy of Sixties' activists and radicals, many of whom embraced the peace movement, the civil rights movement, the women's movement, the rank and file labor movement, etc., as forms of an emancipatory counterculture. An awareness of the intersectionality of our interdependencies and vulnerabilities has come to the fore in recent decades. "Freedom is understood as rooted in these needs, which are sensuous, ethical, and rational in one" (Marcuse 1972, 16-17).

The radical rather than minimum goals of socialism

Marcuse argued that the Sixties' spirit of rebelliousness expressed a visceral repugnance at the totality of the efficiently functioning social order of advanced industrial society. Marcuse described this opposition as a "Great Refusal" (1969, viii-ix) which constituted a multidimensional expression of *system negation*. Capitalism represents the irrational perfection of waste and the degradation of the earth; profitable plastic litter, air pollution, trash (planned obsolescence), toxic dumping, air and water pollution, resource depletion, etc. Ubiquitous advertising adds to the devastation by further boosting sales and the exchange value of a "new" product despite its diminished quality and use-value. We get disposable consumer goods and a society in which lives become disposable as well (Packard 1970).

Marcuse noted that the development of the women's movement and intensifying student anti-war protests were resonant with the ecology and labor movements and that they could be united in protesting against the capitalist "violation of the earth" (Marcuse [1972] 2005, 174; Sukhov 2020, 372-73). The extraordinary value of Marcuse's strategy—*against* the sociopathic disregard for our future; *for* our common humanity—is that *system negation* can have the appeal of a *new general-interest*—offering a constellation of goals and forces made viable through the decommodification of labor and technology and the elimination of profitable waste and destructive divisions—moving toward racial equality, women's equality, the liberation of labor, the restoration of nature, leisure, abundance, and peace. These goals, and the means to them, can bring together a global alliance of transformative forces. Such a strategy forms the key to the *emancipatory universalization of resistance*—the revolt of youth as a global phenomenon—against guns, war, militarism, women's oppression, police violence against minorities and protesters, labor force precarity, and capitalism's many varieties of exploitation. Moral and aesthetic needs become basic vital needs and drive toward new relationships between the sexes, between the generations, between human beings and nature. (Marcuse 1972, 16-17)

Socialism's minimum standards require the provision of adequate social needs-oriented programs and services such as housing, health care, childcare, and education, to everyone, as well as government policy, law enforcement, and public media that ensure the optimization of the human material condition. Still, to be substantial and fully sustainable radical ecosocialist policies must do more. A fuller perspective consistent with Marcuse's vision would emphasize policies that eliminate universal commodity dependency through the decommodification / socialization of the economy; forgive labor force debt; expropriate the expropriators; and redistribute property/land. The decommodification of production overall supplies a socialist alternative with its essential economic and ecological viability. At the conclusion of Marcuse's *Paris Lectures* (2015), he calls for:

> a new form of socialism, namely socialism as in any and every respect qualitatively different and a break with capitalism . . . and it seems to me that only a decisive redirection of production itself would in this sense be a revolutionary development. A total redirection of production, first of all, of course, towards the abolition of poverty and scarcity wherever it exists in the world today. Secondly, a total reconstruction of the environment and the creation of space and time for creative work; space and time for creative work instead of alienated labor as a full-time occupation. (Marcuse 2015, 69)

For Marcuse, however, "the issue is not the purification of the existing society but its replacement" (Marcuse [1972] 2005, 175).

> The inner dynamic of capitalism changes, with the changes in its structure, the pattern of revolution changes: far from reducing, it extends the potential mass base for revolution, and it necessitates a revival of the radical rather than the minimum goals of socialism. (Marcuse 1972, 5)

As I have stressed before, the evidence today of impending natural catastrophe is mounting; so too our awareness that the climate crisis is the outcome of economic and governmental business as usual. Without an adamant commitment to ecosocialism's most radical goals—I like to refer to them as an *EarthCommonWealth Counteroffensive*—there is no sufficient negation, and there will be no sufficient transformation from oligarchy toward a new world system when conditions are ripe for revolution. Marcuse was the critical theorist to develop a uniquely explicit ecosocialist critique of capitalism and develop a strategy of revolutionary ecological liberation. He also knew that an array of artists is needed to assist any culture in the transvaluation of values. Great Art, including tragedy, has the power to engender an elevated sense of calm and love of life and enhance our desire to abide in a serene *("erhaben"*—Schiller) existence on the stately surface of planet earth. Art can help human beings transform a society. It brings us to a knowledge of ourselves as sensuous living labor and to the beauty of consecrated effort (as in the latter life stages of Buddhism and Hinduism, to be discussed in chapter 6 below) offering, in the fullest composure key abilities in service to the community. *Commonwealth* is humanity's (that is, sensuous living labor's) aesthetic form: workmanship and artistry, emancipated from repression, taking place "in accordance with the laws of beauty" (Marx [1844] 1982, 114, also a tribute to Schiller). Human labor is *the* resource that sustains the human community. Change starts with the pleasure we find in meaningful work, mindful of our need to be of service to humanity. We need more than to be merely making a living; we need to be modestly elated and grateful that we are making a life of love and justice, leisure, abundance, and peace.

> [W]e have to become aware of the real possibility of a revolution in the most advanced industrial countries taking place not on a basis of poverty and misery, but rather on the basis of wasted abundance. And if this paradoxical concept is correct, it would mean that we have to become aware of new motives for revolution—new motives for revolution and new goals of revolution that no longer focus on the possibility or necessity of revolution born of misery and material privation, but a revolution on the basis of increasing social wealth for increasing strata of the population. (Marcuse [1974] 2015, 49).

From Marcuse's perspective, the world needs a strategy to oppose resurgent racism, bigoted nationalism, and warlike patriotism. It needs to be able to negate the negations that are damaging lives and to go on the offensive for the changes that can support and extend race and gender equality, labor freedom, economic abundance, peace, and communal well-being. Marcuse's Great Refusal (more on this in chapters 3 and 10 below) can be seen as a template for a global alliance of transformational forces in pursuit of a life-affirming and humanist future of intercultural solidarity within a new ecosocialist order.

Sensuous living labor and EarthCommonWealth

The latent power of labor is central to emancipatory theory and praxis. In this regard, my analysis extends the dialectical philosophical perspective on the material human condition of both Marcuse and Charles Woolfson's *Labor Theory of Culture* (1982). This stresses the cultural context of cooperation and caring in the earliest human societies which fostered interdependence and an awareness of the customary power of partnership. Partnership customs and behaviors had the capacity to ensure survival. Subsistence needs were met with relatively little time spent in the collaborative acquisition of necessities, i.e. three to four hours a day (Sahlins [1968] 2017); thus, the foundation was established for the fuller species' life to flourish within the human community. This included the development of language as a derivative of the communal human condition (Leakey 1994, 124). The "global labor majority [is] constituted by women, peasants, and indigenous people" (Salleh 2017).

The radically socialist logic of commonwealth production, ownership, and stewardship can facilitate a movement for social transformation that can, within the realm of necessity, construct an architecture of intercultural equality, disalienation, ecological balance, abundance, and freedom. Marx and Marcuse emphasized that collective effort is what makes us prosperous: labour occurs in social relationships and is a communal project of social beings to meet human needs and promote human flourishing. Furthermore, social productivity is the political-philosophical foundation of the call for socialized, ownership. Yet capitalism's fetish for commodity production and for growth in exchange values (enhancing surplus value) has become the be-all and end-all of the business system (no limits to profit accumulation). At the same time, the workforce is a resource with programmatic power. It is the creative force in the economy. We live in a massive built environment: this embodies a human community's social labor exteriorized in curbs, pavement—every square inch around us, including gardens, parks, etc.—worked by human hands. This aggregate historical effort constitutes an ecology of a laboring commonwealth, undergirded by the resources of nature. Wealth derives from this collective production process (as was notably described by Adam Smith on the power of the division of labor). Included in the outputs of this collective process is also our common human heritage of science, technology, math, etc., even language, each of which develops primarily within the context of social labor. When these multiple efforts at labor combine judiciously with our common earthly comrades, the land, wildlife, flora, sea, air, etc., humanity's CommonWealth emerges. Conditioned upon proper respect for the earth's rights and resources, laboring humanity, as society's foundational collective, has a legitimate right to the control, disposition, and ownership of this socially produced wealth. This is a *supply-side* economic theory. In contrast to the conservative capitalist fable that economic growth is driven through corporate tax breaks and business deregulation; supply-side here draws attention to the economic significance of the expanded production of real output increasing the society's supply of use-values, *not* the paper wealth of asset price inflation as pursued in financialized capitalism. Commonwealth productivity indicates what social living labor accomplishes in terms of real tangible value creation. Our very humanity is grounded in the legacy we have inherited from our earliest forms of production in partnership societies with their ecologies of caregiving and commonwealth.

There will be no restoration of nature and no re-humanization of our coarsened and divided culture, our damaged and precarious world, without the radical regulation of globally financialized monopoly capitalism—or its *elimination*. Socialism's minimum standards require the provision of adequate social needsoriented programs and services such as housing, health care, child care, and education, to everyone, as well as government policy, law enforcement, and public media that ensure the optimization of the human material condition.

Today's global capitalist crisis is also a huge legitimation crisis, to be discussed in chapter 10, as well as a crucial opportunity for a new political beginning. The goal of building a universal human community on the foundation of universal human well-being must acknowledge the fundamental role of the labor process in the sustenance of human social life. Human labor has the irreplaceable power to build the commonwealth, past and future. Our current conditions of insecurity and risk make it imperative that we undertake a deeper understanding of the necessity of a humanist commonwealth alternative: radical ecosocialism as an egalitarian, abundant, and green political-economy, through which humanity may govern itself honorably and handsomely in terms of our fullest potentials, mindful of the care and gratitude we owe to planet earth.

Works cited

Amnesty International. 1998. *United States of America: Rights for All*. New York: Amnesty International USA.

Bevins, Vincent. 2020. *The Jakarta Method: Washington's Anticommunist Crusade & the Mass Murder Program that Shaped our World*. New York: Public Affairs/ Perseus/Hachette Book Group.

Bogel-Burroughs, Nicholas, John Eligon, and Will Wright. 2021. "Los Angeles Police Exacerbated Chaos at Protests, Report Says" *The New York Times*, March 12, 2021. A-1, A-19.

Domhoff, G. William. 2022, *Who Rules America?* Eighth Edition.*The Corporate Rich, White Nationalist Republicans, and the Inclusionary Democrats in the 2020s*. New York: Routledge.

Dunbar-Ortiz, Roxanne. 2014. *An Indigenous Peoples' History of the United States*. Boston, MA: Beacon Press.

Farr, Arnold L. 2009. *Critical Theory and Democratic Vision: Herbert Marcuse and Recent Liberation Philosophies*. Lanham, MD: Lexington Books.

Feenberg, Andrew. 2014. *The Philosophy of Praxis: Marx, Lukacs, and the Frankfurt School*. London: Verso.

González, Marcial. 2018. "Herbert Marcuse's Repudiation of Dialectics," *Science & Society*, Vol. 82, No. 3, July.

Greene, Felix. 1970. *The Enemy: What Every American Should Know About Imperialism*. New York: Random House.

Harcourt, Bernard E. 2018. *The Counterrevolution: How Our Government Went to War Against Its Own Citizens*. New York: Basic Books/Hachette Book Group.

Horkheimer, Max and Theodor W. Adorno. [1947] 1972. *Dialectic of Enlightenment*. New York: Herder and Herder.

Jansen, Peter-Erwin (ed). [1998–] 2009. Herbert Marcuse, *Nachgelassene Schriften*. Six volumes, edited by Peter-Erwin Jansen. Springe, Germany: zu Klampen Verlag.

Kellner, Douglas. [1998–] 2014. *Collected Papers of Herbert Marcuse*. Six volumes, edited by Douglas Kellner. New York and London: Routledge.

Kellner, Douglas. (ed.). 2005. Herbert Marcuse, *Collected Papers of Herbert Marcuse*. Volume 3, *The New Left and the 1960s*. New York and London: Routledge.

Kellner, Douglas. 2003. *From 9/11 to Terror War*. Lanham, MD: Rowman & Littlefield.

Lamas, Andrew, Todd Wolfson, and Peter N. Funke (Eds.). 2017. *The Great Refusal: Herbert Marcuse and Contemporary Social Movements*. Philadelphia, PA: Temple University Press.

Leakey, Richard. 1994. *The Origin of Humankind*. New York: Basic Books.

Langman, Lauren and George Lundskow. 2016. *God, Guns, Gold, and Glory*. Chicago: Haymarket Books.

Maley, Terry (Ed.). 2017. *One-Dimensional Man 50 Years On: The Struggle Continues*. Halifax: Fernwood Publishing.

Marcuse, Herbert. [1974] 2015. *Paris Lectures at Vincennes University, 1974*. Edited by Peter-Erwin Jansen and Charles Reitz. Philadelphia, PA: International Herbert Marcuse Society.

Marcuse, Herbert. [1979] 2011. "Ecology and the Critique of Modern Society," in Douglas Kellner and Clayton Pierce (Eds.) *Herbert Marcuse, Collected Papers of Herbert Marcuse*. Volume 5, *Philosophy, Psychoanalysis and Emancipation*. New York and London: Routledge.

Marcuse, Herbert. [1972] 2005. "Ecology and Revolution," in Douglas Kellner (Ed.) *Herbert Marcuse, Collected Papers of Herbert Marcuse*. Volume 3, *The New Left and the 1960s*. New York and London: Routledge.

Marcuse, Herbert. [1933] 1973. "On the Philosophical Foundation of the Concept of Labor in Economics," *Telos*, No. 16, Summer.

Marcuse, Herbert. 1972. *Counterrevolution and Revolt*. Boston, MA: Beacon Press.

Marcuse, Herbert. 1969. *An Essay on Liberation*. Boston, MA: Beacon Press.

Marcuse, Herbert. 1965. "Repressive Tolerance," in R.P. Wolff, B. Moore, and H. Marcuse (Eds.). *A Critique of Pure Tolerance*. Boston, MA: Beacon Press.

Marcuse, Herbert. 1964. *One-Dimensional Man: Studies in the Ideology of Advanced Industrial Society*. Boston, MA: Beacon Press.

Marx, Karl. [1844] 1982. *The Economic & Philosophical Manuscripts of 1844*. Edited by Dirk Struik. New York: International Publishers.

McCann, Allison, Blacki Magliozzi, Andy Newman, Larry Buchanan and Aaron Byrd. 2020. "Caught on Over 60 Videos: Police Using Force on Protesters," *The New York Times*, May 31, A-1, A-18-19.

Packard, Vance. 1960. *The Waste Makers*. New York: David McKay Publishing.

Petrou, Karen. 2021. *Engine of Inequality*. Hoboken, NJ: Wiley and Sons.

Reitz, Charles. 2021. "Herbert Marcuse Today: On Ecological Destruction, Neofascism, White Supremacy, Hate Speech, Racist Police Killings, and the Radical Goals of Socialism," *Theory, Culture & Society*. December, Vol. 38(7-8).

Reitz, Charles. 2020. "A Note on Marcial González' 'Herbert Marcuse's Repudiation of Dialectics'," *Science & Society*, 84:2 April.
Reitz, Charles. 2019. *Ecology and Revolution: Herbert Marcuse and the Challenge of a New World System Today*. New York and London: Routledge.
Reitz, Charles. 2016a. "Celebrating Herbert Marcuse's One-Dimensional Man." *Radical Philosophy Review*. Volume 19, Number 1.
Reitz, Charles. 2016b. "Accounting for Inequality: Questioning Piketty on National Income Accounts and the Capital-Labor Split." *Review of Radical Political Economics*. Volume 48, Number 2, Summer.
Reitz, Charles. 2009. "Herbert Marcuse and the New Culture Wars," in Douglas Kellner, Tyson Lewis, Clayton Pierce, K. Daniel Cho, *Marcuse's Challenge to Education*. Lanham, MD: Rowman & Littlefield.
Reitz, Charles. 2000. *Art, Alienation, and the Humanities: A Critical Engagement with Herbert Marcuse*. Albany, NY: State University of New York Press.
Reitz, Charles and Stephen Spartan. [2013] 2015. "The Political Economy of Predation and Counterrevolution: Recalling Marcuse on the Radical Goals of Socialism," in Charles Reitz (ed). *Crisis and Commonwealth: Marcuse, Marx, McLaren*. Lanham, MD: Lexington Books.
Robinson, William I. 2020. *The Global Police State*. London: Pluto Press. Ruschig, Ulrich. 2020. *Die Befreiung der Natur: Zum Verhältnis von Natur und Freiheit bei Herbert Marcuse*. Köln: PapyRossa Verlag.
Sahlins, Marshall. [1968] 2017. "The Original Affluent Society," in *Stone Age Economics*. New York and London: Routledge.
Salleh, Ariel. [1997] 2017. *Ecofeminism as Politics: Nature, Marx and the Postmodern*. London: Zed Books.
Scalia, Antonin. 1992. *R.A.V. v. City of St. Paul, Minnesota*. No. 90-7675.
Sethness Castro, Javier. 2018. *Eros and Revolution: The Critical Philosophy of Herbert Marcuse*. Chicago: Haymarket Books.
Stanley, Jason. 2016. "The Free Speech Fallacy," in *The Chronicle Review*, March 18.
Steel, Ronald. 1971. *Imperialists and Other Heroes: A Chronicle of American Empire*. New York: Random House.
Stone, Oliver and Peter Kuznik. 2019. *The Untold History of the United States*. New York: Simon & Schuster Gallery Books.
Sukhov, Michael J. 2020. "Herbert Marcuse on Radical Subjectivity and the 'New Activism': Today's Climate and Black Lives Matter Movements," *Radical Philosophy Review*, Volume 23, Number 2.
Surak, Sarah and Robert Kirsch (co-editors). 2016. *New Political Science*, Volume 38, Number 4, Special Issue: Marcuse in the Twenty-First Century: Radical Politics, Critical Theory, and Revolutionary Praxis.
Vine, David. 2015. *Base Nation*. New York: Metropolitan Books, Henry Holt & Company.
Visic, Maroje. 2019. "Renaissance of Herbert Marcuse: A Study on Present Interest in Marcuse's Interdisciplinary Critical Theory," *Interdisciplinary Description of Complex Systems*. Volume 17, Number 3-B, Dubrovnik, Croatia. https://bityl.co/CeQC
Winter, Rainer. 2020. "Review: Bernard E. Harcourt, The Counterrevolution," *Theory, Culture & Society*. 37:7-8, December.
Woolfson, Charles. 1982. *The Labor Theory of Culture: A Re-examination of Engels's Theory of Human Origins*. London: Routledge and Kegan Paul.

3

Marcuse on Fascism, Antifascism (Antifa), and the "New Sensibility"

Herbert Marcuse first wrote of the future threat of *neofascism* in the U.S. in an essay titled "33 Theses" ([1947] 1998, 215). This was presented to Max Horkheimer as Marcuse's contribution to the proposed resumption of the publication of the *Zeitschrift für Sozialforschung* after WW2. But the *Zeitschrift* did not reappear, and this essay was not translated or published until fifty years later. Originally titled "33 Theses toward the Military Defeat of Hitler-Fascism," it was found in the Max Horkheimer archive and published by Jansen (1998) and Kellner (1998). It theorizes neofascism as the emergent political expression of totalitarian governance in the advanced industrial countries of the *anti-Soviet post-war West*.

> [T]he world is dividing into a neofascist and a Soviet camp. ... [T]here is only one alternative for revolutionary theory: to ruthlessly and openly criticize both systems and to uphold without compromise orthodox Marxist theory against both. (Marcuse [1947] 1998, 217).

Marcuse's essay stresses that the structural economic forces of corporate capitalism ultimately undergird counterrevolutionary interests. Marcuse thus did not attribute fascist behavior to a "Mass Psychology of Fascism" alone, as did Wilhelm Reich ([1946] 1980), Max Horkheimer, and Erich Fromm. There did exist widespread eliminationist antisemitism among the ordinary German people, as described by Daniel Goldhagen in his much-publicized *Hitler's Willing Executioners* (1996). Nazism did not *create* this bigotry, rather it *endorsed* its expression beyond all customary constraints. Marcuse's analysis, however, stressing structural forces in Germany's political economy sustaining the stigmatization and abuse of Jews is more akin to that of Franz Neumann's *Behemoth* ([1944] 2009) and Robert Brady's (1937) *Spirit and Structure of German Fascism* ([1941] 1960, 410).

Marcuse's still earlier anti-fascist piece, "The New German Mentality," (Marcuse [1942] 1998b) links an ostensibly psychological discussion of the authoritarian mentality of fascism to the material social forces that made it possible:

> The submissive and authoritarian character of man under the Nazi system is not an unchangeable natural property but an historical form of thought and behavior, concomitant with the transformation of largescale industry into a directly political dominion. This character will therefore dissolve when the social forces are defeated which are responsible for the transformation of an industrial into an authoritarian society. In National Socialist Germany, these forces are clearly distinguishable: they are the great industrial combines on which the economic organization of the Reich centers, and the upper strata of the governmental and party bureaucracy. The breaking up of their dominion is the prerequisite and the chief content of re-education. (Marcuse [1942] 1998b, 171)

This archival Marcuse source material is not simply of antiquarian interest. It makes important contributions to the Marxist analysis of fascism and offers a strategic advantage to us today during our own period of political turbulence. For example, it contrasts in a fundamental way with Jason Stanley's recent study, *How Fascism Works; The Politics of Us and Them* (2020). Stanley's account is particularly insightful on current forms of fascist ideology, anti-immigrant rhetoric, propaganda, and police violence: Bolsonaro, Orbán, Trump, the Hindu Nationalist Party (BJP), Germany's AfD. He is strongest on new state institutions like Homeland Security and ICE etc.; also his critique of the free speech fallacy as this protects racist rhetoric and conduct. In contrast to Marcuse, Neumann, Horkheimer, and Brady, however, Stanley's discussion of politics is bereft of political economy. The "forces of capital" are mentioned once (Stanley 2020, xix). The genesis of fascism is ostensibly rooted in a popular nostalgia for hierarchy, purity, and authoritarianism. Hitler's obsession with the destruction of labor unions is discussed, but not in relation to capital accumulation (Stanley 2020, 5, 172). In terms of what it has omitted, his argument lacks the fuller cogency it might have had.

Working with the U.S. government's wartime Office of Strategic Services during World War II to combat German fascism, Marcuse's unpublished papers and publications have uncanny currency given the rise of neofascism in the U.S.A. today. Jansen (2020) also brings to mind the *Studies in Prejudice* undertaken by members of the Frankfurt School in the U.S. in partnership with the American Jewish Committee in California. Volume 5 in the series *Prophets of Deceit*, written by Leo Löwenthal and Norbert Guterman ([1949] 1970), emphasized that any individual antisemitic or racist demagogue must be understood concretely in the social context of the contradictory economic and political conditions of the historical time period. This was stressed by Herbert Marcuse in his "Foreword" added to the 1970 paperback edition of this volume of *Studies*. Racism, involving hate speech and hate crime, thus always needs to be seen in connection with the institutional structures that support and promote it.

Marcuse's most militant and lengthy critique of fascism/neofascism is in a 1972 piece, "The Historical Fate of Bourgeois Democracy," never published until Kellner's 2001 volume 2 of Marcuse's archival papers. Terry Maley turned our attention to this otherwise rarely discussed essay underscoring liberal democracy's susceptibility to proto-fascist populism (Maley 2017, 209). Marcuse defines fascism as the "totalitarian organization of society for the preservation and expansion of capitalism in a situation where this is no longer attainable by the normal functioning of the market" ([1972] 2001, 185). "With the monopolistic concentration of economic power" (ibid, 167) the extraction of surplusvalue is extended upward also towards the middle classes through the intensified appropriation of unpaid labor time. In the context of the Vietnam war and the Nixon presidency, Marcuse concluded that "bourgeois democracy no longer presents an effective barrier to fascism" (ibid, 176). Law and morality no longer stand in the way.

> It is as if capitalism now feels safe enough to throw off the brakes on its productive destruction—legal, moral, political brakes. ... Its own behavior demonstrates daily the truth of Marxian theory. Engels' Third Part of *Anti-Dühring*,[1] Lenin's analysis of imperialism are tame and restrained in comparison with reality. (Marcuse [1972] 2001, 176)

It is a "regressive development of bourgeois democracy, its self-transformation into a police and warfare state" (ibid, 165) supported by

---

1 Which was later published separately as *Socialism, Utopian and Scientific*.

the sadomasochistic tolerance of a "free" people—"tolerance of the crooks and maniacs who govern them" (ibid, 171). The ongoing relevance of Marcuse's Vietnam era analysis to contemporary conditions is vividly revealed in the following comment:

> In free elections with universal suffrage, the people have elected (not for the first time!) a warfare government, engaged for long years in a war which is but a series of unprecedented crimes against humanity—a government of the representatives of the big corporation (and big labor!), a government unable (or unwilling) to halt inflation and eliminate unemployment, a government cutting down welfare and education, a government permeated with corruption, propped up by a Congress which has reduced itself to a yes-machine. (Marcuse [1972] 2001, 168)

Marcuse emphasizes the role racism has played in U.S, elections, especially that of Nixon, and the reactionary segregationist ideology of the antibusing movement. "On the road to fascism, advanced capitalism draws largely on primary aggressiveness.... cruelty, injustice, and vice are invariably rewarded" (ibid, 172-173). He proposes on the other hand that a socialist morality can become a political force. Here the student anti-war movement and the women's movement, as well as the rank-and-file opposition within the union movement become key; weaving them together is our future strategic challenge, i.e., as a New Sensibility, discussed more fully below, culminating in the Great Refusal as a unifying project. Militant activism against today's neo-Nazis and white supremacists also belongs to this Great Refusal. Marcuse dedicates *One-Dimensional Man* "to those who, without hope have given and give their life to the Great Refusal" (1964, 257). In the next line, he refers to "the fascist era" of WW2 and Walter Benjamin's deeply dialectical revolutionary awareness: "It is only for the sake of those without hope that hope is given to us." In chapter 10 below I shall elaborate Marcuse's notion of the Great Refusal as a unifying project, a multidimensional expression of *negation against systems of domination.*

Marcuse repeatedly criticized neofascist tendencies within the context of U.S. politics in *An Essay on Liberation* (1969) and *Counterrevolution and Revolt* (1972), warning against them especially his *Paris Lectures at Vincennes University* ([1974] 2015a, 10). Liberal forms of government are ostensibly forms of democracy, but at a deeper level, systems in which practically everyone is nearly totally dependent upon commodity exchange and markets, i.e. subtle yet substantive forms of economic and political unfreedom when meeting fundamental human needs. What Marx called the commodity fetish means the "worship" of commodity production and commodity dependency by those who have accumultated large capital holdings and who are thus structurally compelled to accumulate more or lose out to capitalist rivals.

Neofascist culture wars: The alt-right and white supremacy

In his 1972 book *Counterrevolution and Revolt*, Herbert Marcuse called attention to an intensifying conservative assault on liberal democracies by right-wing political forces. We are experiencing a transition from liberal democratic forms of unfreedom to reactionary, in many places actually fascist or neofascist, forms of unfreedom (some of them up to now more clandestine [as until recently in the U.S.A.], some of them more overt [as in Hungary, Brazil]). Marcuse's analysis of German fascism is a key component of his overall radical social critique. *Counterrevolution and Revolt* (1972) warned of the emergence of an (albeit stealthy) assault by an increasingly predatory capitalist system against liberal democratic change,[2] not only against its radical opposition (Marcuse, 1972; [1975] 1987, 172). The right-wing's culture wars accelerated through Ronald Reagan, Newt Gingrich, Lynn and Dick Cheney, and Antonin Scalia. First the New Right, then the Alt-Right (Steve Bannon, William S. Lind [2020], Donald Trump), asserted that an ostensibly democratic society must maintain an absolute freedom/tolerance of race and gender-based speech in abusive and even assaultive forms—as protected modes of dissent (Scalia 1992; Kors and Silverglate 1998, 48; Reitz 2000, 257-58).

The Alt-Right's culture wars have manufactured several imaginary conspiracies bent on taking over U.S. public education and manipulating the mainstream media and government policies. Hence their attacks on *The New York Times's* "1619 Project," "cancel culture," "political correctness," "cultural Marxism," and "critical race theory." Their larger project is to mobilize state governments and corporations for their neofascist agenda. Decades after his death (1978) Marcuse has been singled out for derision in at least four publications, notably Bloom (1987), Kors and Silverglate (1998), Buchanan (2002), and Wheeler (2021). Speaking of

---

2 Aaron Blake, "Trump promoted N.M. official's comment that 'the only good Democrat is a dead Democrat.' Now the man is arrested in the Capitol riot," *The Washington Post,* January 18, 2021.

the counterrevolution Marcuse is clear: "[T]he capitalist welfare/warfare state ... must always have an Enemy, with a capital E, a total enemy, because the perpetuation of [our] servitude ...activates and intensifies ... a primary aggressiveness. ... Therefore, the need for an Enemy, who must be there, and who must be created if he does not exist" (Marcuse 1968, 181-182). Of course what was true of Marcuse as enemy writ small was also true of the Enemy writ large, communism, part of an establishment strategy of foreign and domestic political aggression.

Today, as the U.S. Border Patrol allows paramilitary militias to detain and intimidate asylum seekers at the New Mexico/Mexico border and stream live videos of these actions over the internet to maximize the sense of threat to the "homeland,"[3] there has also been a spike in hate crimes directed against AsianAmericans in the wake of Donald Trump calling Covid-19 the "Wuhan virus" or the "China virus." A neofascist rhetoric of hate and fear has emboldened open demonstrations of militarized white supremacy, culminating in Donald Trump's overt and covert mobilization of neofascist America-First Republicans and white power forces for the events at the U.S. Capitol of January 6, 2021.

According to Douglas Dowd, the militarization and brutalization of American culture, along with its right-wing populist politics of grievance and bitterness had its roots especially during the Cold War. Here the Nixon White House successfully developed a public relations campaign that launched a "politics of resentment" (Gary Wills in Dowd 1997, 222). The "silent majority" saw itself as ardently aggrieved against the student anti-war mobilization and the civil rights movement (Dowd 1997, 121). Ronald Reagan and Donald Trump followed this playbook closely, intensifying the strategy's counterrevolutionary power. After the 1989 structural conversion of the USSR and Soviet bloc, the U.S. treated the end of the Cold War "as an occasion demanding the ratification of American global might" (Moyn 2021, 226). "U.S. presidents ordered not fewer but more wars: more than 80 percent of all U.S. military interventions since 1946 came *after* 1989" (Moyn 2021, 226 emphasis in original). Huntington (1996) came to call a central component of this change a "clash of civilizations" and/or a culture war. Enemies are "needed" to be sure, in Marcuse's view, to consolidate consensus in support of established powers and prejudices.

---

3 Nausicaa Renner, "Border Theater" *The New York Times Magazine*, Sunday, May 12, 2019, pp. 9-12.

Herbert Marcuse fled Germany's Nazis in 1933 because of his radical politics and Jewish background. In New York City he developed a remarkable series of books, each published as an English-language original, that represented to the world what would become a potent new perspective, the refugee Frankfurt School's critical social theory: *Reason and Revolution* (1941), *Eros and Civilization* (1955), *One-Dimensional Man* (1964), *An Essay on Liberation* (1969a), and *Counterrevolution and Revolt* (1972). "Critical theory" for Marcuse was not an Aesopian alternative or substitute for Marxism. He sought to raise the philosophy of Marx to its highest level.

As I have mentioned earlier, political and philosophical tendencies that are often referred to as "neoliberalism" and/or "neoconservatism" in much analytical work today, were understood back then as organized counterrevolution by Marcuse (Marcuse 1972; Harcourt 2018; Winter 2020). Today this counterrevolution entails: the police-state U.S.A. Patriot Act; global "Terror War" (Kellner 2003) amounting to a "Reign of Terror" (Ackerman 2021) that has terrified millions, tortured hundreds, created a global surveillance dragnet, created 21 million refugees, and spent $6 trillion on its operations (Ackerman in Tepperman 2021). Likewise, the U.S. quickly had a "money-is-speech" Supreme Court, and intensifying political economic inequalities. Twenty years after September 11, 2001, when the last U.S. troops were withdrawn from Afghanistan, *The New York Times'* editorial board proclaimed "The War on Terror Was Corrupt. ... Corruption was not a design flaw in the war. It was a design feature."[4] Furthermore, a U.S. Senate select committee's investigation into torture inflicted by CIA agents and operatives documented widespread unreported brutal, yet ineffective, interrogation techniques ostensibly contrary to official policy yet known and abetted by senior CIA officials.[5]

---

4 Farah Stockman, "The War on Terror Was Corrupt," *The New York Times*, September 15, 2021. The U.S. spent $5 billion on reconstruction aid and $7 billion on war fighting. "Who won the war on terror? American defense contractors, many of which were politically connected companies that had donated to George W. Bush's presidential campaign, according to the Center for Public Integrity. ... A forensic accountant who served on a military task force that analyzed $6 billion worth of Pentagon contracts estimated that 40 percent of the money ended up in the pockets of 'insurgents, criminal syndicates or corrupt Afghan officials,' according to *The Washington Post*." https://www.nytimes.com/2021/09/13/opinion/afghanistan-war-economy.html?searchResultPosition=2

5 Jeremy Askenhas, Hannah Fairfield, Josh Keller, and Paul Volpe, "7 Key Points from the C.I.A. Torture Report," *The New York Times*, December 9, 2014. https://www.nytimes.com/interactive/2014/12/09/world/cia-torture-report-key-points.html. See also, Carol Rosenberg, "Military Jurors Say Torture is a Moral Stain" *The New York Times*, November 1, 2021 A1. https://www.nytimes.com/2021/10/31/us/politics/guantanamo-torture-letter.html?searchRe sultPosition=1

This is what a police state looks like

Significant U.S. protest actions rattled the U.S. security apparatus well before September 11, 2001. The 1999 "Battle of Seattle" reminds us of the comparative strength and militance of the protest movement against the World Trade Organization. It was an action by "Teamsters and Turtles"—organized labor was out in strength as well as the environmentalist forces. The Black Bloc (or *antifa* movement)[6] also made a first U.S. appearance there. The protest was a huge success in spite of the massive deployment of militarized police. Soon thereafter, in 2001, the World Trade Center's Twin Towers were attacked in NYC. In the aftermath, the U.S. passed the U.S.A. Patriot Act having the excuse they were already seeking to legalize police repression in a neofascist build-up of police power against possible protesters. The Occupy movement felt this in many U.S. cities as protest encampments were destroyed. The BLM protests made this brutal police state-type power well known.[7] Today the preventive counterrevolution entails intensifying wealth and income inequalities, many of which derive from financial and monetary policies of the Federal Reserve bank (Petrou, 2021) and political-economic repression that is now more widely recognized as such (see Kellner 2003, 2012; Harcourt 2018; Bevins 2020).

Marcuse understood the capitalist state is an expression of material inequalities, never neutral, having been captured by the forces of class, race, and gender exploitation. Within the current forms of unfreedom that are yet called democracies, real crimes by the right (years before September 11th, as well as in its aftermath) are tolerated by the state in practice—such as systematic police brutality, depriving millions of Americans from comprehensive health care, treating asylum seekers as criminals, implementing the death penalty in a racially biased manner, supplying arms and training to governments and armed groups around the world that commit torture, political killings, and other human rights abuses, etc. (Amnesty International, 1998). Marxist geographer, David Harvey, explains neoliberal ideology as serving the principle, familiar since the days

---

6 "Antifa" is short for the German term *antifascististische Aktion (*antifascist militance), first abbreviated as such by German anti-Nazi activists in the 1930s though not found in Marcuse's own lexicon. It was reprised in the protest against the advent of German neo-Nazism in the 1980s. Today there is no *antifa* group as such, rather it is a new sensibility that connotes antiracist and antifascist protest in general through mass demonstrations or more militant direct action in self-defense against neo-Nazis and the Klan

7 Sean Kitchen, "This is What a Police State Looks Like," *Raging Chicken Press*, February 15, 2012. https://ragingchickenpress.org/2012/02/15/this-is-what-a-police-state-looks-like/

of Plato's Thrasymachus, that the only *real* meaning of justice is found by always acting in the interest of the stronger parties:

> There shall be no serious challenge to the absolute power of money to rule absolutely. And that power is to be exercised with one objective: Those possessed of money shall not only be privileged to accumulate wealth endlessly at will, but they shall have the right to inherit the earth, taking either direct or indirect dominion, not only of the land and all the resources and productive capacities that reside therein, but also assume absolute command, directly or indirectly, over the labor and creative capacities of all those others it needs. The rest of humanity shall be deemed disposable. (Harvey in Olsen 2021)

The U.S. Supreme Court ruled in 1992 that the first amendment of the U.S. Constitution protected the actual burning of a Ku Klux Klan cross on the front lawn of a Black resident St. Paul, Minnesota. Antonin Scalia and the Supreme Court majority would no doubt publicly abhor overt racist intimidation, as Donald Trump ostensibly also did when pressed in public (Proud Boys "stand back and stand by" wink, wink, nudge, nudge). The Klan got off, and the law against hate speech was ruled unconstitutional because it supposedly limited free speech, forcing the racists to fight *in Scalia's words* with "one-hand tied behind their back" (Scalia 1992), while the forces fighting against racism could use both hands!

Such was the wisdom of the Supreme Court as represented by Scalia (1992). For years the Supreme Court has also ruled on the issues of systemic racism in higher education as these have condensed around affirmative action policies six times voting against any explicit numerical formula to redress past discrimination. Instead, as Nicholas Lehmann points out, because white students brought the suit that they were being passed over for minority students with lower test standardized scores, the only constitutional rationale in the Court's opinion for intentionally recruiting and admitting minority students was to create an intellectually richer campus environment (see its *Bakke*, and *De Funis* decisions). Promoting "diversity" was seen as acceptable since it was a way to broaden the experience of *white* students.[8]

---
8 Nicholas Lehmann, "The Diversity Verdict," *The New Yorker*, August 2, 2021.

Today we are witnessing the mobilization of the ideology and practice of murderous racism in the U.S., now aimed in particular against the Black Lives Matter movement and its allies including the antifascist left. At the same time, former President Trump's appointee to the U.S. Supreme Court, Amy Coney Barrett, takes pride in her adherence to Antonin Scalia's perspective on the Constitution. Scalia's record on racial justice matters as we have seen is atrocious. His 2013 remarks during oral arguments in the Supreme Court's review of the Voter Rights Act also indicated his scorn for what he called a politics of "racial entitlement."[9] A key provision of this Voter Rights Act, the federal government's oversight of election procedures in states with histories of overt discrimination (against Black voters in particular), was struck down by the Court's 2013 decision.

According to *The New Yorker's* Jane Mayer, this ruling "initiated a new era of election manipulation" in which non-profits like the Bradley and Heritage Foundations, sustained by wealthy conservatives, asserted that U.S. elections were rife with the fraud perpetrated by Democratic elections officials who had introduced an expansion of voting rights and opportunities.[10] In her estimation, these well-funded reactionary organizations stand behind ex-president Donald Trump's false assertion that the 2020 Presidential election was stolen from him. Mayer points out that Supreme Court Justices Antonin Scalia, William Rehnquist, and Clarence Thomas developed an Independent Legislature Doctrine in the context of the Court's *Bush v. Gore* decision regarding the troubled 2000 Presidential election. According to this doctrine, "the Justices urged that state legislatures have the plenary power to run elections and even pass laws giving themselves the right to appoint electors."[11] This, she says, informs Donald Trump's and the right's ongoing efforts to use Republican-controlled legislatures to overrule the popular will.[12]

One last note on the Supreme Court must be made concerning the damage done to its reputation during the confirmation hearings of two notorious male justices, Clarence Thomas (in 1991) and Brett Kavanaugh (in 2018). Their toxic masculinity was excused as natural and expected; their sexual harassment and victim shaming was denied. This occurred on three

---

9 Amy Davidson, "In Voting Rights, Scalia Sees a 'Racial Entitlement,'" in the "Close Read" blog of *The New Yorker*, February 28, 2013. http://www.newyorker.com/online/blogs/closeread/2013/02/in-voting-rights-scalia-sees-a-racial-entitlement.html#ixzz2Mriqv04Y.
10 Jane Mayer, "The Big Money Behind the Big Lie," *The New Yorker*, August 9, 2021
11 Ibid.
12 Ibid.

distinct societal levels according to Anita Hill: "individual, institutional, and structural" (Hill 2021, 56). Thomas and Kavanaugh 1) *personally* disparaged their accusers; 2) there was *a shoddy investigation* of charges by politicians who also belittled the complainants, and 3) the *hearing process itself* confirmed the pretense of legitimacy. Hill emphasizes that when fitness for a lifetime judicial appointment is deferred to reactionary political convenience, we have clear cases of institutional neglect and structural complicity in reinforcing and spreading gender-based aggression. She also calls for the Supreme Court decision of 2000 *United States v. Morrison* to be overturned because faulty reasoning ruled aspects of the 1994 Violence Against Women Act unconstitutional (Hill 210).

Institutional forces behind a resurgence of inequality, racial and otherwise, also include the Federal Reserve Bank (Petrou 2021). Petrou's critique shows that U.S. income and wealth inequality grew worse after the crisis of 2008 due to one factor above all others: the way monetary and regulatory policy was dictated by the Federal Reserve Board through rules written by the Fed and financial regulators. Such abuse of power in the interests of this society's monied and investment sectors has intensified the nation's economic inequalities. This has had effects that are wide-ranging and encompass U.S. institutions across the board: family, government, economy, education, religion, health care, the media, law enforcement; most notably also systemic racism.

The New Sensibility: Discontent from the left

If in some quarters today's idols remain money, fame, thrills and power, this reveals a still dominant side of the American character. Langman and Lundskow's work (2016) recognizes that there is another side even if this has been generally repressed. The U.S. has witnessed significant historical struggles: progressive social forces in opposition to slavery, for women's suffrage, a populist anti-monopoly radicalism, for socialism, co-ops, collectives, and communes like New Harmony and Oneida. U.S. culture has been influenced by empathetic and critical writers like Walt Whitman, Mark Twain, as well as the subaltern blues and jazz traditions of Black America. As I have highlighted earlier, during the 1960s new sensibilities of the sort Marcuse described in *An Essay on Liberation* (1969, 23-48) emerged that prefigure a sane socialist society. Marcuse thorized that these were becoming a potent new subversive political factor. As *praxis* ...

> ... the New Sensibility ... emerges in the struggle against violence and exploitation where this struggle is waged for essentially new ways and forms of life: negation of the entire Establishment, its morality, culture; affirmation of the right to build a society in which the abolition of poverty and toil and terminates in a universe where the sensuous, the playful, the calm, and the beautiful become forms of existence and thereby the *Form* of society itself... the aesthetic as a possible Form of the society itself ... a new vision of socialism ... (Marcuse 1969, 25-26)

Marcuse's hopeful activism (which enabled him to be heralded as the philosopher of the student revolts of the late 1960s and 1970s) was rooted in the "transvaluation of values" which he considered to have been represented by the radical opposition forces of the time. Even a one-dimensional society could see protest groups emerge among students, women, and civil rights activists, who developed an oppositional philosophy and politics that represented this New Sensibility.

> These developments reflect the steady growth among the youth of the New Sensibility—new needs, generated under capitalism, but which capitalism cannot fulfill, for gender equality, ecological economics, and anti-racism. The general form of the internal contradictions of capitalism has never been more blatant, more cruel, more costly of human lives and happiness. And—this is the significance of the Sixties—this blatant irrationality has not only penetrated the consciousness of a large part of the population, it has also caused, mainly among the young people, a radical transformation of needs and values which may prove to be incompatible with the capitalist system, its hierarchy, priorities, morality, symbols (the counter-culture, ecology). (Marcuse [1975] 2015b, 304-307)

One-dimensional American liberalism was oblivious to the problematic nature of foundational U.S. social and economic relations and its flattening-out of life's internal inconsistencies and contradictions. Yet pockets of protest emerged within the prevailing U.S. culture of conformity giving rise to a militant, antifastyle, oppositional philosophy and politics.

By the 2020s in the U.S, a resurgent philosophy of state-sanctioned force has been promoted by both politicians and the police. According to William I. Robinson's latest volume, *The Global Police State*: "Savage global inequalities are politically explosive and to the extent that the system is simply unable to incorporate surplus humanity it turns to ever more violent forms of containment" (Robinson 2020, 3). *The New York Times* reported, for example, on the basis of voluminous video evidence, that in New York City during the BLM protests:

> the department said it exercised restraint. The videos tell a different story. . . many of the police attacks, often led by high-ranking officers, were not warranted. ... Philip M. Stinson, a Bowling Green State University criminologist and former police officer who studies the use of force by police, offered a blunt assessment of the behavior shown in the videos. "A lot of this was 'street justice,' he said 'gratuitous acts of extrajudicial violence doled out by police officers on the street to teach someone a lesson."[13]

This deployment of state-sponsored violence, unwarranted as it was, was neither accidental nor incidental. After the George Floyd protests against police killings, unyielding enforcement of "Law and Order" is again demanded by conservatives (and mainstream Democrats like Joe Biden as well) against unruly antiracist protesters. Donald Trump has repeatedly incited his followers to violence against his opponents.[14]

In 1965, Marcuse ([1965] 2014) commented on the issue of police violence (and also violence when used by protesters). This was in his postscript to Walter Benjamin's *Zur Kritik der Gewalt* [*A Critique of Force/Domination/Violence/Power*] (Benjamin, [1921] 1965). Like Benjamin, Marcuse holds that within the framework of the established reality, peaceful protest runs up against the limits that police power sets against it, after which it will encounter the force of police violence. Between May 26 and July 27, 2020, 115 U.S. protesters, for example, were shot in the head with kinetic impact projectiles (rubber bullets, etc.) according to Physicians for Human Rights (2020).[15] Older U.S. readers may well remember the

---

13 Allison McCann, Blacki Magliozzi, Andy Newman, Larry Buchanan and Aaron Byrd, "Caught on Over 60 Videos: Police Using Force on Protesters," *The New York Times*, A-1, A-18-19.
14 Trip Gabriel, Zolan Kanno-Youngs, and Katie Benner, "Fears of Political Violence Rise as Trump's Language Heats Up," *The New York Times*, October 16, 2020. A-25
15 Physicians for Human Rights, "Shot in the Head," September 14, 2020. https://storymaps.arcgis.com/stories/29cbf2e87b914dbaabdec2f3d350839e See also: Shaila Dewan and Mike Baker, "Facing Protests Over Use of Force, Police Respond With More Force," *The New York Times*, May 31, 2020. Updated June 2, 2020, see: https://www.nytimes.com/2020/05/31/us/police-tactics-floyd-protests.html?searchResultPosition=4

law enforcement violence implicated in the deaths of non-violent activists Andrew Goodman, Michael Schwerner, and James Chaney 1964; the brutality of Selma's Black Sunday 1965 and Chicago's Democratic Convention ["police riot"] 1968; not to mention the killing of student protesters by national guardsmen at Kent State 1970.

Analogous to the orchestrated police violence against antiracism protesters, violence against peaceful environmental protest actions has roused an even greater awareness of systemic police brutality. Chase Hobbs-Morgan (2015) has cogently argued that widespread ravages of climate change, arising from the usual business practices of early and late-capitalist systems of production, should actually be understood as forms of *structural violence* and structural injustice. This violence may occur slowly, yet it damages wide swaths of the population unevenly, and police action in support of corporate resource owners has generated a substantial level of violence against non-violent protesters from Greenpeace to Standing Rock.

When Benjamin wrote, the political conditions of the time were not yet ripe for revolution. Marcuse emphasizes that gauging when they are, or will be, is of the utmost importance.

> Insight into the power of what exists prohibits illusions. ... The theory that can stand up against the contemporary established reality, without falling into ideology, must move through the negativity that renders visible the foundations of this established reality's *Gewalt* (power/violence/domination). Only then can the possibility of superseding this *Gewalt* be recognized once more. (Marcuse [1965] 2014, 166)

Benjamin's critique of oppressive establishment violence is accompanied by a defense of emancipatory revolutionary force. This resonates with Marcuse's defense of the "right of resistance," which he reminds us is one of the most venerable elements of Western Civilization (Marcuse [1967] 2005, 62), and he thus also distinguishes between *repressive* violence and *emancipatory* violence. The conventional understanding of armed conflict in the history of the United States—from Lexington and Concord, to Nat Turner, John Brown, and to Appomattox Courthouse—regards emancipatory force as an historical necessity in the defense and expansion of political freedom against repressive violence. "So from the start the opposition is placed in the field of violence. Right stands against right, not only as an abstract claim but as action" (Marcuse [1967] 2005, 62). Our current epoch epitomizes the brutal and reactionary side of U.S. politics (Harcourt, 2018) that has regularly resurfaced in this culture after upswings in progressive activism. "The end of violence is still to be fought for" (Marcuse 1972, 78). Still, Marcuse cautions that revolutionary violence will be defeated so long as the revolutionary opposition does not have *the force of a new general interest*.

Marcuse emphasizes that in spite of the violence of domination and this destructive institutional context, an emancipatory "radical character structure" emerges from advanced industrial society in which subversive needs come to supersede the repressive compensatory needs of the established order: "the potential forces of social change are there" (Marcuse [1979] 2011, 209-210).

> [Changed] needs are present, here and now. They permeate the lives of individuals. ... First, the need for drastically reducing socially necessary alienated labor and replacing it with creative work. Second, the need for autonomous free time instead of directed leisure. Third, the need for an end of role playing [i.e., inauthentic conformity]. Fourth, the need for receptivity, tranquility and abounding joy, instead of the constant noise of production. ... The specter which haunts advanced industrial society today is the obsolescence of full-time alienation. (Marcuse [1979] 2011, 211)

Marcuse regarded the environmental movement of his day as a critical intervention against institutional destructiveness and as the embodiment of an erotic life-affirming energy directed towards the protection of Earth and the pacification of our human existence. Marcuse scholar Javier Sethness Castro emphasizes: "Marcuse did not think that Eros contradicted Logos ... , the two can very much reinforce one another, once their practitioners overcome the indelible connection often made between the concept of reason and instrumental thinking" (Sethness Castro 2018, 4). He stresses Marcuse's characteristic synthesis of Eros and Logos as represented by the term "Orphic Marxism" (Sethness Castro 2018, 96). This gets at Marcuse's own love for nature, quietude, and peace, and how he came to see nature as an *ally* in the struggle against the exploitative societies in which the violation of nature aggravates the violation of man (Marcuse 1972, 59). His *Eros and Civilization: A Philosophical Inquiry into Freud* (Marcuse

1955) proposed a consideration of the mythical figures of Orpheus and Narcissus as aesthetic symbols of an essentially non-repressive Eros and philosophical pantheism in which humanity longs for nature and an ego restored to oneness with the world: "A successful environmentalism will, within individuals, subordinate destructive energy to erotic energy" (Marcuse [1979] 2011, 212).

Reclaiming radical humanism after Auschwitz

In the period after World War II Karl Jaspers was part of a tendency in European philosophy that saw an upsurge in interest in our this-worldly human existence and understood religion anew, largely in humanist terms. The existentialism of Heidegger's *Being and Time* [1927] and Sartre's *Being and Nothingness* [1943] (deeply indebted to Heidegger), inclined philosophy in a non-theistic or atheistic direction. Sartre stressed that our human existence is epistemologically prior to thought and speech and emotions and sense. He popularized the phrase "existence precedes essence" and also the notion that existentialism is a humanism. He believed that the former captured a new, more modest sense of humanism as being also and internally conflicted. Heidegger wondered if philosophers needed the word *humanism* any longer (Heidegger [1947] 1954, 56), though he described it as "sensing and caring that humanity remains humane, not inhuman, i.e., outside its essence" (Heidegger 1954, 61). Hannah Arendt's *The Human Condition* [1958] carried forward her own sense of the phenomenology of human existence of her former mentor and paramour Martin Heidegger. Her book centered a new discussion of the human material condition around labor and work and alienation, though it was not really articulated as a form of critical social theory. In contrast, Erich Fromm's *Marx's Concept of Man* (1961) focused on Marx's *1844 Philosophical Manuscripts* and the explanation of alienation articulated there, grounded in a fourfold distortion of the labor process. Marcuse, who had also studied under Heidegger, advanced philosophy's close connection to critical social theory in *One-Dimensional Man* (1964). This and subsequent works challenged corporate capitalism's illusions of democracy characterized by consumerism, cultural anaesthetization, intellectual compliance, environmental degradation, and war, as untenable forms of wasted abundance and political unfreedom.

Humanism has classically been thought to require a study of the humanities. Indeed, conservative reform approaches to the humanities and a liberal arts education traditionally see them as serving universal aims and goals but fail to acknowledge that a discriminatory politics of race, gender, and class have distorted not only the curriculum, but also patterns of faculty hiring and student recruitment and support. To this degree, the humanities have incorporated a false universalism of Eurocentrism and Anglo-conformity to be more fully discussed in chapter 5 below. Conservative humanists condemn opposition to the Anglo-conformist curriculum as "identity politics" which is derided as narrowly one-sided and restricted in scope. As Marcuse knew, this is doubly ironic because of the one-dimensional Eurocentrism of the humanities tradition and because the liberation movements, which resisted multiple forms of political oppression in the classically understood Western canon were inspired *not* primarily by a politics of difference and special interests, but rather an intercultural politics of solidarity and hope for human understanding universally.

The philosophy of *EarthCommonWealth*, as I formulate it here, envisions an egalitarian intercultural cohabitation of Earth, where commonwealth becomes the universal human condition. I want to develop a viable theoretical paradigm that can overcome both a sense of false (monocultural) universalism and the postmodern despondencies of moral relativism and nihilism. My aim is to build an intercultural sense of human solidarity and commonwealth, underpinning—in ethics, economics, and education—a realistic aspiration to human flourishing. Such a vision is grounded in universalizable value criteria such as the reciprocity, cooperation, shared ownership, and hospitality, as these are also embodied in traditional African proverbs. Marcuse brings a dialectical perspective to bear: "The universal comprehends in one idea the possibilities which are realized, and at the same time arrested, in reality" (Marcuse 1964, 210). Our cultural, political, and emotional conditions can be considered authentic when consistent with the fullest potentials of our species-being, i.e., with what Marx called our *Gattungswesen,* or alienated when social power structurally distorts or denies humanity such authenticity.

Jeremy Rifkin builds upon the eminently needy and caring view of human nature emerging anew in the natural and social sciences and the humanities in the late 20th Century through the work of Harlow, Bowlby, Gimbutas, de Waal, and others, who generally "argue that children are born with a reality principle, and that principle is to seek affection, companionship, intimacy, and a sense of belonging" (Rifkin 2009, 21). His revelatory volume, *The Empathic Civilization: The Race to Global Consciousness in a World in Crisis,* is one I regard as precursor to my own work insofar as his description of the renewed philosophical impetus after World War II echoes what I have written above:

> We rushed to universalize empathy after the last half of the twentieth century. In the aftermath of the Holocaust in World War II, humanity said "never again." We extended empathy to large numbers of our fellow human beings previously considered to be less than human—including women, homosexuals, the disabled, people of color, and ethnic and religious minorities. ... (Rifkin 2009, 26)

Empathy also needs to be seen as an *outcome* of epoch-making historical protest against racism, sexism, poverty, war, and imperialism. Rifkin plays down the fact that a recognition of minority rights and egalitarian policies has been won through struggle. The social movements of our age have been its civilizing forces. Such movements have educated this nation following World War II about alienation, oppression, power, and empowerment. The professoriate, as such, did not lead in this educational effort, although many individual college teachers, like Herbert Marcuse and Peter McLaren, played important and even key activist roles. Rifkin's prescriptions for the future diverge from mine, eschewing as he does any explicit reference to ecosocialism in favor of a utopian capitalism, a "collaborative and caring world ... beginning to slowly penetrate ... some of the world's global companies" (Rifkin 543).

Learning from real world struggles aims at an understanding of the principles of action required for human beings, as sensuous living labor, to grasp theoretically, and possess politically, the productive processes that today divest us from our own creative work and communal power. It is precisely these economic processes that must be restructured to eliminate political inequality and alienation and reclaim our common humanity.

How shall we best protect human life and humane values in this era of white extremist mass shootings, police killings, acrid backlash against public health measures as well as against multicultural reform efforts—all this amid reactionary redefinitions of freedom, i.e. "The Exploitation of Freedom'" (Anker 2022) via anti-maskers, anti-vaxxers, and antisemitic khaki-clad klansmen and paramilitaries)? Racism and the attacks on the supposed enemies—multiculturalism, immigration, and political correctness—play a central role in the right-wing's strategy to build up its own internal muscle by directing its hostility toward scapegoats.

Super-exploitation under the worldwide regime of capital is intensifying inequalities. We are "worlds apart" locally and globally (Sernau 2006). The real estate bust of 2008 saw the destruction of middle class wealth and increasing economic precariousness; yet the system is served by intensifying racist scapegoating as an escape valve. Imperial America has been in decline and retreat since its defeat in Vietnam in the 1960s. Since September 11, 2001 and the 2021 defeat in Afghanistan, it has been meaningfully weakened.[16] At the same time, in the inner empire of the U.S., political animosities are again dramatically polarized. We see a record-high number of hate groups (1,020 according to the Southern Poverty Law Center) and upwards of 60 racist murders since 2018 in the U.S. alone,[17] and more than 50 deaths in a single incident in 2019 in New Zealand. Why is this happening now? Hate crimes had been falling for several years prior to the 2014.[18] "America is reeling backwards, strangled by the past, nasty and uncaring, with everyone at one another's throats."[19]

Freedom of speech as J. S. Mill conceived it originally intended to protect political minorities from domination. This has newly been twisted to protect hate speech and facilitate hate crimes, and as such, Marcuse argued, is not to be tolerated (Marcuse 1965).

Much as Hannah Arendt (1963) called out the "banality of evil" with regard to the Nazi era's push for *Lebensraum* and its engineering of genocide, Ijeoma Oluo's *Mediocre* (2020) vividly recounts the dangerous legacy of white male America during the period of westward expansion, settlement, and manifest destiny. In sharp contrast to the ideology of white superiority, she argues the mediocrity of the average white American male (Oluo 2020, 15-45). Oluo argues that versions of this founding mode of white male mediocrity in the U.S. were subsequently carried over into the 19th century's movements for secession, Jim Crow, the 20th century's system of higher education, its workplaces, its entertainment, its sports, its

---

16 Ross Douthat, "The American Empire in Retreat," *The New York Times*, September 5, 2021, SR-9.
17 SPLC (Southern Poverty Law Center) Report, Spring 2019, page 1. See www.splcenter.org
18 Ibid.
19 Maureen Dowd, "Drowning Our Future in the Past," *The New York Times*, September 5, 2021, SR-9

segregationist politics, and even in its social justice movements. Success is linked to an unearned yet presumed caste status ascribed as white masculine superiority versus women and people of color. If this caste status is breaking down and no longer delivering its unmerited yet ostensibly called-for power and rewards, the formerly entitled white males can become *angry with the world* (Oluo 2020, 270 my emphasis) given their bitter disappointment at their own mediocrity. They may believe their status has been stolen from them. Oluo proposes a crucial theme for a research topic: "Can White Manhood Be More Than This?" (Oluo 2020, 265-278). Can we work toward a new version/vision of masculinity? She believes the current intensified opposition to race and gender-based intimidation and violence indicates that a path forward is definitely feasible. Likewise, Anita Hill emphasizes the need for intentional action against race and gender-based forms of violence and oppression. "[A] systemic, cultural reckoning is called for ... victims and survivors and the rest of society will be better off for it ... [utilizing] an approach to systemic change that is survivor-centered and led" (Hill, 304).

The centrality of radical struggle:
Against white supremacy and neofascism

Herbert Marcuse's sharp critique of the counterrevolutionary power of U.S. militarism and cold war empire-building in foreign policy stems in part because Marcuse witnessed Germany's loss of Weimar democracy to a politics of ethnic national identity, an imagined community of blood and soil. Marcuse's "Repressive Tolerance" (1965) essay was a product of his critique of German fascism and right-wing activism, genocide. It expressed opposition to fascism as well as the liberal doctrines of tolerance that made the Third Reich possible. It contains insights and elements that make it extremely pertinent in our present era of counterrevolutionary backlash against the progress of the civil rights struggles and multicultural educational reform movement. This was written after Marcuse met Brandeis student Angela Davis and began an intellectual/political relationship that lasted well-beyond her student years (Davis, 1974; 2013; 2004). Today Davis continues to criticize racist police brutality and connect the antiracist uprising in Ferguson with the self-defense struggles in Palestine (Davis, 2016). Davis has points out that Marxists in the 1950s and early 60s, like few others in the U.S. except the direct victims themselves, publicly challenged genocide[20] and the resurgent racism in law enforcement, housing, employment, and education.

"Repressive Tolerance" condemned the violence that actually prevails in the ostensibly peaceful centers of civilization: "it is practiced by the police, in the prisons and the mental institutions, in the fight against racial minorities. ...This violence indeed breeds violence" (Marcuse 1965, 105). Marcuse is clear that antiracist protesters are easily and customarily defamed in dominant media accounts as looters and rioters. Yet, in his estimation, if demonstrators do engage in violence, this is usually directed against property as an indignant counterforce to the overwhelming force of domination that directly and wantonly destroys human life.

In the U.S. today white supremacist rhetoric and attacks are on the rise because they are reactionary economic and political weapons of oligarchic capitalist power in a period when U.S. control of the world economy is waning. Threatening the conditions of existence of minority communities around the globe dis-empowers the entire human population, nearly all of which is made up of persons who must work for a living. Marcuse's point was that the intensification of such deeply damaging hate speech and hate crime must be halted in any society that wishes to think of itself as a liberal social order because the ability to protect minorities is the key criterion of any liberal form of government: no protection of minorities, no liberal democracy.

Ethical standards annulled through tolerance complicity

Tolerance complicity is often defended today through the perverse assertion that racist and sexist views contribute necessary components of cultural diversity! They are said to belong within an inclusive pluralism, and this is an example of a vicious cultural and political doublespeak.

> When one person directly harms another, we have a simple case of wrongdoing. A person is *complicit* when causing harm indirectly by being involved in the wrongdoing of others. ...[T]olerance complicity ... does not involve participating in wrongdoing with others, instead, it involves tolerating their wrongdoing by seeming to endorse or failing to denounce it.[21]

---

20 Angela Davis, *Freedom is a Constant Struggle: Ferguson, Palestine, and the Foundations of a Movement* (Chicago: Haymarket Books, 2016) p. 132.
21 Sasha Mudd, "The Ethical Dilemma of Watching the Olympics," *The New York Times*, July 30, 2021, A-23

A "new normal" has been unleashed through changes in the media, the law, the economy, education, etc. Donald Trump's ascendency was only the most recent brash expression of the predatory political economy of race, class, and gender—and the earth-killing tendencies latent in the essential contradictions of capitalism. Brutal forms of racial and other kinds of oppression (including crusading military invasions in order to "extend democracy") are politically tolerated in service to the established system of unfreedom.

Marcuse believed that the doctrine of pure tolerance was systematically utilized by reactionary and liberal forces to abuse equality guarantees and derail or destroy the possibility of democratic egalitarianism. As I have noted above, this is now more widely recognized and criticized as "the free speech fallacy" (Stanley, 2016). Marcuse's arguments undergird the right to an harassment-free environment in the public sphere and specifically on the nation's campuses.

Sethness Castro highlights "Repressive Tolerance" as a militant "philosophical justification for insurrection and active suppression of fascism and militarism from below" (Sethness Castro 2018, 6). This interpretation is distinctive and extends the usual reading of Marcuse in an explicitly revolutionary way. Sethness Castro links Marcuse's call for the withdrawal of tolerance from chauvinistic groups to a justification of the active suppression of fascism and militarism from below, i.e. to revolutionary praxis, as a "militant endorsement of insurrection and counter-violence against the established system" (Sethness Castro 2018, 169).

Interrupting lethal liberties: Hate speech and gun terror

"This pure tolerance of sense and nonsense ... " practiced under the conditions prevailing in the United States today ". . . cannot fulfill the civilizing function attributed to it by the liberal protagonists of democracy, namely protection of dissent" (Marcuse 1965, 94, 117). "To treat the great crusades against humanity... with the same impartiality as the desperate struggles for humanity means neutralizing their opposite historical function, reconciling the executioners with their victims, distorting the record" (Marcuse 1965, 113). Marcuse's partisanship is clear: "The small and powerless minorities which struggle against the false consciousness and its beneficiaries must be helped: their continued existence is more important than the preservation of abused rights and liberties which grant constitutional powers to those who oppress these minorities" (Marcuse

1965, 110). Writing of the Nazi organizers of institutionalized violence, Marcuse said:

> ... if democratic tolerance had been withdrawn when the future leaders started their campaign, mankind would have had a chance of avoiding Auschwitz and a World War. ... Such extreme suspension of the right of free speech and free assembly is indeed justified only if the whole of society is in extreme danger. ... Withdrawal of tolerance from regressive movements *before* they can become active; intolerance even toward thought, opinion, and word, and finally intolerance in the opposite direction, that is toward the self-styled conservatives, to the political Right—these anti-democratic notions respond to the actual development of the democratic society which has destroyed the basis for universal tolerance. The conditions under which tolerance can again become a liberating force have still to be created. (Marcuse 1965, 110-111)

It is a tacit tribute to Marcuse that a strategy for the defense of equal civil rights and intercultural solidarity with victims of hate speech has been developed by authors like Dolores Calderón (2009), Christine Sleeter and Dolores Delgado Bernal (2003), Richard Delgado and Jean Stefancic (1997), Mari Matsuda, Charles Lawrence, Richard Delgado and Kimberlé Williams Crenshaw (1993), and John K. Wilson (1995). They argue effectively that freedom of speech is not absolute, and must be viewed in the context of its real political consequences.

Utilizing Marcuse's critical historical perspective we can get at the truth about our vaunted freedom of speech in the USA, namely that we do *not* now, nor have we ever had it. What we *do* have in our advanced industrial society is a contest of ideas and a contest for control within cultures generally and within educational institutions in particular (Finan, 2007). If we all have a de jure right to express any opinion in public, the de facto condition is that Left opinions are usually marginalized and often suppressed, while right-wing ones, which benefit the ruling class, are given free play. The problem today is really one of which ideas are distributed and amplified by the mass media, so that through repetition and placement in powerful media sources they become dominant, legitimized, and authoritative. Marcuse emphasized that the formation of public opinion in the West (and now nearly everywhere) is largely controlled by oligopolistic media.

Dissenters had but a slim chance of influencing the debate. Furthermore, any state doctrine that purported to be neutral served to reinforce the conventional pretense to freedom while obscuring its factual absence.

"Everyday fascism" in the U.S.

Reinhard Lettau, as a young radical German philosopher, paid a lengthy visit to Marcuse in California in 1970 and published a volume describing police-statelike conditions in Los Angeles under the title "Everyday Fascism" (Lettau 1971). He kept a scrapbook of clippings from the *L.A. Times* of gratuitous violence by police during encounters with Black and Latinx Angelenos. In the later 1970s socially conscious rap artists in LA and NYC likewise criticized and contested the regularity of such confrontations the bitterness of which, since the George Floyd killing in Minneapolis, the world has now learned more fully to recognize.

This was also the period when former Marcuse student Angela Davis, who had become a philosophy professor at UCLA, had a history of activism (and arrest for) opposing the war in Vietnam, protesting the police brutality and killings of Black men by the LAPD, and of politically supporting a series of Black political prisoners, among them Black Panthers Huey Newton and Bobby Seal. She had directed a liberation school for the Student Non-Violent Coordinating Committee (SNCC), but was relieved of her position after she became a communist in 1968. This was same the year that Martin Luther King, Jr., Malcolm X, and Robert Kennedy had been assassinated and the Chicago Black Panthers Fred Hampton and Mark Clark had been killed by the FBI.

In her autobiography Davis (1974) recounts that in 1969 the Panthers planned to build an organization called United Front Against Fascism which (perhaps unexpectedly from our vantage point today) she *opposed* saying "Certainly we had to fight the mounting threat of fascism, but it was incorrect and misleading to inform people that we were already living under fascism" (Davis 1974, 198-199). During a subsequent protest however: "The police motorcycle corps ... gunned the motors of their cycles, thinking the roar was the sound of their own power. At that moment, I saw in this scene historical traces of Hitler's troops trying to terrorize the Jews into submission" (Davis 1974, 229). Davis was put on the FBI's most wanted list when three prisoners whom she had supported, known as the Soledad Brothers, used guns belonging to her in a courtroom escape attempt that eventuated in the killing of a judge. Davis fled the country but was arrested and held in jail for over a year until acquitted of all charges in 1972. Throughout the long academic career that followed she persisted with research and writing on feminism, prisoner support, and the abolition of the carceral state.

Neofascism countered by Antifa in Charlottesville

Following a line of thinking from *Eros and Civilization* (1955), Marcuse theorizes consumerism as a factor in the "... mobilization and administration of libido [that] may account for much of the voluntary compliance ... with the established society. Pleasure, thus adjusted, generates submission" (Marcuse 1964, 75). He explains that society's control mechanisms become even more powerful when they integrate sexually suggestive and explicitly erotic and violent content into advertising and the mass media and infuse these into the content of mass entertainment and popular culture. The unrestrained use of sex and violence by large-scale commercial interests—repressive *de*sublimation— accomplishes more effective social manipulation and control in the interest of capital accumulation than had repressive *sublimation*. It fuels counterrevolution by substituting reactionary emotional release in place of rebellion, and counterrevolutionary illusion in place of freedom.

Marcuse posed the question of whether the ascendency of a neofascist regime in the U.S.A. can be prevented. Among the reasons why he asked this was his conviction that since at least 1972 the U.S.A. had entered a period of preventive counter-revolution.

> According to Freud, the destructive tendency in society will gain momentum as civilization necessitates intensified repression in order to maintain domination in the face of ever more realistic possibilities of liberation, and intensified repression in turn leads to the activation of surplus aggressiveness, and its channeling into socially useful aggression. This total mobilization of aggressiveness is only too familiar to us today: militarization, brutalization of the forces of law and order, fusion of sexuality and violence, direct attack on the Life Instincts in their attempt to save the environment, attack on the legislation against pollution and so on. (Marcuse [1974] 2005, 167).

Amy Goodman of *Democracy Now!* reported on the infamous "Unite the Right" demonstration of Klansmen, neo-Nazis, and other antisemites and white supremacists at Charlottesville, Virginia, in August 2017. Chief among their chants was "Jews shall not replace us!" Non-violent antiracist counter-protesters were physically assaulted, one killed and several injured in an act of vehicular homicide. Cornel West, who was there, described the scene in "Anti-fascists and Anarchists Saved Our Lives in Charlottesville:"

> You had a number of the courageous students, of all colors, at the University of Virginia who were protesting against the neofascists themselves. The neofascists had their own ammunition. And this is very important to keep in mind, because the police, for the most part, pulled back. The next day, for example, those 20 of us who were standing, many of them clergy, we would have been crushed like cockroaches if it were not for the anarchists and the anti-fascists who approached, over 300, 350 anti-fascists. We just had 20. And we're singing "This Little light of Mine," you know what I mean? . . . The anti-fascists, and then, crucial, the anarchists, because they saved our lives, actually. We would have been completely crushed, and I'll never forget that. (West 2017)

Let it be noted that in 1919 a revolutionary uprising of soldiers and striking workers, with whom Marcuse empathized, sought to establish a self-governing socialist republic in Berlin and Munich. These efforts ended in defeat, and Marcuse became politically demoralized by what he understood as the complicity of the conservatively Marxist Social Democrats (SPD) led by Friedrich Ebert in the assassination of the revolutionary communist leaders Karl Liebknecht and Rosa Luxemburg. Ebert struck a Faustian bargain with General William Groener, second-in-command of the German army. Groener would allow the SPD to rule if Ebert allowed the army to crush the massive, armed street demonstrations led by the revolutionary Spartacists, Luxemburg and Liebknecht. The army, thus secure, betrayed the SPD to the Nazis (Shirer 1960, 83-89).

Marcuse said he refused to further support the SPD "not because it believed that it could work with the framework of the established order, for we all do this. ...The reason was rather that it worked in alliance with reactionary, destructive, and repressive forces" (Marcuse [1967] 1970, 102-103). In similar socialist confrontations against fascist aggression in Ethiopia and Spain in the late 1930s, support for the socialist fighters was withheld and considered "premature antifascism" by politically moderate Popular Front and New Deal Democrats even after the rise of Hitler. The strategy of gradual progress toward greater freedoms was a constant struggle for people of African descent in the U.S. until change was impelled by rebellions in Watts, Chicago, New York, 1967-68. At the 2017 antifascist counterdemonstration in Charlottesville, not the police, but antifa fighting forces protected the liberal Christians and mainstream Democrats from serious injury. Marcuse, like Chase-Dunn and Nagy (2018, 262-263), knew we needed a "New Global Left" for "The World Revolution of 20XX."

Antifascism and the Marxist-Anarchist dialectic

Javier Sethness Castro (2018) offers a critical treatment of Marcuse's littleknown essay, "Thoughts on the Defense of Gracchus Babeuf" (Marcuse 1967). The Gracchi were Roman reformers who attempted to counter the Roman aristocracy's propertied interests on behalf of the unpropertied Roman people. Similarly, François-Noel Babeuf favored an egalitarian redistribution of property during the French Revolution; this linked him to the heroism of the Gracchi in support of the poor, yet it also brought him into a confrontation with the revolution's Directory. Marcuse attempts to understand the radicalism of Babeuf who wished to mobilize revolutionary violence to challenge even the provisional government of the successful 1789 revolutionaries. In the end Marcuse concludes that Babeuf's strategy "which was quite unrealistic but not utopian in 1796 appears as utterly utopian today." (Marcuse 1967, 104).

Marcuse's discussion of Babeuf gives rise to a vivid instance of the Marxistanarchist dialectic within Marcuse's larger perspective. Javier Sethness Castro sees Marcuse's essay on Babeuf as evincing support for a vanguardist Leninist/ Bolshevik perspective on strategy, but as also raising the possibility that the Babouvist message of uncompromising commitment to the people might be better advanced by less centralized and authoritarian political approaches ranging from the "Spanish and Russian anarchist movements" to the more contemporary "Zapatistas and Magonistas of the Mexican Revolution" (Sethness Castro 2018, 181). I tend to look for as much common ground as can be found in this two-way conversation between Marcuse's Marxism and anarchism. David Laibman (2016), though not explicitly considering Marcuse, asks with regard to the same general issue: "Within the mix of central-to-decentral forms and loci of operation, is a central *component* necessary?" He inquires further: how can the democratic character of the revolutionary movement be strengthened, both at the de-central and central levels, given that neither level will be automatically free of corruption? Sethness Castro sees the two strains as presenting an unresolved conflict within Marcuse's thought, and he leans more to Marcuse's philosophical anarchism. He characterizes Marcuse's philosophy as a "life-long anti-authoritarianism" (2018, 8). Still, Sethness Castro is clear that Marcuse "describes his own politics in life as Marxist ... though Marcuse was far from being enthralled to Marx" (2018, 11).

Some prominent contemporary anarchists, like Murray Bookchin, however, are clear about their theoretical opposition to, and rejection of, Marxists and Marxism. In his scornful essay *"Listen Marxist!"*, he writes disparagingly of Marxists and Marxist political strategies: "Let us contrast two approaches, the Marxian and the revolutionary" (Bookchin 2018, 118). Nonetheless, even Bookchin finds *Marcuse's* Marxism to have a unique quality: "Marcuse is the most original of the thinkers who still call themselves Marxists" (Bookchin 2018, 159). And Marcuse (1972, 61) recommends a reading of Bookchin's "Ecology and Revolutionary Thought" ([1971] 2018). Where some see a sharp divide between Marxism and anarchism, Marcuse's work is thus regarded by both Bookchin and Sethness Castro as braiding together these two contrasting strands of revolutionary thinking. Early on in his book (page 7) Sethness Castro stresses that it is correct to raise the rarely made comparison between Marcuse and Mikhail Bakunin. These two political theorists are said to converge philosophically in the Hegelian idea of negation, such that the revolution must fully destroy the established social order. "[O]ver the nearly sixty years which spanned Marcuse's writing career, the thinker's political philosophy was seen to have been informed by and in turn advance two somewhat contradictory viewpoints: that of a libertarian socialism or social anarchism which follows left-Hegelianism and the original 'Marxian concept' in tension with a more authoritarian tendency informed by Plato, Rousseau, Jacobinism, and Leninism" (Sethness Castro 2018, 331). "On the other hand though, it is clear that Marcuse embraced the anarchical tactics of the 1960s counterculture and the New Left, as is reflected well in the ... endorsements he would make in terms of councilism and spontaneity late in life (Sethness Castro 2018, 332).

Among the antifascist pieces Marcuse wrote in the 1940s, "33 Theses" as we have seen above is pivotal. Sethness Castro finds that Marcuse weighs the anarcho-syndicalist strategy but "anarchist reflections aside, Marcuse ends these theses by seemingly abandoning a syndicalist orientation in favor of the Leninist model..." (Sethness Castro 2018, 103). Marcuse's larger philosophical vision clearly holds that a central component is necessary among the central-todecentral elements of revolutionary strategy, while understanding that the democratic character of revolutionary struggle is key and must be defended and enhanced.

Marcuse proposes an antifascist vision of *intercultural solidarity against* the resurgent politics of white supremacy, oligarchic wealth idolization, profitable waste, as well as the toxic masculinity characteristic of authoritarian populism. In his ecosocialist view, *the radical transformation of the labor process itself*—labor's liberation from commodification and alienation—*stands centermost. As a species* we have endured because of our sensuous appreciation of our emergent powers: *the power to subsist cooperatively; to create, to communicate, and to care communally within that form of society that we may rightly call a commonwealth.*

The liberation of labor from commodification is the ground of authentic disalienation and freedom "within the realm of necessity," where satisfaction is restored to the processes of social labor and social wealth production, not in terms of greater, more efficient production, but in terms of an ethics of partnership, racial and gender equality, and gratification through work, earth admiration, and ecological responsibility. The convergence of the environmentalist and labor movements is essential in terms of a unified emancipatory praxis if the human species is not only to endure but to flourish. A philosophical and political recognition of the meaning of commonwealth labor serves as the fundamental legitimation of a socialist philosophy and its promise of abundance and leisure for all within a context of respect for the earth.

Marcuse's writings contain essential philosophical resources for critical social theory and revolutionary ecological liberation. His work models the path by which we, an international political force of "the 99 percent," can be politically prepared and strengthened. With his insights, we can reconceptualize our understanding of our world and our work in order collectively to retake and repossess a common world—characterized by racial equality, women's equality, the liberation of labor, the restoration of nature, leisure, abundance, and peace.

Works cited

Ackerman, Spencer. 2021. *Reign of Terror: How the September 11th Era Destabilized America and Produced Trump.* New York: Viking.
Amnesty International. 1998. *United States of America: Rights for All.* New York: Amnesty International USA.
Anker, Elizabeth. 2022. "The Exploitation of 'Freedom,'" *The New York Times.* February 6 SR6.
Arendt, Hannah. 1963. *Eichmann in Jerusalem: A Report on the Banality of Evil.* New York: Viking.
Arendt, Hannah. [1958] 1998. *The Human Condition,* Chicago: University of Chicago Press.
Benjamin, Walter. [1921] 1965. *Zur Kritik der Gewalt und andere Aufsätze.* Frankfurt: Suhrkamp.
Bevins, Vincent. 2020. *The Jakarta Method: Washington's Anticommunist Crusade & the Mass Murder Program that Shaped our World.* New York: Public Affairs/ Perseus/Hachette Book Group.
Bloom, Allan. 1987. *The Closing of the American Mind.* New York: Simon & Schuster.
Bookchin, Murray. 2018. *Post-Scarcity Anarchism.* Chico and Edinboro: AK Press.
Brady, Robert. [1937] 1971. *Spirit and Structure of German Fascism.* New York: Lyle Stuart.
Buchanan, Patrick J. 2002. *The Death of the West: How Dying Populations and Immigrant Invasions Imperial Our Country and Civilization.* New York: St. Martin's Griffin Thomas Dunne Books.
Calderón, Dolores. 2009. "One-Dimensionality and Whiteness," in Douglas Kellner, Tyson Lewis, Clayton Pierce, K. Daniel Cho (Eds.) *Marcuse's Challenge to Education.* Lanham, MD: Rowman & Littlefield.
Chase-Dunn, Christopher and Sandor Nagy. 2018. "The Piketty Challenge: Global Inequality and World Revolution," in Lauren Langman and David A. Smith (eds.), *Twenty-First Century Inequality & Capitalism.* Chicago: Haymarket Books.
Davis, Angela. 1974. *An Autobiography.* New York: Random House.
Davis, Angela. 2016. *Freedom Is a Constant Struggle: Ferguson, Palestine, and the Foundations of a Movement.* Chicago: Haymarket Books.
Davis, Angela. 2013. "Critical Refusals and Occupy," *Radical Philosophy Review,* 16:2
Davis, Angela. 2004. "Marcuse's Legacies," in John Abromeit and W. Mark Cobb (Eds.) *Herbert Marcuse: A Critical Reader.* New York: Routledge.
Delgado, Richard and Jean Stefancic. 1997. *Must We Defend Nazis? Hate Speech, Pornography and the New First Amendment.* New York: New York University Press.
Dowd, Douglas. 1997. *Blues for America.* New York: Monthly Review Press.
Feinstein, Andrew. 2012. *The Shadow World: Inside the Global Arms Trade.* New York: Picador [Farrar, Straus, and Giroux].
Finan, Christopher M. 2007. *From the Palmer Raids to the Patriot Act: A History of the Fight for Free Speech in America.* Boston: Beacon Press.
Fromm, Erich. 1961. *Marx's Concept of Man.* New York: Frederick Ungar.
Goldhagen, Daniel Jonah. *Hitler's Willing Executioners: Ordinary Germans and the Holocaust.* New York: Vintage.
Greene, Felix. 1970. *The Enemy: What Every American Should Know About Imperialism.* New York: Random House.

Harcourt, Bernard E. 2018. *The Counterrevolution: How Our Government Went to War Against Its Own Citizens*. New York: Basic Books/Hachette Book Group.

Heidegger, Martin. [1947] 1954. *Platons Lehre von der Wahrheit, mit einem Brief über den 'Humanismus.'* Bern: Franke Verlag.

Hill, Anita. 2021. *Believing: Our Thirty-Year Journey to End Gender Violence*. New York: Viking.

Hobbs-Morgan, Chase. 2015. "Climate Change, Violence, and Film" *Political Theory* 1-21 https://bityl.co/CeQX

Huntington, Samuel P. 1996. *The Clash of Civilizations and the Remaking of World Order*. New York: Simon & Schuster.

Jansen, Peter-Erwin, 2020. "Mobilization of Bias Today: The Renewed Use of Established Techniques; Reconsideration of Two Studies on Prejudice from the Institute of Social Research," translated by Charles Reitz, in Jeremiah Morelock (ed) *Critical Theory and Authoritarian Populism*. London: University of Westminster Press.

Jansen, Peter-Erwin (ed). [1998–] 2009. Herbert Marcuse, *Nachgelassene Schriften*. Six volumes edited by Peter-Erwin Jansen. Springe, Germany: zu Klampen Verlag.

Kellner, Douglas. 2003. *From September 11th to Terror War*. Lanham, MD: Rowman & Littlefield.

Kellner, Douglas. [1998–] 2014. *Collected Papers of Herbert Marcuse*. Six volumes edited by Douglas Kellner. New York and London: Routledge.

Kellner, Douglas. 2012. *Media Spectacle and Insurrection 2011: From the Arab Uprisings to Occupy Everywhere*. London: Bloomsbury.

Kors, Alan. C. & Silverglate, Harvey. 1998. *The Shadow University: The Betrayal of Liberty on American Campuses*. New York: The Free Press.

Laibman, David. 2016. "Marxist-Anarchist Dialog: A Two-Way Learning Curve," *Science & Society*, Volume 80, Number 3, July.

Langman, Lauren and George Lundskow. 2016. *God, Guns, Gold, and Glory*. Chicago: Haymarket.

Lettau, Reinhard. 1971. *Täglicher Faschismus: Amerikanische Evidenz aus 6 Monaten*. Munich: Carl Hanser Verlag.

Lind, William S. 2020. "Cultural Marxism," cultureshield.com. https://bityl.co/ CeQd

Löwenthal, Leo and Norbert Guterman. [1949] 1970. *Prophets of Deceit, Studies in Prejudice Series*, Volume 5. New York: Harper & Brothers, Copyright American Jewish Committee, Palo Alto, CA: Pacific Books.

Maley, Terry. 2017. "Human Emancipation and the 'Historical Fate of Bourgeois Democracy,'" in his edited collection *One-Dimensional Man 60 Years On: The Struggle Continues*. Halifax and Winnipeg: Fernwood Publishing.

Marcuse, Herbert. [1974] 2015a. *Paris Lectures at Vincennes University*, 1974. Philadelphia, PA: International Herbert Marcuse Society.

Marcuse, Herbert. [1975] 2015b. "Why Talk on Socialism?" in Charles Reitz (Ed.). *Crisis and Commonwealth: Marcuse, Marx, McLaren*. Lanham, MD: Lexington Books.

Marcuse, Herbert. [1979] 2011. "Ecology and the Critique of Modern Society," in Douglas Kellner and Clayton Pierce (Eds.) Herbert Marcuse, *Collected Papers of Herbert Marcuse*. Volume 5, *Philosophy, Psychoanalysis and Emancipation*. New York and London: Routledge.

Marcuse, Herbert. [1972] 2005. "Ecology and Revolution," in Douglas Kellner (Ed.) Herbert Marcuse, *Collected Papers of Herbert Marcuse*. Volume 3, *The New Left and the 1960s*. New York and London: Routledge.

Marcuse, Herbert. [1974] 2005. "Marxism and Feminism" in Douglas Kellner (Ed.) Herbert Marcuse, *Collected Papers of Herbert Marcuse*. Volume 3, *The New Left and the 1960s*. New York and London: Routledge.

Marcuse, Herbert. [1947] 1998. "33 Theses toward the Military Defeat of HitlerFascism," in Douglas Kellner (Ed.) Herbert Marcuse, *Collected Papers of Herbert Marcuse*. Volume 1, *Technology. War, and Fascism*. New York: Routledge.

Marcuse, Herbert. [1942] 1998. "The New German Mentality" in Douglas Kellner (Ed.) Herbert Marcuse, *Collected Papers of Herbert Marcuse*. Volume 1, *Technology. War, and Fascism*. New York: Routledge.

Marcuse, Herbert. [1975] 1987. *Zeit-Messungen*, Herbert Marcuse *Schriften* 9. Frankfurt: Suhrkamp.

Marcuse, Herbert. [1955] 1966. *Eros and Civilization*. Boston, MA: Beacon Press.

Marcuse, Herbert. 1972. *Counterrevolution and Revolt*. Boston, MA: Beacon Press.

Marcuse, Herbert. [1972] 2001. "The Historical Fate of Bourgeois Democracy," in Douglas Kellner (Ed.) Herbert Marcuse, *Collected Papers of Herbert Marcuse*. Volume 2, *Towards a Critical Theory of Society*. New York: Routledge.

Marcuse, Herbert. [1967] 2005. "The Problem of Violence and the Radical Opposition," in Douglas Kellner (Ed.) Herbert Marcuse, *Collected Papers of Herbert Marcuse*. Volume 3, *The New Left and the 1960s*. New York: Routledge.

Marcuse, Herbert. 1970. *Five Lectures: Psychoanalysis, Politics, ana Utopia*. Boston, MA: Beacon Press.

Marcuse, Herbert. 1969. *An Essay on Liberation*. Boston, MA: Beacon Press.

Marcuse. Herbert. 1968. "Liberation from the Affluent Society," in *To Free a Generation: The Dialectics of Liberation*. David Cooper (ed.) New York: Collier Books.

Marcuse, Herbert. 1967. "Thoughts on the Defense of Gracchus Babeuf" in *The Defense of Gracchus Babeuf* edited by John Anthony Scott. Amherst. MA: University of Massachusetts Press.

Marcuse, Herbert. 1965. "Repressive Tolerance," in R.P. Wolff, B. Moore, and H. Marcuse (Eds.). *A Critique of Pure Tolerance*. Boston, MA: Beacon Press.

Marcuse, Herbert. [1965] 2014. "*Afterword* to Walter Benjamin's *Critique of Violence*" in Douglas Kellner and Clayton Pierce (Eds.) Herbert Marcuse, *Collected Papers of Herbert Marcuse*. Volume 6, *Marxism, Revolution, and Utopia*. New York and London: Routledge.

Marcuse, Herbert. 1964. *One-Dimensional Man: Studies in the Ideology of Advanced Industrial Society*. Boston, MA: Beacon Press.

Marcuse, Herbert. [1941] 1960. *Reason and Revolution*. Boston, MA: Beacon Press.

Matsuda, Mari J., Lawrence, C. R., Delgado, R., & Crenshaw, K. W. 1993. *Words That Wound: Critical Race Theory, Assaultive Speech, and the First Amendment*. Boulder, CO: Westview Press.

Moyn, Samuel. 2021. *Humane: How the United States Abandoned Peace and Reinvented War*. New York: Ferrar, Straus, and Giroux.

Neumann, Franz. 1942. *Behemoth: The Structure and Practice of National Socialism 1933–1944*. London: Victor Gollancz.

Olsen, Gary. 2021. "Will Neoliberalism Morph into Fascism in the United States?" *CounterPunch,* March 5.

Oluo, Ijeoma. 2020. *MEDIOCRE: The Dangerous Legacy of White Male America*. New York: Seal Press/Hachette Book Group.

Packard, Vance. 1960. *The Waste Makers*. New York: David McKay Publishing.
Petrou, Karen. 2021. *Engine of Inequality: The Fed and the Future of Wealth in America*. Hoboken, NJ: John Wiley & Sons.
Physicians for Human Rights. 2020. "Shot in the Head," September 14 https://bityl.co/CeQh
Reich, Wilhelm. [1946] 1980. *The Mass Psychology of Fascism*. New York: Farrar, Straus and Giroux.
Reitz, Charles. 2000. *Art, Alienation, and the Humanities: A Critical Engagement with Herbert Marcuse*. Albany, NY: State University of New York Press.
Rifkin, Jeremy. 2009. *The Empathic Civilization: The Race to Global Consciousness in a World in Crisis*. New York: Penguin.
Robinson, William I. 2020. *The Global Police State*. London: Pluto Press. Scalia, Antonin. 1992. *R.A.V. vs. City of St. Paul* 505 U.S. 377.
Sernau, Scott. 2006. *Worlds Apart: Social Inequalities in a New Century*. Thousand Oaks CA: Pine Forge Press.
Sethness Castro, Javier. 2018. *Eros and Revolution: The Critical Philosophy of Herbert Marcuse*. Chicago: Haymarket Books.
Shirer, William L. 1960. *The Rise and Fall of the Third Reich*. Greenwich, CT: Fawcett.
Sleeter, Christine and Delores Degaldo Bernal. 2003. "Critical Pedagogy, Critical Race Theory, and Anti-Racist Education," in James A. Banks and Cherry A. Banks (Eds.). *Handbook of Research on Multicultural Education*. San Francisco, CA: Jossey-Bass.
Stanley, Jason. 2016. "The Free Speech Fallacy," in *The Chronicle Review*, March 18.
Stanley, Jason. 2020. *How Fascism Works; The Politics of Us and Them*. New York: Random House.
Sukhov, Michael J. (2020) "Herbert Marcuse on Radical Subjectivity and the 'New Activism': Today's Climate and Black Lives Matter movements." *Radical Philosophy Review* 23(2). DOI: 10.5840/radphilrev2020813115.
Tepperman, Jonathan. 2021. "America Traumatized," *The New York Times Book Review*, September 5. 13.
West, Cornel. 2017. "Anti-fascists and anarchists saved our lives in Charlottesville," *Democracy Now!* Monday, Aug 14, 2017. https://bityl.co/CeQl
Wheeler, Liz. 2021. "Critical Race Theory is Repackaged Marxism," *Newsweek,* June 14, https://www.newsweek.com/critical-race-theory-repackaged-marxism-opinion- 1599557
Wilson, J. K. 1995. *The Myth of Political Correctness: The Conservative Attack on Higher Education*. Durham, NC: Duke University Press.
Winter, Rainer. 2020. "Review: Bernard E. Harcourt, *The Counterrevolution*," *Theory, Culture & Society*. 37:7-8, December.

4

Nature as Ally: Against Global Catastrophe(s)

> Marxist theory has the least justification to ignore the metabolism
> between the human being and nature ...
> —Herbert Marcuse, *The Aesthetic Dimension* (1978, 16)

The global system of advanced capitalism is poisoning and depleting the resources of our material environment; an intercontinental politics of neofascism is contorting our political lives. Refugees migrate from the Middle East to Europe, from the Global South to the U.S.A., only to be denied their rights to asylum. Derelict political leadership at the highest levels in the U.S. throughout the Covid-19 crisis led to surplus destruction and death compared to other nations.[1] Establishment politicians in various parties promote racial animosity and anti-immigrant scapegoating as they orchestrate social control policies in service to this system. There can be no escape from the pandemic or the refugee crisis, ecological devastation, and the generalized economics of despair worldwide without a global movement representing individual well-being as also embedded within and dependent upon communal well-being.

Herbert Marcuse's ecological writings emphasize how both the earth and human life are stressed under the conditions of global financial capital. His little-known essays "Ecology and the Criticism of Society" ([1979] 2011a) and "Ecology and Revolution" ([1972] 2005) need to

---

[1] "The American coronavirus fiasco has exposed the country's incoherent leadership, self-defeating political polarization, a lack of investment in public health, and persistent socioeconomic and racial inequities that have left millions of people vulnerable to disease and death." —Joel Achenbach, William Wan, Karin Brulliard and Chelsea Janes, "The Crisis that Shocked the World: America's Response to the Coronavirus," *The Washington Post*, July 19, 2020. See also, David Leonhardt, "U.S. is Alone Among Peers in Failing to Contain Virus," *The New York Times*, August 7, 2020, A-1. The Covid Crisis Group [Philip Zelikow, ed.], *Lessons Learned from Covid War: An Investigative Report.* New York: *Public Affairs*, 2023).

be recognized as decisive for his vision of radical socialism. Marcuse is the only figure of the first-generation Frankfurt School who developed writings directly concerned with ecological and feminist problems or the counterstrategies to confront and overcome them. His essays on ecology are eminently aware of the interconnectedness of the biosphere and the negative impacts of the capitalist political economy. Environmentalist criticisms of extractive and polluting economic policies tended implicitly or explicitly to involve system negations and epitomize his strategy of the Great Refusal against the established order. The Great Refusal meant demonstration, confrontation, and rebellion to protest repression and negate advanced industrial society globally (Marcuse [1955] 1966, 149; 1969 ix; Marcuse [1964] 1991, 257; Lamas, Wolfson, and Funke 2017). Marcuse argued that the Sixties' spirit of rebelliousness expressed a visceral repugnance at the totality of the efficiently functioning social order as such. The ecology movement represented a driving force within this Great Refusal (Marcuse 1972, 61).

> This society is obscene in producing and indecently exposing a stifling abundance of wares while depriving its victims abroad of the necessities of life; obscene in stuffing itself and its garbage cans while poisoning and burning the scarce foodstuffs in the fields of its aggression; obscene in the words and smiles of its politicians and entertainers; its prayers, in its ignorance, and in the wisdom of its kept intellectuals. (Marcuse 1969, 7-8)
>
> [O]pposition is directed against the totality of a well-functioning, prosperous society—a protest against its Form—the commodity form of men and things. (Marcuse 1972, 49, 51)

Capitalism's fetish with commodity production and profit is poisoning the earth. Profit comes before all else: gun manufacturers before victims in schools and churches. Drug manufacturers before diabetics and opioid addicts. This obsession is a many-headed hydra: cut off one head and five more appear, e.g., control cigarettes then vaping generates renewed profits for the tobacco industry.

Under capitalism, our primary drives, *sex* for procreation and species survival and *aggression* as self-protection are repressively bent toward controlled forms of behavior compatible with the commodity form: gratuitous sex and violence. The New Left found nature valuable because it represented a nonrepressive social, sexual, and political order. "[N]ature was the very negation of the market society, with its values of profit and utility" (Marcuse [1972] 2005, 174). It assists in "the recovery of the life-enhancing forces in nature, the sensuous aesthetic qualities which are foreign to a life wasted in unending competitive performances ..." (Marcuse 1972, 60).

> If the New Left emphasizes the struggle for the restoration of nature, for public parks and beaches, for spaces of tranquility and beauty; if it demands a new sexual morality, the liberation of women, then it fights against material conditions imposed by the capitalist system and reproducing this system. (Marcuse 1972, 17)

Marcuse's political-philosophical vision continues to offer intelligent strategic perspectives on current concerns—especially issues of neofascist white supremacy, hate speech, hate crimes, police brutality, environmental destruction, and education as monocultural social manipulation. These troubles are profound, yet they can be countered through a Marcusean strategy of revolutionary ecological liberation and women's emancipation—radical socialism as I will attempt to show in my concluding chapter 10 below.

Marcuse's posthumously published *Paris Lectures at Vincennes University, 1974* underscored his belief that the women's movement was one of the most important political forces for system change. He saw this movement as key in the transformation of civilization's traditionally patriarchal values, and this as *central* to what he saw as the "context of the enlarged depth and scope of the revolution, of the new goals and possibilities of the revolution" (Marcuse [1974] 2015a) such that the movement for the liberation of women finds momentous significance in his overall perspective. Marcuse was one of the first critical Marxists to write on feminism ("Marxism and Feminism" [1974] 2005). This appeared in the same year in which he delivered his Paris lectures.

Commercialized Nature, Polluted Nature, Militarized Nature: May Day! May Day!

Human beings uniquely appreciate the radical power of the earth and its remarkable beauty. Within the dialectics of nature, ecological reciprocity can be a creative force. We now recognize that we have the capacity to transform our estate on the face of the planet, such that we can regain a place of honor within our world while attaining our own fullest ethical and intellectual potential. Because we need a new world system, we also need to see that nature can be our ally.

In 1972 Marcuse began to criticize explicitly the ways in which nature was under attack: "Commercialized nature, polluted nature, militarized nature cut down the life environment of man, not only in an ecological, but also in a very existential sense" (Marcuse 1972, 60).

Marcuse regarded the environmental movement of his time as the embodiment of life-affirming energy directed toward the protection of Earth and peaceful human existence overall. He recognized the importance of ecology to the revolutionary movement and the importance of the revolutionary movement for ecology. Both are linked through Eros into a campaign for revolutionary ecological liberation. To him this reflected the vernal spirit of "May Day" (ribbons and flowers, etc.), while embodying also the combative spirit of the revolutionary international labor force. May Day, as a revolutionary holiday, means protesting particular wrongs—and fighting for reform struggles within capitalism is part of the struggle for system change. But this is also a fight at a higher level of engagement, protesting a political-economic wrong in general—capitalism—and having fateful implications for our future on the face of the planet. He advocated not only the Great Refusal, but what he called "revolutionary ecological liberation" (Marcuse [1972] 2005, 174). Wasted abundance and environmental degradation required a radical systems-critique and a form of political opposition that needed to become a revolutionary force.

Nature's power to soothe and quiet our souls and bring peace to the human heart was famously praised in 19th Century German Romanticism via poems like Goethe's classic *Über allen Gipfeln ist Ruh* [Wanderer's Night Song] and his Song of May—*O wie herrlich leuchtet mir die Natur* — "Oh how Nature's splendor radiates within me!" In sharp contrast (in 1944 after Auschwitz) the critical theorists Max Horkheimer and Theodor Adorno considered that the grand-sounding nature veneration in German high culture now rang hollow. A much-quoted passage from their *Dialectic of Enlightenment* reads: "Dominant practice and its inescapable alternatives are not threatened by nature, which tends rather to coincide with them, but by the fact that nature is remembered" (Horkheimer and Adorno [1944] 1972, 255). Nature required the reflective powers of the human mind to itself be understood and liberated. For Horkheimer and

Adorno, *not* nature, but its *remembrance*, was key. This contains the idea that the mind of human beings must rise above nature in an almost dualistic manner. This perspective almost sees *nature as an adversary*, viewing the environing world with a pronounced sense of doom—as a catastrophe waiting to happen. Horkheimer and Adorno criticize humanity's separation from nature, but their *Dialectic of Enlightenment* is permeated by post-war disgust and resentment against all of humankind and the world. It discharges high-voltage literary sarcasm and exudes haughty intellectual self-absorption, giving up on the educative and political promise of human rationality as such. They resort to extremely cutting and pessimistic aphoristic remarks; reason is not just problematic, it is tragic and sick.

Herbert Marcuse, on the other hand, continued to hold reason and *nature itself* in high esteem. In 1972 his *Counterrevolution and Revolt* contained the notable chapter on "Nature and Revolution." He theorized in a less demoralized, dualistic, and more hopeful vein:

> What is happening is the discovery (or rather, rediscovery) of *nature as an ally* in the struggle against the exploitative societies in which the violation of nature aggravates the violation of man. The discovery of the liberating forces of nature and their vital role in the construction of a free society becomes a new force in social change. (Marcuse 1972, 59, emphasis added)

How singular and extraordinary that Marcuse saw nature as an *ally*, its liberating power as a new force in the struggle for liberation! Plato had quite famously scoffed that the countryside and the trees had nothing to teach him (*Phaedrus* 230d). But Aristotle had gazed in awe at nature and praised the benefits of walking outdoors as easing the thought process (thus his *Peripatetic* school). Hobbes infamously imagined human beings in a 'war of each against all' in his hypostatized "state of nature." It was such a perfect excuse for his monarch's imposition of 'law and order.' Rousseau, on the other hand, theorized nature as a harbinger of freedom and equality.

Nature as ally 1: Emerson, Ecuador and Mother Earth

Like Aristotle and Rousseau, Marcuse could still marvel without irony at nature. He saw it as resilient and possessing a force that can be liberating. It was not as if nature were a *subject* that could choose to act on our behalf (or not) giving us "following seas" or a tail wind—one might just as often be randomly becalmed or swamped. Nature is in motion; it is dynamic, and it is because humanity and nature are *dialectically interdependent* that the "liberation of nature" can be a "vehicle for the liberation of man" (Marcuse 1972, 59). Marcuse rejects the pessimism of Horkheimer and Adorno as well as the theology implied if one holds that nature can be a "manifestation of subjectivity" (Marcuse 1972, 65).

Ralph Waldo Emerson, like Rousseau, Goethe and Schiller, *did* classically propose certain advantages we owe to nature: refreshed sensations and awareness, our essential bond with both the living and the non-living features and creatures of the material world. "To the body and mind which have been cramped by noxious work or company, nature is medicinal and restores their tone ... [T]he universe is the property of every individual in it. Every rational creature has all nature for his dowry and estate ... he is entitled to the world by his constitution" (Emerson [1836] 2009, 6-8). To Emerson we are also *educated* through the study of the environment: "To the young mind, everything is individual, stands by itself. By and by, it finds how to join two things and see in them one nature ... it goes on tying things together, diminishing anomalies, discovering roots running underground, whereby contrary and remote things cohere, and flower out from one stem" (Emerson [1837] 2009, 151). One might say with Emerson that such education affords insights into an incipient *dialectics of nature*. But Emerson, for all his social engagement and philosophy of nature, is no Engels. Nonetheless, we stand to benefit as an historical materialist when re-reading Emerson's work on nature: we can both negate and elevate Emerson's pantheistic and proprietary weaknesses in sublated form as well as preserve and promote his ecological strengths.

Marcuse's philosophy helps in this regard with his recognition of the humanizing propensities of nature. Nature needs us as an ally to prevent its destruction and we need nature as an ally given its power to ensure that we can endure. "[T]he restoration of the earth as a human environment, is not just a romantic, aesthetic, poetic idea which is a matter of concern only to the privileged; today, it is a question of survival" (Marcuse [1972] 2005, 175).

Marcuse emphasizes that human beings and the earth are enmeshed in an ecological web of mutuality and interdependence that critical reason can comprehend. Today however Marcuse asserts that both human beings and nature are governed by the forces of capital (Ruschig 2020).

Nature will "help" liberate us—if we help liberate *it*. Nature itself requires liberation because we now encounter nature "as transformed by society, subjected to a specific rationality which became, to an ever-increasing extent, technical, instrumentalist rationality bent to the requirements of capitalism" (Marcuse 1972, 59-60). Marcuse *does* say that in a sense we must recognize "nature as a subject in its own right—a subject with which to live in a common universe" (Marcuse 1972, 60). From this perspective nature must be made whole where it has been damaged. Alex Khasnabish (2017) has linked Marcuse's radical ecological thinking to "the persistence of Indigenous struggle after five centuries of colonialism" in Central and South America (Khasnabish 2017, 101). The 2008 Preamble to the Constitution of Ecuador includes such an explicit provision: "We hereby decide to build a new form of public coexistence, in diversity and harmony with nature, to achieve the good way of living [buen vivir, sumac kawsay]." Marcuse is likeminded: "The Marxian conception understands nature as a universe which becomes the congenial medium for human gratification to the degree to which nature's *own* gratifying qualities and forces are recovered and released" (Marcuse 1972, 67).

According to Indigenous author Daniel R. Wildcat (of whom much more later), Mother Earth herself is trying to tell us something today: she is undergoing dramatic change. She has issued a Red Alert telling us that "Humankind does not stand above or outside of Earth's life system ... [H]opefulness resides with those who are willing to imaginatively reconstitute lifeways emergent from the nature-culture complex" (Wildcat 2009, 21). The Red Alert is intended to bring not fear but hope. Nonetheless, the message from nature is telling us that climate catastrophe is of *human* origin, unfolding *now* (not in terms of long-wave geological time), i.e., so rapidly that we humans can perceive it and know it (Wildcat 2009, 46-47). Yet it is not nature, but human culture, that is the source of our problems. Hope can be found in taking seriously the lifeways of indigenous peoples worldwide. Scientists are increasingly doing so, and "it is time to make a strategic alliance" (Wildcat 2009, 52). We need to listen to indigenous voices: It is not our human nature, but specific human cultural practices that have disturbed nature profoundly. Nature is not a resource; it is a relative and, with respectful interaction, an ally (Wildcat 2009, 64).

David Bedford and Tom Cheney explicitly linked Marcuse's work to Native American philosophy in "One-Dimensional Man and Indigenous

Struggles" (2017). "Like many Indigenous movements, Marcuse envisions a way of understanding and interacting with nature that is qualitatively different from that which occurs in modern, industrial, one-dimensional capitalism" (Bedford and Cheney 2017, 68). They argue that for many First Nations the idea of nature has an aesthetic power the revolutionary potential of which has been recognized by Marcuse. "It is here that Marcuse's aesthetic theory comes to bear on Indigenous struggles… It is not necessary that the representation of nature be perfectly accurate. Indeed, it may even be partly mythical. Its significance is of an alternative dimension, a beautiful image of a different reality that breaks apart the prevailing way of being and thereby creates the possibility of a better future" (Bedford and Cheney 2017, 71).

Nature as ally 2: John Dewey, naturalism, and "Modern Materialism"

Marcuse was not the first 20th Century philosopher of social reform and revolution to see nature as a realistic ally in humanity's struggle. John Dewey had an exceptional appreciation of the accommodating qualities of nature, especially as articulated in his classic works *Human Nature and Conduct* (1922), *Experience and Nature* (1925), and *Logic, The Theory of Inquiry* (1938). He was renowned during the Progressive Era in American history for having demonstrated that the scientific study of *nature* opened up new ways to study and transform the *social order*. The reflective methods used in the study of nature in turn had the power to elucidate and ameliorate society's problems. He was reviled in conservative religious circles for his emphasis on social science in public education and on a secular curriculum. "Misunderstood by most first-generation critical theorists [including the early Marcuse[2] —CR] recent critical theorists (e.g. Habermas and Fraser) have shown increased appreciation of John Dewey's thought" (Antonio 2021, 74). Marcuse's many valid criticisms of Dewey revolved around questions of experimentalist logic and pragmatic valuation (Marcuse 1939a; 1939b), *not* his philosophical naturalism. In an early review of Dewey's work Marcuse writes approvingly: "The subject of research is never an isolated I, consciousness, or spirit. Rather, it is a living

---

[2] "Marcuse unfairly lumps Dewey into the positivist camp …" (Kellner, Pierce, and Lewis 2011, 88). Marcuse's sound criticisms of Dewey are discussed in depth by Douglas Kellner, Clayton Pierce, and Tyson Lewis (2011, 39-48), "Introduction," to Herbert Marcuse, *Philosophy, Psychoanalysis and Emancipation* Volume 5, *Collected Papers of Herbert Marcuse*, Douglas Kellner and Clayton Pierce, eds. (New York: Routledge, 2011) pp. 39-48.

organism with 'natural' actions and reactions to and on the environment" (Marcuse [1939a] 2011c, 82). "Dewey's logic ... remains ... naturalistic" (ibid., 87). Years later Marcuse would also note: "There seems to be a close affinity between Marx's and Dewey's reorientation of theory on practice" (Marcuse [1958] 1961, 210). I will argue in chapter 6 below that through reflective historical practice human beings have become moral, consistent with the ecological materialism of Marx, Dewey, and Marcuse.

Dewey's intellectual legacy includes the work of Marvin Farber, a Harvard philosophy PhD in 1925 who had also studied in Freiburg, Germany, under Husserl and Heidegger. In 1937 he became chair of philosophy at the University of Buffalo (now State University of New York at Buffalo). He published widely on phenomenology, critical of Husserl's opposition to naturalism and its tendencies toward subjectivism and idealism (Farber [1959] 1968, *Naturalism and Subjectivism*). His critique of Husserl stems in large part from a Deweyan view of nature (1949, 607; [1959] 1968, 24ff), though his own critical philosophical views are fully developed and quite distinctively his. He was founder and editor of what became the illustrious international journal, *Philosophy and Phenomenological Research*. One of Marcuse's early essays (a criticism of Sartre) was published there. Like Marcuse, Farber became profoundly critical of also of Heidegger and existentialism. Michael L. Simmons, Jr., a former colleague of Farber, similarly specializing in Dewey and critical realism's aesthetic and social theory, emphasizes Farber's shift in philosophical terminology from that of naturalism to materialism (Simmons 1982, 2) and Farber's recognition of "the truth of historical materialism" (Farber in Simmons 1982, 21; Farber 1984). "Farber obviously has read Marx. I find Farber's description and analysis of our social system more telling than Dewey's ..." (Simmons 1982, 23). Farber's erudition and that of the journal earned the respect of philosophers around the world, including, by "marvelous coincidence" his last generation of graduate students, the original *Telos* group at Buffalo (D'Amico, Kim, Piccone 1980-81, 168).[3]

---

[3] Decades after its relocation away from Buffalo because of internal political splits a reconstituted Telos group began to attack liberal democracy from the right, turning to the philosophy of Carl Schmitt and rejecting liberalism's multicultural reform, egalitarian ideas, and universal human rights. See Robert J. Antonio's critique of this shift in "When History Fails Us" in Jeremiah Morelock (ed.) *How To Critique Authoritarian Populism* (Leiden: Brill, 2021, pp. 62-70)

"Dialectic of Enlightenment" vs. "Philosophy for the Future"

In contrast to Horkheimer and Adorno's political pessimism in *Dialectic of Enlightenment* (1944), with its attendant rejection of naturalism and materialism, there appeared in the U.S. shortly thereafter (1949) a volume rarely given the appreciation it deserves today, edited by three of the most prominent American philosophers advancing both John Dewey's naturalist legacy and the historical materialism of Marx, Engels, Lenin. Marvin Farber, with Roy Wood Sellers and V.J. McGill, published their essay collection, *Philosophy for the Future: The Quest of Modern Materialism* (1949). This contains contributions from prominent intellectuals, many of whose names are familiar to those who know the history of Marxist critical thought in America and Europe: August Cornu, Dirk J. Struik, J.B.S. Haldane, Bernard Stern, Maurice Dobb, J.D. Bernal, Abraham Edel, Maurice Cornforth, and Georg Lukács.

The foreword, collectively written by the editors, makes clear that their modern materialism rejects mechanistic interpretations, is both scientific and humane, emphasizes the interrelatedness of things, and "forgoes the comfort ... of imagining that the order of nature is attuned to [human] purposes or endowed with sensitivity and beneficence" (Sellers, McGill and Farber [henceforth SMF] 1949, vii,). By *dis*connecting modern philosophy at the outset from theology, and enfolding it instead within the perspective of the social and natural sciences, the volume's consideration of the human material condition holds up well. It contains rich veins of modern materialist insight despite its now recognizable lapses and limitations. Auguste Cornu (SMF 57), for example, elaborates the view that modern materialism is historical and that historical materialism is dialectical. Dirk Struik interprets the history of mathematics from a social and materialist perspective. J.B.S. Haldane elucidates naturalism and a modern materialism in astonishing and vivid fashion by comparing living organisms to a seemingly immaterial flame: "[T]he flame, like a living organism, is a pattern of chemical changes rather than a pattern of molecules" (SMF 207). Historical sociologist Bernard Stern similarly distinguishes integrative levels of material organization in the complex layered structures of life and non-life (much as Roy Bhaskar will to do in greater depth fifty years later, see chapter 7 below). Stern likewise stresses, consistent with the budding U.S. Civil Rights movement, that "racial and physiographic determinist explanations of human behavior have been discredited as the significance of the culture concept has come to be appreciated" (SMF 340). Maurice Dobb criticizes the "orthodoxy that had fastened upon the world of academic economics" (SMF 326) in terms of its fetishism of prices and exchange values despite monopoly conditions having undercut any application of its theory of price competition on supply or demand. J.D. Bernal turned to the ways in which capital in monopoly form tends to distort even science: "Every university scientist is in fact dependent upon the monopolists for grants which make his academic research possible . . ." (SMF 406). Brandon Absher's *The Rise of Neoliberal Philosophy* (2021) as well as David N. Smith's *Who Rules the Universities* (1974) document the ongoing validity of this. Abraham Edel brings to the discussion of monopoly and imperialism Rudolf Hilferding's recognition that finance capital weaponizes racism (SMF 423). "Thus in racial ideology there emerges a scientifically-cloaked foundation for the power-lust of finance capital" (Hilferding in Edel, SMF 423). Maurice Cornforth elucidates the repressive limitations for philosophical work of the modern mathematical logic and empiricism of Russell and Whitehead, as well as the inadequacies Wittgenstein's linguistic analysis. Marcuse, it must be noted, likewise undertakes essential criticisms of empiricism, positivism, and Wittgenstein's language philosophy in *One-Dimensional Man* chapter 7, where he sees them as components of one-dimensional thought and the logic of domination. Lastly, let me recall how Georg Lukács focuses critical remarks in this volume against the apparent radicality of the existentialism of Martin Heidegger and Jean-Paul Sartre, in which he takes apart in particular the "myth of nothingness" (SMF 577). Human alienation cannot be superseded through the "free" creation of meaning out of the supposed meaninglessness of the objective world, but rather through an analysis of the world's political crises, including those of empire, war, and fascism.

Like the authors listed above Marcuse pushes beyond Dewey's social liberalism and social reform to the more radical goals of socialism. For Marcuse, Farber, and Simmons, science and technology must be enlisted in the service of humanity, *not* capital accumulation. All three understood commercialized exploitation of the earth as the source of social injustice and environmental violations of the planet that must be ended:

> The general form of the internal contradictions of capitalism has never been more blatant, more cruel, more costly of human lives and happiness. And—this is the significance of the Sixties—this blatant irrationality has not only penetrated the consciousness of a large part of the population, it has also caused, mainly among the young people, a radical transformation of needs and values which may prove to be incompatible with the capitalist system, its hierarchy, priorities, morality, symbols (the counter-culture, ecology) ... (Marcuse [1975] 2015b, 114-115)

Increasingly, the ecological struggle comes into conflict with the laws which govern the capitalist system: the law of increased accumulation of capital, of the creation of sufficient surplus-value, of profit, of the necessity of perpetuating alienated labor and exploitation ... [T]he ecological logic is purely and simply the negation of capitalist logic; the earth can't be saved within the framework of capitalism, the Third World [Global South] can't be developed according to the model of capitalism (Marcuse [1972] 2005, 175).

Daniel R. Wildcat reminds us that Dewey's philosophy was dedicated to the beneficial supersession of the dualistic disjunction of culture from nature (Wildcat 2009, 104). John R. Shook (2017) recalls Dewey on nature:

> Although nature is perilous, nature's intelligibility beneficially supports the pursuits of social intelligence to fulfill ends and realize ideals ... Human individuality is developed through participation in social intelligence's realization of ideals through cultural advancement, where communication and art are predominant ... Cultural/moral progress through intelligence increases the intelligibility of nature and increases the degree of unity with nature's intelligibility ... Though life is short and full of struggle, one's reasonable life has the support of the growing cosmic order and the significance of contributing to that order. (Shook 2017, 26).

Roberta Dreon (2015) explicitly emphasizes the affinity of Marcuse to Dewey's naturalism, especially within the aesthetics developed by both.

> [The] ... naturalistic stance [is] oriented towards the biological roots of the aesthetic with a focus on the one hand on human organic dependence on a natural and naturally social environment

and on the other on human instinctual nature ... [I]n both Dewey and Marcuse a kind of anthropologically oriented stance can be found which has to do with the dynamic historical and even social configurations of our structurally dependent human nature of our ultimately being living creatures. In this sense ... for both authors the aesthetic is ultimately connected to a tendency to enhance life. (Dreon 2015, 79)

For Dewey nature was supportive, intelligence was social, and scientific method, the reflective process, could assist in the reconstruction of the exploitative political-economic order. "Philosophy is thinking what the known demands of us ... It is an idea of what is possible, not a record of accomplished fact. . . it is hypothetical like all thinking. It presents us an assignment of something to be done—something to be tried" (Dewey [1915]1966, 326). The new British critical realists, Roy Bhaskar, Sean Sayers, and Rom Harré worked out fascinating contemporary elaborations of these positions. Bhaskar's contributions to naturalism and critical realism will be discussed in chapter 7 below.

Nature as ally 3: Our political Eros — Against corporate capitalism, global inequality, global warming, the global pandemic

Populations are reeling the world over—from poverty, war, ethnic oppression, and corrupt economic profiteering. Corporate globalization has intensified social inequality and cultural polarization worldwide. Increasing globalization correlates directly with growing economic disparities both within and between nations (Sernau, 2006). This is intensifying through the "race to the bottom" as capitalism searches the globe for the lowest wage labor markets. Douglas Dowd (2009, 11) has called this dynamic capitalism's imperative of exploitation. Business priorities in social affairs are a delusional and eminently destructive perversion of economics. "Nowhere has the distribution of the pie become more equitable .... [A]mong the more unequal regions of the world—the United States, say, or Russia—income disparities are reaching levels not before seen in modern history."[4] "The three richest people in the U.S. own the same wealth as the bottom half of the U.S. population (roughly 160 million people)."[5]

---

4 Eduardo Porter and Karl Russell, "It's an Unequal World; It Doesn't Have to Be," *The New York Times*, December 14, 2017
5 Oxfam International, *Reward Work, Not Wealth, Briefing Paper for Davos World Economic*

The extraction of surplus value under capitalism gives rise also to an excess of destruction and repression of human freedom in advanced industrial societies.[6] We have seen that racial minorities have been hardest hit by the deadliest effects of Covid-19. In the midst of this Covid-19 crisis, the 2020 uprising against systemic racism, precipitated by the police killing of George Floyd, has ignited a global movement for the equality of Black lives.

The White House of ex-president Trump emboldened neofascist rhetoric of hate and fear and mobilized militarized white supremacist kill squads (including those who encouraged Kyle Rittenhouse to use his military-style automatic weapon to threaten and shoot down antiracist protestors in Kenosha, Wisconsin, in late August 2020).[7] The governmental policies and paramilitary tactics of "ICE" (Immigration and Customs Enforcement) directed at undocumented immigrants, have rounded-up hundreds of immigrants in one month, August 2019.[8]

An awareness of the intersectionality of our interdependencies and vulnerabilities has vividly come to the fore. Movement protests linking our social and ecological precariousness, led by Greta Thunberg, Extinction Rebellion, the Sunrise Movement, and others have elevated the struggle for the environment just as ecological justice has also come under siege by the U.S. government.[9] This is the stirring of our political Eros today against the forces of destruction. Ecological devastation and massive fatalities from Covid-19 have been multiplied by "deaths of despair;" oxycontin overdoses are now known to have been enabled by Big Pharma (Case and Deaton 2020; Sandel 2020, 197-222). For those of us without immense personal wealth, these conditions are a matter of our very survival. Chris Hedges and Joe Sacco make clear in *Days of Destruction, Days of Revolt* (2012) that the nation's essential, but lowest paid, workers are lethally confronted by this system's institutional failures: political, economic, educational, health care, law enforcement, etc. "Corporate capitalism will,

---

Forum, released January 22, 2018.https://policy-practice.oxfam.org/resources/reward-work-not-wealthto-end-the-inequality-crisis-we-must-build-an-economy-fo-620396/

6 Herbert Marcuse, *Eros and Civilization: A Philosophical Inquiry into Freud* (Boston: Beacon Press [1955] 1966) p. 35. Even under egalitarian and partnership conditions, basic repression of instincts and desires is required to sustain ethical human life and civilization. The emergence of dominator power in highly unequal class-divided societies entails "surplus repression."

7 See Paige Williams, "American Vigilante," *The New Yorker,* July 5, 2021.

8 Miriam Jordan, "ICE Arrests Hundreds in Mississippi Raids Targeting Immigrant Workers," *The New York Times*, August 7, 2019.

9 Nadja Popovich, Livia Albeck-Ripka, and Kendra Pierre-Louis, "The Trump Administration Is Reversing 100 Environmental Rules," *The New York Times*, July 15, 2020.

quite literally, kill us, as it has killed Native Americans, African Americans trapped in our internal colonies, in the inner cities, those left behind in the devastated coal fields, and those who live as serfs in our nation's produce fields" (Hedges and Sacco 2012, xii).

Despite massive devastation, the 2020 Covid-19 crisis has unpredictably unveiled several potentially emancipatory philosophical truths and political realities. The largely employer-based U.S. health insurance system stands revealed as utterly dysfunctional: leaving vast swaths of a population uninsured, even under normal circumstances, it puts everyone at risk during the viral pandemic that the world is enduring in the 2020s. Cities, provinces, and nations out-bidding one another for protective equipment, testing equipment, ventilators, is plainly outrageous. We see that such a crisis demands radical collaboration rather than competition. Our current epoch, however, epitomizes the brutal and reactionary side of U.S. politics that has regularly re-surfaced in this culture after upswings in progressive activism.

In the run-up to the Covid-19 crisis we were already living in extraordinary times: intensifying economic and political polarization, reckless saber-rattling, resurgent white supremacy, anti-immigrant racism, the rise of authoritarian populism and anti-intellectualism exemplified by relentless defense of Donald Trump by his ardent supporters throughout his presidency and the impeachment process. What we have in the U.S. today is a total surveillance state, an alarming rise in hate crimes, the impunity of police using racist deadly force, armed forces using torture, etc., just those sorts of things Marcuse called out and warned against in 1972: "[T]he capitalist system requires the organization of counterrevolution at home and abroad ... Torture has become a normal instrument of 'interrogation' around the world ..." (Marcuse 1972, 1).

Importantly, since the onset of the pandemic, we have at long last come to acknowledge the essential role of the lower-wage labor force in our society: truck drivers, grocery stockers, cashiers, and of course higher-paid medical professionals: these workers and the workforce overall are the crucial force sustaining the economy. *We have seen that private ownership of business is not necessary for the essentials of economic production, distribution, and exchange. The key component is labor and everything depends on labor.* Like Marx, Marcuse argued philosophically that labor *is ontologically significant*—it is the *human mode of being in the world* (Marcuse [1933] 1973; John Bellamy

Foster, 2000). Labor in this sense is not to be reduced to any form of class circumstance: it's part of our nature as human beings. Social productivity is the political-philosophical foundation to the call for socialized ownership.[10] Marx had explored these philosophical foundations earlier.

> Labor is, in the first place, a process in which both man and Nature participate, and in which man of his own accord starts, regulates, and controls the material reactions between himself and Nature. (Marx *Capital*, Vol I [1867] 1976, 283)

> In creating a world of objects by his practical activity, in his work upon inorganic nature, man proves himself a conscious species-being, i.e., as a being that treats the species as its own essential being, or that treats itself as a species-being. (Marx *1844 Manuscripts* 1982, 113)

Marcuse, like Marx, asserted a radically materialist conception of the species essence of socially active human beings: seen from the outside, we are the ensemble of our social relations; seen from the inside, we are sensuous living labor. Sensuous living labor is the substrate of our being as humans. It is the foundation of our affective and intellectual capacities (and vulnerabilities), bioecologically developed within history. Humanity's earliest proverbs, fables, and riddles teach the survival power of partnership and cooperation and the categorical ethical advantages of empathy, reciprocity, hospitality, and respect for the good in common. Humanity experiences the satisfactions / dissatisfactions derived from our economic, aesthetic, intellectual, and moral standards, gravitating toward the humanism of a communally laboring commonwealth. Both Marx and Marcuse understood human alienation as estranged labor: sensuous living labor's separation from: 1) its product, 2) the process of production, 3) from our species need for the gratification of our sensuous, intellectual, political and ethical faculties [our species being or *Gattungswesen*], and 4) our separation from other producers, whom we tend to see as competitive units of commodified labor (Marx [1844] 1982, 106-116).

---

10 Marcuse's ideas with regard to the workforce and the concept of labor underwent significant shifts and modifications over the course of his career. In one of his final publications, he stressed "The working class still is the 'ontological' antagonist of capital, and the potential revolutionary Subject; but it is a vastly expanded working class, which no longer corresponds directly to the Marxian proletariat" (Marcuse [1979] 2014, 392). In *One-Dimensional Man* (1964) Marcuse had theorized that a "comfortable, smooth, democratic unfreedom" was to be found in advanced industrial society, in which the workforce had been absorbed into consumer society and labor's potential for opposition paralyzed.

Nature As Ally 4: Family and community well-being: Against surplus destruction and wasted abundance

Capitalism represents the irrational perfection of waste and the degradation of the earth; profitable plastic litter, air pollution, trash (planned obsolescence), toxic dumping, air and water pollution, resource depletion, etc. Ubiquitous advertising adds to the devastation by further boosting sales and the exchange value of a "new" product despite its diminished quality and use-value. We get disposable consumer goods and a society in which lives become disposable too (as described decades ago by Vance Packard in *The Waste Makers*, 1960).

If *economics* is (as Aristotle held) the study and practice of improving the human material condition enabling human families and communities to flourish, the capitalist system is obviously *dis*-economic in its extreme inequalities of immiseration and wealth, limitations on quality of life, and undemocratic monopolization of power. In economics and ethics, Aristotle (in contrast to Thrasymachus who viewed justice as whatever satisfied individual self-interest) believed the chief vice was the boundless pursuit of property accumulation; the chief virtue, the pursuit of the well-being of the family and community (*Politics,* Chapter IX).

Former U.S. President Donald Trump unilaterally pulled the U.S. out of the Paris climate accords, and the USA's reigning right-wing politicians during the Trump era have indulged in a loathsome defense of the fossil fuel industries: coal, gas, and oil. They rolled back the admittedly insufficient regulations of the Environmental Protection Agency. Waste-making in capitalist economies, especially within the productive system, is globally destructive (Magdoff and Williams 2017).

Decades ago, critical economist Douglas Dowd wrote: "at least *half* of our gross domestic product may be classified as waste of goods and services" (Dowd 1997, 123). He considered economic waste per the understanding of Thorstein Veblen as the waste of capital, labor, and resources to produce the opposite of socially useful goods and services. Its immensity was due in large measure to overspending on the military and warfare. Today, after having delivered 363 tons of shrink-wrapped $100 bills to oligarchs and warlords in Iraq—and more ($837 billion spent on war fighting) in Afghanistan—with nothing to show for it but widespread destruction, death, and military defeat, we see again this bitter and disgusting truth.[11]

---

11 "How the U.S. sent bn in cash to Iraq. And watched it vanish," *The Guardian*, February 8, 2007.

U.S. militarism and U.S.-led global capitalism are hostile to nature

Excessive military spending illustrates this vice catering to the owners of the U.S. suppliers to military-industrial complex most vividly. The fuller costs of U.S. wars in terms of lives lost, government lies and illegalities, and torture, are repeatedly emphasized by Marcuse (1969, 1972, 2019). The U.S. military budget is far greater than needed, and in fact, could be reduced if the sole goal were national defense. In reality, the military budget does more than provide for defense, it is a major mechanism to subsidize owners of the military-industrial complex and thus keep the nearly unbounded profits flowing (Melman 1970; 1985). Military spending is one of the most wasteful projects in the U.S. and elsewhere around the globe. It could be substantially reduced and public welfare would not be impaired.

Seymour Melman writes in *Pentagon Capitalism* of the "depleting consequences" of military spending for the U.S. economy and society: "Since the end of the Second World War, the United States government has spent an astronomical $1,000 billion for military purposes" (1970, 184). His *Permanent War Economy* establishes the thesis that "Industrial productivity, the foundation of every nation's economic growth, is eroded by the relentlessly predatory effects of the military economy" (1985, 7). Andrew Feinstein (2012) comments on contemporary world military spending: "An inestimably large amount of public money is expended on the arms trade. This is not only in direct government expenditure, which totals trillions of dollars a year, but in the massive state subsidization of R&D, export and other incentives, wastage on unnecessary weapons systems, overspending by contractors and bailouts to badly run companies" (Feinstein 2012, 524-525; see also Boggs 2005, 26-27). Marcuse had his own commentary in 1974 on U.S. militarism (Marcuse [1974] 2015a): "[I]f you throw together—which as an orthodox Marxist you might well do—unemployment and employment for the military services, you arrive at the following numbers: a total of over 25% of the labor force, i.e. 22.3 million, were either unemployed or dependent on military spending directly or indirectly" (Marcuse [1974] 2015a, 42). This is a capitalism of wasted abundance.

https://www.theguardian.com/world/2007/feb/08/usa.iraq1 "Afghanistan collapsed because corruption had hollowed out the state," *The Guardian*, August 30, 2021. https://www.theguardian.com/commentisfree/2021/aug/30/afghanistan-us-corruption-taliban. Fahrah Stockman, "The War on Terror Was Corrupt From the Start" *The New York Times*. September 13, 2021. https://www.nytimes.com/2021/09/13/opinion/afghanistan-war-economy.html?searchResultPosition=1

The U.S. military is the largest single source of greenhouse gasses, yet the U.S. media are generally uncritical about the U.S. military being the largest polluter in the world. According to FAIR (Fairness and Accuracy in Reporting), "Major Media Bury Groundbreaking Studies of Pentagon's Massive Carbon Bootprint" (FAIR October 10, 2019). In December 2021 the U.S. Congress passed its annual military spending bill costing $778 billion and providing a bipartisan $25 billion more in Pentagon funding than requested by President Joe Biden and nearly $38 billion more than the last such bill of former President Donald Trump's tenure. Democratic socialist, Senator Bernie Sanders, stated his opposition: "At a time when the scientists are telling us that we face an existential threat in terms of climate change, we are told that we just don't have enough money to transform our energy system away from fossil fuel and create a planet that will be healthy and habitable for our kids and future generations" (Sanders 2021). Unlike the generous bipartisan support for military spending in 2021, crucial social-needs-oriented infrastructure legislation has been killed by its opponents in Congress. This is a capitalism that has become more and more militarist and predatory; superprofits are generated by wasteful war production. Likewise, any limited prosperity among war production workers is eluding masses of people whose conditions of life are becoming increasingly precarious.

Common menace, common earth:
The EarthCommonWealth alternative

In the foregoing pages, Marcuse's view that capitalism represents the irrational perfection of waste, earth degradation, profitable plastic litter, trash (planned obsolescence), toxic dumping, air and water pollution, resource depletion, etc. has been emphasized. He alerted us to the fact that advanced industrial society gives us throwaway consumer goods and throwaway lives as well. Today, such corporate practices underlie the full spectrum of sales, from single-use plastics clogging landfills, rivers, and oceans—to such contemporary innovations as Monsanto's seeds that produce crops artificially made sterile, such that the seeds are under monopoly control and must always be purchased anew. The economy is dominated by the fetish with production for sale, for exchange value rather than use-value. This has given us the twisted dis-economics of profit growth through planned obsolescence, waste, and advertising. Ostensibly durable goods, like automobiles, washing machines, etc., are engineered with the predictable premature breakdown built right in.

EarthCommonWealth is not Marcuse's term but my way to denote and elaborate his comprehensive vision of an *ecosocialist system-alternative* calling for the elimination the capitalist economy's core fetish with production for exchange value and profit rather than use-value. Having such an alternative perspective is a prerequisite for overcoming the climate crisis and launching the restoration of our too-much abused nature and the renewal of our human nature from its alienated condition. EarthCommonWealth envisions the displacement and transcendence of capitalist oligarchy as such, not simply its most bestial and destructive components. It is a concept explored in preliminary form in *Ecology & Revolution* (Reitz 2019). This is a *green* economic alternative because its ecological vision sees all living things and their non-living earthly surroundings as a global community capable of a dignified, deliberate coexistence. The ecological work of Aldo Leopold (1942; 1949) also comes into play for me here.

Understanding Earth in global ecological terms Leopold saw it is not merely soil and rock; it is a biotic pyramid, a fountain of energy flowing through a circuit of land, minerals, air, water, plants, and animals including the human species. He proposed a dialectical and materialist "land ethic" as a call to conservation and cooperation, in which the individual's rights to private property in land are contrasted with historical patterns of communal ownership (Leopold 1949). The EarthCommonWealth Alternative seeks to restore nature's bounty and beauty by opposing the profitable misuse of limited natural resources, in large measure by negating planned obsolescence and its attendant wasted abundance, negating the capitalist fetish of exchange value, and by liberating commonwealth labor by eliminating its commodity or wage form. Ending the crisis of the environment is not primarily a proposition involving massive new social costs and investments to cleanse our ecology of the detritus left by an otherwise rampantly polluting corporate capitalism. Nature is an ally, a model and inspiration for conservation and social savings by ending profitable waste and protecting the earth, air, and water as reserves for life.

In addition to being a green alternative, this is a *commonwealth alternative* because 1) it opts for a new system of ecological production, egalitarian distribution, partnership/humanist values, shared ownership, liberated (i.e. nonalienated) labor, and democratized governance having its foundation in the ethics of partnership labor and partnership productivity, and 2) because of its ecosocialist and humanist commitment to living our lives on the planet consistent with the most honorable and aesthetic forms of human social and political fulfillment. The *EarthCommonWealth Alternative* would entail the "expropriation of the expropriators." It would eliminate rent-seeking and the for-profit financial industry and eliminate universal commodity dependency through the decommodification / socialization of the economy. It decouples income both from individual labor activity and from property ownership through an ecosocialist form of universal guaranteed incomes. Incomes are distributed without reference to individual productivity, according to need, and as equally as feasible. Hours of labor are substantially reduced. The well-rounded scientific and philosophical development of the young is made possible through a system of multicultural general education privileging no single culture, religion, or language. EarthCommonWealth represents a social-political philosophy with the determinate potential to fulfill humanity's species-being.

Ecosocialism offers a *counteroffensive* against the dis-economics of cultural polarization, the destruction of nature, and humanity's dread prospect of extinction. Writing about the post-colonial realities in Africa from an indigenous perspective, my colleague Ewa Unoke emphasizes the contemporary relevance of African social teachings as offering "a new path of abundance, peace, progress, and partnership." The "foundation for the future ... [must be] anchored on a solid culture of justice and a shared humanity—Ubuntu" (Unoke 2012, 35, 45). I shall explore the emancipatory possibilities of this perspective in depth in chapter 5. For Unoke political structures and cultures established for exploitative purposes must be challenged with a program for radical change. Even after the defeat of Nazism and apartheid, the victors' human rights model of justice has been fundamentally flawed: "Until *human security* replaces *national security* in the 21st Century strategic thinking, the search for durable peace and sustainable global security will remain elusive" (Unoke 2021, 338).

The evidence of impending economic, governmental, and/or natural catastrophe is mounting. Without a well-defined ideology like EarthCommonWealth, there is no suffcient negation, and there will be no sufficient transformation away from oligarchy, when conditions are ripe for revolution, toward the new world system we seek, respectful of the material conditions of life on our planet and commensurate with the essential caretaking capacities of the human species.

Marcuse described this opposition as a "Great Refusal" (1969, ix) which constituted a multidimensional expression of *system negation*. We have indeed much to learn from Marcuse's systemic analysis, especially in terms of the contemporary challenge of building the theory and practice for an alternate world system. Marcuse's critique of the rise of counterrevolutionary cultural power in the U.S. stood in sharp contrast to the conventional U.S. wisdom on topics of the military, race, and the business orientation of society (Marcuse 1969, 1972). In this volume I emphasize Marcuse's revolutionary philosophical perspectives on labor and the economy, racism, and ecology.

The Children of Prometheus:
Revolutionary Ecological Liberation and Women's Equality

During the last year of his life, Marcuse offered an upbeat and optimistic reassessment of the Prometheanism that he had vividly rejected as a manifestation of capitalism's performance principle in Eros and Civilization (1955). Marcuse's final lecture was presented at a Frankfurt conference on the anxieties associated with advancing technology. The conference theme was somewhat melancholy: "The Sorrow of Prometheus: Senseless Progress." Marcuse's title, "Children of Prometheus: 25 Theses on Technology and Society" ([1979] 2011b), indicated his refusal to be disconsolate. His focus was on social transformation toward a better future condition for humanity. Technology tends to facilitate forces of domination, true, but Marcuse makes clear that it also has the capacity to overcome alienated labor and bring qualitative change to our lives with generous amounts of leisure and free time if propelled by ecosocialist politics as we build a new world system. Marcuse finds that by 1979 the children of Prometheus have experienced the "New Sensibility" that he memorably described in 1969 in An Essay on Liberation as emerging from the imaginative utopian tendencies in Marx and Nietzsche to see the process of production as a process of creation and the ingression of freedom within the realm of necessity in a new socialist society (1969, 20-22). The New Sensibility reflects the steady growth among young people of new needs, generated under capitalism, but which capitalism cannot fulfill, for gender equality, ecological economics, and antiracism. The children of Prometheus have developed a view of technology as a means of liberation from the struggle for existence, part of the "apparatus of freedom" in a post-capitalist future. The convergence of the environmental movement with the labor movement and imaginative aesthetic movements is essential in terms of a unified emancipatory praxis if the human species is to go on living.

> The revolt of youth (students, workers, women), undertaken in the name of the values of freedom and happiness, is an attack on all the values which govern the capitalist system. And this revolt is oriented toward the pursuit of a radically different natural and technical environment; this perspective has become the basis for subversive experiments such as the attempts by American "communes" to establish non-alienated relations between the sexes, between generations, between man and nature—attempts to sustain the consciousness of refusal and of renovation. (Marcuse [1972] 2005, 174)

> [W]hat is at stake in the socialist revolution is not merely the extension of satisfaction within the existing universe of needs, nor the shift of satisfaction from one (lower) level to a higher one, but the rupture with this universe, the qualitative leap. The revolution involves a radical transformation of the needs and aspirations themselves, cultural as well as material; of consciousness and sensibility; of the work process as well as leisure. The transformation appears in the fight against the fragmentation of work, the necessity and productivity of stupid performances and stupid merchandise, against the acquisitive bourgeois individual, against the servitude in the guise of technology, deprivation in the guise of the good life, against pollution as a way of life. Moral and aesthetic needs become basic, vital needs and drive toward new relationships between the sexes, between the generations, between men and women and nature. Freedom is understood as rooted in these needs, which are sensuous, ethical, and rational in one. (Marcuse 1972, 16-17)

Marcuse's insights into the power of sensuous living labor (i.e. our human nature) to liberate itself from commodification and exploitation in order to make commonwealth a universal human condition are underappreciated. As a species we have endured because of our sensuous appreciation of our emergent powers: the power to subsist cooperatively; to create, to communicate, and to care communally within that form of society that we may rightly call a commonwealth. In Marcuse's ecosocialist view, the radical transformation of the labor process itself—the liberation of laboring humanity from commodification and alienation—stands centermost.

> The liberation of nature cannot mean returning to a pre-technological stage, but advancing to the use of the achievements of technological civilization for freeing man and nature from the destructive abuse of science and technology in the service of exploitation ... [C]ertain lost qualities of artisan work may well reappear on the new technological base. (Marcuse 1972, 60)

Humanity's rights to a commonwealth economy, politics, and culture reside in our commonwork. This involves sensuous living labor authentically actualizing itself through humanist activism and creativity—humanity remaking itself through a social labor process in accordance with the commonwealth promise at the core of our material reality. This requires a new system of shared ownership, democratized ownership, and common ownership: EarthCommonWealth is living labor's repressed but natural promise. The radically socialist logic of commonwealth production, ownership, and stewardship can bring to fruition, within the realm of necessity, an intercultural architecture of equality, disalienation, ecological balance, freedom, and abundance.

The liberation of labor from commodification is the ground of authentic dis-alienation and freedom "within the realm of necessity," where satisfaction is restored to the processes of social labor and social wealth production in terms of an ethics of partnership, racial and gender equality, and gratification through work, earth admiration, and ecological responsibility, and *not* solely or even primarily in terms of greater, more efficient production. The convergence of the environmentalist and labor movements is essential for revolutionary change. A philosophical and political recognition of the meaning of commonwealth labor serves as the fundamental legitimation of a socialist philosophy and its promise of abundance and leisure for all within a context of respect for the earth.

Works cited

Absher, Brandon D., 2021. *The Rise of Neoliberal Philosophy*. Lanham, MD: Lexington Books.

Antonio, Robert J. 2021. "When History Fails Us," in Jeremiah Morelock (ed,), *How to Critique Authoritarian Populism*. Leiden: Brill.

Azenabor, Godwin. 2008. *QUEST: An African Journal of Philosophy / Revue Africaine de Philosophie*, No. XXI: 229–240.

Bedford, David and Tom Cheney. 2017. "One-Dimensional Man and Indigenous Struggles," in Terry Maley (ed). *One-Dimensional Man 50 Years On: The Struggle Continues*. Halifax and Winnipeg: Fernwood Publishing.

Boggs, Carl. 2005. *Imperial Delusions: American Militarism and Endless War*. Lanham, MD: Rowman & Littlefield.

Case, Ann and Angus Deaton. 2021. *Deaths of Despair and the Future of Capitalism*. Princeton: Princeton University Press.

D'Amico, Robert, Sang-ki Kim, Paul Piccone. 1980-81. "Marvin Farber 1901-1980" *Telos*, Number 46, Winter.

Dewey, John. 1925. *Experience and Nature*. Chicago: Open Court.

Dewey, John. [1915] 1966. *Democracy and Education*. New York: The Free Press.

Dowd, Douglas. 1997. *Blues for America*. New York: Monthly Review Press.

Dreon, Roberta. 2015. "Aesthetic Issues in Human Emancipation Between Dewey and Marcuse," *Pragmatism Today*. Volume 6, Issue 2.

Emerson, Ralph Waldo. [1836] 2009. "Nature" in *Nature and Other Essays*. Mineola, NY: Dover Publications.

Emerson, Ralph Waldo. [1837] 2009. "The American Scholar" in *Nature and Other Essays*. Mineola, NY: Dover Publications.

Farber, Marvin. 1984. *The Search for an Alternative*. Philadelphia: University of Pennsylvania Press.

Farber, Marvin. [1959] 1968. *Naturalism and Subjectivism*. Albany: SUNY Press. Farber, Marvin. 1949. "Experience and Subjectivism" in *Philosophy for the Future: The Quest of Modern Materialism*. New York: The Macmillan Company.

Feinstein, Andrew. 2012. *The Shadow World: Inside the Global Arms Trade*. New York: Picador [Farrar, Straus, and Giroux].

Foster, John Bellamy. 2000. *Marx's Ecology: Materialism and Nature*. New York: Monthly Review Press.

Hedges, Chris and Joe Sacco. 2012. *Days of Destruction, Days of Revolt*. New York: The Nation Press.

Horkheimer, Max and Theodor W. Adorno. [1947] 1972. *Dialectic of Enlightenment*. New York: Herder and Herder.

Khasnabish, Alex. 2017. "The Radical Imagination Beyond Refusal," in Terry Maley (ed). *One-Dimensional Man 50 Years On: The Struggle Continues*. Halifax and Winnipeg: Fernwood Publishing.

Kellner, Douglas, Clayton Pierce, and Tyson Lewis. 2011. "Introduction," to Herbert Marcuse, *Philosophy, Psychoanalysis and Emancipation,* Volume 5, *Collected Papers of Herbert Marcuse,* edited by Douglas Kellner and Clayton Pierce. New York: Routledge.

Leopold, Aldo. [1953] 1993. *Round River*. New York: Oxford University Press. Leopold, Aldo. [1942] 1991. "The Role of Wildlife in Liberal Education," in Susan L. Flader and J. Baird Callicott (Eds.). *The River of the Mother of God and Other Essays* by Aldo Leopold. Madison, WI: University of Wisconsin Press.

Leopold, Aldo. [1953] 1966. "The Land Ethic," in *A Sand County Almanac*. New York: Oxford University Press.

Leopold, Aldo. [1949] 1966. *A Sand County Almanac*. New York: Oxford University Press.

Magdoff, Fred and Chris Williams. 2017. *Creating an Ecological Society*. New York: Monthly Review Press.

Marcuse, Herbert. [1979] 2019. *Ecology and the Critique of Society Today*. Peter-Erwin Jansen, Sarah Surak, and Charles Reitz (eds). Philadelphia: International Herbert Marcuse Society.

Marcuse, Herbert. [1974] 2015a. *Paris Lectures at Vincennes University, 1974*. Edited by Peter-Erwin Jansen and Charles Reitz. Philadelphia, PA: International Herbert Marcuse Society.

Marcuse, Herbert. 1978. *The Aesthetic Dimension*. Boston, MA: Beacon Press.

Marcuse, Herbert. [1975] 2015b. "Why Talk on Socialism? in Charles Reitz (ed). *Crisis and Commonwealth: Marcuse, Marx, McLaren*. Lanham, MD: Lexington Books.

Marcuse, Herbert. [1979] 2014. "The Reification of the Proletariat," in Douglas Kellner and Clayton Pierce (Eds.) Herbert Marcuse, *Collected Papers of Herbert Marcuse*. Volume 6, *Marxism, Revolution, and Utopia*. New York and London: Routledge.

Marcuse, Herbert. [1979] 2011a. "Ecology and the Critique of Modern Society," in Douglas Kellner and Clayton Pierce (Eds.) Herbert Marcuse, *Collected Papers of Herbert Marcuse*. Volume 5, *Philosophy, Psychoanalysis and Emancipation*. New York and London: Routledge.

Marcuse, Herbert. [1979] 2011b. "Children of Prometheus: 25 Theses on Technology and Society" in Douglas Kellner and Clayton Pierce (Eds.) Herbert Marcuse, *Collected Papers of Herbert Marcuse*. Volume 5, *Philosophy, Psychoanalysis and Emancipation*. New York and London: Routledge.

Marcuse, Herbert. [1939a] 2011c. "Review of John Dewey's *Logic: The Theory of Inquiry*," in Douglas Kellner and Clayton Pierce (Eds.) Herbert Marcuse, *Collected Papers of Herbert Marcuse*. Volume 5, *Philosophy, Psychoanalysis and Emancipation*. New York and London: Routledge.

Marcuse, Herbert. [1939b] 2011d. "Critique of John Dewey's *Theory of Valuation*," in Douglas Kellner and Clayton Pierce (Eds.) Herbert Marcuse, *Collected Papers of Herbert Marcuse*. Volume 5, *Philosophy, Psychoanalysis and Emancipation*. New York and London: Routledge.

Marcuse, Herbert. [1974] 2005. "Marxism and Feminism" in Douglas Kellner (Ed.) Herbert Marcuse, *Collected Papers of Herbert Marcuse*. Volume 3, *The New Left and the 1960s*. New York and London: Routledge.

Marcuse, Herbert. [1972] 2005. "Ecology and Revolution," in Douglas Kellner (Ed.) Herbert Marcuse, *Collected Papers of Herbert Marcuse*. Volume 3, *The New Left and the 1960s*. New York and London: Routledge.

Marcuse, Herbert. [1933] 1973. "On the Philosophical Foundation of the Concept of Labor in Economics," *Telos*, No. 16, Summer.

Marcuse, Herbert. 1972. *Counterrevolution and Revolt*. Boston, MA: Beacon Press

Marcuse, Herbert. 1969. *An Essay on Liberation*. Boston, MA: Beacon Press

Marcuse, Herbert. 1965. "Repressive Tolerance," in R.P. Wolff, B. Moore, and H. Marcuse (Eds.). *A Critique of Pure Tolerance*. Boston, MA: Beacon Press.

Marcuse, Herbert. 1964. *One-Dimensional Man: Studies in the Ideology of Advanced Industrial Society*. Boston, MA: Beacon Press.

Marcuse, Herbert. [1958] 1961. *Soviet Marxism: A Critical Analysis*. New York: Random House.

Marx, Karl. [1869] 1976. *Capital*, Volume 1, London: Penguin.
Marx, Karl. [1844] 1982. *The Economic & Philosophical Manuscripts of 1844*. Edited by Dirk Struik. New York: International Publishers.
Melman, Seymour. 1970. *Pentagon Capitalism: The Political-Economy of War*. New York: McGraw-Hill.
Melman, Seymour. 1985. *The Permanent War Economy*. New York: Simon & Schuster.
Packard, Vance. 1960. *The Waste Makers*. New York: David McKay Publishing.
Reitz, Charles. 2019. *Ecology and Revolution: Herbert Marcuse and the Challenge of a New World System Today*. New York and London: Routledge.
Reitz, Charles. 2000. *Art, Alienation and the Humanities: A Critical Engagement with Herbert Marcuse*. Albany, NY: SUNY Press.
Reitz, Charles and Stephen Spartan. [2013] 2015. "The Political Economy of Predation and Counterrevolution: Recalling Marcuse on the Radical Goals of Socialism," in Charles Reitz (ed). *Crisis and Commonwealth: Marcuse, Marx, McLaren*. Lanham, MD: Lexington Books.
Ruschig, Ulrich. 2020. *Die Befreiung der Natur: Zum Verhältnis von Natur und Freiheit bei Herbert Marcuse*. Köln: PapyRossa Verlag.
Sandel, Michael J. 2020. *The Tyranny of Merit: What's Become of the Common Good?* New York: Ferrar, Straus and Giroux.
Sanders, Bernie. 2021. *Congressional Record* Vol. 167, No. 200, Legislative Session, Senate, November 17.
Sellers, Roy Wood, McGill, V.J. and Farber, Marvin (Eds). 1949. *Philosophy for the Future: The Quest of Modern Materialism*. New York: Macmillan.
Sernau, Scott. 2006. *Worlds Apart: Social Inequalities in a New Century*. Thousand Oaks CA, London, New Delhi: Pine Forge Press.
Shook, John R. 2017. "The Nature Philosophy of John Dewey," *Dewey Studies*. Vol 1, No. 1, pp. 13-43. https://bityl.co/CeQv
Simmons, Michael L. Jr. 1982. "The Present Position of Marvin Farber's Materialism," paper presented at International Conference on Philosophy and Science in Phenomenological Perspective: Dedicated to Memory of Marvin Farber, State University of New York at Buffalo, March 11-13. Personal copy.
Smith, David N. 1974. *Who Rules the Universities?* New York: Monthly Review Press.
Unoke, Ewa. 2012. *Global Security After Evil: Assumptions, Fallacies, Myths, and Realities of the Post-Colonial State*. Saarbrücken, Germany: Lambert Academic Publishing.
Wildcat, Daniel R. 2009. *Red Alert! Saving the Planet with Indigenous Knowledge*. Golden, CO: Fulcrum Publishers.

5
Recovering Our Commonwealth Sense

> Everyone knows that the shape of the world in which we are now living is not its final form. .... It is the hope of humanity to find peace, not through transcendence, but by changing the world
> —*believing in the possibility of earthly perfection.*
> —Karl Jaspers, *Die geistige Situation der Zeit* ([1931] 1999, 5-6)

Humanity's first teachings on ethics are to be found in ancient Africana philosophy. A commonwealth sense is present in them which has continued as a moral guide to social behavior up to the present. I argue that a commonwealth ethos is the intercultural core of humanity's historical wisdom traditions and that it is at the heart of a future ecosocialist society.

Francis B. Nyamnjoh, Patrick U. Nwosu, and Hassan M. Yosimbom (2021, henceforth NNY) have recently edited an especially insightful collection of essays delineating the contemporary interpretations and usages of proverbs in Africa. According to a piece by Edmund Akwasi Agyeman, "African philosophers, sociologists and social anthropologists have for decades asserted that African social organization is communal" (NNY, 61). Agyeman points out that African philosophy's renowned Zulu principle of *ubuntu* underscores the sociality of personhood: "I am because we are, and since we are, therefore I am" (NNY, 63, 154), in contrast to Descartes' theory of human personhood that begins with an asocial and ahistorical "I think therefore I am." The conviction that each of us needs the other for survival is key to Africana philosophy and undergirds its communal ethic.

Emerita professor of African American Studies at Syracuse University, Mîcere Gîthae Mũgo, extends the concept of *ubuntu* linking it to the Kiswahli term *utu*—"the capacity to exhibit behavior that is humane" (Mũgo 2021, 6). She stresses "an *utu/ubuntu* imperative" in African indigenous knowledge that also applies to scholarly research and writing. She emphasizes the obligation of the Africana professoriate to create "liberated academic zones" in which scholarship is to be animated through "the heart of the mind" (2021, 10, 20). As this volume moves forward, I shall argue [utilizing also insights from Ato SekyiOtu (2019)] that *ubuntu* and *utu* offer universalizable moral principles of general education and an impeccable idea also of what makes higher education *higher*.

Today many observers consider contemporary African cultures to be notoriously religious, some also profoundly misogynistic. Yet the secular humanistic foundations of Africana moral philosophy are soundly attested to by scholars such as Kwame Gyekye (2010), Kwasi Wiredu (1991) and Alfred T. Kisubi (2015). They emphasize that culture is *not* to be seen as an export from "enlightened" Europe to Africa, quite the contrary. African proverbs represent for one thing the first formulations of the golden rule. Philosophy professor, Godwin Azenabor (2008, 234), of the University of Lagos has argued for the underlying identity of African proverbs and Kant's categorical imperative. Today we are also aware of the African and Asian roots of Plato's now not purely Greek view of the world (Bernal 1991): how the *Republic* and the *Meno*, especially, share with Egyptian, Indian, and Buddhist philosophies cultural notions of enlightenment and equanimity, the transmigration of souls and reincarnation making societal harmonization possible.

The materiality of Africa's earliest proverbs

Researchers and editors Nyamnjoh, Nwosu, and Yosimbom (NNY 2021) emphasize the *materiality* of Africa's earliest indigenous and ongoing ways of knowing. This materiality has to do with the content and meaning of a language act beyond its stylistic or aesthetic appeal. Proverbs are regarded as the condensed wisdom of experience that reflects the realities of human existence. As repositories of norms and values passed on in an oral tradition from generation to generation, the proverbs serve as a cultural force shaping social behavior. Communal social systems were the material ground giving rise to these traditional sayings, serving as the political-economic base for the wisdom and practices of "sharing, mutual aid, caring for others, interdependence, solidarity, reciprocal obligation and social harmony" (Edmund Akwasi Agyeman in NNY, 59). The proverbs are also seen as materially relevant to the authentic indigenous conduct of moral life.

These editors note that several recent collections of Africana proverbs have been published, some with upwards of four thousand entries, documenting their impact with regard to "being and becoming" an African. Associated with diverse cultures in several geographic localities, the proverbs come from the Igbo, Yorùbá, and Otukpo peoples of Nigeria; Ghana's Akan and Nawuri cultures; the Amhara of Ethiopia, and the Malinka of Mali. The proverbs address the full spectrum of life's many dimensions: impermanence, fragility, religion, fighting, hierarchy, danger, disability, the natural environment, women, marriage, and death. Some proverbs are cryptic and problematic; some have become Christianized. They provide a wide range of understandings and these are inevitably contested and reconstituted (Elias Bongma in NNY, xix).

Several Africana scholars in this collection make crucial selections from the many hundreds of proverbs and center their work particularly on the aphorisms and maxims emphasizing community, belonging, and moral education. "African philosophers, such as Kwame Gyekye, have drawn on proverbs to extract the communitarian ethos embedded therein to defend that Africans are communitarian in nature" (Husein Inusah and Michael Segbefia in NNY, 335). Gyekye's communitarianism stands in sharp contrast with the socialism of African leaders Kwame Nkrumah, Leopold Senghor, Julius Nyerere, and Kamauzu Banda because he considered that their versions of African socialism inhibited personal freedoms (Agyeman in NNY, 63). Nonetheless, Geyeke proclaimed that the contemporary study of traditional proverbs represents "the reassertion by Africans of their humanity, and as human beings, as makers of history, as contributors to the history of human emancipation" (Firoze Manji in NNY, 7).

Postcolonial African writers like Chinua Achebe and the towering African critics, Chinweizu (1975, 1988) and Frantz Fanon (1961), offer caustic condemnations of colonial-era misinterpretations of African folkways and morés as "primitive." Instead, they used an understanding of indigenous African proverbs as an intervention against Eurocentric views, such as those of Hegel and Joseph Conrad, that diminished the importance of rationality in African thought. According to commentator Divine Fuh, "There are the kind of knees that Derek Chauvin placed on George Floyd's neck in Minneapolis, USA, on 25 May 2020, [also] placed around the neck of the knowledge ecosystem across Africa ...." (Fuh in NNY, 432). Achebe, who wrote in English, has had his work compared to that of James Baldwin for its "bellwether effect" on contemporary African critical literary art with its rigorous thinking about racialized colonial oppression and inequality (Yosimbon in NNY, 301). "Achebe's approach to African proverbs was to study the themes critically and highlight their relevance to the leadership and politics of the time" (Nwosu in NNY, 179).

According to Patrick U. Nwosu, authentic leadership in African cultures accrues to elders due to "lifelong hard work and honesty" (NNY, 183), as well as their genuine humility and modesty. The present generation is linked to its ancestors; their knowledge of appropriate proverbs being among the root sources of societal cohesion. These proverbs reinforce the view that good governance transcends acquisitive egoism and is anchored in a form of collective decision-making. In his view, Achebe stressed that any ostensible universality of a proverb emerges from its comprehensive inclusivity encompassing that which is needed to attain the temporal well-being of the community.

Hissein Inusah and Michael Segbifia sort the proverbs even further focusing on those stressing intellectual and moral virtue. In the Akan culture of Ghana, these intellectual proverbs revolve around the capacity to learn, curiosity, thoroughness, and scholarly integrity; the moral virtues stress compassion, benevolence, generosity, etc., as forms of active regard for the well-being of others (Inusah and Segbifia in NNY, 337-338, 352).

My reflections on the traditional proverbs of Africa also select and highlight a range of aphorisms and maxims. These address collective approaches to *work* in society and thus also vividly illustrate the philosophical materiality of traditional African thought. Today such proverbs remind us that "effort is expected on the part of community members for their welfare and for the welfare of the community at large" (Agyeman in NNY, 71) and even the rich and powerful "need to be constantly mindful that their fortune and authority result not so much from the individual effort but from the labor and sacrifice of others and see themselves more as custodians and servants than as owners and masters" (Nyamnjoh in NNY, 33).

Some of the most renowned and primordial proverbs about collective labor undergird my critical theory of labor as this impacts our being and becoming human.

- The cotton thread says that it is only as a team that you can carry a stone.
- Many hands make light work.
- It takes a whole village to raise a child.

These constitute universalizable humanist, i.e. not narrowly tribal, teachings for the guidance of practical life. According to Ghanaian-born Ato Sekyi-Otu, a professor of social and political thought at York University Toronto who recently retired, we must understand "that indigenous ethical judgments are already universalizing in their justificatory grounds, inescapably humanist in their critical vocabulary" (Sekyi-Otu 2019, 18). Further, they can in no way be confused with purely religious teachings. Not gods, but communally laboring humanity can be seen as the source of ethics here. Like Marx, Sekyi-Otu holds that religion is not relevant in terms of its truth value, but rather in terms of the human needs it may disclose as a haven in a heartless world. He sees moral universals as embodied in the African sense of righteous indignation, and a "vernacular Kantianism" (Sekyi-Otu 2019, 18) as being native to every culture. Among humanity's earliest proverbs, fables, and riddles are those that teach the survival power of partnership and cooperation, gravitating toward the humanist happiness of a communally laboring commonwealth. It takes a village to make humanity humane.

Rejecting relativism

Because of the diversity of religions and the existence of multiple modes of moral reasoning around the world today, contemporary philosophy has often nurtured an almost all-pervasive moral relativism, a development with significant intellectual and social implications. My aim in this *EarthCommonWealth* volume is to articulate an alternative to relativism in ethics while simultaneously rendering justice to the fact that many moral and religious traditions do exist.

Sekyi-Otu (2019) has assembled perhaps the strongest arguments against regarding Africa-centric wisdom of the sort discussed above as somehow also a relativist rejection of universalism. He defends multiculturalism and its appreciation of difference, individual singularity and dignity. Rejecting the traditionally Anglo-European version of possessive individualism, he presents a view of individuality compatible with commitment to an egalitarian community. He calls this a *Left individualism*, emphasizing responsible agency and engagement to "combat capital's dominion" and its "violent contempt for local needs" (Sekyi-Otu 2019, 2). Never forgetting that race matters, he demands that "things, in the most materialistic meaning of the word, [be] restored to their proper places" (Sekyi-Otu 2019, 5).

Rejecting false (imperial) universalism

In this way, Sekyi-Otu develops the idea of *Left Universalism* and a left humanism which he considers to be the philosophical foundations of critical race work. Africacentric universalism is said to be a testimony to this Left universalism—the universality of morality as well as a practice of universalism *for Africa's sake*. Sekyi-Otu, like Frantz Fanon and many other postcolonial African thinkers, opposed the infamous European empire-builders in Africa as white predators and white destroyers. He unmasked the coercive and counterfeit universalism of Eurocentrism (worldwide white supremacy and imperialism's distorted vision of economic growth) as a "parochialism bearing arms" (2019, 13; see also Losurdo 2021, 949). Fanon concluded that under such forms of false universalism even interracial sexual desire could become pathological and selfdestructive. This added an extra dimension to alienation. Sekyi-Otu finds a kind of radical Left individualism in Fanon's philosophy compatible with the strenuous pursuit of the common good, in which it becomes "each citizen's individual responsibility for the choice, design, and stewardship of the civil commons of postcolonial society" (Sekyi-Otu, 185).

Sekyi-Otu's critical philosophy is also clear about rejecting the absolute validity of colonial forms of Western Christianity, seeing these instead as too often misanthropic and totalitarian (Sekyi-Otu, 230). Echoing Plato's *Euthyphro,* he raises the issue of behavior being both religious and *un*ethical. Plato framed this matter in its classic form: the arbitrary or capricious will of a God or gods cannot the *foundation* of moral action, because even a divine will if it is to be good, must *derive* its determinations and course from a logically prior philosophical understanding of the idea of Goodness itself. Plato's *Republic* likewise sees justice as a property of the ideal city/state insofar as it is ruled by men and women educated to the (conflicted) human condition, living communally (communal marriage, communal child care) with intelligence moderating appetite and spirit, disinterested and detached from lust for property, power, fame, etc devoutly acting in accordance (not with God's will but) with Goodness in itself.

Historical realities of the invasion of Africa brought the imposition of Anglo norms, mores and customs; language hierarchy; military occupation, racist control through law and politics and extralegal violence. Sekyi-Otu thus stresses that his own radicalism does *not* consider colonial class exploitation an outrage because his thinking is *African;* rather, because such exploitation is and was an objective worldwide abomination, he is obligated, African or not, to anti-imperialism. Following African literary artist Ayi Kwei Armah, he propounds a deontological argument for communism, seeing communism as an ethical imperative. A principle of connectedness undergirds what he considers to be timeless ideals of reciprocity and equality showing "the way" of justice. In this vein, the young Marx himself had also written that moral criticism finds its culmination in "... the *categorical imperative to overthrow all those conditions* in which man is an abased, enslaved, abandoned, contemptible being. ... Theory is only realized in a people so far as it fulfills the needs of the people" (Marx [1844] 1964, 52, 53, emphasis in original).

Sekyi-Otu goes on to say "[T]he commons, or more concretely the 'civil commons,' which *ubuntu* in essence requires, ...has now become what Marcuse might have called a 'historical imperative' ...." (Sekyi-Otu 2019, 35). Marcuse knew that the material pressures toward the emancipatory struggle for commonwealth are irrepressible long-term. He not only described the obscenities of global inequality, domination, alienation, and war in an extraordinarily vivid and effective manner, but more importantly, his writing evoked solidarity among subaltern groups across traditional barriers of culture. He elucidated the social change strategy of united action (Marcuse [1971] 2005, 149-151) to extend the base, as well as building united fronts, to bring together intersectional movements for racial equality, women's equality, and the liberation of labor (Marcuse [1974] 2015, 46, 60). Marcuse wanted to help labor reclaim its humanist potential, where, with gratitude for all things made and appreciation for all things of this earth, we struggle to become more fully who we are. Marcuse had argued in *One-Dimensional Man* that universals must be understood as both historical and substantive. "The substantive universal intends qualities which surpass all particular experience, but persist in the mind, not as a figment of the imagination nor as mere logical possibilities, but as the 'stuff' of which our world consists" (Marcuse 1964, 213).

Sekyi-Otu likewise valorizes a further assessment Marcuse made concerning historical materialism: finding that it preserved the best of philosophical idealism as well as the concept of essence (Sekyi-Otu 2019, 108, 3). Marcuse's 1972 *Counterrevolution and Revolt* defended the "*idealistic core* of dialectical materialism" at the same time as he wrote of the "perpetual *materialistic* core of *idealism*" (Marcuse 1972, 70, emphasis in original). Marcuse, as I have said before, has a radically new conception of the essence of socially active human beings: seen from the outside, we are the ensemble of our social relations; seen from the inside, we are sensuous living labor. Overall, in accordance with what he sees as the rationality of philosophy and the fuller reality of concept of human essence, he finds that there are technological and intellectual grounds for a new world system actualizing the radical promise of a socialist commonwealth.

At the same time, Sekyi-Otu's perspective stands apart from both the African socialism of Leopold Senghor (Senegal) and Julius Nyerere (Tanzania) as well as certain classical precepts of Marx and Engels. His moral argument for communism disconnects revolution from the actions of a particular class and decouples it from any presumed historical necessity in the "unwilled ripeness of time" (Sekyi-Otu 2019, 108, 114). His Left universalism primarily offers a critical mode of ethical reasoning with a philosophically materialist concern for "native *human* necessities" and for "what Engels called the human being's 'native thirst for freedom'" (Sekyi-Otu 2019, 6, 31).

Intercultural ethical commonalities

A celebration of humanity's multicultural diversity needs also to be accompanied by an appreciation for our *inter*cultural commonalities. A memorable and insightful account of these intercultural areas of overlap in philosophy, particularly ethics, occurs in a key work of Karl Jaspers, *The Origin and Goal of History* ([1949] 2021). I use his work as a stepping-stone in the direction I am going in order to establish a moral unity at the heart of the world's enduring wisdom traditions—Daoism, Confucianism, Vedantism, Buddhism, Judaism, Islam, Christianity, and humanism—on the historical/anthropological plane and in terms of the material human condition. Jürgen Habermas has recently published a two-volume history of philosophy which devotes two massive chapters to what Jaspers called "The Axial Age" (Habermas 2019, Vol. 1, 175-460). Habermas's discussion ranges widely over the anthropological, historical, and philosophical contexts. The strength of his account centers on his elaboration of the epistemological shift from mythology to a transcendental perspective that permits a moral critique of established customs. I share this assessment, yet our accounts differ substantially in terms of emphasis on other essential worldview comparisons. I offer my own insights here and in chapter 6 below, which I believe deepen an appreciation of Jaspers' awareness of the ethical convergences linking the separate philosophies of Buddha, Kongfuzi, and Socrates/Plato.

Although Jaspers is seen as a non-Marxist liberal humanist, writing in the context of the Cold War in the new Federal Republic of Germany, he nonetheless presented a provocative, historically grounded thesis regarding the meaning of what he called the ancient *axial period* or Axial Age for the development of the human intellect around 500 BCE. His perspective argues "that, in the period lasting approximately from 800 to 200 BCE, a number of thinkers had emerged in different parts of the world, who brought human consciousness to a common state of reflexivity and defined the fundamental, enduring patterns of human thinking" (Thornhill 2021, xv). He theorizes the almost simultaneous appearance of common intellectual insights and developments in geographically widely separated societies with virtually no means of cross-communication.

Jaspers recounts the perspectives of two historians whose work prompted his own inquiries—Viktor von Strauss, who asserted that:

> During the centuries when Lao-tse [Laozi] and Confucius [Kongfuzi] were living in China, a strange movement of the spirit passed through all civilized peoples. Jeremiah, Habakkuk, Daniel and Ezekiel were prophesying and in a renowned generation (521-516 [BCE]) the second temple was erected in Jerusalem. Among the Greeks, Thales was still living, Anaximander, Pythagoras, Heraclitus and Xeophanes appeared, and Parmenides was born. In Persia an important reformation of Zarathustra's ancient teaching seems to have been carried through, and India produced Sakyamuni [Gautama], the founder of Buddhism. (von Strauss in Jaspers [1949] 2021, 16)

Likewise, the conclusions of historian Ernst von Lasaux:

> It cannot be an accident that, six hundred years before Christ, Zarathustra in Persia, Gautama Buddha in India, Confucius in China, the prophets in Israel, King Numa of Rome and the first philosophers—Ionians, Dorians and Eleatics—in Hellas, all made their appearance pretty well simultaneously as reformers of the national religion. (Lasaux in Jaspers [1949] 2021, 16)

Viewing the Axial Age as the outcome of earlier historical stages, Jaspers explains that it followed upon a) archaic prehistory and b) the period of the ancient civilizations of Egypt, Babylon, and China's Yellow River. The first epoch Jaspers held to be of "inapprehensibly profound significance" (Jaspers [1949] 2021, 40). In it humanity lived in meaningful communities in which our primary motives and vital impulses are said to have emerged (regulating sexuality, etc.) along with language and myths; so too, did the use of fire and tools. Prehistory, he says, gave humanity its "characteristic stamp," even if essential qualities lay dormant far into the future. Still, he concludes that it gave us "no core of tenable knowledge" (Jaspers [1949] 2021, 40); it did not enable humanity to yet know itself.

While appreciating Jaspers's perspective, I have already countered this above. The second stage, "civilization," prior to the axial period was characterized by river control, the development of writing, magnificent and various architectural forms, sculpture, and the hierarchical organization of public and social life in the form of world empires. Humanity's future powers were faintly visible, glimpsed as possible, not actual. In both of these epochs the generic human intellect was thought to be *alienated from itself* because the human mind was molded by folklore, legend, mythos, and religion instead of reason, explanation, and wisdom. Here Jaspers, in his own unique fashion, tacitly follows Hegel's *Phenomenology,* Chapter VI, B, on the enlightenment's challenge to superstition. I challenge Jaspers as he asserts that—in the Axial Age—"for the first time *philosophers* appeared" (Jaspers [1949] 2021, 10; emphasis in original). He is as Euro-centric as Hegel in asserting the inappropriate colonialist view that while philosophy learned from the past, it also stood in contrast to "the old, stable, unawakened matriarchal powers" of prehistory and the mythologies of the empires of the early civilizations (Jaspers [1949] 2021, 24).

An opponent of Soviet communism, Jaspers thought of himself as a democratic socialist. "The socialization of the means of production in large-scale undertakings, to abolish the private appropriation of surplus value, is a goal that one can deem just and strive after without being a believing Marxist" (Jaspers [1949] 2021, 183-184). "Socialism is the universal tendency of contemporary mankind toward an organization of labor and of participation in the products of labor that will make it possible for all men to be free. To this extent almost everyone is a socialist today" (Jaspers [1949] 2021, 192).

Within the diverse cultures of China, India, and the West (Hellas, Palestine, Persia) Jaspers says *sociological* conditions were remarkably analogous: social power was concentrated in wealthy cities and small states, often at war with one another. The misery caused by war and political conflict meant that for most people catastrophe loomed at every juncture, yet exceptional individuals "*desired* to help through insight, education, and reform" (Jaspers [1949] 2021, 12; emphasis in original). The academic enterprises of Kongfuzi and Plato both had the same purpose: political leadership informed by an enlightened view of the conflicted human condition and learning with regard to justice. Their philosophies "did not become common property" (Jaspers [1949] 2021, 12) however, and Jaspers was concerned that history could "sink back again into the magical and demonological" (Jaspers [1949] 2021, 71). The epoch lost its creativeness and is seen as an interregnum between two ages of great imperial states, with the emergence of the Macedonian and the Roman empires made mighty through conquest.

Jaspers' Axial Age hypothesis does shed our most familiar form of *mono*culturalism: it radically de-centers Christianity and religious forms of thought in general. He says consideration of the Axial Age is an attempt to "gain possession of something *common to all mankind*, beyond all differences of creed" (Jaspers [1949] 2021, 27). It represents a "venture into boundless communication" that is key to "becoming-human" (Jaspers [1949] 2021, 27). "The truth is that which links us to one another" (Jaspers [1949] 2021, 18). Jaspers maintains that a "*profound mutual comprehension was possible*" (Jaspers [1949] 2021, 15; emphasis in original). I have likewise indicated the materialist and communal basis for a synoptic view grounded in social labor and a labor theory of ethics, to be elaborated in greater detail in the next chapter.

What caused the Axial Age? Jaspers says no meaningful explanations have emerged. He emphasizes that whether one accepts or rejects the Axial Age hypothesis, it raises the "question of the manner in which the unity of mankind becomes a concrete reality for us" (Jaspers [1949] 2021, 29) —given that the world is now a single unit of communications" (Jaspers [1949] 2021, 32). "Since the whole sphere of the earth is more accessible to the technology of communications ...the political unity of the earth can only be a matter of time" (Jaspers [1949] 2021, 213).

CommonWealth: Intercultural labor solidarity

Earlier it was noted that in economics and ethics Aristotle believed the chief *vice* was the boundless pursuit of property accumulation; the chief *virtue*, the pursuit of the well-being of the community (*Politics* Chapter IX). According to Pauline Yu, former President of the American Council of Learned Societies, in *Our Cultural Commonwealth* (2006), "commonwealth" is defined both as "a body or number of persons united by a common interest," and as the "public welfare, general good or advantage." As the following chapters will make clear, I build upon these core meanings extending them on the basis of my multicultural research in philosophy, political economy, and sociology, drawing especially on the critical social theory of Herbert Marcuse. Recent literature ostensibly related to the ideas of commonwealth and the liberation of labor has been disappointing, including works by Michael Hardt and Antonio Negri (2009, 2000), and Gar Alperowitz (2013).

My aim is to build an intercultural sense of human solidarity and commonwealth, underpinning—in ethics, economics, and education—a realistic telos of human flourishing. A new intercultural architecture of commonwealth production, ownership, and stewardship can bring to fruition, within the realm of necessity, the revolutionary goals of rehumanization (disalienation): economic and political equality, labor freedom, ecological balance, leisure, abundance, and peace. My thesis is that there is a commonwealth promise at the core of humanity's material reality as sensuous living labor. I have connected the theory of commonwealth developed here to the core values of the world's wisdom traditions. An intercultural labor force humanism is an alternative world system, and not only necessary but feasible: it is the gravitational center holding social life together despite flare-ups and explosions caused by the massive forces of careening corporate capitalism. The labor force must rely upon itself and the world's commonwealth traditions to mobilize its fullest revolutionary power.

I appreciate the utopian use of the term commonwealth by the Danish immigrant and socialist, Laurence Gronlund, of Milwaukee and Chicago, in his 1884 *Cooperative Commonwealth*. Marcuse would recognize it as well. Commonwealth "is not to be regarded as a personal conceit, but as *an historical product*, as a product in which our whole people are unconscious partakers" (Gronlund [1884] 1965, 90, emphasis in original).

> [T]he Cooperative Commonwealth will be highly promotive of social welfare by securing to all its citizens abundance; by furnishing them leisure; and by enabling them to follow their natural bent. Work will no longer be a tribute to physical necessity but a glad performance of social office. (Gronlund [1884] 1965, 103)

Hardt and Negri, in *Commonwealth* (2009) and *Empire* (2000), appear to offer exciting prospects regarding alternative systems of freedom, yet they displace socialist humanism and labor humanism with allegedly radical accounts of biopolitics and biopower. As they see it, wealth is created through biopolitical production, yet their postmodernist philosophical perspective follows a Wittgensteinian linguistic turn, privileging an antifoundationalist discussion of language games and eschewing a discussion of human beings as sensuous living labor. Both *Commonwealth* and *Empire* displace critical sociological analysis and dematerialize labor as a variable, seeing industrial production as supplanted by the intellectual, immaterial, and communicative dimensions of production, thereby dematerializing their political economy, and replacing a theory of labor force empowerment with the theory of the multitude against empire.

Roxanne Dunbar-Ortiz points to Hardt and Negri's concept of "the commons" in their 2009 volume *Commonwealth* as being inattentive to the unique situation of Native Americans for whom nationhood and sovereignty were/are matters of importance: "Most writings about the commons barely mention the fate of the Indigenous peoples in the call for all land to be shared" (DunbarOrtiz, 2014, 230). She emphasizes that Native peoples—as original stewards of the American lands—tended, managed, and owned these lands communally. Petroglyphs and cliff art from Chaco Canyon to Lascaux testify to an ethical and aesthetic awareness of the mutual interconnectedness and interdependencies ontologically binding humanity, earth, and sky. For ninety-nine percent of human history principles of mutuality, solidarity, protection of the earth, and rarity of war were [are] central to the cultural traditions of the small, mobile, self-governing, Indigenous communal bands (Fry & Souilliac 2017, 5). As I have shown above such principles may be widened beyond small group membership and even beyond national identity. I build upon Aldo Leopold's ecological writing, which extends this perspective arguing that humanity needs to adhere to such an Indigenous-informed, partnership-oriented land ethic and land aesthetic. Thus, ecological insights are fundamental to my call for a cosmopolitan EarthCommonWealth.

Several books by Gar Alperovitz raise the profile of the commonwealth idea; he demonstrates historically how this has inspired numerous, small-scale, cooperative efforts. His 2013 volume, *What Then Must We Do? Straight Talk about the Next American Revolution, Democratizing Wealth and Building a Community-Sustaining Economy from the Ground Up* focuses on the system as the problem and calls for system change in a manner that resonates well with my analysis. I agree explicitly with his stated purpose: devising a change in ownership modes in order to effect system change. I see Alperovitz's emphasis on co-ops etc. as inspiring, yet also as piecemeal gradualism. The enduring power of large-scale privately-owned economic enterprises will inevitably limit and distort what coops can accomplish.

Chapters 6 and 7 will develop my perspective on a commonwealth form of labor derived from Marx and Marcuse, just as this chapter connects my idea of commonwealth with the foundational values of the world's wisdom traditions. Commonwealth labor is not only a social and productive force but also labor that is liberated, labor that is meaningful, labor even in aesthetic form. Thus, I see commonwealth as a kind of ethico-aesthetic as well as a social-ecological formation. I understand commonwealth (in reliance on the metabolic relation between human society and nature that Marx describes) as a particular kind of human partnership relation and as a particular kind of socio-ecological formation in the tradition of Aldo Leopold's land ethic discussed more fully in chapter 6 below. I move from the concept of public ownership to the concept of commonwealth ownership, a form of eco-humanist governmental stewardship, consistent with the basic democratic tenets of Marxism, not necessarily as a dictatorship of the proletariat. My concept has a special affinity with Marcuse, who thought of himself as a Marxist, and was very interested in council communism and in humanism as the radical form of socialism. I encompass within my notion of EarthCommonWealth the multiple dimensions of racial equality, women's equality, the liberation of labor, the restoration of nature, leisure, abundance, and peace.

Marcuse proposes a vision of *intercultural solidarity against* the resurgent politics of white supremacy, oligarchic wealth idolization, profitable waste, as well as the toxic masculinity characteristic of authoritarian populism. In his (and my) ecosocialist view *the radical transformation of the labor process itself*—labor's liberation from commodification and alienation—*stands centermost.* Marcuse's philosophy of labor did not reduce it to a narrowly understood class circumstance. *As a species* we have endured because of our sensuous appreciation of our emergent powers: the power to subsist cooperatively, to create, communicate, and care communally. I argue elsewhere that the very foundation of ethics is to be found in commonwealth labor (Reitz 2019, 93-118). Humanity's earliest customs, i.e. communal production, shared ownership, and solidarity assured that the needs of all were met, i.e. including those not directly involved in production, such as children, the disabled, and the elderly.

The right of the commonwealth to govern itself, and humanity's earliest ethic of holding property in common, derive only secondarily from factual individual contributions to production. They are rooted primarily in our essentially shared species life and our being *as humans*, not solely in terms of being rational animals, but as *social* animals, as Aristotle stressed, for whom moral and political accomplishments were sources of our highest happiness. In my view elaborated in chapters 6 and 9 below we are *sensuous living labor—possessing a promesse du boneur commun*. We live as essentially laboring beings engaged in a metabolism with nature and inescapably living with others in both an Aristotelian and even more fundamentally a *ubuntu* or commonwealth sense.

Humanity's rights to a commonwealth economy, politics, and culture reside in our commonwork. Our earliest proverbs, fables, and riddles from the oldest African cultures teach the power of partnership and cooperation. Humanity experiences the satisfactions / dissatisfactions derived from our bio-ecologically generated economic, aesthetic, intellectual, and moral standards gravitating toward the humanism of a communally laboring commonwealth. Humanism in ancient times (Plato and Aristotle) was not a philosophy of the natural and unmediated goodness of human beings, as in the Romanticism of a latter-day Rousseau. Humanity had a metabolism with nature mediated through labor and a metabolism with other humans mediated by culture. Ancient Greek philosophy stressed the humanizing influence of parents and teachers, customs, culture, and laws within a societal context. As a species we have endured because of our sensuous appreciation of our emergent powers: the power to cooperatively procure our livelihoods; to create, communicate, and care communally within a form of society that we may now rightly understand to be an intercultural humanist commonwealth.

Works cited

Azenabor, Godwin. 2008. *QUEST: An African Journal of Philosophy / Revue Africaine de Philosophie*, No. XXI: 229–240.
Bahro, Rudolf. 1977a. *Die Alternative*. Cologne/Frankfurt: Europäische Verlagsanstalt.
Bahro, Rudolf. 1977b. "The Alternative in Eastern Europe," *New Left Review*, No. 106. November–December.
Bernal, Martin. 1991. *Black Athena: The Afroasiatic Roots of Classical Civilization: The Fabrication of Ancient Greece 1785–1985*. New York: Random House.
Bose, Nirmal Kumar. 1965. "Gandhi: Humanist and Socialist," in Erich Fromm (Ed.), *Socialist Humanism*. Garden City, NY: Doubleday.
Buck, William. 1973. *Mahabharata*. New York: New American Library.
Chan, Peter M.K. 2012. *The Six Patriarchs of Chinese Humanism*. Lulu.com. www.lulu.com/shop/peter-mk-chan/the-six-patriarchs-of-chinese-humanism/ebook/product-20158012.html.
Dart, Raymond A. 1956. *Cultural Status of the South African Man-Apes*. Washington, DC: The Smithsonian Institution.
de Waal, Frans. 2013. *The Bonobo and the Atheist: In Search of Humanism among the Primates*. New York: W.W. Norton.
de Waal, Frans. 2009. *The Age of Empathy*. New York: Random House.
de Waal, Frans. 2006. *Primates and Philosophers*. Princeton, NJ: Princeton University Press.
Dunbar-Ortiz, Roxanne. 2014. *An Indigenous Peoples' History of the United States*. Boston, MA: Beacon Press.
Eisler, Riane. 1987. *The Chalice and the Blade*. New York: HarperCollins.
Engels, Frederick. [1872-1882] 1973. *Dialectics of Nature*. New York: International Publishers.
Engels, Frederick. [1884] 1972. *The Origin of the Family, Private Property and the State*. New York: International Publishers.
Fry, Douglas P. and Geneviève Souillac. 2017. "The Original Partnership Societies: Evolved Propensities for Equality, Prosociality, and Peace," *Interdisciplinary Journal of Partnership Studies*, Vol. 4, No. I, March.
Gronlund, Laurence. [1884] 1965. *The Cooperative Commonwealth*. Cambridge, MA: Harvard University Press
Gyekye, Kwame. 2010. "African Ethics," in *The Stanford Encyclopedia of Philosophy*, No. 2011, Fall.
Habermas, Jurgen. 2019. *Auch eine Geschichte der Philosophie*, Band 1. Frankfurt: Suhrkamp.
Heidegger, Martin. [1927] 1967. *Sein und Zeit*. Tübingen: Max Niemeyer Verlag.
Igloliorte, Heather. 2016. *Inuit Art. The Brousseau Collection*. Quebec City: Musée national des beaux-arts du Quebec.
Jaspers, Karl. [1931] 1999. *Die geistige Situation der Zeit*. Berlin: Walter de Gruyter.
Jaspers, Karl. [1949] 2021. *The Origin and Goal of History*. London and New York: Routledge.
Jolley, Dorothy R. 2011. *Ubuntu: A Person is a Person Through Other Persons*. Masters Thesis. Southern Utah University.
Kant, Immanuel. [1795] 1983. "To Perpetual Peace: A Philosophical Sketch," in *Perpetual Peace and Other Essays*. Translated by Ted Humphrey (with a dedication to Herbert Marcuse). Indianapolis, IN: Hackett Publishing.
Kant, Immanuel. [1784] 1983. "Idea for a Universal History with a Cosmopolitan Intent," in *Perpetual Peace and Other Essays*. Translated by Ted Humphrey (with a dedication to Herbert Marcuse). Indianapolis, IN: Hackett Publishing.

Kant, Immanuel. Posthumous papers, cited in Will Durant, 1967. *The Story of Civilization,* Volume X, New York: Simon & Schuster.

Kellner, Douglas. 1984. *Herbert Marcuse and the Crisis of Marxism.* Berkeley, CA: University of California Press.

Kellner, Douglas. 1973. "Introduction to 'On the Philosophical Foundation of the Concept of Labor,'" *Telos,* No. 16, Summer.

Kisubi, Alfred Taligoola. 2015. "Cultural Origins of African Humanism and Socialism (Ujamaa)," in Charles Reitz (Ed.). *Crisis and Commonwealth: Marcuse, Marx, McLaren.* Lanham, MD: Lexington Books.

Leacock, Elinore Burke. 1972. "Introduction" to Frederick Engels, *The Origin of the Family, Private Property, and the State.* New York: International Publishers.

Leakey, Richard. 1994. *The Origin of Humankind.* New York: Basic Books.

Leakey, Richard and Roger Lewin. 1978. *People of the Lake.* Garden City, NY: Anchor/Doubleday.

Losurdo, Domenico. 2021. *Nietzsche the Aristocratic Rebel.* Chicago: Haymarket.

Marcuse, Herbert. 1979. "The Reification of the Proletariat," *Canadian Journal of Political and Social Theory / Revue canadienne de théorie politique et sociale,* Vol. 3, No. 1 (Winter/Hiver).

Marcuse, Herbert. [1974] 2015. *Paris Lectures at Vincennes University, 1974.* Edited by Peter-Erwin Jansen and Charles Reitz. Philadelphia, PA: International Herbert Marcuse Society.

Marcuse, Herbert. [1971] 2005. "The Movement in a New Era of Repression," in Douglas Kellner (Ed.) Herbert Marcuse, Collected Papers of Herbert Marcuse. Volume 3, *The New Left and the 1960s.* New York and London: Routledge.

Marcuse, Herbert. [1930] 1976. "On the Problem of the Dialectic," *Telos,* No. 27, Spring.

Marcuse, Herbert. [1932] 1973. "The Foundation of Historical Materialism," in his *Studies in Critical Philosophy.* Boston, MA: Beacon Press.

Marcuse, Herbert. [1933] 1973. "On the Philosophical Foundation of the Concept of Labor in Economics," *Telos,* No. 16, Summer.

Marcuse, Herbert. [1964] 1991. *One-Dimensional Man.* Boston, MA: Beacon Press.

Marcuse, Herbert. [1941] 1960. *Reason and Revolution.* Boston, MA: Beacon Press.

Marcuse, Herbert. [1937] 1968. "The Affirmative Character of Culture," in *Negations: Essays in Critical Theory.* Boston, MA: Beacon Press.

Marx, Karl. [1867] 1964. *Capital.* Vol. 1. London: Penguin.

Marx, Karl. [1844] 1975. "Contribution to the Critique of Hegel's Philosophy of Law," in Karl Marx, *Early Writings* edited by T.B. Bottomore. New York: McGraw-Hill.

McLaren, Peter. 1994. *Critical Pedagogy and Predatory Culture: Oppositional Politics in a Postmodern Era.* London and New York: Routledge.

Mūgo, Micere Githae. 2021. *The Imperative of Utu / Ubuntu in Africana Scholarship.* Ottawa, CA: Daraja Press.

NNY: Nyamnjoh, Francis B., Patrick U. Nwosu, and Hassan M. Yosimbom (eds). 2021. *Being and Becoming African as a Permanent Work in Progress: Inspiration from Chinua Achebe's Proverbs.* Bamenda, Cameroon: Langaa Research & Publishing Common Initiative Group.

Nyamnjoh, Francis B., Patrick U. Nwosu, and Hassan M. Yosimbom (eds). 2021. *Being and Becoming African as a Permanent Work in Progress: Inspiration from Chinua Achebe's Proverbs.* Bamenda, Cameroon: Langaa Research & Publishing Common Initiative Group.

Russell, Bertrand. [1927] 1967. *Why I am Not a Christian and Other Essays*. New York: Touchstone.
Sahlins, Marshall. [1968] 2017. "The Original Affluent Society," in *Stone Age Economics*. London and New York: Routledge.
Sahlins, Marshall. 2017. *Stone Age Economics*. London and New York: Routledge.
Sapolsky, Robert M. 2018. *Behave: The Biology of Humans at our Best and Worst*. New York: Penguin Books.
Sekyi-Otu, Ato. 2019. *Left Universalism, Africacentric Essays*. New York: Routledge.
Suchting, W.A. 1986. *Marx and Philosophy*. New York: New York University Press.
Tauber, Zvi. [2013] 2015. "Art as a Manifestation of the Struggle for Human Liberation," in Charles Reitz (Ed.). *Crisis and Commonwealth: Marcuse, Marx, McLaren*. Lanham, MD: Lexington Books.
Thornhill, Chris. 2021. "Foreword to the Routledge Classics Edition." of Karl Jaspers, [1949] 2021. *The Origin and Goal of History*. London and New York: Routledge.
Wiredu, Kwasi. 1991. "Morality and Religion in Akan Thought," in Norm R. Allen, Jr. *African-American Humanism*. Buffalo: Prometheus Press.
Woolfson, Charles. 1982. T*he Labor Theory of Culture: A Re-examination of Engels's Theory of Human Origins*. London: Routledge and Kegan Paul.

6
Labor Theory of Ethics

The core functions of philosophy, science, and religion can be authentically disclosed by examining the historical nature of *socially active human beings*. We are the ensemble of our social relations, and likewise, seen from the inside, we are *sensuous living labor*. This core sensuousness is cultivated by our empathic human capacity to care, a capacity more primordial than Heidegger's *Sorgestruktur* [i.e. his existentialist theory of the human *individual* as a caring yet distressed being, caring and distressed about our very being in time] (Heidegger, *Sein und Zeit* §65). My view goes back to the *social* behavior of primates in which an empathic "humanism" can be found. Primatologist Frans de Waal (2013, 2009, 2006) has demonstrated and explained the emergence of an instinctual sense of empathy in certain primates and humans: "distress at the sight of another's pain is an impulse over which we exert little or no control; it grabs us instantaneously, like a reflex, with no time to weigh the pros and cons" (de Waal 2006, 51). "Emotion and social intuition ... anchor some of the few moral judgments most humans agree on" (Sapolsky 2018, 488). Likewise, Herbert Marcuse has emphasized that discontent with practical social problems can give rise dialectically to sensations and ideas subversive to the established reality, our political Eros standing with nature as an ally. The source may be said to be within us insofar as social customs of empathy and solidarity find instinctual expression in the life-preserving force, longing for the pacification of the struggle for existence. More on this in chapter 9 to follow.

Distress and desperation characterize much of life on earth today. Society is no longer anaesthetized into the one-dimensionality that Marcuse famously called "a comfortable, smooth, reasonable, democratic unfreedom" (Marcuse [1964] 1991, 1). The beguiling but false impression of 1960s America as an everexpanding realm of affluence is now long gone. Can philosophers consider themselves critically minded and at the same time be oblivious to this widespread precarity and questions about how society perpetuates it? Marcuse was of the opinion that critical social theorists are "given hope" precisely for the sake of those who have none.

My work embodies this hope, grounded in the *labor theory of ethics*, in which I hypothesize a humanist core morality common to a range of major religions, non-theistic humanist philosophy, and to the history of anthropological social science. Humanistic sensibilities characterize the social core of our being, our sensuous practical activities, our livelihood strategies, and our communal labor. I owe much to the work of Charles Woolfson, particularly his reexamination of Engels's theory of human origins. He makes a well-documented case for what he calls *The Labor Theory of Culture* (1982). I shall highlight the major features of his study here as they undergird my own understanding.

Humanity's earliest work customs, i.e. communal production, shared ownership, and social solidarity assured that the needs of all were met, i.e. including those not directly involved in production like children, the disabled, and the elderly. As chapter 3 endeavored to explain, humanity's earliest proverbs, fables, and riddles from the oldest African cultures teach the survival power of partnership and cooperation and the categorical ethical advantages of empathy, reciprocity, hospitality, and respect for the good in common (Kisubi 2015; Sekyi-Otu 2019).

Woolfson's volume discusses in this regard Engels's "The Part Played by Labor in the Transition from Ape to Man" (Engels [1876] 1973, 248-264). Our primate ancestors adapted to labor and were themselves adapted by labor, developing rudimentary linguistic skills in the process (Woolfson, 3). Engels's theory is fairly well-known and summarized as follows:

> [W]ith the adoption of an erect posture and bipedal locomotion, the hand of early man was *freed* to acquire an increasing facility in tool-use and tool-making which led in turn over time to further changes in the structure of the hand, such that the hand became not only "the organ of labor," but also the "product of labor." (Woolfson, 6)

Engels engaged with what were at the time the newest research developments in archeology, anthropology, and primatology. These have profoundly suggestive implications even today for the theory of human development. His extensive investigations ultimately furnish *a critical theory of labor* as *the* formative factor in human origins. Woolfson finds that contemporary research confirms the broad outlines of Engels's theory: there is a crucial connection between the hand to brain development, and that this influence is forged through labor.

A materialist analysis of human development thus begins with how human communities produce their means of livelihood. In obtaining sustenance there was feedback to humanity's mental faculties that impacted discursive planning and the division of labor within a cooperative context. According to Engels, humanity became "*humanized* through labor" (Woolfson, 7). Ingenuity in labor in this view is a cultural accomplishment. Through it our own being, as a part of nature, becomes more humane.

Woolfson brings Marx's *Capital* to mind with regard to social forms of labor and our relationship to nature:

> Technology discloses man's mode of dealing with Nature, the process of production by which he sustains his life, and thereby also lays bare the mode of formation of his social relations and of the mental conceptions that flow from them. (Marx in Woolfson, 10)

Marx also connected the human labor process with human insight into forms of the ideal, even an aesthetic ideal:

> A spider conducts operations which resemble those of the weaver, and a bee would put many an architect to shame by the construction of its honeycomb cells. But what distinguishes the worst architect from the best of bees is that the architect builds the cell in his mind before he constructs it in wax. At the end of every labor process, a result emerges which had already been conceived by the worker at the beginning, hence already existed ideally. (Marx [1867] 1976, 284)

Production through human labor is the process of human making by which new tangible values are added to the economy. Wealth derives from this collective production process (notably described by Adam Smith on the division of labor). In addition outputs of this collective process include our common human heritage of science, technology, math, etc., and even language, each of which develops primarily within the context of commonwealth labor. When these multiple efforts at labor combine respectfully and judiciously with our common earthly reserves of land, sea, air, etc., humanity's CommonWealth emerges. We live in a massive built-environment: this built-environment embodies a human community's social labor exteriorized (*veräussert*) in curbs, pavement—every square inch around us, including gardens, parks, etc.—worked by human hands. This aggregate historical effort constitutes an *ecology of commonwealth labor*, yet we are largely oblivious of this circumstance. The workforce is the creative force in the economy. Laboring humanity, as society's foundational collective, has a legitimate right to the control, disposition, and ownership of this socially produced wealth.

Frederick Engels also reproduced and elaborated Karl Marx's notes on the work of the early American ethnographer Lewis Henry Morgan in his *Origin of the Family, Private Property and the State* (Engels [1884] 1972). With regard to his materialist conception of history, Marx was interested in Morgan's anthropological assessments (in *Ancient Society* published in 1877 by the Charles Kerr Cooperative in Chicago) of early forms of human life, politics, and government, particularly as reported with regard to the Iroquois of North America. Marx and Engels wished to compare earlier and later forms of social organization, and Engels acknowledges that he owes to Morgan a revolution in his ideas (Engels [1884] 1972, 83).

What was key for Morgan as well as Marx and Engels was their attention to differential forms of labor and ownership and the emergence of private property (Leacock 1972, 9-14). There is much that is outmoded and by today's standards even racist, in Morgan's terms "savagery," "barbarism," and "civilization" in the analysis of developmental stages in social evolution and as used by Marx and Engels. Still, the question of the material basis for the emergence of new and successive social formations remains pertinent. The theory of successive stages is to be considered even if only preliminary to a fuller study of historical processes.

Engels's volume also retains a definite value with regard to what anthropologists are increasingly recognizing as the *indigenous critique of Euro-American life*. Morgan's research showed that Iroquois households were communistic and characterized by pairing (rather than group) marriage and the leadership of women: "there is often much more respect for women than among our Europeans" (Engels [1884] 1972, 113). Group marriage "if it ever existed, belongs to such a remote epoch that we can hardly expect to prove its existence directly..." (Engels [1884] 1972, 97). Anthropology's critical assumptions about group marriage in early societies considered it a form of male supremacy involving a degradation of women, suppressing their aversions and inclinations if they had to be sexually available to all men. Engels contested this view, but insisted also that women's suppression intensified with the advent of class society. Most significantly, in early societies there was a reciprocity and partnership quality to women's and men's roles within communal family relations. Women and children were not dependent on individual men and women held partnership decision-making powers. Engels emphasized Morgan's insight that men and women elders in Iroquois society could together select the male sachems and depose them at will. Among the Seneca, prisoners of war were not enslaved but regularly adopted into the tribe with full rights (Engels [1884] 1972, 148-150). Engels quotes Morgan extensively on the ethics, rights and privileges of individuals among the Iroquois:

> All the members of an Iroquois gens [family group] were personally free. And they were bound to defend each other's freedom: they were equal in privileges and in personal rights, the sachem and chiefs claiming no superiority; and they were a brotherhood bound together by the ties of kin. Liberty, equality, fraternity though never formulated were cardinal principles of the gens. These facts are material, because the gens was the unit of a social and governmental system, the foundation upon which Indian society was organized .... (Engels [1884] 1972, 151).
>
> That is what men and society were before the division into classes. And when we compare their position with that of the overwhelming majority of civilized men today, an enormous gulf separates the present-day proletarian and small peasant from the free member of the old gentile society (Engels [1884] 1972, 160).

Engels concludes *Origins* with Morgan's words summarizing what is of greatest significance in understanding the dynamics of society.

> [A] career of which property is the end and aim ... contains the elements of self-destruction. Democracy in government, brotherhood in society, equality in rights and privileges, and universal education, foreshadow the next higher plane of society to which experience, intelligence, and knowledge are steadily tending. *It will be a revival, in higher form, of the liberty, equality, and fraternity of the ancient gentes* [Engels's italics]. (Morgan in Engels [1884] 1972, 237)

"The original affluent society"

Marshall Sahlins quite famously revolutionized anthropology in the late 1960s in the tradition of Engels's orientation to the egalitarian and partnership qualities of social life in the neolithic. His essays in this tradition have been collected as *Stone Age Economics* ([1968] 2017). These challenged received academic wisdom characterizing early societies as engaged in an all-consuming struggle for survival against food scarcity with his authoritative review of the then-current primary sources of ethnographic and anthropological research on early human life in "The Original Affluent Society." This led him to egalitarian conclusions with regard to an ethics of partnership power, abundance, leisure, and peace among early hunting and gathering societies.

Like Marcuse, Sahlins was sickened by what he saw in the "affluent" 1960s as the widespread precarity of human life around the world despite our epoch's technological advances and ostensible abundance. In his considered estimation the economics of the stone age hunting and gathering societies functioned in a manner providing material plenty with extraordinary relief from economic cares. The livelihood of all was rather easily obtained with minimal time expended in the quest for food. Women's harvesting and gathering was the central economic activity, with hunting more peripheral. Life was largely unhurried and unstressed with much leisure and daytime sleep. Economic resources to the outsider might have seemed underutilized, with no food storage facilities, with even indifference to material goods, and utensils. Property holdings were small and portable and easily replaced. With no one expropriating product from any producers by force of domination, there was no conception of "surplus," economic growth, or private accumulation. For Sahlins the so-called 'arts of subsistence' met early humanity's felt needs quite fully. Because these arts afforded much free space, enough for modest forms of prosperity, leisured childcare, conversation, visiting, travel, and dancing, the phrase 'arts of livelihood' came to supplant what was too often taken as the unembroidered quality of mode of *subsistence* as an inevitably austere existence.

Marcuse early on developed a critical study of work and social alienation looking at economic activity within the total complexity of other human activities and human existence in general. In his 1933 essay "On the Philosophical Foundation of the Concept of Labor in Economics" labor is seen as the key *activity* by which *humanity exteriorizes itself* and also *humanizes the world*. In addition to persons directly involved in production, others like politicians, artists, researchers, and clergy also *do work*, and in his estimation are members of the labor force. He contends that "labor is an ontological concept of human existence as such" (Marcuse [1933] 1973, 11). We enhance our self-expression and flourishing through labor, and this can take many forms. Marcuse builds upon Hegel's theory of the laboring consciousness overcoming its alienated existence and attaining an emancipated perception of its authentic self (Marcuse [1930] 1976, 36). He tied this also to Marx's historical and dialectical theory of socialist revolution as having the primary purpose of the supersession of "capitalist commodity production" (ibid., 38), and the aim especially of overcoming labor's deformation and commodification. Marcuse likewise honors Marx's philosophical humanism as "The Foundation of Historical Materialism." In his essay having that title Marcuse emphasizes that Marx in the *1844 Manuscripts*, as is now widely known, repeatedly identifies a genuine concept of communism with a humanist worldview and that the alienation theory articulated there by Marx looks to its supersession through the actualization of the human essence (Marcuse [1932] 1973, 7-8).

I have indicated above that human beings are not only the ensemble of our social relations, we are sensuous living labor, a view I derive from Marx and Marcuse in the following manner. Marx's first thesis on Feuerbach reads: "The chief defect of all hitherto existing materialism—that of Feuerbach included—is that the thing, reality, sensuousness, is conceived only in the form of the *object or of contemplation*, but not as *sensuous human activity, practice*, not subjectively" (emphasis in original). Marx criticizes the lack of labor theory in the sensualism of Feuerbach, and Marcuse cites Marx in *Reason and Revolution* ([1941] 1960) on the centrality of *labor* to human existence.

Humanity's earliest proverbs, fables, and riddles (as I have endeavored to show in chapter 5 above) teach the survival power of partnership and cooperation and the categorical ethical advantages of empathy, reciprocity, hospitality, and respect for the good in common. Humanity experiences the satisfactions/dissatisfactions derived from our bio-ecologically generated economic, aesthetic, intellectual, and moral standards gravitating toward the humanism of a communally laboring commonwealth. Having brought into being these universalizable value criteria, our cultural, political, and emotional conditions can be characterized as *authentic* (when consistent with the *fullest potentials* of our species-being, i.e. what Marx called our *Gattungswesen*) or as *alienated* (when social power structurally distorts or denies humanity such authenticity).

Marcuse has been perhaps most famously noted for his contention that the actually existing labor force lacks a critical appreciation of the potential of a philosophy of labor to transcend existing society. "Under the conditions of a rising standard of living, non-conformity with the system appears to be socially useless, and the more so when it entails tangible economic and political disadvantages and threatens the smooth operation of the whole" (Marcuse [1964] 1991, 2). Given capitalism's tendency toward periodic crisis, Marcuse certainly understood that this "smooth operation of the whole" is *not*, however, a permanent condition. In spite of the dominant state of system stability, regular episodes of economic collapse disclose that: "...forces and tendencies exist which may break this containment and explode the society" (Marcuse [1964] 1991. xv).

Marcuse's analysis of the alienation and commodfication of labor acknowledges the power of the workforce to enact and lead social change. His assessment undergirds a theory of labor humanism aiming at the disalienation of our essentially sensuous and creative practical and productive activities. Public ownership of socially produced wealth is *the* revolutionary starting point for labor that can transform the contemporary human condition and re-create the labor process to reflect fully our human potential. I stress in addition that incomes must be de-linked from private property ownership and reconnected to human needs, public work, and *public wealth*.

According to Marcuse, socialism in its most *radical* sense is more than a theory of democratic government. It is a philosophy of authentically human existence and the fulfillment of both human needs and the political promise of our human nature, where creative freedom provides the foundation for satisfaction in all of our works. As I have noted above, Marcuse and Marx asserted *a radically materialist conception of the essence of socially active human beings*: we are *sensuous living labor*.

Douglas Kellner's 1973 essay with regard to *the concept of labor* in the development of Marcuse's thought is a remarkable exception to a general neglect of this material, and has been a key stimulus to my own commentary. During the 1930s and '40s Marcuse ([1933] 1973) elaborated an "ontology of labor"—a philosophy grounded in the human condition as living labor.

This ontology of labor is said to have its source, not in Heidegger, but in Marx and Hegel themselves, and this is reprised in Marcuse's little-known last publication dealing with the nature of the "proletariat," and his final thoughts reinforce the labor humanist and commonwealth foundations of the critical philosophy that he shares with Marx: "The working class still is the 'ontological' antagonist of capital ...." (Marcuse 1979).

> Because he conceived human existence in terms of sense, Feuerbach disregarded this material function of labor altogether. 'Not satisfied with abstract thought, Feuerbach appeals to sense perception [Anschauung]; but *he does not understand our sensuous nature as practical, human-sensuous activity.*' Labor transforms the natural conditions of human existence into social ones. By omitting the labor process from his philosophy of freedom, therefore, Feuerbach omitted the decisive factor through which nature might become the medium for freedom. (Marx in Marcuse [1941] 1960, 272, emphasis added)

Like Marx, Marcuse emphasized that labor must be seen as a central dimension of human life beyond its narrow confines within a commodified economy. They both understood human alienation as estranged labor: sensuous living labor's separation from: 1) its product, 2) the process of production, 3) other producers, and 4) from our species need for the gratification of our sensuous, intellectual, political and ethical faculties.

Marx's labor theory of culture is vividly expressed in *Capital* Volume 1, chapter 7, on the labor process. He connects his theory to that of Benjamin Franklin, whom he credits with defining humanity as a tool-making animal.

> As soon as the labor process has undergone the slightest development, it requires specially prepared instruments. Thus we find stone implements and weapons in the oldest caves. In the earliest period of human history, domesticated animals, i.e. animals that have undergone modification by means of labor, that have been bred specially, play the chief part as instruments of labor along with stones, wood, bones, and shells, which have also had work done on them. The use and construction of instruments of labor, although present in germ among certain species of animals, is characteristic of the specifically human labor

process, and Franklin therefore defines man as a "tool-making animal. (Marx [1867] 1976, 286)

Marx and Marcuse saw *capital* as congealed labor or dead labor—*living labor* that had been objectified into productive equipment, the means and tools of production. Abraham Lincoln expressed the same view—consistent with Locke, Smith and Marx—of the relationship of labor to capital: "Labor is prior to, and independent of, capital. Capital is only the fruit of labor, and could never have existed if labor had not first existed. Labor is the superior of capital, and deserves much the higher consideration."[1] Lincoln, like Marx, recognized and renewed the dignity of work.

Employing Rudolf Bahro's theory of "surplus consciousness" (Bahro 1977a, 376ff; 1977b) Marcuse argues *against* his previous emphasis in *One-Dimensional Man* (1964) on the system-integration of the consciousness of the workforce. Bahro held that often even state functionaries in the U.S.S.R. or Eastern Bloc did not fully identify with the apparatus of government or its political imperatives. System-thinking in those places was easily undermined when social contradictions became politically heightened, and a surplus consciousness (*überschüssiges Bewußtsein*, literally an "overflow" of consciousness) ensued in a widely disseminated fashion (Bahro 1977a, 381). During the final stages of his own intellectual development, Marcuse believed Bahro's insight was immensely significant. Douglas Kellner concludes: "In effect, Bahro and Marcuse are arguing that critical consciousness and emancipatory needs *are* being developed by the contradictions in the social conditions of advanced industrial society—capitalist and state socialist." (Kellner 1984, 308-09, emphasis added). Under the changed socio-economic conditions of 1977-78, what Marcuse called a "counter-consciousness" was already emerging that made it possible for the consciousness "of the underlying population [to be] penetrated by the inherent contradictions of capitalism" (Marcuse 1979, 21). This echoes his essays on labor humanism (1932) and the concept of labor in economics (1933) discussed above. Zvi Tauber's 2013 essay on Marcuse's aesthetics of liberation focuses on an appreciation of the trans-historical dimension of art within its specific-historical content. He develops an understanding of the classic question of how the existence

---

[1] Lincoln's "Annual Message to Congress" December 3, 1961. Cited in Michael Parenti, *Democracy for the Few.* (New York: St. Martin's Press, 1988) p. 10.

and consciousness of modern humans and the ancient Greeks, for example, can be interlinked such that we can recognize and enjoy the art of antiquity. Utilizing Hegel, Marx, and Marcuse as sources, Tauber highlights Hegel's view that the phenomena of human existence in their historical totality develop a sense of truth about the human condition that is trans-historical, general, and universal. He then explains how Hegel's historical analysis of the phenomena of human existence is translated by Marx into sociological language. The conscious expression of this sense of humanity's real social existence in great art, such as in Greek tragedy, is to be seen as both a disclosure of life's real possibilities and a denunciation of life's real limitations.

I would like to propose in a manner of my own, yet analogous to Tauber's treatment of art, those trans-historical insights can also emerge from a *non-religious, demystifying reading of the history of ethical thought in the world's traditions of moral philosophy*. Marx and Engels asserted a radically materialist conception of the essence of socially active human beings: the material nature of the human being stresses the cultural context of cooperation and caring in the earliest human societies which fostered interdependence and an awareness of the customary power of partnership. Partnership customs and behaviors had the capacity to ensure survival. As Sahlins pointed out, the livelihood needs were met with relatively little time spent in the collaborative acquisition of necessities (three to four hours a day); thus, the foundation was established for the fuller species life to flourish within the human community. This included the development of language as a derivative of the communal human condition (Leakey 1994, 124).

Labor mediates between human beings and nature

"Humankind's primary relation to the world is an *active* one, specifically the relation involved in *labor*" (Suchting 1986, 12). The "labor theory of culture" (Woolfson 1982) is grounded in Marx's *Capital* Volume 1. As Marx writes, "Labor ... is a condition of human existence which is independent of all forms of society; it is an eternal natural necessity which mediates the metabolism between man and nature" (Marx [1867] 1976, 133). Sensuous living labor represents the metabolism between human beings and nature.

Following Woolfson's *Labor Theory of Culture* (1982), I understand ethics here as rooted in specific-historical realities and practices and at the same time as a negation of these realities raised to a higher, ideal level. The ideals are themselves practical: aiming at the transformation and pacification of everyday conflict. Understanding such ideals in social and historical terms is pivotal to a materialist theory of ethics and commonwealth.

I also follow the anthropological theorists, Douglas P. Fry and Geneviève Souillac (2017), Riane Eisler (1987), Richard Leakey (1994; Leakey and Lewin 1978), and primatologist Frans de Waal (2013, 2009) in departing from masculinist mythic accounts of human origins in any Golden Age or Garden of Eden and/or from accounts of 'Man the Killer Ape' (Dart 1956).

As this chapter will demonstrate, I am further oriented within a world-historical frame and committed to understanding the multiple wisdom traditions of a globally diverse humanity. My analysis utilizes a dialectical and materialist perspective to develop its understanding of an ethical core common to the wisdom traditions of the world's major religions as well as non-theistic humanist philosophy. Through an examination of the essentially economic features of the human condition and the history of our species as socially active human beings, I am seeking the pivotal principles of conscience that can ascertain the concrete common goods undergirding the evaluation of moral practice. On the basis of my interpretation of Marcuse's early work on labor as an ontological concept (Marcuse [1933] 1973), these common goods are understood to have emerged from our sensuous practical activities, our subsistence strategies, and our earliest forms of communal labor in egalitarian partnership societies. Humanity's earliest customs, i.e. communal production, shared ownership, and solidarity assured that the needs of all were met, i.e. including those not directly involved in production like children, the disabled, and the elderly. This right of the commonwealth to govern itself, and humanity's earliest ethic of holding property in common, derive only secondarily from factual individual contributions to production; they are rooted in our essentially shared species life and our being as humans, as sensuous living labor.

Africa and China: A universal humanism of partnership, reciprocity and benevolence

Knowing the right thing to do and actually doing it are often enough two entirely different matters; faltering in the latter does not invalidate the former. Humanity's first explicitly ethical maxims emerged as the proverbs that in a general way regulated life in the earliest African partnership cultures. These cultures centered on the customary sense of ubuntu or showing "humanity toward others," through empathy and principles of reciprocity and solidarity in communal life, teamwork, modesty, and mutuality. African proverbs included the first formulations of the golden rule. Philosophy professor, Godwin Azenabor (2008, 234), of the University of Lagos has argued for the underlying identity of African proverbs and Kant's categorical imperative. Of course, there could be conflict within and between tribes. Nonetheless, these proverbs constituted universalizable humanist, i.e. not narrowly tribal, teachings for the guidance of practical life, and can in no way be confused with purely religious teachings. "The cotton thread says that it is only as a team that you can carry a stone." "Many hands make light work." "It takes a whole village to raise a child." Not gods, but communally laboring humanity can be seen as the source of ethics here. "I am who I am because of who we all are." We work for the good in common because it is through our community that we each flourish (see Dorothy R. Jolley, 2011). The the secular humanistic foundations of African moral philosophy are soundly attested to by scholars such as Kwame Gyekye (2010), Kwasi Wiredu (1991) and Alfred T. Kisubi (2015).

In ancient China, the Dao was regarded as the "way" of the world. Opposites interpenetrated and emerged out of the other in a dialectical manner (centuries before Hegel and Marx developed their elaborations of the notion). Understanding the interconnectedness of all things, the yin/yang dynamics of both nature and human life, was necessary for concrete thinking and itself a social product. "Lay plans for the accomplishment of the difficult before it becomes difficult; make something big by starting with it when small" (Dao De Jing, LXIII). Today information processing would call this methodology a form of enhanced decision-making through systems analysis. Daoism's dialectical naturalism and humanism taught harmony, balance, gentleness, and equanimity with regard to life's changes. It accepted significant social inequalities yet was skeptical of official knowledge. Political authority was considered legitimate only if it assured the material well-being of the masses as the "mandate of heaven" required. Heaven was thus a metaphor for the satisfaction through politics of human needs. When the policies of the prevailing powers did not or could not meet the economic needs of the people, the people's rights of rebellion and overthrow were to be exercised (Mengzı[Mencius], in Chan 2012).

For Kong Fuzi (Confucius) "heaven's" mandate regarding the welfare of the common people also defined the purpose of government. An early form of a labor theory of ethics and justice may also be extrapolated from his Analects: "The head of a state or noble family worries not about underpopulation but about uneven distribution ... where there is even distribution there is no such thing as poverty" (Analects XVI.1). Humanist principles of benevolence, mutual regard, fairness, and humility are elaborated as ren or "human-heartedness." This was illustrated through the Principle of the Measuring Square: if there are those behind you, treat them as you would have those in front of you treat you; if there are those below you, treat them as you would have those above you treat you. With regard to religious practices, Kong Fuzi advised: "[W]ork for the things the common people have a right to and keep one's distance from gods and spirits while showing them reverence" (Analects VI.22). If one does not know how to serve one's comrades, how can one presume to serve the gods (Analects XI.12). Rites in ancient China were observed in virtually all human affairs. They clearly went well beyond religion and were part of everyday etiquette. Kong Fuzi taught open-mindedness, even in religion, with regard to these rites: "The asking of questions is in itself the correct rite" (Analects III.15). The golden rule appears as the injunction: "Do not impose upon others what you yourself do not desire" (Analects XV.24).

Plato and dialectical humanism

Plato's dialectics were borrowed from Socrates and derived from the highlevel conversations, actually social debates, which could arrive at truth. Plato, as political educator in the Republic, furnishes us with his key cave allegory. Its first sentence raises the issue: to what extent have we become enlightened or unenlightened about our being? "Let me tell you in a parable about whether the mind of humans is educated or uneducated about human nature and the human condition" (Steph. VII, 514a). Plato understands the propensities of our sensuous living substance toward illusion, delusion, dishonor, and disgrace. At the same time, his dialectical humanism stresses that to be enlightened/educated about our being and reality means we are capable of constructing from within ourselves dialectical rationality addressing our uncertain general condition and resolving the dissatisfaction / fulfillment conundrum in terms of an idea or model of the moral good to be pursued and obtained in our individual lives—including a "platonic love" or heartfelt care for learning, wisdom, the good society, and the good life.

In sharp contrast to divine command theories of ethics and politics, which taught obedience to a supernatural protective authority above all else, Plato taught that critical thinking, rather than the unfathomable and arbitrary will of the gods, could determine morally careful conduct. Plato argued that conventional beliefs about the visible and intelligible worlds are subject to question, and if not examined, they often lead to a shallow, disillusioned life. Education should remove the chains of illusion. An education to ideals as criteria of judgment makes possible the realization of our dignity and our greatest (intellectual and political) satisfactions. Rational minds learn through dialogue and debate as well as through logical deduction (mathematical reasoning). Study and inquiry can disclose how the best possible human relations and human communities may be constituted. He theorizes that justice is the characteristic of the public work of the leaders of the ideal city/state insofar as this political entity is governed by equal numbers of men and women educated to awareness of the (conflicted) human condition, living communally, with intelligence moderating appetite and spirit, disinterested and detached from lust for property, power, fame, etc., devoutly acting in accordance (not with God's will, but) with principles we have deciphered as to what is substantively advantageous for the pacification through fulfillment of our conflicted species life. Today we are aware of the African and Asian roots of Plato's view of the world (Bernal 1991): how the Republic and the Meno, especially, share with Egyptian, Indian, and Buddhist philosophies cultural notions of communal harmonization, transmigration of souls/reincarnation in a caste system, enlightenment and equanimity. Plato's Republic did not include the general public as participants at any level of government unless they first met educational qualifications, and this reflected existing aristocratic practice. Thus, many have seen his particular political and educational recommendations as authoritarian and conservative. His guardians seem legitimated as elite human beings. Still, in the Meno, Socrates was able to help a common slave boy fully comprehend the highest forms of mathematical reasoning; thus, if virtue and justice are knowledge, they might likewise be taught. Ordinary children might thus learn of the ideal of the Good as well and hence participate in political leadership. An early work of Plato, the Meno holds that no teachers of virtue are to be found, however. Persons who exemplify virtue seem to get this through divine dispensation. Plato's Republic, on the other hand, does acknowledge that virtue and the ideal of the Good can be imparted: dialectical pedagogy can make this and a vision of the just society possible. Marcuse stresses the practical and subversive nature of Plato's philosophy: "[T]he authentic, basic demand of idealism is that this material world be transformed and improved by knowledge of the Ideas. Plato's answer to this demand is his program for a reorganization of society" ([1937] 1968, 91–92).

Judaism, Hinduism and Buddhism on enlightenment and consecrated labor

Likewise, we need to comprehend the proto-humanistic elements embedded in other ancient wisdom traditions such as Judaism and Hinduism. Judaism requires us to do well the labor that confronts us as a necessity, to make amends annually to those we may have offended or to whom we may owe a debt, and it also supplies dozens of proverbs for right conduct. So too its veneration of the exodus from oppression and escape from slavery (a political-economic denunciation and liberation ethic which also abides in Islam and Christianity).

Hinduism teaches the ideal and power of Dharma: that benevolence is to be engraved in human hearts, and people are to live such that they might become worthy of immortal bliss. The instrument of this ideal is the ostensible power of karma, the doctrine of reciprocity and the rise in the long run of the indestructible human species essence (Atman) within an individual to attain fulfilment, happiness, and nirvana. Only honest labor/action, consecrated by good will in work/struggle, detached from consequences, can lead to good fortune. A version of the golden rule rises once more in the Mahabharata in Dharma's famous questioning of Yudhishthira (in the "Virata"): "What is honesty?—That is to look and see every living creature as yourself, bearing your own will to live, and your own fear of death … . What is it that humanity calls good fortune?—That is the result of what they have done honestly" (Buck 1973, 221). The doctrine of karma has legitimated dramatic and devastating social inequality. Like the caste system itself, these features have been negated and superseded through struggle in modern India. The idea of karma may nevertheless be seen as a metaphor for the real social interconnectedness of the conditions facing newer generations as these have been impacted by the work, for better or worse, of older generations. This may also be seen as a token of the moral principle of reciprocity analogous to the Confucian doctrine of the Measuring Square. Nirmal Kumar Bose has stressed a view of Gandhi as a humanist and socialist, emphasizing his classic practice of satyagraha, the refusal to cooperate with unethical social conventions, and his belief that honest labor undergirds a life worth living (Bose 1965, 90-91).

Buddhism, as a view of the world without gods, pursues the cessation of human suffering. Gotama Siddhartha, its founder, taught that we might become enlightened as to the human condition. At its root, therefore, Buddhism is an ethics of humanism, expressed most concisely in its Four Noble Truths [Proverbs]: life is suffering; suffering has its cause(s); these causes can be overcome; act/work/live in that manner which relieves the suffering in oneself—and that of others (as does the socially activist figure of the Bodhisattva).

Aristotle and the ecology of care

Buddha, Socrates, and Kong Fuzi preceded Aristotle by a full generation or more. Ancient humanism in each of the forms above, was not a philosophy of the natural and unmediated goodness of human beings, as in the Romanticism of Rousseau. It was a philosophy of the humanizing influence of parents and teachers, customs, culture, and laws within a conflictual societal context. Aristotle likewise saw humanity as a political animal, the zoon politikon, and politics the master art in the proper fashioning of human life and human society. As Marcuse explains:

> The doctrine that all human knowledge is oriented toward practice belonged to the nucleus of ancient philosophy. It was Aristotle's view that the truths arrived at through knowledge should direct practice in daily life as in the arts and sciences. In the struggle for existence, men need the effort of knowledge, the search for truth, because what is good, beneficial, and right for them is not immediately evident. (Marcuse [1937] 1968, 88)

Aristotle theorized that our highest happiness derived from the actualization of our essentially human capacities, powers, and potentials: speech/thought; worthy conduct, integrity, character, and moderation by way of the golden mean. Our task was to become intellectually and politically accomplished. To this end, one's upbringing, parenting, education, and the social structure supportive of these nurturing forces, were the most crucial factors. Aristotle's naturalism and humanism inquired into the ways and means by which our species might thrive and flourish. In economics and ethics, a chief vice was the boundless pursuit of property accumulation; a chief virtue, is the pursuit of the well-being of the community (*Politics* Chapter IX).

Among the key social teachings of medieval Islam, Christianity, and Judaism were those that preserved essential elements of Aristotle's philosophy of moderation in economic pursuits (condemning excess and insufficiency, the charging of interest, etc.). Ibn Khaldun is said to have adapted Aristotle's concept of moderation to politics in the fourteenth century. His central notion of asabiyyah emphasized the sense of shared social purpose and solidarity making for community cohesion, and he developed a perspective on political economy rooted in the idea that all earnings derive from the value created through labor. Bertrand Russell's essay, "Why I am Not a Christian," ([1927] 1967) treats Jesus as a non-divine, human teacher. In the Sermon on the Mount, once again, the golden rule holds an honored position. This and other precepts and proverbs are attested to by Russell as, by and large, a reprise of earlier teachings of the Daoist master, Laozi, as well as Buddha and Socrates on humility, forgiveness, loving-kindness, generosity to the stranger (*xenia*), as well as to the poor.

According to Heather Igloliorte (2016) of Concordia University, Montreal, the Inuit of the North American Arctic are direct descendants of the Thule people, who lived in the circumpolar region from 900 to 1200 CE. Their traditional knowledge and value system is known as the Inuit Qaujimajatuqangit. This encompasses ecological and environmental knowledge, societal values, and cosmology. It focuses on social and collective well-being. "It is a knowledge gained from time on the land and in the company of elders and family members.... . [I]t emphasizes respect, reciprocity, sharing and serving others" (Igloliorte 2016, 8). Consensus-based decisions are based on the collaborative group dynamics of fishing and sealing parties. Contributions to the common good are regarded as the highest form of leadership.

Kantian enlightenment humanism

In the modern epoch, Kant is thought to have philosophized about benevolence, goodwill, and the golden rule most prodigiously. He transfigures these into the proverbial categorical imperative: Never act except in such a way that your practice models what you would desire as the universal behavioral ideal.

Against the notion of the supernatural origin of ethical standards, in his view, humanist standards are the origin of everything that might be called truly "sacred"—

> God is not a substance existing outside me, but merely a moral relation within me ... The categorical imperative does not assume a substance issuing its commands from on high, conceived therefore as outside me, but is a commandment or a prohibition of my own reason ... The categorical imperative represents human duties as divine commandments not in the historical sense, as if [a divine being] had given commands to men, but in the sense that reason ... has the power to command with the authority and in the guise of a divine person ... . The Idea of such a being, before whom all bend the knee, etc. arises out of the categorical imperative, and not vice versa. (Kant in Durant 1967, 550)

Kant saw enlightenment as education to autonomy and freedom. Individuals, having formerly been content to remain silent with regard to political affairs and policies, could emerge from this consensual subordination and disfranchisement by using their own intellectual faculties to weigh and evaluate circumstances free of the partisan political guidance of the prevailing religious and governmental authorities. A chapter criticizing the traditional arguments for the existence of god is included in his *Critique of Pure Reason* and is considered a high point of that volume. Enlightenment autonomy and freedom, attained on a person-by-person basis, could gradually bring humanity closer to a constitution establishing world citizenship. This is indispensable for the attainment and maintenance of the global public's human rights, and hence also world peace. Though there was no talk of rights in early forms of ethical thinking, there is today a common language of human rights epitomized in the *UN Universal Declaration* (1948). Kant's 1784 "Idea for a Universal History with a Cosmopolitan Intent" argues the theoretical warrant for the emergence of a "universal cosmopolitan state" (Kant [1784] 1983, 38). In "Perpetual Peace: A Philosophical Sketch" he acknowledges in advance that this proposal will inevitably be met by "worldlywise statesmen" with smugness (Kant [1795] 1983, 107) and that they would deride and dismiss his political views as "mere theory." The "practical politician" would mock Kant's theory of the human duty towards peace and assert instead the "right" of the strong to make the weak obey them.

> Nonetheless, ... reason absolutely condemns war as a means of determining right and makes seeking the state of peace a matter of unmitigated duty ... . A league of a special sort must therefore be established, one that we can call a league of peace ... to end all wars forever. (Kant [1795] 1983, 116-117)

Hegel and Marx further developed the logic and strategy that undergirds today's commonwealth aspirations. Hegel taught that history is a way of learning, and he raised the contemporary philosophical issue of why humanity's social and intellectual life is still controlled by the powerful few rather than by the multitude. Hegel argued the social evolution of reason from lower to higher would absorb and complete the limited and alienated products of an earlier form of culture and education, attaining thereby an advanced level of intelligence, art, and civilization. Hegel's theory proposed that dis-alienation had to be the work of the alienated elements themselves, educationally and politically. It remained for Marx's labor theory of history to buttress Hegel on alienation and to call attention to the appropriative and expropriative economic and political processes of the past and those which we continue to confront today in advanced capitalist modes, as well as the re-appropriation challenges facing the global workforce. The tenth Feuerbach thesis tells us: "The standpoint of the old materialism is civil society; the standpoint of the new is human society or social humanity." Marx replaces the bourgeois notion of civil society (which claims a spurious social status separate from the government and the economy) with the notion of social humanity as a governmental and economic power, i.e. human society as commonwealth.

Multiple modes of moral reasoning (and rationalization) have emerged over the course of human history. These can be rivals to what I have called the labor theory of ethics. The latter, as humanism, negates divine command theory, yet absorbs and preserves aspects of character-based and duty-based approaches, as well as essential elements the social utilitarianism of Mill. The personal utility calculus of Bentham is regarded by Marx as a form of moral egoism consistent only with bourgeois philistinism, as was the theory that even private economic evils can contribute—through the magic of the market—to the public good. Max Stirner, Friedrich Nietzsche, and Ayn Rand fall into similar categories of egoist illegitimacy.

Marx was aware, in an insight derived from Aristotle that the pursuit of private accumulation—beyond all bounds—was not compatible with the meaning of oikonomia, economics. Oikonomia referred to the concrete considerations undertaken to ensure the well-being or flourishing of the household, and by extension, the community.

A dialectics of the particular and universal is the pre-condition for the fulfillment of our species-being. Marcuse's perspective on the historical reality of universals is likewise essential for liberation. "The universal comprehends in one idea the possibilities which are realized, and at the same time arrested, in reality" (Marcuse 1964, 210). "The substantive universal intends qualities which surpass all particular experience, but persist in the mind, not as a figment of the imagination nor as mere logical possibilities, but as the 'stuff' of which our world consists" (Marcuse 1964, 213).

My emphasis on the internal/intrinsic ethical core of the world's wisdom traditions is a matter of our very survival. The labor movement must be able to explain this praxis and the necessity of socialism and humanism. Today's intensifying levels of global economic oppression necessitate intellectual and political growth. The ethic of intercultural solidarity today is essential in terms of praxis if the human species is to go on living.

Works cited

Azenabor, Godwin. 2008. *QUEST: An African Journal of Philosophy / Revue Africaine de Philosophie*, No. XXI: 229–240.
Bahro, Rudolf. 1977a. *Die Alternative*. Cologne/Frankfurt: Europäische Verlagsanstalt.
Bahro, Rudolf. 1977b. "The Alternative in Eastern Europe," *New Left Review*, No. 106. November–December.
Bernal, Martin. 1991. *Black Athena: The Afroasiatic Roots of Classical Civilization: The Fabrication of Ancient Greece 1785–1985*. New York: Random House.
Bose, Nirmal Kumar. 1965. "Gandhi: Humanist and Socialist," in Erich Fromm (Ed.), *Socialist Humanism*. Garden City, NY: Doubleday.
Buck, William. 1973. *Mahabharata*. New York: New American Library.
Chan, Peter M. K. 2012. *The Six Patriarchs of Chinese Humanism*. Lulu.com. www.lulu.com/shop/peter-mk-chan/the-six-patriarchs-of-chinese-humanism/ebook/product-20158012.html.
Dart, Raymond A. 1956. *Cultural Status of the South African Man-Apes*. Washington, DC: The Smithsonian Institution.
de Waal, Frans. 2013. *The Bonobo and the Atheist: In Search of Humanism among the Primates*. New York: W.W. Norton.
de Waal, Frans. 2009. *The Age of Empathy*. New York: Random House.
de Waal, Frans. 2006. *Primates and Philosophers*. Princeton, NJ: Princeton University Press.
Eisler, Riane. 1987. *The Chalice and the Blade*. New York: HarperCollins.
Engels, Frederick. [1872-1882] 1973. *Dialectics of Nature*. New York: International Publishers.
Engels, Frederick. [1884] 1972. *The Origin of the Family, Private Property and the State*. New York: International Publishers.

Fry, Douglas P. and Geneviève Souillac. 2017. "The Original Partnership Societies: Evolved Propensities for Equality, Prosociality, and Peace," *Interdisciplinary Journal of Partnership Studies*, Vol. 4, No. I, March.
Gyekye, Kwame. 2010. "African Ethics," in *The Stanford Encyclopedia of Philosophy*, No. 2011, Fall.
Heidegger, Martin. [1927] 1967. *Sein und Zeit*. Tübingen: Max Niemeyer Verlag.
Igloliorte, Heather. 2016. *Inuit Art. The Brousseau Collection*. Quebec City: Musée national des beaux-arts du Quebec.
Jolley, Dorothy R. 2011. *Ubuntu: A Person is a Person Through Other Persons*. Masters Thesis. Southern Utah University.
Kant, Immanuel. [1795] 1983. "To Perpetual Peace: A Philosophical Sketch," in *Perpetual Peace and Other Essays*. Translated by Ted Humphrey (with a dedication to Herbert Marcuse). Indianapolis, IN: Hackett Publishing.
Kant, Immanuel. [1784] 1983. "Idea for a Universal History with a Cosmopolitan Intent," in *Perpetual Peace and Other Essays*. Translated by Ted Humphrey (with a dedication to Herbert Marcuse). Indianapolis, IN: Hackett Publishing.
Kant, Immanuel. Posthumous papers, cited in Will Durant, 1967. *The Story of Civilization*, Volume X, New York: Simon & Schuster.
Kellner, Douglas. 1984. *Herbert Marcuse and the Crisis of Marxism*. Berkeley, CA: University of California Press.
Kellner, Douglas. 1973. "Introduction to 'On the Philosophical Foundation of the Concept of Labor,'" *Telos*, No. 16, Summer.
Kisubi, Alfred Taligoola. 2015. "Cultural Origins of African Humanism and Socialism (Ujamaa)," in Charles Reitz (Ed.). *Crisis and Commonwealth: Marcuse, Marx, McLaren*. Lanham, MD: Lexington Books.
Leacock, Elinore Burke. 1972. "Introduction" to Frederick Engels, *The Origin of the Family, Private Property, and the State*. New York: International Publishers.
Leakey, Richard. 1994. *The Origin of Humankind*. New York: Basic Books.
Leakey, Richard and Roger Lewin. 1978. *People of the Lake*. Garden City, NY: Anchor/Doubleday.
Marcuse, Herbert. 1979. "The Reification of the Proletariat," *Canadian Journal of Political and Social Theory / Revue canadienne de théorie politique et sociale*, Vol. 3, No. 1 (Winter/Hiver).
Marcuse, Herbert. [1930] 1976. "On the Problem of the Dialectic," *Telos*, No. 27, Spring.
Marcuse, Herbert. [1932] 1973. "The Foundation of Historical Materialism," in his *Studies in Critical Philosophy*. Boston, MA: Beacon Press.
Marcuse, Herbert. [1933] 1973. "On the Philosophical Foundation of the Concept of Labor in Economics," *Telos*, No. 16, Summer.
Marcuse, Herbert. [1964] 1991. *One-Dimensional Man*. Boston, MA: Beacon Press.
Marcuse, Herbert. [1941] 1960. *Reason and Revolution*. Boston, MA: Beacon Press.
Marcuse, Herbert. [1937] 1968. "The Affirmative Character of Culture," in *Negations: Essays in Critical Theory*. Boston, MA: Beacon Press.
Marx, Karl. [1867] 1976. *Capital*. Vol. 1. London: Penguin.
Marx, Karl. [1844] 1975. "Contribution to the Critique of Hegel's Philosophy of Law," in Karl Marx, *Early Writings* edited by T.B. Bottomore. New York: McGraw-Hill.
McLaren, Peter. 1994. *Critical Pedagogy and Predatory Culture: Oppositional Politics in a Postmodern Era*. London and New York: Routledge.
NNY: Nyamnjoh, Francis B., Patrick U. Nwosu, and Hassan M. Yosimoom (eds). 2021. *Being and Becoming African as a Permanent Work in Progress: Inspiration from Chinua Achebe's Proverbs*. Bamenda, Cameroon: Langaa Research & Publishing Common Initiative Group.

Nyamnjoh, Francis B., Patrick J. Nwosu, and Hassan M. Yosimbom (eds). 2021. *Being and Becoming African as a Permanent Work in Progress: Inspiration from Chinua Achebe's Proverbs*. Bamenda, Cameroon: Langaa Research & Publishing Common Initiative Group.

Russell, Bertrand. [1927] 1967. *Why I am Not a Christian and Other Essays*. New York: Touchstone.

Sahlins, Marshall. [1968] 2017. "The Original Affluent Society," in *Stone Age Economics*. London and New York: Routledge.

Sahlins, Marshall. 2017. *Stone Age Economics*. London and New York: Routledge.

Sapolsky, Robert M. 2018. *Behave: The Biology of Humans at our Best and Worst*. New York: Penguin Books.

Sekyi-Otu, Ato. 2019. *Left Universalism, Africacentric Essays*. New York: Routledge. Suchting, W.A. 1986. *Marx and Philosophy*. New York: New York University Press.

Tauber, Zvi. [2013] 2015. "Art as a Manifestation of the Struggle for Human Liberation," in Charles Reitz (Ed.). *Crisis and Commonwealth: Marcuse, Marx, McLaren*. Lanham, MD: Lexington Books.

Wiredu, Kwasi. 1991. "Morality and Religion in Akan Thought," in Norm R. Allen, Jr. *African-American Humanism*. Buffalo: Prometheus Press.

Woolfson, Charles. 1982. *The Labor Theory of Culture: A Re-examination of Engels's Theory of Human Origins*. London: Routledge and Kegan Paul.

7
Ecological Materialism

In the last few years, two very popular books have elaborated an ecological materialist perspective extremely effectively: *The Hidden Life of Trees: What They Feel, How They Communicate—Discoveries from a Secret World* by German forester Peter Wohlleben (2015) and *The Overstory*, a novel by Richard Powers (2019). These have had a wide impact with their ecological materialist message. "This is what the ecosystem achieves: the fullness of life with tens of thousands of species interwoven and interdependent" (Wohlleben, 245). Trees are social beings exchanging information with fungi, grasses, shrubs and insects. "[T]rees communicate by means of olfactory, visual, and electrical signals ..." and trees are "more than just a commodity" (Wohlleben, 12 and 241). They provide key benefits to humanity above lumber production.

A similar message is contained in *The Overstory*. Narrated with a homespun Lake Wobegone wistfulness—interwoven with threads of science fiction—it conveys in its own way a modern grasp of nature's dynamism and history and interconnectedness such that it has been found worthy of a Pulitzer Prize. It reports that halfway up the length of Sweden is Old Tjikko, a Norway spruce a few hundred years old, but "below in the microbe-riddled soil he reaches back nine thousand years or more" (Powers, 221). The book's vision is nonetheless pessimistic. "A group of backpackers ... all trying to bail out the ocean of capitalism with an acorn cup" (Powers, 239). We neither make nor understand reality: "We just evade it. So far. By looting natural capital and hiding the costs. But the bill is coming, and we won't be able to pay" (Powers, 320). Nonetheless, the environmentalist influence these volumes have had on the public imagination is exceptionally beneficial. I hope to add to their efforts an understanding of the larger philosophical foundations and presuppositions that undergird their work—the ecological materialist *understory*.

A philharmonic performance also has its understory. Imagine all the instruments on the stage without players. Consider each violin or French horn or clarinet in terms of its *matter and form and its developmental history*, each different in sound, shape, and structure from its predecessors in centuries past. Observe the modern piano, emergent from the clavichord, the harp, even the lyre. Now it has eighty-eight steel cord filaments, each a specific thickness and length to make eight-eight notes. If a hammer strikes and a string is vibrating, waves of air molecules may impact our ears loudly or softly, high frequency or low. All these historical and material dimensions will influence the sound. Enter the musicians with their parts under their arms, perhaps for Strauss's *Death and Transfiguration*, perhaps Puccini's *La Bohème*. Cooperating as their scores configure, their concerted effort does emotionally *move* the receptive audience, human bodies sensing and appreciating a humane and joyful sadness in common. Historically conditioned materials and minds in motion are dialectically interconnected here. Nothing *purely* mechanical is involved. And while there is an existential independence of nature from human beings, it is human beings alone who can appreciate the powers of nature and our own place within the natural realm.

Philosophical perspectives, emergent over centuries, have endeavored to understand and comprehend the dynamic material conditions that have generated the history of nature, society, and thought. Historical materialism is a name relatively recently given to this endeavor within Marxism (Plekanov [1897] 2020; Marcuse [1932] 1973). This chapter undertakes a re-examination of this historical materialism in the work of Marx, Engels, and Marcuse. Historical materialism signals the intellectual emergence of the recognition (held to be central to philosophical rationality) that the natural world, as well as social life, have undergone multiple transformations over time in terms of patterns of geological change, bio-ecological development, and socioeconomic transformations. Frederick Engels confides something to us about the ontology (or dialectics) of things in nature as well as those constructed through human ingenuity, like buildings, books, and governments:

> [T]he world is not to be comprehended as a complex of ready-made *things*, but as a complex of *processes*, in which the things apparently stable... go through uninterrupted change of coming into being and passing away, in which in spite of all seeming

accidentality and all temporary retrogression, a progressive element asserts itself in the end ... (Engels [1888] 1974, 44)

The new conception of nature [is] complete in all its main features; all rigidity [is] dissolved, all fixity dissipated, all particularity that had been regarded as eternal became transient, the whole of nature shown as moving in eternal flux and cyclical course. (Engels [1872-1882] 1973, 13)

Engels is elaborating the dynamics and the dialectics of matter and nature, the unity of body and mind, with an emphasis on human creativity (and intelligence itself) as "the highest product of matter" (Engels [1888] 1974, 25). Modern science and philosophy have emphasized humankind as a part of nature and thought as a social product. In contemporary sociology, an *ecological-evolutionary* perspective stresses that human societies are embedded in the natural world and humans are part of the global ecosystem—influenced by such things as soil, water and mineral resources, climate, terrain, plants, animals, and other features of the territory in which they live (Nolen and Lenski 2011). An *ecological materialism* sees the world and human societies in terms of systems of interrelated parts, the whole often being greater than the sum. In societies, the basic needs of the system are met through cooperation of one sort or another, often a customary solidarity and egalitarian partnership, sometimes compulsion or coercion. This cooperation is reproduced by the basic forms of social learning, an enculturation; the mode of cooperation can also be challenged and transformed, sometimes successfully. Fundamental conflicts are endemic to most modern human societies existing within a globalized political-economic system, a world system that has tended towards patterns of dominator power and inequality.

Because it is so important it bears repeating that the methodologies of ecology, critical philosophy, and sociology take interconnected *systems* to be the focus of analysis (in terms of statics and dynamics, structures and processes), rather than primarily on isolated particular units, individuals, experiences, or inert machinery. Georg Lukács thematized these approaches in his treatment of totality and reification, the whole being greater than the sum of the parts (Lukács [1924] 1971). Hegel and Marx studied the systemic interconnectivities in nature and the social world in terms of reciprocities and mutualities, as well as tensions, conflicts, and antagonisms, where opposition can lead to contradiction as well as qualitative transformation, progress or regress, as the case may be. These are the methodologies of dialectical materialism. For Michael L. Simmons, Jr., emeritus professor of educational theory at the University of Buffalo:

> Dialectic treats existence, whatever its domain, size, form, importance, as a totality (or a unity) comprising elements or factors that stand in opposition, in conflict, even contradiction, to each other. Movement of the object results primarily from the oppositions, etc. The particular relations of any oppositions, conflicts, or contradictions are the necessary condition of the existence and particular nature of the very totality which contains them; it is [sic] them. (Simmons in Reitz 2019, 138)

Simmons explains further that the materialist dialectic understands real inadequacies and absences in light of real and better human possibilities in order that these "be realized in restructured social relations." Higher learning *is* dialectical understanding, incipient critical social science and radical political education. Where science looks for lawfulness, Simmons acknowledges the critical realism of Roy Bhaskar (*The Possibility of Naturalism*, 1975)—as well as the naturalism of Dewey (*Human Nature and Conduct* 1922; *Experience and Nature* 1925) and Marvin Farber (*Naturalism and Subjectivism* 1959)—allow us to understand these "laws" as *tendencies* within the underlying structures internal to nature and social reality that generate empirical data. For Bhaskar the tendencies can be understood dialectically as actualized and as not actualized depending on conditions, time, and place. From the perspective of the critical realists and naturalists mentioned above, science and philosophy inherently entail a dialectical logic supporting emancipatory cultural action for freedom and justice.

Societies have a history: So does Nature

Even a stone has a history (Lenin [1914] 1972, 111) as does every species of life; geology and biology must explain this history as well as describe it. Nature is *not* a collection of inert hunks of matter or molecules, but an interactive ecological totality of material forces and processes engaged in various interrelated sets and schemes of protracted and/or rapid change in living and nonliving systems. As Marx, Engels, and critical Marxist materialists like Herbert Marcuse were well aware, the interactive and dynamic qualities of the material world were evident in the ancient Greek writings of Heraclitus, Thales, Democritus and Leucippus. Likewise, the works of the elder Pliny and Lucretius in the Roman era. Renewed publications of these writers during the Renaissance marked the modern beginning of a unified theory of the material world.

Science was attempting to eliminate the "meta" from metaphysics, and stress the "uni" in universe. Mind and humankind were starting to be understood as integral parts of nature. Comprehension, itself, was thought to require broadly based scientific knowledge of the macrocosm, as well as humanistic expertise in such fields as art and anatomy. Indeed, the Renaissance recognition of the inherent interconnections linking different areas of theoretical endeavor and practical concern was the most remarkable event of all.

Historical materialism attempts to understand the philosophical problem central to human history and human liberation: theoretical explanation and its relation to reality. Alexander Humboldt's "everything is interconnected" approach (especially in *Kosmos*), recognized how humanity's inner capacities adapt to the world's ecosystems, and that our insight into these ecosystems builds our fuller, more comprehensive understanding of life as a whole, i.e., including aesthetics, ethics, and politics. Humboldt's writing on plant ecology, geography, geology, and much more, of necessity also condemned sugar plantation slavery as a denatured and disfiguring economic form where he found it in Cuba. Humboldt maintained the unity of the human race, against Agassiz, who promoted racial hierarchy. Humboldt's work also was a manifest or a latent background influence on Henry David Thoreau, John Muir, Friedrich Engels, and a generation later, Herbert Marcuse and Aldo Leopold.

Aldo Leopold's ecological materialism: Our ethical relationship to land

Earlier in this volume, Marcuse's ecological writings were examined in detail. His final monograph links his materialism and his critical Marxism. "Marxist theory has the least justification to ignore the metabolism between the human being and nature ...." (Marcuse 1978, 16). Aldo Leopold, a forester, nature writer, and the nation's first professor of wildlife management at the University of Wisconsin in 1933 is renowned as one of the world's foremost philosophers of conservation and ecology. Leopold's philosophy was not a narrow instrumental rationality of resource management, but rather in dialectical sympathy with wildlife, plant life, ice, water, air, and the land (Brennan 2007, 519). He understood earth (i.e. land) scientifically as a biotic system. "Land ... is not merely soil, it is a fountain of energy flowing through a circuit of soils, plants, and animals" (Leopold [1953] 1966, 231). It is a fundamental constituent of a "biotic pyramid."

> Plants absorb energy from the sun. This energy flows through a circuit called the biota... A plant layer rests on the soil, an insect layer on the plants, a bird and rodent layer on the insects, and so on up through various animal groups to the apex layer, which consists of the larger carnivores... Each successive layer depends upon those below it for food and often for other services, and each in turn furnishes food and services to those above ...lines of dependency for food and other services are called food-chains. Thus soil-oak-deer-Indian is a chain that has largely been converted to soil-corn-cow-farmer (Leopold [1953] 1966, 230–231).

Above and beyond nature's beauty, Leopold saw that living on the face of our planet with dignity is possible. Our historical and material condition holds the promise of ethical, political, and aesthetic meaning for human communities. To Leopold, nature was considered to be a community to which humanity belongs. "The culture of primitive peoples is often based on wildlife. Thus, the plains Indian not only ate buffalo, but buffalo largely determined his architecture, dress, language, arts, and religion" (Leopold [1949] 1966, 195).

Ultimately, Leopold comes to replace the term "wildlife" with the term "land" because he sees the former as inextricably bound to the latter. Leopold explicitly developed what he called a "land ethic" that led him to a logic of protection, love, and respect for nature—both in recreation and in social production. "That the land is a community is a basic concept of ecology. But that the land is to be loved and protected is an extension of ethics" (Leopold, 1966, x). He replaced a view of humanity as conqueror of the land-community with a vision of the planet's inhabitants as a commonwealth of earth. "EarthCommonWealth" is my term, not his, but it encapsulates his conviction that ecological science can lead to ecological conscience: to conservation and cooperation.

"Ecology is the science of communities, and the ecological conscience is therefore the ethics of community life" (Leopold [1947] 1991, 340).

Ecological science discloses "the tendency of interdependent individuals or groups to evolve modes of cooperation ... All ethics so far evolved rest upon a single premise: that the individual is a member of a community of interdependent parts" (Leopold [1949] 1966, 218–219). Leopold argues that "for the purposes of a liberal education ecology is superior to evolution as a window through which to view the world" (Leopold [1942] 1991, 305). "Much of the damage inflicted on land is quite invisible to laymen. An ecologist ... must be the doctor who sees the marks of death in a community that believes itself well and does not want to be told otherwise" (Leopold 1993, 165).

Let us build upon the hitherto largely unheralded ecological vision of Aldo Leopold that embraces all living things as an earthly community capable of measured and dignified coexistence with our planet and its surroundings. Leopold, like Humboldt and Engels, did not limit himself to the description of immediate abuses or the observation of ecological marvels. His analysis was grounded in an appreciation-in-depth of the dynamism and mediated dialectical interdependencies of nature that could also make recovery and ecological/ ethical advance possible. Leopold developed an ecological critique of private property rights in land ownership since such rights undergirded social and environmental destruction:

> When god-like Odysseus returned from the wars in Troy, he hanged all on one rope a dozen slave-girls of his household whom he suspected of misbehavior during his absence ... The girls were property. The disposal of property was then, as now, a matter of expediency, not right and wrong ... The ethical structure of that day covered wives, but had not yet been extended to human chattels ... Land, like Odysseus' slave girls, is still property. (Leopold 1966, 217–218)

> [E]thics, so far studied only by philosophers, is actually a process in ecological evolution. Its sequences may be described in ecological as well as in philosophical terms. An ethic, ecologically, is a limitation on freedom of action in the struggle for existence. An ethic, philosophically, is a differentiation of social from anti-social conduct. These are two definitions of one thing. The thing has its origin in the tendency of interdependent individuals or groups to evolve modes of cooperation ... cooperative mechanisms with an ethical content. (Leopold 1966, 217-218)

Leopold's Land Ethic contains a critique of private property ownership leads him to valorize commonality and cooperation given our societal interdependence. He connects the aesthetic realm also to the land: "What is art? Only the drama of the land's workings" (Leopold [1942] 1991, 303). Aside from humans, does any other living being on the face of the planet appreciate its beauty, its ethical promise?

> The practice of conservation must spring from a conviction of what is ethically and aesthetically right, as well as what is economically expedient. A thing is right only when it tends to preserve the integrity, stability, and beauty of the community, and the community includes the soil, waters, fauna, and flora, as well as people ... Economic provocation is no longer a satisfactory excuse for unsocial land use ... for ecological atrocities ... I have no illusions about the speed or accuracy with which an ecological conscience can become functional. (Leopold [1947] 1991, 345)

An ecology and ethics of commonwealth epitomize what Aldo Leopold had in common with Vine Deloria, Jr. (1992), one of the most highly-regarded literary and political figures of the Standing Rock Sioux. Humans, wildlife, plants, and land form a larger inclusive community relationship—one to be respected and held in the highest regard.

Deloria writes with wry irony: "[I]t is the white man with his careless attitude toward life who is actually in danger of extinction" (Deloria [1992] 1995, 250). "The native peoples of the American continents ...have managed to survive. Now, at a time when the virtues they represented, and continue to represent, are badly needed by the biosphere struggling to remain alive, they must be given the participatory role which they might have had in the world if the past five centuries had been different" (Deloria [1992] 1995, 252). The *participatory role* of indigenous leadership is needed now more than ever.

Caution: "Everything You Know About Indians Is Wrong"

Paul Chaat Smith, a droll and indigenous essayist, wrote a series of searing critiques of even the most well-meaning interpretations of Native American life in *Everything You Know About Indians Is Wrong* (2009). "We are witnessing a new age in the objectification of American Indian history and culture, one that doesn't even need Indians except as endorsers" (Chaat Smith 2009, 16). By this he meant that non-Native interests have continued with a colonial appropriation of indigenous philosophy to suit their (our?) own "feel good" purposes: "Today the equation is Indian equals spiritualism and environmentalism" (20). "Our designated place today ...we are the keepers of the earth, of the zoos, of the skies and the stars and plants and animals and insects. We are spiritual teachers, wise elders, and environmentalists par excellence. We are wonderful artists and gifted storytellers" (185). For Chaat Smith, this wistfulness tinged with romanticism and racism is a matter of revulsion and loathing. We are warned against it. Smith leaves the issues unresolved, offering instead a narrative of his seemingly unremarkable, yet contradictory life experiences: suburban upbringing, erstwhile AIM activism, to the curator at the National Museum of the American Indian. Such a life makes, as he says, for "lousy television" but a waggish memoir.

"When Will America Be Discovered?"

"Columbus arrived in the New World in 1492, but America has yet to be discovered" (Weatherford 1988, 255). Fortunately, one of Vine Deloria Jr.'s closest collaborators, Daniel R. Wildcat, professor of sociology and academic administrator at Haskell Indian Nations University in Lawrence, Kansas, offers us a set of exceptionally worthy resources allowing serious readers to discover America's indigenous ecological ingenuity.

> Those expecting to find reassuring romantic reveries about noble savages living close to nature should turn elsewhere for their reading pleasure... New Age secrets and formulae, and exoticized platitudes of mythological tribal origin, are absent in these pages. (Wildcat, 2009, 20, 74)

Wildcat's volume, *Red Alert!: Saving the Planet with Indigenous Knowledge* (2009), cogently makes the case for an "Indigenous Realism." To know reality we need to respect the dynamic material relationships that constitute the complex web of life. This

> ...is *not* a call to anthropology and archeology as these disciplines have been practiced throughout much of their Western academic existence, but a challenge to replace a search for humankind's general development along a Western-inspired universal timeline with a rethinking of our diverse human cultural development as shaped by places. (Wildcat 2009, 11)

Daniel R. Wildcat's perspective on saving the planet with indigenous knowledge delves into the historic American sources on the "web of life" from which Leopold unfolded his own appreciation of indigenous ecophilosophy: humanity needs to adhere to a partnership-oriented land ethic and land aesthetic.

> In order to deal with the array of social and ecological issues we will face across nearly every dimension of the complex life system of Mother Earth, we must begin to understand our lives as essentially *not* only about us but about our human selves in what environmental scientists and ecologists, without the least hint of romanticism, call the web of life. (Wildcat 2009, 5)
>
> [W]e have no tradition of religious writings .... [W]e have saved ourselves from religious wars.... [W]e are, as my northern plains friends say *mitakua oysin*, "all related." (Wildcat 2009, 57-59)

Wildcat's writing also takes us behind Marcuse's 1972 insight that *nature is an ally,* reminding us that it is *Mother Earth herself* who has been admonishing us to act boldly to stop the climate catastrophe that he calls "global burning." We are immersed in a global fossil fuel economy in which greenhouse gas emissions are the source of the ecological damage being done in terms of droughts, water shortages, sea-level rise, floods, and biodiversity loss through (polar bear, sea turtle) extinction. He stresses that it is Native voices that need to be heard as we engage in difficult discussions about the *institutions* responsible for this environmental damage:

> After a centuries-long colonial imposition of Eurocentric notions of civilization and progress on indigenous peoples ...continuing global "development" with the same worldview and institutions that have produced the deadly global situation ... [is] ...insanity. (Wildcat 2009, 79)

The indigenous critique stresses that we, in all our biological diversity, cultural diversity, and *earthen* diversity, are all interconnected. This requires respectful stewardship of land and life in terms of communal responsibility and communal possession. It admonishes us to treat nature 'like a relative, not a resource.' So too, my own conceptions of EarthCommonWealth and ecological materialism want us to pay attention to our lives within the nature-culture nexus. What is needed is a kind of *indigenized ecosocialism*.

The history of human origins

In 2022, as I write this, David Graeber's and David Wengrow's blockbuster volume, *The Dawn of Everything: A New History of Humanity* is being widely heralded as a 704-page tome that alters our understanding of human socio-cultural evolution completely. Graeber and Wengrow (2021) have very important new anthropological insights to propose, especially about what they highlight as an indigenous American critique of European political and economic tendencies in the Americas and in Europe. As mentioned in chapter 1, they introduce us to the writing of early 18th Century Baron Lahontan, deputy Governor-General of French Canada, who has preserved the reproachful words of the Wyandot (Huron) philosopher-statesman, Kandiaronk (1703), on the inhumanity of the French, whose "distinctions of 'mine' and 'thine'" and love of money were seen as undergirding French bloodthirst and their propensity towards tyranny (Graeber and Wengrow 2021, 54-55; numbers in parenthesis hereafter refer to this volume). Americans of European descent today need to know that the Wyandots considered themselves better than the French, that they lived peaceably with greater ease and comfort, were more generous and hospitable, treated their children better, and benefitted from having women in leadership roles. Much the same case in this indigenous critique, including reference to Baron Lahontan and the "mine and thine" statement, had been made by anthropologist Jack Weatherford (1988) thirty years earlier. His work is not mentioned by Graeber and Wengrow though they do argue strenuously on their own that anthropology needs to value in particular this critique by indigenous Americans:

> What we are suggesting is that indigenous doctrines of individual liberty, mutual aid, and political equality, which made such an impression on French Enlightenment thinkers, were ...the product of a specific political history: a history in which questions of hereditary power, revealed religion, personal freedom, and the independence of women were still very much matters of self-conscious debate. (Graeber and Wengrow, 482)

Like Morgan and Engels, Graeber and Wengrow recount this history in terms of anthropological studies of the woodland Iroquois Confederation of the 17th Century. As context, they add descriptions of the urban Mississippians of Cahokia of the 10th to 12th Centuries. They juxtapose the proto-democratic politics of the Iroquoian Wyandots over against the authoritarian and hierarchal Cahokians, whose mound-building culture had an upper class that possessed a pronounced sense of sovereignty. This offers us a serious and exciting new historical understanding. Their book is worth it for its stunning proposition about Iroquoian protest alone, though this is evocative, not definitive, speculative and debatable. They also turn our attention importantly and correctly also towards what we can learn from a monumental and grand city, that was without lords or overlords, Teotihuacan in Mexico, with its project of massive classless social housing supporting communal social life.

Their volume becomes problematic and distressing, however, when it moves to a broad criticism of lines of reasoning and evidence having to do with the world's earliest types of societies composed of gatherers and hunters, i.e. small peaceful egalitarian partnership communities. Feminist philosopher/anthropologist Riane Eisler's *The Chalice and the Blade* (1987) introduced the term "partnership power" to describe cultural patterns in which men and women have different roles, yet these are *not* unequal. Eisler relies on studies by James Mellaart (1975) and Maria Gimbutas (1991) of paleolithic cultures and cultures even after the advent of agriculture (in Knossos and Çatalhöyük) in which all persons were more alike than different. Similar qualities of solidarity and partnership power generally characterize human relationships in studies of the gathering and hunting societies, prior to what Eisler criticizes as the later appearance of dominator power. Douglas P. Fry and Geneviève Souillac (2017) have reported research findings that resonate with Eisler under the title "The Original Partnership Societies: Evolved Propensities for Equality, Prosociality, and Peace:"

> [W]e are now at the threshold of an evolutionary paradigm shift that fully recognizes how cooperation, sharing, caring, reconciliation, and restraint against violence also have strong evolutionary bases [de Waal 2009; Fry 2012; Fry et al. 2010; Fuentes 2004; Hrdy 2009; Verbeek 2008]. (Fry and Souillac 2017, 2)
>
> On the basis of the extant nomadic forager data, it seems likely that humans have in fact evolved predilections for using restraint against lethal aggression; developed species-typical inclinations to empathize, care, share, and cooperate in prosocial activities ranging from communal childcare to the quest for food; engaged

in reciprocal exchanges of goods and services which resulted in net gains for the participants; favored nonviolent conflict resolution and avoidance over violence; employed social control mechanisms to maintain cooperation, equality, and peaceful social life; and respected the personal autonomy of the individual [Fry 2006; 2012; Fry & Szala 2013; Hrdy 2009]. (Fry and Souillac 2017, 3–4.)

Nowak (2011) recently dubs human beings "SuperCooperators" and reviews multiple lines of evidence as to why cooperation actually represents the centerpiece on the human evolutionary table (see also Dyble et al., 2015). Obviously, humans possess the capacity for competition, cruelty, and violence, but a growing corpus of evidence shows that human nature is much less violent and selfish than has long been presumed under the traditional evolutionary paradigm [de Waal 2009; Ferguson 2011; Fry 2006; Hart & Sussman 2009; 2011; Nowak 2011]. (Fry and Souillac 2017, 2).

The work of Eisler, Fry and Souillac stressing the egalitarianism and concord in early human societies is not explicitly addressed by Graeber and Wengrow. Instead, their criticisms land with greatest force upon Marshall Sahlins's "The Original Affluent Society." Graeber and Wengrow deplore that "Sahlins's essay [is] perhaps the last truly great example of that genre of 'speculative prehistory' invented by Rousseau ...." (Graeber and Wengrow, 136).

Graeber completed his dissertation under Sahlins, and he and Wengrow even add an oddly paradoxical disclaimer "[I]t's worth saying that the broad picture Sahlins presented appears to be correct" as they overwhelm his work with irrelevancies and indignities. Any discussion of the actual results of Sahlins's appraisal of primary source materials on early societies is displaced by a purported demystification of Sahlins's Rousseauian or Marxist "mythology." They believe they have thus invalidated Sahlin's "speculative prehistory" and have turned "social evolution on its head" (Graeber and Wengrow, 141).

Their criticisms actually emerge from a 1980s postmodern philosophical backlash that developed in some conservative quarters against the theoretical radicalism of the 1960s. The 'postmodern turn' was characteristically skeptical of historical materialism, bidding farewell to Marxism and the Left for employing ostensibly grand narratives, linear progress, material infrastructures of social formations, and historical necessity in philosophical and scientific explanation altogether. As fascinating as many of their findings are, they do not honestly invalidate anthropology's hitherto well-developed understanding of socio-cultural change, especially since current practitioners know that knotty factors can lead to regression and *de*volution. Postmodernism evaded serious theoretical explanation by criticizing nearly all received wisdom and conventional science as being only comprised of language games and/or myth-making. It is now itself quite extensively discredited for having characterized knowledge *not* as knowledge, but as bias and preconception. Thus, in the postmodern view, long-entrenched habits of speaking with regard to the "State of Nature" and "Childhood of Humanity" are mere "Semantic Snares and Metaphysical Mirages" (Graeber and Wengrow, 247). They proudly proclaim these will collapse with due consideration of actual evidence.

Engels's *Origin of the Family, Private Property and the State* also receives a postmodern rebuff in a lengthy Graeber and Wengrow chapter: "The State Has No Origin" (Graeber and Wengrow, 359-440). So too, modes of production are rejected as explanations of social stratification: "Why Even Very Sophisticated Researchers Still Find Ways to Cling to the Idea that Social Inequality has an 'Origin'" (Graeber and Wengrow, 85). Inequality and property relations simply drop away as analytical social concerns for Graeber and Wengrow, displaced by higher priority issues of individual liberty and personal freedom. Engels's notion of primitive communism is also casually de-materialized and recast as a "baseline" communism that "applies in all societies" where any decent person would help a drowning person if asked to throw them a rope [!] (Graeber and Wengrow, 47).

Graeber's and Wengrow's explicit goal is to "lay down foundations for a new world history." They present nothing like the materialist critical theory of society of Charles Woolfson's *Labor Theory of Culture* (1982) or the primatological insights of Frans de Waal's *The Bonobo and the Atheist: In Search of Humanism Among the Primates* (2013), in place of the Rousseau-Hobbes oscillations, they fetishize and mock. Their work curiously acknowledges the tradition of V. Gordon Childe's venerable *Man Makes Himself* ([1936] 1951). This volume earned its reputation because it *did* hold that human beings "learned to cooperate and act together in getting their livelihood" (Childe, 48), i.e. through common work. Childe also embraced as progress successive modes of production. Graeber and Wengrow say they wish to invoke his intellectual spirit, but this is rather incongruous with their own anti-foundational postmodernism. They agree with Childe as do I: "We are projects of collective self-creation" (Graeber and Wengrow, 9). However, they offer an account of human history *without political economy, without a critique of the structural drivers of unequal life chances, without a materialist theory of power* that can hold accountable the predatory enforcement of extractive and exploitative economic relations grounded in the substantive differentials between propertied and non-propertied segments of the population. They deflect critical attention away from central concerns of radical anthropology and social theory, namely equality and political economy, communal caring for commonwork and commonwealth, towards a conservative redefinition of freedom in terms of individual autonomy and personal liberty that would be compatible even with forms of vast social inequality and massive ownership of private income-producing property. This is the axial political quarrel between philosophical anarchism and historical materialism. Graeber and Wengrow's purported "new history of humanity" adheres to postmodern premises fallaciously belittling as "romanticism" the research conclusions that Sahlins, Engels, Eisler, Fry and Souillac, and others have long found to be especially worthy of note in early human societies, namely political egalitarianism, partnership, and peace.

Ecological materialism as naturalism as critical realism

Roy Bhaskar's philosophical project develops a dialectical and naturalist ontological critique of reality and challenge to empiricism and positivism in social science. He has made an extraordinary impact in philosophical circles today discussing this multifaceted problematic in ten major books, written in two different stages. The first five volumes on naturalism and critical realism, written between 1975 and 1993, aim to clarify compellingly how our endeavors to know and explain the real world may transpire soundly. In my estimation, these volumes extend and deepen the naturalism and realism of classical Marxist philosophy (historical materialism and dialectics) in a manner that demonstrates the validity of critical realism and naturalism as a unified philosophy of science. This prospect is especially exciting in its appeal and promise, yet his writing is immensely difficult. What I get from it seems particularly enlightening and useful. I acknowledge that my understanding is partial, yet what I have learned is of great value. Several secondary sources have immeasurably helped (Andrew Collier, Margaret Archer, and Sean Sayers); here I rely chiefly on Merwyn Hartwig (2020), Savita Singh (2020), and Morteza Ardebili (2016). Clearly I will have missed substantive subtleties, but my account may be useful nonetheless.

Bhaskar was intellectually dissatisfied with philosophy's antifoundationalist postmodern turn, as well as mainstream scientific realism (empiricism, behaviorism, body/mind split). He became the advocate of a new form of critical realism (beyond that of Roy Wood Sellers's *Evolutionary Naturalism* 1922) that he considered necessary to shed new light on the theory of reality, i.e. the ontology, undergirding both science and social science. Critical realism also has implications for ethics.

Mainstream realism's empiricist reductionism and or mechanical materialism is challenged by critical realism in that it explains *ontological* issues (i.e. our understanding of the material foundations of the natural world) in a new way. Bhaskar's chief contribution is his conception that the natural world is a *layered* or *stratified* composite reality: the empirical layer, the actual event layer, and a generative layer; all three must be considered for a comprehensive understanding of nature and the real. Our empirical observations, while factual, do not represent the real world wholly, but only partially. Reality is deeper and is composed of generative processes and structures that produce manifest phenomena. These processes and structures, while not visible, are knowable. They are open rather than closed systems, and they contain event possibilities that may be actualized or *not* actualized. Reality is composed of the empirical, the actual, and the underlying structural generative mechanisms (the dynamics of nature). The generative layer gives rise to the actual events and to the empirical phenomena; some real possibilities remain absent. Real systems are open, having multiple dimensions and depth. Consciousness "...is a complex or set of powers ...historically emergent from and present only in association with (certain complex forms of) matter" (Bhaskar [1979] 2015, 98).

Likewise critical realism understands human existence in a manner that challenges the methodological individualism of much contemporary social science, especially economics. Bhaskar sees the subject matter of sociology as the *relations* that obtain between people not simply the agency of individuals, even masses of individuals. In this view, societies are irreducible to people, irreducible to data points along a supply curve or a demand curve, and irreducible to a "rational" utilitarian calculation of advantage. As with Aristotle, Marx, and Durkheim *nothing* done by any individual is *not* social. As the *zoon politikon*, humanity is social in speech, labor, wisdom, and politics. Methodological individualism has hindered us from appreciating what is essential to our freely flourishing well-being, and thus it has contributed to our alienation. Bhaskar seeks to emancipate social theory such that it might transform rather than reproduce contemporary social structures of domination. Here he has a particular affinity to the philosophical designs of Herbert Marcuse and Karl Marx. With regard to our labor and modes of subsistence, he says:

> [P]eople in their social activity must perform a double function: they must not only make social products, but make the conditions of their making, that is reproduce (or to a greater or lesser extent transform) the structures governing their substantive activities of production. (Bhaskar [1979] 2015, 38)

Social structures are understood as coercive, but also enabling. Within reality, the "is" and the "ought" interpenetrate dialectically. There is a realism rather than a relativism in ethics and politics.

Reality and Its Depths is the title Roy Bhaskar and Savita Singh have selected to indicate what they emphasize as the subject matter of the recorded series of interviews between them during late 2001 and early 2002. Transcriptions of these recordings have been skillfully edited for publication by Mervyn Hartwig. After 2000, Bhaskar's theorizing entered a second stage that followed until his death in 2014 in which he fused critical realism with a distinctively materialist reading of elements of Vedic ontology. Bhaskar called this recombination *metaReality*—a step that cost him many former adherents.

Savita Singh is a much-published feminist poet. Born in India, she is a professor in the School of Gender and Development Studies at the Indira Gandhi National Open University in New Delhi. She is a scholar of critical social theory in a version she calls "creative critical theory," and is active in the International Herbert Marcuse Society.

As we have already seen Herbert Marcuse is renowned for his description of the pitfalls of living as a *One-Dimensional Man* (1964). This meant living an alienated and damaged life entranced in a world of fabricated consumerist satisfactions devoid of any awareness of society's profound contradictions or humanity's fuller and more authentic potentialities. Marcuse's critical social theory thus has much in common with Bhaskar's critical realism. For example, in *One-Dimensional Man* (1964) he argues *for the historical reality of universals*. The theory of the underlying reality and historical substance of universals is analogous in some ways to Bhaskar's generative layer of reality. "The universal comprehends in one idea the possibilities which are realized and at the same time arrested in reality" (Marcuse [1964] 1991, 210). To Marcuse, discourse in advanced industrial societies is reduced to operational terms. It is oriented toward the priorities of a commercialized, profit-oriented political economy. He writes with a certain poetic sensibility for reality's complexities and ironies: this operationalism comprises a "comfortable, smooth, reasonable, democratic *unfreedom*" (Marcuse [1964] 1991, 1, emphasis added). Historically real universals provide a context that transforms our understanding of actuality and empirical reality:

> The larger context of experience, this real empirical experience today is still that of gas chambers and concentration camps, of Hiroshima and Nagasaki, of American Cadillacs and German Mercedes, of the Pentagon and the Kremlin, of the nuclear cities and the Chinese communes, of Cuba, of brainwashing, of massacres. But the real empirical world is also that in which all these things are taken for granted or forgotten or repressed or unknown, in which people are free. (Marcuse [1964] 1991, 180)

Savita Singh offers the following comment on Bhaskar's noticeable relationship to Marxism: "People who don't know a lot about critical realism tend to think that it's an extension of the critical theory of Adorno and Horkheimer. But it's different, it seems more closely aligned with Marxism" (Singh 2020, 19). To which Bhaskar replies, "Yes. But I think critical theory and the Frankfurt School is extremely interesting... The first generation of critical theorists ...[was] ... still engaged in a project, which they saw as a project of emancipation, or revolutionary praxis .... Habermas completely dissociated himself from any real vision of a better society other than one which would be produced through communicative interaction" (2020, 19-20). Bhaskar, to my knowledge, never refers explicitly to Marcuse.

In spite of several references to Marx's failures and inadequacies, however, he *did* during the sixties self-identify as a Marxist in theory

(Bhaskar 2020, 14) and he does lionize Marx for his analysis of commodity exchange in *Capital:* "the crucial transaction in this realm appears to be an exchange of equivalents, but it actually is not. It is not an exchange, it is an appropriation... This scientific realist approach informs Marx's understanding ...of the empirical and received world" (2020, 57). "Marx himself was in important ways implicitly a critical realist avant la lettre" (2020, 237). The point of philosophy for Bhaskar, as for Marx and Marcuse, is to make the deeper levels of reality intellectually visible.

Reality and Its Depths serves primarily as an orientation to the several dimensions of Bhaskar's critical realism. However, the record of the conversation of Bhaskar with Savita Singh even more importantly discloses much about Bhaskar's personal life and his political positions rarely discussed elsewhere. Savita Singh begins her exploration of Bhaskar's life and work with questions about his childhood and his student years. Bhaskar discloses that on account of his Indian heritage, flagged by his name, he was bullied as a child in the extremely racist society of Britain in the 1950s. He was also bullied by his authoritarian father. This abuse, he says, gave him a lifelong sense of solidarity with the oppressed.

The first half of this record of the conversation between Bhaskar and Singh culminates in the book's fifth chapter under the headings of "Recovering Truth" and "Escaping from Mystification (2020, 83)." Echoing Marcuse on the historical truth of universals, Bhaskar's recovery of truth is equally political and radical.

> Our world, the planet, which is the habitat of the human species, is in ecological crisis and chronic economic imbalance and is afflicted by alienation and anomie, and many other things that threaten its survival, including the ever-continuing possibility of a holocaust .... No century before the twentieth has known more killing ...as a result of conscious intentional decisions at the level of military chiefs of staff and governments. No century has seen more killing of civilians by both armies and other people. (Bhaskar 2020, 83)

The road to this recovery of truth may seem to be a fairly improbable result of Bhaskar's first steps toward a counter-positivist theory of the generative systems undergirding empirical data in *A Realist Theory of Science* (1975) and *The Possibility of Naturalism* (1979). Most discussions of these works eschew explicit political considerations. Savita Singh's particular techniques of inquiry have, in contrast, drawn-out many new and weighty disclosures from Bhaskar himself.

Bhaskar challenges what he calls the "taboo" against a theory of reality—an ontology—within conventional accounts of positivism and hermeneutics, the reigning philosophies of science and social science. He criticizes the actualism of both mainstream natural science and conventional sociology: "describing the world in terms of the prevailing pattern of events" (2020, 79) and being utterly complacent about current affairs and conditions rather than understanding what the prevailing order negates and renders absent in them. He regards usual scientific perspectives as being officially agnostic about the nature of reality as such. Empiricism denies the existence and the reality of the unseen causal nexus in favor of observable constant correlations of theoretically discrete phenomena. Hermeneutics likewise eschews an objective account of the make-up of the social world, in and of itself, in favor of a study of the subjective meanings we attach to what we observe. Bhaskar, on the other hand, provides an account of the logic of scientific discovery (2020, 27) that reveals a "plausible picture ...of how reality works to explain the causal law" (2020, 27). Bhaskar emphasizes the "intransitive" (2020, 28) nature of this reality: "being exists apart from our knowledge" of it (2020, 35). Critical realism is presented as bringing out the fuller truth of positivism and hermeneutics through a greater appreciation of the whole, "transcendental," obdurate, independent nature of a dynamic historical and material reality. In Bhaskar's view ethics is likewise not a matter of subjective values (2020, 38), but real universalizable virtues such as loving-kindness and caring (2020, 185).

Bhaskar's secular reverence for materialism's metaReality

The second half of the conversation between Bhaskar and Singh, produced primarily for an Indian audience (2020, 55), focuses on his philosophy after a period of lengthy and severe illness (broken shoulder, multiple colds) and after having been scammed by criminal New Agers of much of his savings. A philosophical turn has taken place, and Bhaskar's next several books slowly develop a generic concept of God, as a power within our lives, without identifying any particulars, knowing full well that it would be misunderstood and that he would be pilloried for it.

Savita Singh is deeply skeptical if not appalled: "...finding God, what does it do? I really want to understand this. Look at the practices of Hindu society, look at the practices of Islamic society" (2020, 113). Bhaskar contends that his Vedic perspective can lead to a further transcendental deepening of critical realism (2020, 102), rather than to anything like religious sectarianism. He describes his spirituality as *secular, new, and bold* (2020, 215). He sees himself as "breaking the taboo put on discussing God by very important people in the West..." (2020, 115). At the same time, he argues that his revised theory of *metaReality* can offer a rapprochement between East and West philosophically, as an extension of critical realism which continues to be "reconcilable with science" (2020, 106). The traditional Vedic concepts of "smaller self" and "bigger self" help him to recapture a classical Hindu perspective on the human person and the human material condition. In this view each of us has our personal smaller self (which we identify with our name, birthplace, age, current residence, etc.); but we also partake in the larger universal species essence (what Marx in the 1844 Manuscripts called our *Gattungswesen*). In Vedic philosophy, this species being is our *atman*, which we need to aspire to know (2020, 210). Additionally, our lives are enmeshed within an extensive web of relationships, such that we are all related within "the cosmic envelope, which binds everything" (2020, 110). This also seems an enlargement of Marx's materialist view that humans are an ensemble of social relations and that our lives depend upon our metabolism with nature. "[M]atter evolves to the point where it eventually gives rise to, first life, and then consciousness. [This] is a materialist view" (2020, 111).

Bhaskar also theorizes in Vedic fashion that every human being has a real "ground state" (2020, 65) in which we spontaneously perform creative and loving, right actions. Ethical understanding and partnership behavior is said to be intrinsic to our generic nature as humans. Furthermore, "... saving yourself and ourselves from this social crisis that we are all in won't wait until you develop the theory [of human emancipation]. Rather, you need to work on, pare your-self down and do what you feel is correct, operating from your ground state in as pure and clear a way as you can" (2020, 192).

Anthropologists Riane Eisler and Richard Leakey and primatologist Frans de Waal have emphasized the extemporaneous cooperation and caring featured in the earliest human societies. This fostered communal interdependence and an awareness of the customary power of partnership. Communal customs and behaviors had the capacity to ensure survival.

So Bhaskar's theory of the ground state may also be elaborating the fundamental human capacity to care in a materialist and dialectical fashion.

Savita Singh thoughtfully follows up by asking Bhaskar to extend commentary explicitly to the "Question of Women" (2020, 181). He begins by citing the basic economic circumstance of women under capitalism: "women's labor is not recognized" (2020, 181), even though it is necessary for the reproduction of the social order. He emphasizes that women should instead be credited "in their role as a binding force within the family ...unconditionally manifesting holistic, intuitive, tacit, totalizing, noninstrumental, loving, creativity" (2020, 182). But here he is beginning to romanticize women's roles. He asserts that the characteristic labor of women (childcare, care for the sick, care for the family and community) is a prefiguration of the good society. He praises women as spiritual teachers in India (2020, 183) and as representing the soul in Islam (2020, 184). Savita Singh is compelled to challenge him: "I do think that your view of Hindu women is very flabby and lofty ...[i]f you think that women are very much in touch with their ground state—" (2020, 187). She had already expressed her exasperation at the practices of Islamic societies today.

Bhaskar was clearly making an effort to understand the oppression of women, yet within limitations, he was not equipped to acknowledge. Savita Singh advised that further research, learning, and discussion is needed to adequately evaluate the power of the ground state and theory of *metaReality* to understand the condition of women. Her ability to elicit frank, intimate, and thoughtful responses from Roy Bhaskar on all of this is extraordinary.

Bhaskar's early work developing critical realism is quite ingenious, and his influence substantial. His emphasis on ontology importantly expanded and deepened our understanding of historical materialism and the philosophy of science. His conversation with Savita Singh offers readers a first-hand personal encounter with one of philosophy's most evocative contemporary voices. It provides a rare glimpse of Bhaskar on Bhaskar before and after his Vedic turn. His identification of his perspective on Vedic philosophy with his secular and material philosophical commitments is not as unsettling as it is both curious, thought-provoking, and plausible.

Sensuous living labor is my term for the essential manner of being human that I find theorized within the materialist conception of Marx and Marcuse. Sensuous living labor is the substrate of our ontology as humans. It is the foundation of our affective and intellectual capacities (and vulnerabilities), bio-ecologically developed within history. As a species we have endured because of our sensuous appreciation of our emergent powers: the power to live cooperatively; to create, communicate, and care communally within what I call a *commonwealth*.

Marx referred to this as our species-being *(Gattungswesen)*, with potentialities that may have been socially actualized or arrested under any definite set of economic and political circumstances. When arrested, our alienation as humans from our larger self is gauged by having our labor exploited, being in competition with others for work, being excluded from the decision-making processes at work, and being deprived of a life of freedom and dignity. Realizing the promise of our human selves is also the measure of what is sanctified as worthy of respect in the indigenous view of Dan Wildcat. An assessment of such sanctity can only be made by a larger view encompassing the well-being of the nature-culture nexus of our extensive ecological kinship relations. This means in the context of our larger self: our lives expressed over seven generations, three before us and three after us, as this self has been shaped by the past and is shaping the future (Wildcat 2009, 99, 125-126).

We need in the end to return to Eisler: two logics have characterized the patterns of social life on earth, the partnership model and the dominator model. She has coined the word "gylany" to characterize the partnership model with regard to the roles of women (gy) and men (an). When these roles are different, yet not unequal, she characterizes the social circumstances as *gylanic*. In contrast, rigid male domination within the social order is said to be *androcracy*. She stresses that even though androcracy has proved adaptive, this does *not* mean it is a higher development. Instead, it is regressive and represents a tendency toward devolution. She speaks of "... Western culture ...[as] ...a bloody five-thousand year dominator detour" with the advent of 'might makes right' masculinist power (Eisler 1987, xxiii). Yet it is also true that some agricultural societies were unstratified, egalitarian, and not class divided. In the art of Minoan Crete, there is no idealization of warfare. So too, in palaeolithic art, there is an absence of armed might and a representation rather of the strength of nature's most impressive creatures of the commons. Butterflies and serpents represented the powers of metamorphosis and regeneration. Serpents, like those intertwined in the physician's caduceus, symbolize health and well-being.

Eisler and Tamara Agha-Jaffar (2002) highlight the work of feminist historian Gerda Lerner in *The Creation of Patriarchy* (1986). Lerner maps out the historical transformation of the female as the emblem of the generative powers of earth to the male as progenitor in ancient Greek mythology. Similarly in the monotheistic Pentateuch:

> [T]hrough [the] unique act of reversing the natural order of creation, a reversal that had never before or since been duplicated, a male not only "gives birth" to a female—thereby establishing his precedence over her—but he has sovereignty over her .... by virtue of the fact that he is given authority to name her. (Agha-Jaffar 2002, 41)

Eisler is troubled by yet another androcratic business-dominated solution to today's problems of mass precarity. As she sees it, when politicians tell us that business investment and the free market will bring prosperity, the material needs of millions are ignored, minimized, and denied. Elected male leaders are likely to be heading us toward a "totalitarian solution" emphasizing violence and strong-man rule (Eisler 1987, 179-18).

Herbert Marcuse sees a radical socialist feminism as the needed counterforce against androcratic neofascism. Ecological materialism is bringing forth the radical visions of both ecosocialism and feminism to bear on a new critical understanding of nature, society, and thought: an ecology of commonwealth, an ecology of care.

Works cited

Agha-Jaffar, Tamara. 2002. *Demeter and Persephone: Lessons from a Myth*. London: McFarland & Co.

Ardebili, Morteza. 2016. "Reorienting Socio-Economic Theory—A Critique of Ontological Foundations," in Charles Reitz (ed). *Reflections on Science and the Human Material Condition*. Kansas City, MO: Kindle Direct Publishing.

Bhaskar, Roy, Savita Singh, Mervyn Hartwig. [2001] 2020. *Reality and Its Depths: A Conversation Between Savita Singh and Roy Bhaskar*. Singapore: Springer.

Bhaskar, Roy. [1979] 2015. *The Possibility of Naturalism: A Philosophical Critique of the Contemporary Human Sciences*. London and New York: Routledge.

Brennan, Jason. 2007. "Dominating Nature," *Environmental Values*, Vol. 16. No. 4. Childe, V. Gordon. [1936] 1951. *Man Makes Himself*. New York: The New American Library.

de Waal, Frans. 2013. *The Bonobo and the Atheist: In Search of Humanism among the Primates*. New York: W.W. Norton.

de Waal, Frans. 2009. *The Age of Empathy*. New York: Random House.

Deloria, Jr. Vine. [1992] 1995. "Afterword" to *America in 1492* edited by Alvin Josephy in *Voices of Diversity*, edited by Pat Andrews. Guilford, CT: The Dushkin Publishing Group.

Eisler, Riane. 2007. *The Real Wealth of Nations: Creating a Caring Economics*. San Francisco: BK Publishing.
Eisler, Riane. 1987. *The Chalice and the Blade*. New York: HarperCollins.
Engels, Frederick. [1888] 1974. *Ludwig Feuerbach and the Outcome of Classical German Philosophy*. New York: International Publishers.
Engels, Frederick. [1884] 1973. *The Origin of the Family, Private Property and the State*. New York: International Publishers.
Engels, Frederick. [1872-1882] 1973. *Dialectics of Nature*. New York International Publishers.
Fry, Douglas P. and Geneviève Souillac. 2017. "The Original Partnership Societies: Evolved Propensities for Equality, Prosociality, and Peace," *Interdisciplinary Journal of Partnership Studies*, Vol. 4, No. I, March.
Gimbutas, Maria. 1981. "The Image of Woman in Prehistoric Art" in *The Quarterly Review of Archeology*. December.
Graeber, David and David Wengrow. 2021. *The Dawn of Everything: A New History of Humanity*. New York: Ferrar, Straus and Giroux.
Hartwig, Mervyn, Savita Singh, Roy Bhaskar. [2001] 2020. *Reality and Its Depths: A Conversation Between Savita Singh and Roy Bhaskar*. Singapore: Springer.
Lenin, V.I. [1914] 1972. *Philosophical Notebooks*. Moscow: Progress.
Leopold, Aldo. [1949] 1966. *A Sand County Almanac*. New York: Oxford University Press.
Leopold, Aldo. [1942] 1991. "The Role of Wildlife in Liberal Education" in Susan L. Flader and J. Baird Callicott (Eds.). *The River of the Mother of God and Other Essays by Aldo Leopold*. Madison, WI: University of Wisconsin Press.
Leopold, Aldo. [1953] 1993. *Round River*. New York: Oxford University Press.
Leopold, Aldo. [1953] 1966. "The Land Ethic," in *A Sand County Almanac*. New York: Oxford University Press.
Lukács, George. [1924] 1971. *History and Class Consciousness*. Cambridge, MA: MIT Press.
Marcuse, Herbert. [1964] 1991. *One-Dimensional Man: Studies in the Ideology of Advanced Industrial Society*. Boston, MA: Beacon Press.
Marcuse, Herbert. 1978. *The Aesthetic Dimension*. Boston, MA: Beacon Press.
Marcuse, Herbert. [1932] 1973. "The Foundation of Historical Materialism," in his *Studies in Critical Philosophy*. Boston, MA: Beacon Press.
Mellaart, James. 1975. *The Neolithic of the Near East*. New York: Scribner.
Nolan, Patrick and Gerhard Lenski. 2011. *Human Societies*. Boulder, CO: Paradigm Publishers.
Plekhanov, George. [1897, 1940] 2020. *Essays in Historical Materialism*. Paris: Foreign Languages Press.
Sellars, Roy Wood. 1922. *Evolutionary Naturalism*. Chicago: Open Court Publishing.
Powers, Richard. 2019. *The Overstory*. New York: W.W. Norton.
Simmons, Michael L., Jr. 2019. "Dialectic: Philosophy of Education's Missing Essence," conference paper at State University of New York at Buffalo, n.d. in Charles Reitz, *Ecology and Revolution: Herbert Marcuse and the Challenge of a New World System Today*. New York: Routledge.
Singh, Savita, Roy Bhaskar, Mervyn Hartwig. [2001] 2020. *Reality and Its Depths: A Conversation Between Savita Singh and Roy Bhaskar*. Singapore: Springer.
Smith, Paul Chaat. 2009. *Everything You Know About Indians Is Wrong*. Minneapolis: University of Minnesota Press.

Wildcat, Daniel R. 2009. *Red Alert! Saving the Planet with Indigenous Knowledge*. Golden, CO: Fulcrum Publishers.
Weatherford, Jack. 1988. *Indian Givers: How the Indians of the Americas Transformed the World*. New York: Fawcett/Columbine.
Wohlleben, Peter. 2015. *The Hidden Life of Trees, What they Feel, How They Communicate, Discoveries from a Secret World*. Berkeley, CA: Greystone Books.
Woolfson, Charles. 1982. *The Labor Theory of Culture: A Re-examination of Engels's Theory of Human Origins*. London: Routledge and Kegan Paul.

8
Critical Political Economy
(with Stephen Spartan)

Carbon and oxygen molecules are not hurt or treated unjustly by burning fossil fuels and producing carbon dioxide. When the environmental crisis is studied only from the point of view of the natural sciences and engineering, the situation is conceived as a technical problem with a technical fix. It's thought to be a largely unintentional misfortune, brought about through a kind of innocent dereliction. This according to emeritus German philosopher Ulrich Ruschig, whose noteworthy recent volume, *Die Befreiung der Natur: Zum Verhältnis von Natur und Freiheit bei Herbert Marcuse* (The Emancipation of Nature: Herbert Marcuse on the Relationship Between Nature and Freedom, 2020) offers a necessary contrast to conventional discussions of the mere scientific data of climate change, etc., highlighting instead the necessity of critical political economy in understanding the origins of today's ecological crisis. Especially now, when environmental catastrophe appears inevitable and human survival is a threat of momentous public concern, professor Ruschig emphasizes with Marcuse and Marx that the origins of these threats are to be found in the way social production is organized, more precisely in the capitalist mode of production. Several of Ruschig's inspired yet stinging insights seem to 'sing the petrified circumstances their own tune and make them dance.' They serve as an apt and vocal accompaniment to the detailed theoretical discussion of political economy my economics colleague Stephen Spartan and I wish to unfold in this chapter,

    Ruschig explains, for example, that capitalists understand that they can reduce payrolls in every sector of production if they minimize the cost of essential foodstuffs. This has given us the industrial food system: confined animal feed operations (CAFOs) for beef and for fast food to feed the nation; hormones in the dairy industry, supersizing bovine udders, leading to early onset of puberty in young female consumers of this product. Ruschig reminds us profit maximization will stop at nothing: open-pit coal and copper and cobalt mines polluting aquafers; genetic engineering with biodiversity loss; fishing the seas barren of Atlantic halibut and salmon. When it comes to the exploitation of labor, global capitalism identifies the "cost" of labor as the cost of reproducing (feeding, housing clothing, educating) the labor force as the labor force. The macroeconomic payroll is profitably reduced when the cost of a subsistence living for the labor force is minimized. This has meant shifting production to lowwage regions like Mexico or China. Revenues above subsistence are retained by business owners as an income flow, which they divide with their financiers and investors. Here capitalists say their money works for them, and incomeproducing properties claim a disproportionate share of the global GNP. The world's labor force is never fully remunerated for the societal wealth it has collectively created. Capitalism is the system in which investment-ready private property, i.e. money, is invested to make more money, and investors, bankers, and financiers control political power. Capitalism cuts nature to pieces in order to monetize the sale of its parts. It dominates both nature and human life. Ecosocialists on the other hand understand the metabolic interdependence of the human species and nature and defend the notion that nature is to be protected in its own right *and* in order to protect ourselves. Today, like the labor force, nature also requires liberation.

The roots of crisis: The capital-labor antagonism

Stephen Spartan and I stress that corporate globalization is intensifying social inequality and cultural polarization worldwide. Increasing globalization correlates directly with growing inequality both within and between nations (Sernau, 2001, 52-55). This global polarization and growing immiseration have brought to an end what Herbert Marcuse (1964) theorized in *One-Dimensional Man* as the totally integrated and completely administered political universe of the liberal welfare/warfare state. Neoliberalism has replaced this "comfortable, smooth, democratic unfreedom" (Marcuse, 1964, 1) with something more openly vicious. Peter McLaren and others call it *predatory* culture. Michael Apple (2001, 18) describes it as "capitalism with the gloves off." David Korten (1995, 195) writes similarly of predatory finance: "The global economy is not, however, a healthy economy. In all too many instances, it rewards *extractive* investors who do not create wealth but simply extract and concentrate existing wealth. The extractive investor's gain is at the expense of other individuals or the society at large."

Douglas Dowd's *Inequality and the Global Economic Crisis* (2009) offers a systemic overview:

> Capitalism is, and must be, not only an economic but also a political and social system whose processes go well beyond production and trade for profit.... Britain was the first to seek and achieve the necessary depth and breadth of the processes *systemic* to capitalism: 1) expansion, 2) exploitation, and 3) oligarchic rule .... The interaction of capitalism's "imperatives" has inexorably produced intermittent crises and threats to its very survival, most destructively the socio-economic upheavals and wars of the twentieth century. (Dowd 2009, 11)

The imperative of exploitation is intensifying today through the "race to the bottom" as capitalism searches the globe for the lowest wage labor markets. Inequalities of income and wealth have been increasing over the last three decades in the United States, a tendency established well before the 2008 economic fiasco in the banking and real estate industries. As we shall see, middlerange households lost the most. Decades of labor speedup facilitated enormous amounts of capital accumulation and the intensification of poverty.[1]

In a tendency that today has only gotten worse, the sharpest wealth declines in the U.S. have hit minority families.[2] Hispanic households suffered asset losses of 66 percent between 2005 and 2009; wealth in Asian American households fell by 54 percent; African American households dropped 53 percent. During 2011, compensation to those in Wall Street's

---

1 See *The New York Times*, July 11, 2011, "Weak Results are Projected for Wall Street" p. B-1. However, by March 8, 2013 Wall Street was again flying high, with a nominal rise to pre-2007 levels, though still 10 percent below that when adjusted for inflation. See Floyd Norris, "A Long Way Back for Dow Industrials" *The New York Times*, March 8, 2013, p. 3-3. See Monika Bauerlein and Clara Jeffery, "Speedup. All Work and No Pay," the cover story in *Mother Jones* July and August 2011, pp. 18-25. Also, Ben Agger, *Speeding Up Fast Capitalism* (Boulder, CO: Paradigm Publishers 2004). See also "Companies Spend on Equipment, Not Workers," *The New York Times*, June 10, 2011, p. A-1. Sabrina Tavernise, "Poverty Reaches 52-Year Peak, Government Says," *The New York Times*, September 14, 2011, p. A-1.
2 Sabrina Tavernise, "Recession Study Finds Hispanics Hit Hardest: Sharp Wealth Decline," *New York Times*, July 26, 2011, p. A-1. The impact of institutional relationships of racial inequality on wage-related income disparities has been classically demonstrated in the study by Michael Reich, *Racial Inequality* (Princeton: Princeton University Press, 1981). See also Sharon Smith, "Race, Class and 'Whiteness Theory'" *International Socialist Review*, Issue 46, March-April 2006.

financial industry in total rose to near record levels, up 4 percent over 2010,[3] and in October 2012 Wells Fargo bank reported a jump of 22 percent in profits, JP Morgan 34 percent.[4]

A critical examination of these kinds of social dynamics is a vital part of radical pedagogy (McLaren 2015a; 2015b; 1997). Anyone who has grown up in the U.S.A. typically has little awareness of the nature of wealth or the pattern of its distribution in society. We also lack insight into the connection of income flows to relations of capitalist property ownership and the commodification[5] of labor and life. According to *The Washington Post's* piece by Christopher Ingraham reporting on the findings of economist Edward N. Wolff, "The richest 1 percent now owns more of the country's wealth than at any time in the past 50 years" (December 6, 2017).[6] He goes on to report on the unequal distribution of the *total wealth in quintiles of all U.S. households*:

- 90% is held by the wealthiest quintile
- 8% by the second-wealthiest quintile
- 2% by the middle quintile
- 0% by the second-lowest quintile
- –1% by the poorest quintile.

When we first started teaching about forty years ago, the top quintile owned significantly less, 78 percent of the total wealth, and the poorest quintile owned a positive, albeit tiny, percentage (1 percent). The second-wealthiest quintile then had 15 percent of the wealth compared to its 8 percent share today.

This pattern of polarization has also transpired with regard to incomes, over time, such that today "income inequality has soared to the

---

3 Susanne Craig and Ben Protess, "A Bigger Paycheck On Wall St.," *The New York Times*, October 10, 2012, p. B-1
4 Ben Protess, "Wells Fargo Reports a 22 percent Jump in Profit," *The New York Times*, October 13, 2012, p. B-2; Jessica Silver-Greenberg, "Mortgage Lending Helps JP Morgan Profit Rise 34 percent," *The New York Times*, October 13, 2012, p. B-1
5 The word *commodity* originally carried the connotation of something that *accommodated* a basic need or desire; something *commodious*, suitable, fitting, convenient. Marx's *Capital* stresses how and why under capitalism this meaning is distorted and superseded by the connotation of *possessing exchange value* that is more important than *use-value*. The *commodification* of the economy means its deformation toward the *production of exchange values rather than use values* and the new circumstance that *markets govern access* to nearly every and all commodities according to the ability to pay; thus the "fetish character of the commodity" under capitalism, with one's ability to work also becoming a commodity sold in a labor market and exchanged for wage.
6 https://www.washingtonpost.com/news/wonk/wp/2017/12/06/the-richest-1-percent-now-owns more-of-the-countrys-wealth-than-at-any-time-in-the-past-50-years/

highest levels since the Great Depression."[7] "The increase in incomes of the top 1 percent from 2003 to 2005 exceeded total income of the poorest 20 percent of Americans..." (U.S. Budget Office in Dowd 2009, 122). On top of this, in February 2013, Emmanuel Saez of the University of California, Berkeley, reports that during the then-current recovery the incomes of the top 1 percent rose 11.2 percent, while the incomes of the remaining 99 percent fell by 0.4 percent.[8] According to economist Saez and his colleague Thomas Piketty of the Paris School of Economics, the general pattern is this: *about half of all income the economy produces accrues to the top 10 percent of income earners.*[9]

If the facts of increasing economic inequality are largely undisputed, the same may not be said of their social significance. The prevailing views among economists and business utopians, represented in the writings of George Gilder (1993) for example, hold that these inequalities are natural and normal, a positive social good. They signify a ladder of opportunity, and meritocratically reward differences in talent, effort, intelligence, perseverance, etc. In their view, it is precisely the possibility of upward mobility that characterizes a democratic economy.

On the other hand, writers in economics like Dowd (2009) and Stiglitz (2012), in sociology like Macionis (2012, 37-39), and political philosophers like John Rawls (1971) characteristically emphasize the profoundly alienating, unequal, and *un*democratic impacts that such wealth and income maldistribution have on *life chances*. "Life chances" is a technical term in sociology used to indicate the relative access a household has to the society's economic resources: decent housing, health care, education, employment, etc. The greater the wealth in one's household, the greater one's life chances. The less wealth in one's household, the fewer life chances. Life chances (as well as wealth and income) are today being transferred away from the vast majority of households and redistributed to the advantage of the wealthiest. Rawls (1971) has argued that departures from universal equality are in principle departures from social justice, and his views are persuasive in terms of social contract theory and a version of Kant's ethical universalism. One might frame an ingenious thought experiment utilizing his methodology and his concept of the "veil of

---
7 Annie Lowrey, "Costs Seen in Income Inequality," *The New York Times*, October 17, 2012, p. B-1.
8 Annie Lowrey, "Incomes Flat in Recovery, but not for the 1%," *The New York Times*, February 16, 2013, p. B-1
9 Ibid., p. B-4.

ignorance" to demonstrate, through abstract logical analysis alone, the advantage (in terms of the sheer probability of enhancing one's life chances) of making the "blind" choice to be born in a perfectly equal society (where each population quintile owned 20 percent of wealth) rather than in one characterized by the stark lopsidedness in the distribution of wealth and life chances as in the U.S. today. In the latter, four out of five quintiles each owns substantially less than 20 percent; only the top quintile owns more. Nonetheless, the abstract philosophical (i.e. ahistorical and asociological) quality of Rawls's theory renders it oblivious to other issues, especially the important impacts of racial inequality. Arnold

L. Farr, a contemporary Marcusean philosopher with a deep appreciation for the work of Charles Mills, makes a trenchant critique of latent racism even in Rawls, liberal democracy's foremost political theoretician (Farr 2009). Above and beyond Rawls, we shall indicate below the outlines of the socialist labor theory of commonwealth ownership and justice utilized by both Marx and Marcuse and which we contend has a greater material and sociological warrant.

Wealth accumulation and workforce remuneration

Seldom discussed among students (or among faculty) is the question of where wealth comes from or the nature of the relationship of wealth to labor. These issues were first formulated, and for many economists settled without controversy, in the classical economic theory of John Locke and Adam Smith. As is well known, they held that a person's labor is the real source of all wealth and property that one might have the right to call one's own. Locke emphasized the natural equality of human beings and that nature was given to humanity in common:

> Though the earth and all inferior creatures be common to all men, yet every man has a property in his own person; this nobody has any right to but himself. The labor of his body and the work of his hands we may say are properly his. Whatsoever, then, he removes out of the state that nature hath provided and left it in, he hath mixed his labor with, and joined to it something that is his own, and thereby makes it his property. –John Locke, 1690. *An Essay Concerning the True Original Extent and End of Civil Government*, Chapter V, Paragraph #27.

Similarly, Adam Smith held:

> The produce of labor constitutes the natural recompense or wages of labor. In that state of things which preceded both the appropriation of land and the accumulation of stock, *the whole produce of labor belongs to the laborer* .... In the arts and manufactures the greater part of the workmen stand in need of a *master* to advance them the materials of their work, and their wages and maintenance till it be completed. *He shares the produce of* their *labor, or the value which it adds to the materials upon which it is bestowed; and in this share consists his profit.* –Adam Smith, 1776. *Wealth of Nations,* Chapter VIII, Paragraphs 1, 2, and 8 (emphasis added).

Marx and Marcuse built upon Locke and Smith, but stressed that labor is a *social* process; that the value created through labor is most genuinely measured by socially necessary labor time; and that its product rightfully *belongs* to the labor force as a *body*, not to individuals as such, i.e. grounding a theory of common ownership and justice, i.e. Common *Wealth*. America was aware of Marx's writing and ideas in large measure via the mediation of socialist Horace Greeley's *New York Tribune,*[10] which published articles under Marx's byline from 1852-1862 (Reitz 2009). Marx and Marcuse encompassed the theories of Locke and Smith within a larger philosophy of labor. Where Locke and Smith saw individual labor as the source of private property, in an atomistic (Robinsonian) manner, Marx recognized that all humans are born into a social context. Humanity's earliest *customs*, i.e. communal production, shared ownership, and solidarity assured that the needs of all were met, i.e. including those not directly involved in production like children, the disabled, and the elderly. This right of the commonwealth to govern itself, and humanity's earliest ethic of holding property in common, derive only secondarily from factual individual contributions to production; they are rooted primarily in our essentially shared species nature as empathic social beings.

Richard Leakey (1994, 60-63; Leakey and Lewin 1978) and Frans de Waal (2013, 2009) stress that the cultural context of cooperation and caring fostered interdependence and an awareness of the power of

---

10 See also John Nichols (2011) and Robin Blackburn (2011). Further, see Kevin B. Anderson (2010) and Charles Reitz (2009)

partnership. These customs and behaviors had the capacity to ensure survival. Communal labor sustained human life and human development. When commodified as it is today, labor's wealth-creating activity is no longer a good in itself. The overall "value" of the activity of the workforce, governed by capitalist property relations, is reduced to its aggregate payroll. Classical political economy (Ricardo, then Marx) called the downward pressures upon the "value" of commodified labor to drop to *dehumanized* levels of bare subsistence "the iron law of wages."

For these reasons we wish to argue, as Marcuse clearly saw, that there can be no *rehumanization* of society and social philosophy without the decommodification of labor. Douglas Kellner called Marcuse's notion of labor decommodification the *"liberation of labor"* (Kellner 1973, 3 emphasis in original). Rehumanization cannot be accomplished without a form of social justice grounded in commonwealth ownership. Kellner (1973, 7) has importantly pointed out that by 1967 Marcuse clearly indicated "the qualitative difference between the free and unfree society is that of letting the realm of freedom appear within the realm of necessity—in labor and not only beyond labor" (Marcuse 1970, 63).

Like Kellner, I (Reitz 2000, 64) have criticized the earlier Marcuse ([1933] 1973) who tended to overemphasize the activity of *play* as a countervailing force to the alienating attributes of work. But play, like art, can be seen as an extension of the essential activity of sensuous living labor, not as qualitatively distinguished from it. Richard Leakey (1994, 93) emphasizes tool-making as humanity's first industry, and that tools became works of art. The urge to produce depictions of animals and humans also seems to have been irresistible. Marcuse recognized this affinity of art with unalienated labor.

Labor theory of value / Critical theory of work

The labor theory of value, even in Locke and Smith, is rejected by most conventional economists who contend that labor is merely a cost of doing business, and that profit accrues from entrepreneurial skill, technological innovation, and risk-taking. These factors may increase profit in the short run in a subdivision of any given industry, where fractions of capital compete, yet in the long run, the innovative production processes and reduced costs and payrolls become the new social average. What has meaning for an individual entrepreneur does not explain the aggregate picture. National income accounts, on the other hand, reveal the structural fundamentals of the value production process. These accounts are insightful and useful in Marxist terms in that they presuppose that labor in each firm (and by extension each branch of production) is paid for through payroll outlays from the total value that is added through the firm's value production process.

Marx's critical philosophical perspective demonstrates that labor has a reality and a capacity beyond its theoretical and practical confinement within its commodified form (i.e. a wage or salary). The fuller potential and power of labor, as recognized also by Locke and Smith, challenges the presumption that capital produces value, the view that profit *unilaterally* accrues as a reward for the contribution of the investor/employer. Labor provides the total value added in the production process. Profit is a *subtraction* from the value produced.

The Americanization of the world-wide economy aims at the overall reduction of payrolls on the global assembly line, no matter the greater levels of manufacturing employment in developing countries. The model we develop in this chapter[11] will illustrate the dynamics of wealth acquisition and accumulation and the generative mechanisms that are the origins of inequality (*Figure 1*). This will substantiate our thesis that inequality is not simply a matter of the gap between rich and poor, but of the structural relationships in the economic arena between propertied and non-propertied segments of populations.

Our model may serve as a small but necessary contribution to the advancement of a more economically informed critical theory of society and indicate how and why *property relations* must be addressed in order to root out recurring crises.

Figure 1 will outline the dynamics of this value *production* process in manufacturing, and disclose the fundamental *distributive* structures of the contemporary business economy: capital acquisition/accumulation and workforce remuneration. If labor creates all wealth, as John Locke and Adam Smith maintained, then labor creates all the value that is distributed as income to the labor force (wages and salaries) and to capital (rent, interest, dividends, and profit).

---

11 Thanks also to Ken Stone, a radical labor activist and friend of long ago in Hamilton, Ontario, who helped me understand Marxist political economy in the 1970s. He has been involved in anti-racism, human rights, and anti-war activities over the years and was formerly a member of the National Steering Committee of the Canadian Peace Alliance and was on the International Central Committee of the Global March to Jerusalem.

FIGURE 1: Production Process

Modelling income flows: the "capital-labor split"
Dynamics and structure of value/wealth production and distribution as income

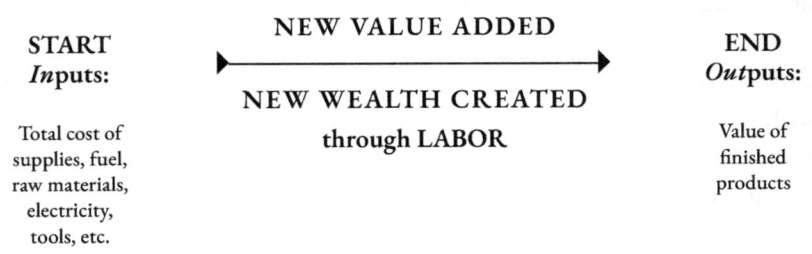

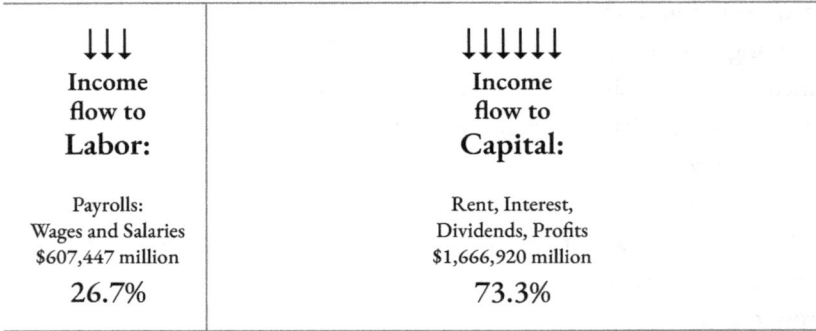

Value added in the production process is calculated by deducting the dollar costs of the *inputs* (supplies, raw materials, tools, fuel, electricity, etc.) from the dollar value of the *outputs*. The social relations of production that organize society's productive forces to produce a surplus product are not merely modes of essential cooperation, they are also power and privilege relations. The power and privilege relations of a society will dominate the productive forces and essential work relations to ensure that the total product be more than the minimum necessary product. We emphasize that incomes returned to capital and labor are *structurally determined*, i.e. conditioned primarily by societal, rather than individual, factors.

The *Statistical Abstract of the United States* includes data from the U.S. Department of Commerce and the Census Bureau. The methodology utilized to calculate the gross domestic product looks at the amount of *new wealth created, i.e. value added* through production in each firm and each industry. This is calculated by deducting the dollar costs of the *inputs* (supplies, raw materials, tools, fuel, electricity, etc.) from the dollar value of the *outputs*. Very importantly, these national income accounts—unlike the prevailing business utopian models—do *not* include the "cost" of labor among the *input* costs in the conception of the production process they utilize. Instead, they treat workforce remuneration as do Locke, Smith, and Marx, above—as an income flow stemming from the *value production process* itself.[12]

The following discussion of the origins and outcomes of income inequality in the manufacturing sector offers several insights that can be useful when considering other sectors of the U.S. and global economies, such as financial and information-based services. We recognize that the financial sector of the economy has been producing increasing shares of GDP: 2.8 percent in 1950, 4.8 percent in 1980, and 7.9 percent in 2007 according to the research of David Scharfstein and Robin Greenwood of Harvard Business School as reported by recently by Gretchen Morgenson.[13]

Joseph E. Stiglitz also emphasizes that growth in the financial sector has contributed "powerfully to our society's current level of inequality," and this largely because it has "developed expertise in a wide variety of forms of rent-seeking" (Stiglitz, 2012, 36-37). Much more needs to be said about rent-seeking, and we shall do so in this chapter below. The analysis of manufacturing data that concerns us here, however, is absolutely necessary in order to build our critical theoretical foundation. This will allow us to clarify and distinguish our views on value production, as we do below,

---

12 Today manufacturing data collected by the U.S. Census Bureau is much less accessible since the dubious discontinuation of its annual publication of the *Statistical Abstract of the United States* (SAUS) in 2012. This substantial handbook had been the convenient reference volume for working social scientists and social science teachers containing 1,400 tables of official government statistics on the social, political, and economic conditions in the United States. Now students, teachers, and social researchers must negotiate complex online sources in which comparable data from the U.S. Census Bureau and Department of Commerce can be needlessly difficult to find. Manufacturing data, specifically of the sort used in our research, is no longer labeled or reported in exactly the same way by the federal government. ProQuest, a privately held LLC, based in Ann Arbor, Michigan (apparently a new iteration of the former dissertation publisher, University Microfilms International) publishes a new annual version of the *SAUS*. This is a reference available in many academic libraries. Adjusting for changes in terminology, and different tables, we can see that the general pattern of unequal remuneration remains.

13 Gretchen Morgenson, *The New York Times*, October 28, 2012, pp. B-1, B-6.

from those of some postmodern and neoliberal theorists who confuse an inflation of asset prices for production of value.

As Morgenson points out,[14] income to money management firms, like mutual funds, hedge funds, and private equity concerns, increases when the *price* of assets that are overseen increases, even though the cost of providing financial services does not increase. This increased income does not derive from the creation of *value* but from an *extraction of wealth* from savers (like pension funds, and institutional investors) to the financial sector. Jodi Dean (2012, 136-54) describes in striking fashion the information and knowledge sector's most novel contemporary elaborations of exploitation and expropriation—including new labor forms that even *dispense* with wage payment (i.e. contests and prize competitions in which only a few are rewarded but all create viable products with their labor).

Our analysis seeks to draw out basic implications latent in standard economic data, and to arrive at certain significant findings that have been avoided in standard economics and business textbooks. In agreement with Marcuse's dialectical analysis, we see the global system of finance and commerce as no longer viable, plunging toward a dreadful reckoning with its own contradictions: attempting to reproduce its mode of privilege at the expense of the reproduction of the productive base (see also Greider 1997, 316).

If businesspeople traditionally speak of income-producing property, *critical political economy* knows it is not the *property* that produces income, rather it is the *property and power relationships* of the business system that allow owners of capital to appropriate income that it has not earned from wealth it has not created. Private ownership of capital is clearly not socially necessary for *value production*. The necessary component is *labor*. We must abstract from the particular qualities of the labor power of any individual person and instead focus on labor power at the average industry rate of productivity, what Marx called socially necessary labor time (see Raj Patel 2009, 66). A *critical* appreciation of work turns "right side 'round" the empiricist assertion that "job creators" are paying their employees, and demonstrates that employ*ees* are paying their employ*ers*. Our analysis of U.S. Census Bureau data undertaken below will demonstrate this. The power of the strike is to withhold these payments to propertied interests; the power of socialism is the reduction/elimination of them. In any society the labor

---

14 Ibid.

force must produce a surplus of value/wealth to maintain infrastructure and provide for social goods such as health care, education, etc., over and above incomes to individuals. Marx's point is that *only the labor force as a social body* has a legitimate right to manage this surplus. When it does, the first condition for a humanist commonwealth has been met.

The *Capital-Labor Split*: this phrase is from Thomas Piketty.[15] Every dollar of the value-added in U.S. manufacturing—for example in 2008, $2,274,367 million[16]—was distributed into one of the two basic reproduction categories: 1) as income to the workforce—as *payroll* (wages and salaries)—$607,447 million; and 2) as income to owners and investors—as *profit, rent, dividends, and interest*—$1,666,920 million.

This sort of division of the added value between labor (26.7 percent) and capital (73.3 percent) is structured by unequal property relations into the dynamics of reproduction in every sector of the economy and into the division of the Gross Domestic Product overall. Figure 1 depicts the three inextricably interconnected activities of production, distribution, and capital accumulation. It discloses how *a system of appropriation is embedded within the relationship of wage labor to capital* in the distribution process. As we have seen, the GDP is completely distributed as income. In the U.S. manufacturing sector in 2008 (not an untypical year) this meant that 73.3 percent of the manufacturing sector's contribution to GDP was returned to capital; 26.7 percent was returned to labor.

Data released 08 Jan 2016 by the U.S. Census updates these numbers: valuea dded in manufacturing in 2014 was $2,400,063 million; the payroll was $618,871 million; thus capital's share was $1,781,192 million. Thus the 2016 capital/labor split in manufacturing: labor *25.7 percent; capital 74.3 percent.*[17] This model is derived from standard approaches to national income accounting, for example in McConnell and Brue (2005) and Parkin (2005). If the raw data change from year to year, the proportionate patterns of unequal distribution have persisted over decades. There is no reason to expect the pattern to do anything but worsen as it has consistently done. Our theoretical contribution here is to bridge the traditional macro-micro separations, which artificially and unnecessarily detach a macro discussion

---

15 Thomas Piketty, *Capital in the Twenty-First Century* (Cambridge, MA: Belknap Press, 2014) pp. 41, 263.
16 This and other figures from: Table 1006. Manufactures—Summary by Selected Industry, 2008. *Statistical Abstract of the United States:* 2011, p. 634.
17 https://factfinder.census.gov/faces/tableservices/jsf/pages/productview.xhtml?pid=ASM_2014_31GS101&prodType=table

FIGURE 2: Calculating Income Flow to Capital

Total Value Added by Manufactures – Total Payroll = Income Flow to Capital
Manufactures – Summary by selected industry, 2008
[12,781.2 represents 12,781.200. Based on the Annual Survey of Manufactures.]

Industry based on shipments	2002 NAICS code [1]	All employees Number (1,000)	Payroll Total (mil. dol.)	Payroll Per employee (dol.)	Production workers (1,000)	Value added by manufactures (mil. dol.)	Value of shipments (mil. dol.)
Manufacturing, total	31–33	12,781.2	607,447	47,527	8,872.9	2,274,367	5,486,266
Food [6]	311	1,437.8	51,818	36,039	1,113.7	246,222	649,056
Grain and oil seed milling	3112	53.2	2,817	52,953	39.5	28,988	94,000
Sugar and confectionery products	3113	61.9	2,625	42,431	47.3	13,184	26,648
Fruit and vegetable preserving and specialty food	3114	167.7	6,232	37,161	138.5	28,045	63,187
Dairy products	3115	132.3	5,899	44,592	95.6	27,072	98,118
Animal slaughtering and processing	3116	505.7	15,217	30,094	438.9	50,823	169,925
Bakeries and tortilla	3118	271.6	9,442	34,760	172.8	34,108	58,701
Beverage and tobacco products	312	152.8	7,322	47,905	87.0	76,292	125,520
Beverage	3121	134.7	6,223	46,196	73.5	44,833	88,085
Textile mills	313	135.6	4,661	34,383	113.1	12,471	31,845
Textile product mills	314	136.3	4,151	30,455	104.9	11,540	26,630
Apparel	315	148.9	3,887	26,112	116.2	9,237	19,596
Cut and sew apparel	3152	118.5	3,075	25,951	92.2	7,385	15,608
Leather and allied products	316	31.7	994	31,361	23.9	2,619	5,411
Wood products	321	461.6	15,619	33,834	365.5	34,577	88,004
Sawmills and wood preservation	3211	91.7	3,394	37,024	76.9	7,278	24,272
Paper	322	403.2	20,546	50,957	311.6	79,175	178,749
Pulp, paper, and paperboard mills	3221	117.8	7,794	66,142	93.6	40,476	82,923
Converted paper products	3222	285.4	12,752	44,687	218.0	38,700	95,826
Printing and related support activities	323	605.9	25,138	41,491	422.4	60,003	99,167
Petroleum and coal products	324	105.9	8,415	79,444	68.2	91,559	769,886
Chemical	325	780.1	50,766	65,074	448.8	355,481	751,030
Basic chemical	3251	151.8	10,880	71,656	92.2	83,629	244,174
Pharmaceutical and medicine	3254	249.1	18,771	75,347	117.8	142,773	194,478
Soap, cleaning compound, and toilet preparation	3256	104.4	5,667	54,259	62.7	46,661	97,431
Plastics and rubber products	326	796.5	31,580	39,651	613.2	91,431	204,679
Plastics products	3261	651.8	25,299	38,815	499.7	76,503	167,423
Rubber product	3262	144.7	6,281	43,415	113.5	14,929	37,256
Nonmetallic mineral products	327	443.4	19,372	43,694	338.0	61,994	115,920
Glass and glass product	3272	93.9	4,227	45,042	74.0	12,562	23,197
Cement and concrete products	3273	213.6	9,106	42,637	161.8	29,774	57,779
Primary metal	331	418.3	22,693	54,245	328.7	93,564	282,141
Iron and steel mills and ferroalloy	3311	109.3	7,668	70,150	87.4	43,036	126,332
Foundries	3315	144.0	6,435	44,689	116.3	15,492	31,842
Fabricated metal products	332	1,572.7	69,231	44,021	1,153.4	188,072	358,363
Forging and stamping	3321	123.5	5,763	46,663	92.0	15,834	34,899
Architectural and structural metals	3323	408.5	17,253	42,239	293.1	44,878	94,980
Machine shops, turned product and screw, nut, and bolt	3327	398.5	17,748	44,537	298.5	39,941	64,064
Coating, engraving, heat treating, and allied activities	3328	136.0	5,360	39,403	104.0	16,432	27,740
Machinery	333	1,127.4	57,212	50,749	726.1	168,153	356,954
Agriculture, construction, and mining machinery	3331	209.2	10,279	49,147	143.0	39,037	94,334
Industrial machinery	3332	127.6	7,648	59,919	67.6	18,703	35,612
Ventilation, heating, air conditioning, and commercial refrigeration equipment	3334	145.8	6,019	41,297	104.7	19,092	40,702
Metalworking machinery	3335	161.3	8,305	51,502	112.1	17,325	29,277
Computer and electronic products	334	1,034.1	66,345	64,156	493.8	234,390	391,082
Computer and peripheral equipment	3341	92.6	5,908	63,792	34.7	38,727	68,110
Communications equipment	3342	132.8	8,961	67,481	53.9	30,504	53,865
Semiconductor and other electronic component	3344	371.6	20,486	55,123	227.9	71,258	116,809
Navigational, measuring, medical, and control instruments	3345	395.1	29,033	73,475	151.3	88,473	139,775
Electrical equipment, appliance, and component	335	411.9	19,038	46,226	285.3	61,975	131,759
Electrical equipment	3353	144.4	6,890	47,705	96.1	21,840	44,301
Transportation equipment	336	1,474.4	82,532	55,976	1,018.6	252,187	666,807
Motor vehicle	3361	163.0	11,318	69,424	139.5	52,337	210,978
Motor vehicle body and trailer	3362	123.5	4,789	38,790	95.0	10,208	29,764
Motor vehicle parts	3363	523.7	24,771	47,297	391.6	62,812	174,646
Aerospace product and parts	3364	439.8	30,892	70,240	235.2	93,036	178,709
Ship and boat building	3366	149.0	6,857	46,016	103.1	16,665	30,430
Furniture and related products	337	459.8	16,344	35,544	343.3	43,965	80,466
Miscellaneous	339	642.9	29,782	46,322	397.1	99,460	153,200
Medical equipment and supplies	3391	313.7	16,151	51,491	188.5	60,424	84,029

North American Industrial Classification System. 2002. Includes employment and payroll at administrative offices and auxiliary units. All employees represents the average of production workers plus all other employees for the payroll period ended nearest the 12th of March. Production workers represent the average of the employment for the payroll periods ended nearest the 12 of March, May, August, and November. Adjusted value added; takes into account (a) value added by merchandising operations (that is, difference between the sales value and cost of merchandise sold without further manufacture, processing, or assembly), plus (b) net change in finished goods and work-in-process inventories between beginning and end of year. Includes extensive and unmeasurable duplication from shipments between establishments in the same industry classification. Includes industries not shown separately.
Source: U.S. Census Bureau, Annual Survey of Manufactures, "Statistics for Industry Groups and Industries: 2008," June 2010.

of national income from a micro consideration of income distribution in terms of wages, salaries, rents, profits, dividends and interest. *Figure 1* shows that income distribution fundamentally occurs in a structurally determined manner (contrary to the prevailing emphasis on the individual features of performance and remuneration).

Figure 2 presents empirical data from the *Statistical Abstract of the United States 2011* measuring wealth created (value-added) in manufacturing. Looking at the data we see, for example, that in category 3152, *cut and sew apparel*, the total value added was (in millions) *$7,385*. The payroll (in millions) was *$3,075*. Therefore the amount returned to capital (in millions) was *$4,310*. This latter figure is an amount equal to 100 percent of what was paid to the workforce *plus* an extra 40 percent. What is true in this sector of the economy holds true in every other branch even more dramatically.

This analysis has examined incomes in the context of political and property relationships that are key to wealth accumulation, emphasizing how property relations account for the basic fact of the U.S. economy— the highly unequal distribution of incomes resulting from the patterns of workforce remuneration and the patterns of returns flowing to capital (via "income-producing wealth").

Intensifying inequality and the capital valorization crisis

Global economic polarization between those with immense property holdings versus the intensified immiseration of those without has led to the deepening crisis of finance capitalism that much of the world is currently witnessing. The 2008 economic debacle in the U.S. resulted in massive investment and job losses stemming directly from the institutional inability of the "world's strongest financial system" (The Financial Crisis Inquiry Commission 2011, xvi) to manage huge U.S. surpluses of capital without reckless speculation and massive waste of societal resources. The brutal consequences of this crisis are well known; its origins, however, are not. It was necessary therefore to impel the analysis *forward* with contemporary data, as we have done above, and *more deeply*, through to a critical understanding of the roots of capitalism's remuneration/ reproduction dynamics and structure, summarized above in our model, *Figure 1*. The global economy is increasingly one world supervised by global finance capital (Greider 1997). Finance capital derives its income from interest payments on massively extended credit (Greider 1997, 285-

289). A governing system of, by, and for finance capital has emerged largely led by U.S. interests, yet it is unsustainable on its own terms.

Austerity budgeting is the preferred social policy of hegemonic U.S. and global financial interests today, and now the primary function of sovereign states is the enforcement of debt payments to Wall Street and its own debt service through structural adjustment policies and budgeting that shifts resources from social needs-oriented programs to financial institutions. Keynesian strategies in support of the U.S. (or Greek or Portugese) labor force are no longer necessary in a political milieu where reactionary politicians will demand and liberal politicians will agree to direct government subsidies to finance capital.[18] Clearly the political terrain is contested, with recent major demonstrations and general strikes in Spain and Greece suppressed with police state tactics in midSeptember, and again in mid-November, 2012.

Predation within the economy has intensified with the emergence of "fast" capitalism—characterized by manic investing unhinged from reality in pursuit of market advantage in financial assets—described by Ben Agger (1989, 2004).

Given deregulation, megamergers of financial institutions, globalized communications technologies facilitating instantaneous capital flows, reckless investment in the real economy (commercial and residential real estate) and synthetic product (unreal derivatives, etc.), huge accumulations of capital (Greider, 232) have been amassed at the pinnacle of the global economy (i.e. largely in the U.S.). The U.S. capital glut led to a condition where investment banks have had to devise ever more speculative strategies to realize profit given the superabundance of wealth accumulated at the top. This is what we refer to as the over-appropriation crisis or the crisis of capital valorization. Today the global capitalist system is hyperactive. It is erratic,[19] desperate, disintegrating, and selfdestructive. We have recently witnessed two typical scandals of desperate and self-destructive finance capital: JP Morgan's enormous hedging designed to distort financial markets in their favor, and the Barclay's scandal of manipulation the Libor (London interbank offered rate) with knowledge of New York Fed regulators.[20]

---

18 See Raphael Minder, "Revolt raises pressure on Spanish government," *International Herald Tribune*, September 26, 2012, p. A-1; also Liz Alderman and Niki Kitsantonis, "Clashes erupt in Athens during anti-austerity strike," *International Herald Tribune,* September 27, 2012, p. A-3.
19 Louise Story and Graham Bowlet, "Market Swings are Becoming the New Standard," *The New York Times* September 12, 2011, p. A-1: "... canny investors could profit from the big swings..."
20 See Michael J. de la Merced and Ben Protess, "New York Fed Knew of False Barclays Reports on

Never content to receive less than maximal returns, capital is today as always hungry for valorization, seeking yields above average rates of profit. Yet the capital valorization process is currently in crisis. Prior to 2008 Wall Street institutions like American International Group (AIG), Bear Stearns, Citigroup, Countrywide Financial, Fannie Mae, Goldman Sachs, Lehman Brothers, Merrill Lynch, Moody's, and Wachovia had huge capital surpluses which they were frantic to valorize.

One strategy of some key financial institutions was to back massively real estate development trusts (REITs) to overbuild both commercial and residential properties. In order to reap big returns this business plan also required that banks recklessly issue enormous amounts of mortgage credit to commercial and residential buyers, even when these were patently unqualified. Investment bankers then hedged their real estate investment bets by insuring themselves against commercial and residential mortgage client default through convoluted over-the-counter derivatives, and credit default swaps.

Many financial institutions designed investment instruments consisting of bundles of the so-called subprime (in fact fraudulent) mortgages, and had them triple-A rated by complicitous auditors,[21] "flipped" the lethal assets for a fee, and shunted them to those less astute (institutional investors, pension plans, credit unions, etc.) who would directly bear the loss.[22] Some investment banks then conducted credit default swaps such that they, not the parties who had been sold the assets, were the beneficiaries when the defective investment products inevitably crashed and burned. Taxpayers covered the insurers' liabilities (AIG was "too big to fail") so that Wall Street, whose reproduction as a mode of privilege within the current social formation is imperative, was guaranteed payment for its worthless investment instruments.

The strategic irrationality of this country's leading investment banking institutions arises from the systemic fetish characteristic of

Rates," *The New York Times* July 14, 2012, p. A-1. Also, Jessica Silver-Greenberg, "New Fraud Inquiry as JP Morgan's Loss Mounts," *The New York Times* July 14, 2012, p. A-1. Further: "The Spreading Scourge of Corporate Corruption," *The New York Times* July 13, 2012, pp. B-1, B-5.

21 A separate, yet indicative, case against a ratings agency has recently made it to court. An Australian judge, Jayne Jagot, found that Standard and Poor's was liable for rating an investment instrument AAA in a manner "no reasonably competent ratings agency" would have. See Floyd Norris, "A Casino Strategy, Rated AAA," *The New York Times* November 9, 2012, p. B-1.

22 JPMorgan Chase and Credit Suisse recently settled for 417 million, government charges that they had packaged and sold troubled mortgage securities to investors, without admitting guilt. In 2010, Goldman Sachs settled a similar suit for 550 million. See Jessica Silver-Greenberg, "2 Banks to Settle Case for 417 Million," *The New York Times* November 17, 2012, p. B-1.

finance capital (as well as of *industrial* capital as emphasized by Marx in *Capital*).²³ This is the obsession with an asset's ostensible price (as a marketable commodity) independent of its value as a function of socially necessary labor time or its use. The bubbles in asset prices in the dot.com area, telecommunications, as in commercial and residential real estate, resulted from finance capital's compulsion under penalty of extinction to seek the valorization of capital (profit acquisition/accumulation) through desperate bets on price fluctuations and volatile market values in speculative transactions independent of values as measured by real factors of production. A highly financialized economy, in which capital seeks valorization without employment, leads to the delusional (inflated, unreal) claims on wealth that are not sustainable. "Real estate values are up! The stock market is up!" These gains are "really there" only if the conditions that inflate these prices persist. Price fetishism confuses selling price growth with real value growth. Investment in U.S. Treasury bonds has also been a traditional haven for surplus capital. After the debt limit showdown of mid-summer 2011, investment ratings agencies like Standard & Poor's have downgraded U.S. bonds. This increases the U.S. government's costs of borrowing and also increases the returns on these investment instruments. From the bondholder/rentier perspective, awash in wealth and wishing to maximize revenues, a bounce in the premiums the U.S. government can be made to pay on its borrowed funds is a desirable prospect.²⁴ Similarly, changes to the U.S. tax code favorable to the biggest corporations and the super-rich have not only relieved them of a significant tax burden: monies spared from taxation in this manner may instead be loaned back to the U.S. Treasury, earning interest, thus providing wealthy individuals and large corporations a positive rather than a negative income flow.

Neoliberal and neoconservative policies today serve what William Greider (1997, 285-289) has termed "The Rentiers' Regime." Joseph E. Stiglitz (2012) has also linked "rent seeking" to his understanding of the world's "1 Percent Problem." Rent-seeking may be seen as a mode of privileged accumulation and surplus over-appropriation.

---

23 On the commodity fetish, see Karl Marx (1968, 87). Capitalist relations involve a paradoxical inversion: "... sachliche Verhältnisse der Personen und gesellschaftliche Verhältnisse der Sachen...." Human beings are valued only as matters of business, and only matters of business are seen as having human value.
24 Binyamin Appelbaum, "Taking a Closer Look At a Downgrade's Result: Treasuries Likely to Still Appeal to Investors," *The New York Times*, July 31, 2011, p. A-13.

The term "rent" was originally used to describe the returns to land, since the owner of land receives these payments by virtue of his ownership and not because of anything he *does*. This stands in contrast to the situation of workers, for example, whose wages are compensation for the *effort* they provide. The term "rent" was then extended to include monopoly profits, or monopoly rents, the income one receives simply from control of a monopoly. Eventually the term was expanded still further to include the returns on similar ownership claims. (Stiglitz 2012, 39)

Marcuse understood what subsequent writers called neoliberal and rentier politics as preemptive counterrevolution. We can see how the neoliberal business utopian model is incapable of liberating humanity because it requires humanity to remain dependent on commodities, markets, and the financial and investment priorities of those who monopolize the capital accumulation process and speculate on the temporary price-fluctuations of assets. Commodity-dependency is the foundation of unfreedom in contemporary societies. Importantly, this dependency on commodities, markets, and finance is not inevitable. Realigning the social order to conform with the highest potentials of our economy, technology, and human nature requires the de-commodification of certain economic minimums: health care, child care, education, food, transportation, housing,—and work, through a guaranteed income. These are pre-revolutionary, *transitional* goals. *Revolutionary* goals envisage a more encompassing view of liberation and human flourishing: the passage from wages and salaries to public work in the public interest—public work for a commonwealth of freedom, with work as life's prime want. "Commonwealth of freedom" is a concept developed by Boyte and Kari (1996) which we extend in the direction of Marcuse's radical goals of socialism.

The vision of rehumanized social action and social ownership developed in this chapter is an extension and refinement of classical philosophical sources: Africana ubuntu principles and proverbs; Aristotle on human beings as the *zoon politikon;* social beings with politics as the key art to the good life; Buddha and Aquinas on good works and relief of suffering; Kant on cosmopolitan humanism; Marx on communism as the actualization of human species potential [Gattungswesen]. It is a mature philosophy of human freedom and fulfillment grounded in human capacities as sensuous living labor. We pursue here also Marcuse's recommendations on ending the material bases of domination, reshaping the productive forces in accordance with aesthetic form, and the free development of human needs and faculties toward peace and gratification. Authentic freedom is ours when we, as sensuous living labor, grasp intellectually and hold politically the resources that we have produced and which can be possessed by all within a decommodified and rehumanized world.

As Marcuse recognizes, the abolition of commodified labor is impossible under capitalism. Hence a critical liberal arts education that helps humanity accomplish its own humanization is inherently limited by the affirmative character of culture (i.e. its tendency to reproduce established inequalities), and is institutionally obstructed today. The Marxist conceptions of *wage-labor* and *commodity fetishism* are the key analytical criteria that measure the underlying dehumanization and commercialization of education and life itself under capitalism. Abolition of these phenomena will be the hallmark of humanist advancement in society and culture.

This society is fully capable of abundance as Marcuse recognized in *OneDimensional Man,* yet the material foundation for the persistence of economic want and political unfreedom is *commodity-dependency.* Work, as the most crucial of all human activities, by which humanity has developed to its present stage of civilization, can be and should be a source of human satisfaction. Under capitalism, it is reduced to a mere means for the receipt of wages. Sensuous living laborers are reduced to being mere containers for the only commodity they can bring to the system of commodity exchange, their ability to work. Necessities of life are available to the public exclusively as commodities through market mechanisms based upon the ability to pay.

Commodified existence is not natural; it is contrived. Significant portions of commodified social life need to be rethought and reconstructed. We need to articulate a common-ground political platform that can unify progressive forces to reclaim our common humanity. (See chapter 10 in this volume.) Consistent with Marcuse's obstinate utopianism ([1937] 1968, 143), we must hammer out what we really desire. What are the most intelligent/wisest uses of labor? We emphasize here the transformation of commodified human labor into *public* work, i.e. work that aims at the public good rather than private accumulation (Boyte and Kari 1996), and how this would undergird progressive political advance. Work in the public interest in the public sector expands areas of the economy traditionally considered the public domain, the public sphere, the commonwealth: social needs-oriented projects like libraries, parks, utilities, the media, telephone service, postal service, transportation, social services.

The decommodification of services in these areas, along with a policy ensuring a guaranteed minimum income, would supply a socialist alternative to its fundamental economic viability. So too is the decommodification of health care, housing, and education. Already we see that areas within the field of information technology are pregnant with the possibility of decommodification: public-domain software and shareware on the internet, etc.

The demand for decommodification sets Marcuse's analysis—and ours—distinctly apart from a *liberal* call for a "politics of recognition" (Taylor 1994; Honneth 1994, 2005) that features *attitudinal* and/or minimal *redistributive* remedies (Fraser and Honneth 2003). While recognition and redistribution are certainly needed, they are not sufficient. The slogan "tax the rich," while helpful in *liberal* terms, misses the *revolutionary socialist* point that the cure for today's harsh distributional inequalities lies in new relationships of common ownership that restructure the very processes of value creation, production, income and wealth distribution, exchange, and consumption.

No non-socialist theory of society or education has any profound quarrel with wage labor or the general system of commodity dependency. Marx admonishes workers: "...instead of the *conservative* motto '*A fair day's wage for a fair day's work!*' they should inscribe on their banner the *revolutionary* watchword, '*Abolition of the wages-system!*'" (Marx [1865] 1965, emphasis in original). We have reiterated above how Marx clarified capitalist society's obsession with production for profit rather than human need. This is its structurally generated fetish/addiction to production for commodity exchange rather than for usevalues. Production for *use* rather than *exchange* would optimize living conditions within the social formation as a whole. Capitalist productive relations are driving global labor to its knees. Only the abolition of wage labor and commodity fetishism in the economy can restore satisfaction and dignity to an uncommodified labor process.

Like Hegel and Marx, Marcuse understood that a subaltern, serving consciousness becomes aware through labor of its own dependency and unmet human needs. Ultimately, it learns also that those it serves are not absolutely independent and free, but rather dependent on it, labor.

This reality is a key source of labor's own political education and the foundation of its philosophy of possibility and hope. The frustration of *our essential sensuous practical activity, labor*, will ultimately propel a *politics of labor ownership of wealth* as the liberation of the repressed political potential of the human species. In the dominator systems that characterize global cultures today, not even the oppressors or their children are capable of coming to self-knowledge strictly through the agency of those educational forces committed institutionally to the reproduction of an oppressive social division of labor. Only through the practical and intellectual opposition to the reproduction patterns of domination can any theorist emancipate himself or herself from even the most consoling mystifications of oppressor systems. And only thus does practice or theory become critical.

We have learned from the movements against racism and sexism that class relations do not wholly demarcate structures of dominator power. Racism, patriarchy, homophobia, and other forms of discrimination, disrespect, and inequality sorely inhibit our powers of actualization. Reactionary forces reinforce bias of every sort in the hoary yet effective strategy of divide and conquer. While the general abolition of the wages system is not absolutely *sufficient* to secure the conditions for each of us to become all that we are capable of being, *the alienation and exploitation of labor is the enabling material core that today requires the dominant culture to target innocent minorities as scapegoats*.[25] Radical social science must empower general education students (i.e. the labor force in a multicultural society) intellectually, politically, and culturally to end these abuses.

A key challenge for the environmentalist movement and the labor movement today is re-thinking economics, building a theory and a practice for a humane world system. The business mind—the logic of marginal advantage within a market society that ostensibly accomplishes widespread prosperity—has been confronted here with its own contradictions: dehumanized production, an overworked and underpaid labor force, and increasing impoverishment. We emphasize the power of the labor movement not only as a source of class contestation over the distribution of the economic value that it has produced but also as a source of learning and advances in theory and social organization. Labor's traditional values have built the common good, and revolutionary critical pedagogy

---

25 See Steven Greenhouse and Steven Yaccino, "Fight Over Immigrant Firings, Strikers Say Pizza Factory Cracked Down to Prevent Union from Organizing," *The New York Times* July 28, 2012, p. B-1.

begins with labor's untold story (see also Boyer and Morais [1955] 1997). Economic processes today divest us from our own creative work, yet these also form the sources of our future social power.

We have recast the discussion of dehumanization and rehumanization in terms of the commodification and decommodification of sensuous living labor. We have thus attempted to furnish the beginnings of a more comprehensive critical social theory stressing the centrality of labor in the economy. Critical philosophy and radical pedagogy must theorize the origins and outcomes of economic and cultural oppression, and be engaged politically with the labor force to end them. This is the logic and manifesto that can liberate the fuller potential of any critical theory of society. As Peter McLaren has emphasized (2015b) critical theory must come to inform the full curriculum, such that its new norms of understanding and justice may enable us to build from within the realities of the present the partnership organizations of the future that will make possible new ways of holding resources and real opportunities for all persons to reclaim the full social power of labor, leadership, and learning.

We have extended some of the most radical components of Marcuse's critical social analysis, and augmented these with our own contributions—primarily through our interpretation and modeling of fact-based observations drawn from the national income accounts and also our work in critical pedagogy, labor education, and in the multicultural education reform movement. We have furnished material for curriculum components that may elicit freshened perceptions of the basic workings of the U.S. economy as well as challenge established patterns of education. Such perceptions can help generate a "new sensibility" (Marcuse 1969) with regard to the origins of social inequality, the irrationality and destructive nature of current patterns in the distribution of income and wealth, and the real possibility of a more humane, just, and abundant future. This new sensibility is a "refusal of the actual" (Marcuse 1969, 34), a form of consciousness in which science, technology, and art are released from service to exploitation and mobilized for a new vision of socialism (Marcuse 1969, 23, 26).

The analytical innovations presented here can be regarded as Marcusean insofar as they embody a form of the "Great Refusal" and disclose truths about our human condition and our human potential that are absent from established patterns of academic and political of discourse. We have attempted to do this in our discussions of the intensifying inequalities in the social distribution of income and wealth, rival interpretations of the meaning of inequality, the implications of the labor theory of value for wealth accumulation, ownership, and justice, and finally, the 2008 financial crisis in the U.S. Of special significance, we feel, is our model of workforce remuneration and capital accumulation. A depth-dimensional understanding of these dynamics undergirds our entire approach to the EarthCommonWealth Project.

Works cited

Agger, Ben. 2004. *Speeding Up Fast Capitalism: Cultures, Jobs, Families, Schools, Bodies*. Boulder, CO: Paradigm Publishers.

Agger, Ben. 1989. *Fast Capitalism*. Urbana, IL: University of Illinois Press.

Anderson, Kevin B. 2010. "Race, Class, and Slavery: The Civil War as Second American Revolution" Chapter 3 in *Marx at the Margins*. Chicago: University of Chicago Press.

Apple, Michael W. 2001. *Educating the 'Right' Way: Markets, Standards, God and Inequality*. New York & London: RoutledgeFalmer.

Blackburn, Robin. 2011. *An Unfinished Revolution: Karl Marx and Abraham Lincoln*. London and New York: Verso Press.

Boyer, Richard O. and Herbert M. Morais. [1955] 1997. *Labor's Untold Story*. United Electrical Radio & Machine Workers of America.

Boyte, Harry C. and Nancy Kari. 1996. *Building America: The Democratic Promise of Public Work*. Philadelphia: Temple University Press.

Dean, Jodi. 2012. *The Communist Horizon*. London: Verso.

de Waal, Frans. 2013. *The Bonobo and the Atheist: In Search of Humanism Among the Primates*. New York: W. W. Norton.

de Waal, Frans. 2009. *The Age of Empathy*. New York: Three Rivers Press.

Dowd, Douglas. 2009. *Inequality and the Global Economic Crisis*. London: Pluto Press.

Dowd, Douglas. 2004. *Capitalism and Its Economics*. London: Pluto Press.

Dowd, Douglas. 1997. *Blues for America*. New York: Monthly Review Press.

Farr, Arnold L. 2009. *Critical Theory and Democratic Vision: Herbert Marcuse and Recent Liberation Philosophies*. Lanham, MD: Lexington Books.

Financial Crisis Inquiry Commission, The. 2011. *The Financial Crisis Inquiry Report: Final Report of the National Commission on the Causes of the Financial and Economic Crisis in the United States*. New York: Public Affairs.

Fraser, Nancy and Axel Honneth. 2003. *Umverteilung oder Anerkennung?* Frankfurt a. M.: Suhrkamp.

Gilder, George. 1993. *Wealth and Poverty*. Oakland, CA: ICS Press.

Greider, William. 1997. *One World, Ready or Not*. New York: Simon & Schuster. Honneth, Axel. 2005. *Verdinglichung*. Frankfurt a. M.: Suhrkamp.

Honneth, Axel. 1994. *Kampf um Anerkennung*. Frankfurt a. M.: Suhrkamp.

Kellner, Douglas. 1973. "Introduction to 'On the Philosophical Foundation of the Concept of Labor,'" *Telos*, No. 16, Summer.

Korten, David C. 1995. *When Corporations Rule the World*. West Hartford, CT: Kumarian Press.
Leakey, Richard. 1994. *The Origin of Humankind*. New York: Basic Books.
Leakey, Richard and Roger Lewin. 1978. *People of the Lake*. Garden City, NY: Anchor/Doubleday.
Macionis, John C. 2012. *Social Problems*. Upper Saddle River, NJ: Pearson/Prentice Hall.
Marcuse, Herbert. [1974] 1987. *Zeit-Messungen*. In *Herbert Marcuse Schriften 9*. Frankfurt: Suhrkamp.
Marcuse, Herbert. [1933] 1973. "On the Philosophical Foundation of the Concept of Labor in Economics," *Telos*, No. 16, Summer 1973.
Marcuse, Herbert. 1972. *Counterrevolution and Revolt*. Boston, MA: Beacon Press.
Marcuse, Herbert. 1970. "The End of Utopia," in his *Five Lectures*. Boston, MA: Beacon Press.
Marcuse, Herbert. 1969. *An Essay On Liberation*. Boston. MA: Beacon Press.
Marcuse, Herbert. [1937] 1968. "Philosophy and Critical Theory," in *Negations, Essays in Critical Theory*. Boston, MA: Beacon Press.
Marcuse, Herbert. 1964. *One-Dimensional Man: Studies in the Ideology of Advanced Industrial Society*. Boston. MA: Beacon Press.
Marx, Karl. [1867] 1968. *Das Kapital*. Erster Band in *Marx-Engels Werke* Band 23. Berlin, East: Dietz Verlag.
Marx, Karl. [1865] 1965. *Wages, Price, and Profit*. Beijing: Foreign Languages Press.
McConnell, Campbell R. and Stanley L. Brue. 2005. *Economics: Principles, Problems, and Policies*. Boston: McGraw-Hill.
McLaren, Peter. 2015a. *Pedagogy of Insurrection*. New York and Bern: Peter Lang Publishing.
McLaren, Peter. 2015b. "Revolutionary Critical Pedagogy for a Socialist Society," in *Crisis and Commonwealth*, Charles Reitz, editor. Lanham, MD: Lexington Books.
McLaren, Peter. 1997. *Revolutionary Multiculturalism: Pedagogies of Dissent for the New Millennium*. Boulder: Westview Press, HarperCollins.
Nichols, John. 2011. "Reading Marx with Abraham Lincoln" Chapter 3 in *The "S" Word: A Short History of an American Tradition*. London and New York: Verso.
Parkin, Michael. 2005. *Economics*. Boston: Pearson Addison Wesley. Parenti, Michael. 1988. *Democracy for the Few*. New York: St. Martin's.
Patel, Raj. 2009. *The Value of Nothing*. New York: A Picador Book of St. Martin's Press.
Rawls, John. 1971. *A Theory of Justice*. Cambridge, MA: Harvard University Press.
Reitz, Charles. 2009. "Horace Greeley, Karl Marx, and German 48ers: AntiRacism in the Kansas Free State Struggle, 1854-64," *Marx-Engels Jahrbuch 2008*. Berlin: Akademie Verlag.
Reitz, Charles. 2000. *Art, Alienation, and the Humanities. A Critical Engagement with Herbert Marcuse*. Albany: SUNY Press.
Reitz, Charles. 1976. "A Critical Outline of the Political Philosophy of Social Reconstructionism," *Cutting-Edge, Journal of the Society for Educational Reconstruction*, 7:4 (Summer).
Ruschig, Ulrich. 2020. *Die Befreiung der Natur: Zum Verhältnis von Natur und Freiheit bei Herbert Marcuse*. Köln: PapyRossa Verlag.
Sernau, Scott. 2001. *Worlds Apart: Social Inequalities in a New Century*. Thousand Oaks, CA: Pine Forge Press.
Stiglitz, Joseph E. 2012. *The Price of Inequality*. New York: W. W. Norton.
Taylor, Charles. 1994. "The Politics of Recognition," in *Multiculturalism* edited by Amy Gutman. Princeton, NJ: Princeton University Press.
U.S. Census Bureau. 2011. *Statistical Abstract of the United States.*, http://www.census.gov/prod/2011pubs/11statab/manufact.pdf (retrieved June 11, 2011).

9
Promesse du Bonheur Commun

Herbert Marcuse never loses sight of critical political economy and structural social analysis. At the same time, the link between the erotic and the political is one of Herbert Marcuse's signature notions. According to Brazilian Marcuse scholar Imaculada Kangussu, Marcuse's hypothesis in this regard is that there is a biological foundation for political practice (Kangussu 2021). Eros is an essential element of his emancipatory philosophical naturalism and ecological materialism. The manner of this erotic and political interconnection was first introduced by Marcuse as the *promesse du bonheur* in an essay written a full decade before his famous 1955 volume, *Eros and Civilization*. "Sensual love gives a *promesse du bonheur* [promise of happiness and fulfillment] which preserves the full materialistic content of freedom. ... Sensuality ... preserves the goal of political action: liberation" (Marcuse [1945] 1998, 204).

Eros and Civilization elaborated the view that the sensuous powers of Eros and beauty could help subordinate humanity's aggressive instincts to life-sustaining, non-destructive, instincts. Beauty assists in the "transformation of sexuality into Eros" (Marcuse [1955] 1966, 197). Eros "implies an enlargement of the meaning of sexuality itself" (ibid., 205). "There is an unbroken ascent in erotic fulfillment from the corporeal love of one to that of others, to the love of beautiful work and play, and ultimately to the love of beautiful knowledge" (ibid., 211). Eros ultimately seeks a serene, stately, noble logic of gratification for humanity, where "the right and true order of the Polis is just as much an Erotic one as the right and true order of love" (ibid., 211). Marcuse did not think socialism could liberate Eros entirely from Thanatos, the death instinct (Marcuse 1978, 72), but that sexuality elevated by beauty to Eros could nonetheless help us attain our freedom-and-happiness-in-common by learning to live with a seasoned maturity and dignity on planet Earth. Socialism's minimal standards require the provision of adequate social-needs-oriented programs and services such as housing, health care, childcare, and education, to everyone, as well as government policy, law enforcement, and public media ensuring the optimization of the human material condition. But, even more importantly we must "revive the *radical* rather than the *minimum* goals of socialism" (Marcuse 1972, 5, emphasis added). For Marcuse, the radical goals of socialism go beyond the elimination of want and poverty through efficient production and distribution of use-values: they involve a "qualitative leap" against "the fragmentation of work, the necessity and productivity of stupid performances and stupid merchandise, against the acquisitive bourgeois individual, against the servitude in the guise of technology, deprivation in the guise of the good life, against pollution as a way of life" (Marcuse 1972, 16-17).

In *The Aesthetic Dimension* Marcuse speaks of the "erotic quality of the Beautiful" (1978, 62). He sees "Beauty in its perhaps most sublimated form: as political Eros" (Marcuse 1978, 64). Thus, he connected the *promesse du bonheur* to the capacity of art and beauty to convey a sense of *political* gratification and serenity. In *One-Dimensional Man* (1964, 210) the *promesse du bonheur* is a token of a fully liberated human future.

Marcuse takes the phrase *promesse du bonheur* from the romantic French writers, Charles Baudelaire and Stendhal (Miles 2017). Stendhal held that this sense of aesthetic elation could at times abruptly convert into complete exhaustion and debilitation, giving rise to the legend of the Stendhal Syndrome: some particularly sensitive visitors to the Uffizi Gallery in Florence were said to have swooned from an overdose of beauty.

The promise of *bonheur* was also heralded decades earlier in European *political* thought: in the first article of French *Declaration of the Rights of Man* (1793). This is traditionally taken as signifying the well-being of all, the general good: "The aim of society is the common welfare [*bonheur commun*]."[1] Marcuse clearly understood the *promesse du bonheur* as encompassing also this *bonheur commun*. Art and beauty proclaim the

---

1 "Le but de la société est le bonheur commun. Le gouvernement est institué pour garantir à l'homme la jouissance de ses droits naturels et imprescriptibles." *Déclaration Française des Droits de l'Homme et du Citoyen du 24 juin 1793.* http://dcalin.fr/internat/declaration_droits_homme_1793.html. I owe this insight to Domenico Losurdo (2021, 46). In this historical (1793) form the idea of the bonheur commun drew upon and reflected the rights of "life, liberty, and pursuit of happiness" as highlighted in the U.S. Declaration of Independence of 1776. The "pursuit of happiness" in the documents of 1776 and 1793 invites our political imagination still today, yet it was then largely a proxy for John Locke's defense of the right to own one's property privately.

possibility of our communal gratification and prompt us to work to fulfill our natural and political needs as non-alienated social beings.

> [T]he development of the productive forces renders possible the material fulfillment of the *promesse du bonheur* expressed in art; political action—the revolution—is to translate this possibility into reality (Marcuse [1958] 1961, 115).

Analogous to the essential extraction of "surplus value" under capitalism according to the Marxist critique, Marcuse theorized that a *surplus* repression of human freedom is exacted from the population in advanced industrial societies ([1955] 1966, 35). Even under egalitarian and partnership conditions, a *basic* repression of instincts and desires is needed to sustain ethical human life and civilization. But the distinction between basic and surplus repression allows him to interpret repression anew: civilization does *not* have to be based *wholly* on repression and sublimation; it can also be based on free libidinous (though predominantly non-genital) relationships within a community. The political sublimation of Eros "*does not repress* or even divert erotic energy, but on the contrary seeks ways of liberating it ..." (Marcuse [1967] 2017, 23; emphasis in original). The political Eros seeks to release forces that can produce a *counteroffensive* against the dis-economics of cultural polarization, the destruction of nature, and the dread prospect of extinction. The emancipatory Eros of the environmentalist movement "confronts the concerted power of big capital, whose vital interests the movement threatens ... " (Marcuse [1979] 2011, 212). On the basis of Fourier's philosophy, he concludes that, after socialist transformation, work itself could be liberated from surplus repression and become attractive due to a pleasant togetherness ([1955] 1966, 216-217).

The transvaluation of values

We have seen how Langman and Lundskow (2016) have argued that today's "gods" in the U.S. tend to be money, fame, thrills and power and that this reveals the dominant side of the American character. At its margins, significant historical struggles have occurred: progressive social forces struggling against slavery, for women's suffrage, a populist anti-monopoly radicalism, socialism, co-ops, collectives, and communes like New Harmony and Oneida, though even the memory of these struggles has been generally repressed. During the 1960s "New Sensibilities" of the sort Marcuse described in *An Essay on Liberation* (Marcuse 1969, 23) emerged that prefigure a sane socialist society in 21st Century America. By 1972, Marcuse recognized that even a one-dimensional society could see protest groups emerge among students, women, and civil rights activists, who developed an oppositional philosophy and politics. His essentially hopeful outlook on social justice activism and his lionization as the philosopher of the student revolts of the 1970s were both rooted in the common transvaluation of values accomplished by a political Eros that was shaping the civil rights struggles, the women's liberation movement, labor militancy, and radical environmentalism.

> The primary *counter-force* to aggressive energy is *erotic* energy: to the degree to which it presses aggression into the service of the Life Instincts—it strives for the unification, pacification, and protection of Life. Here is *the hidden "political" element* in this energy: originating in, but transcending, the personal relationships between individuals—erotic energy *strives to transform* the natural and social environment into one of satisfaction and peace—strives to reduce destructive violence, to undo brutality, cruelty, and ugliness. These are the instinctual, the erotic, and aesthetic elements in any radical historical movement, and vice versa: *without political sublimation*, political transcendence, the moral, sexual, aesthetic *rebellion remains a private affair,* and in the last analysis *selfdefeating.* (Marcuse [1967] 2017, 23; emphasis in original).

During the anti-Vietnam War protests and the civil rights movement, Martin Luther King, Jr., like Marcuse, called for "a radical revolution of values."[2] This was to counteract the predatory adulation of plutocracy and power in the U.S. American *culture* that has been filled with religious zealotry and militarism, and today continues to be threatening, pathologically aggressive, sadomasochistic and punitive, denying legitimate authority in science and government. It is also delusional: seeing itself as free and democratic! Racial animosity, anti-immigrant scapegoating, and resurgent nationalism/patriotism are being orchestrated today in the troubled system of American/global capitalism—as neopopulist/neofascist instrumentalities of social control and economic stabilization.

---

2 Barbara Ransby, "MLK Called for a 'Radical Revolution of Values.' The Movement for Black Lives Delivers One." *In These Times*, April 4, 2017. https://inthesetimes.com/article/mlk-calledfor-a-radical-revolution-of-values-the-movement-for-black-lives

As mentioned earlier, feminist writer Ijeoma Oluo (2020) has argued the *mediocrity* of the average white American male in the context of this country's legacy of dangerous male chauvinism and racism, much as the Hannah Arendt had emphasized the "banality of evil" in fascist Germany. We saw in chapter 3 that Oluo described the American male's brawny vapidity as composed of a false sense of success and superiority linked to an unearned yet presumed caste status ascribed as superior versus women and people of color. As this caste status breaks down, it no longer automatically furnishes its unmerited power and rewards. Formerly entitled white males, believing that their status has been stolen from them, often become angry with the world. At the same time traditional gender roles have never before been so widely questioned and defied in our social order than today. So too, traditionally alienating and oppressive norms in work and employment continue to be challenged with new intensity since the pandemic of 2020.

The commonwealth past and promise

Marcuse sees the necessity of work in society as "ontological." It is the basis and fundamental form of every social formation and applies to the life of every human being. As I have said before, Marcuse, like Marx, asserted a radically materialist conception of the essence of socially active human beings: seen from the outside, we are the ensemble of our social relations; seen from the inside, we are sensuous living labor. Sensuous living labor is the substrate of our being as humans. Imaculada Kangussu has also written that in Marcuse's view "human beings are determined by social structures, *but not only those presently existing* …" (Kangussu 2021, 231, emphasis added). Our affective and intellectual capacities (and vulnerabilities) have been socio-ecologically developed within history. As a species we have endured because of our sensuous appreciation of our emergent powers: *the power to subsist cooperatively; to create, to communicate, and to care communally within that form of society that we may rightly call a commonwealth*. In Marcuse's ecosocialist view, there is the promise of *the radical transformation of the labor process itself* in the future—the liberation of laboring humanity from the surplus repression of commodification and alienation. I am stressing Marcuse's underappreciated insight into the latent power of sensuous living labor to liberate itself from exploitation and to make commonwealth a universal human condition.

Earlier in this volume I have emphasized how humanity's first explicitly ethical maxims emerged as proverbs that generally modulated life in the earliest African partnership cultures. These cultures focused on the traditional habit and feeling of *ubuntu* or "showing humanity to others." This was done through empathy and principles of reciprocity and solidarity in community life, in teamwork, modesty and mutual aid. Those who worked (nearly every ablebodied member of the society) also created the first ethical maxims: "Many hands make light work;" "To raise a child, it takes an entire village;" "Only as a braided cord can the cotton carry the stone." African proverbs contained the first formulations of the golden rule. Of course, conflicts could arise within and between communities. Nevertheless, these proverbs constituted universalizable humanist, i.e. not narrow tribal teachings to guide practical life and cannot in any way be confused with purely religious teachings. Human beings, as sensuous living labor, have in the past and can in the future act in accordance with an egalitarian and partnership sense of the *bonheur commun*.

> Released from the bondage to exploitation, the imagination, sustained by the achievements of science, could turn its productive power to the radical reconstruction of experience ... the aesthetic ... would find expression in the transformation of the Lebenswelt—society as a work of art. (Marcuse 1969, 45)

Our need for the *bonheur commun* has the power to reclaim our intercultural humanity. Our fundamental desire is to gratify human social needs by engaging in a kind of public work for the public good. We know our rights to a commonwealth economy, politics, and culture reside in our commonworks. This involves sensuous living labor authentically actualizing itself through human(ist) activism and creativity—humanity remaking itself through a social labor process in accordance with the commonwealth promise at the core of our material reality. This requires a new system of shared ownership, democratized ownership, common ownership. Commonwealth is the aesthetic form of an alienation-free society with humanity's (that is, sensuous living labor's) essential social activity, workmanship and artistry, emancipated from surplus repression.

Marcuse believed that among the most radical goals of socialism are the aesthetic ones. Our lives need to embody the aesthetic. Not the kind of aesthetic that we could say distinguishes the architecture of Haussmann's Paris or the Venetian Piazza San Marco from that of everyday life at home. However beautiful and emblematic of freedom, these architectural jewels are nonetheless ornaments in high culture that cover societies that are still generally characterized by economic, political, and libidinous repression of the workforce (even if the rulers were allowed transgressive excesses in their lives as less limited individuals).

Paris and Venice do not stand for the deeper aesthetic satisfactions that Marcuse envisions as needed for a truly liberated social formation in which all human lives, associated in egalitarian partnership, access nonrepressive gratification and freedom as the norm in political life. In the chapter on "The Aesthetic Dimension" in *Eros and Civilization* Marcuse combines the aesthetic theories of Kant and Schiller with Freud. From Kant's treatment of imagination as a source of free creativity, he turns to Schiller's *Letters on Aesthetic Education*, in which Schiller, like Kant, describes human *sensuality* as the basis of aesthetics and as an impulse for a "new kind of civilization." Marcuse seeks a new civilization where it is possible to realize the non-alienated self. In this regard, according to philosopher Roberta Dreon, Marcuse sought …

> … a further sphere of meaning of the aesthetic in our life. Marcuse originally developed Schiller's idea of the aesthetic state as an intermediate one, capable of acting as a mediator between sensibility and reason by making reason sensuous and sensibility fruitful, as opposed to merely dissipative. From this point of view, he speaks about a new sensibility and a new aesthetic ethos, capable of contributing to new forms of society and of satisfying the human need to live a more integrated life—a sensuously and imaginatively richer one, not condemned to fear and submission, but based on gratifying relations with other men and women, on living in a respected and nurtured environment, even on working with pleasure. Sensibility must be nurtured by the imagination and by the capacity to take other people's roles, thereby shaping an ethos capable of adequately fulfilling the basic human needs, instead of neglecting or repressing them. (Dreon 2015, 82)

Marcuse also sought a reconciliation between our "self" and our *species-self* or species-essence in which humanity's nature and freedom meet. Schiller's *Letters* are also the source of Marx's statement in the *Paris Manuscripts of 1844* about future production in a perfected communist society occurring beyond the commodity form and "according to the laws of beauty."

Ecosocialism, in Marcuse's view, possesses the potential to bring beauty and sensuous satisfaction to humanity, fulfilling our natural and political essence as human beings. Ecosocialism delivers on art's *promesse de bonheur* and nature's promise that we can attain our happiness-in-common by learning to live with dignity and freedom on planet Earth. Marcuse regarded the environmental movement of his day as a critical intervention of Eros against institutional destructiveness and as the embodiment of a life-affirming energy directed towards the protection of Earth and the pacification of our human existence. "A successful environmentalism will, within individuals, subordinate destructive energy to Erotic energy" (Marcuse [1979] 2011, 212). Marcuse saw this energy as a political Eros in a twofold sense (Marcuse [1955] 1966, 211): First, it is the *"love of beautiful work and play"* —a Platonic, higher level, selfless regard for other humans as humans. Secondly, as the *"love of beautiful knowledge,"* a Platonic desire that culminates in a political struggle against institutional forces of destruction.

Marx's *Paris Manuscripts of 1844* saw communism as represented in two ways: first, new possibilities of production and life occur in a kind of "raw communism"—people liberated from the formerly alienating conditions caused by private property and the private accumulation of the social product. This essential communism is intended to safeguard and increase the income of all workers—as a minimum standard of society. The *fuller development of communism is more radical:* labor is freed from its commodity form (as wages or salaries) to become common*work* for the common*wealth*. The qualitative difference in the community of freedom thus entails the radical transformation of the labor process itself to meet the new social needs as Marcuse stresses. For Marx, a fully perfected communism represents a *"true* resolution of the conflict between existence and being, between producing products and producing self-confidence, between freedom and necessity, between individual and genus. It is the solution to the riddle of history, and knows itself to be this solution" (Marx [1844] 1970, 76). Labor's liberation from the *commodity form* and sublation within its *commonwealth form* also makes it possible for beauty to infuse human life from its foundation up— for the entire society to be a work of art.

This volume has stressed that Marcuse's ecological writings emphasize how both the earth and human life are warped under the exploitative conditions of global financial capital. It has shown that his essays "Ecology and the Criticism of Society" (1979) and "Ecology and Revolution" (1972) are politically decisive and need to be taken to heart. The methodology of ecology focuses on the complex and central underlying structures in nature and the economy. It is eminently cognizant of the interconnectedness of the biosphere and the negative impacts of the capitalist political economy. Ecology provides a critical insight into the generative mechanisms underlying persistent injuries to nature and their effects over time and a strategy for a new world system. He found that countering the extractive and polluting economic policies of global capitalism required system-negations, and that environmentalist criticisms implicitly or explicitly involved the Great Refusal.

Marcuse's *Paris Lectures of 1974* (2015) advocate for a "new form of socialism …"

> … namely socialism as in any and every respect qualitatively different and a break with capitalism … and it seems to me that only a decisive redirection of production itself would in this sense be a revolutionary development. A total redirection of production, first of all, of course, towards the abolition of poverty and scarcity wherever it exists in the world today. Secondly, a total reconstruction of the environment and the creation of space and time for creative work; space and time for creative work instead of alienated labor as a full-time occupation. (Marcuse [1974] 2015, 69)

The *universalization of resistance* that Marcuse sought came from his realization that the women's movement and the intensification of the student anti-war protests were in harmony with ecosocialism and that they could protest together against the capitalist "violation of the earth." The extraordinary value of Marcuse's strategy is that of a "united front," against the sociopathic political disregard for our future—and for our common humanity. The multiplicity of possible refusals, each for the sake of our deepest love of life, could and should be consolidated as a new general interest. In the next (and last) chapter I elaborate on this as "The Great Refusal *Project*." As noted in chapter 4 above, human beings uniquely appreciate the awesome power of the earth and its remarkable beauty. Within the dialectics of nature, ecological reciprocity can be a creative force. We now recognize that we have the capacity to transform our estate on the face of the planet, such that we can regain a place of honor within our world while attaining our own fullest ethical and intellectual potentials. We liberate the *promesse du bonheur commun* through ecosocialism's negation of the current system and its concrete vision of EarthCommonWealth solidarity.

Works cited

Dreon, Roberta. 2015. "Aesthetic Issues in Human Emancipation Between Dewey and Marcuse," *Pragmatism Today*. Volume 6, Issue 2.

Kangussu, Imaculada. 2021. "Marcuse and the Symbolic Roles of the Father: Someone to Watch Over Me" in Jeremiah Morelock (ed.), *How to Critique Authorian Populism*. Leiden: Brill.

Langman, Lauren and George Lundskow. 2016. *God, Guns, Gold, and Glory*. Chicago: Haymarket Books.

Losurdo, Domenico. 2021. *Nietzsche the Aristocratic Rebel*. Chicago: Haymarket.

Marcuse, Herbert. [1967] 2017. "Protest and Futility" in Herbert Marcuse, *Transvaluation of Values and Radical Social Change* edited by Peter-Erwin Jansen, Sarah Surak, and Charles Reitz, Philadelphia, PA: International Herbert Marcuse Society.

Marcuse, Herbert. [1974] 2015. *Paris Lectures at Vincennes University, 1974*. Edited by Peter-Erwin Jansen and Charles Reitz. Philadelphia, PA: International Herbert Marcuse Society.

Marcuse, Herbert. [1979] 2011. "Ecology and the Critique of Modern Society," in Douglas Kellner and Clayton Pierce (Eds.). *Herbert Marcuse, Philosophy, Psychoanalysis and Emancipation*, Volume 5, *Collected Papers of Herbert Marcuse*. New York and London: Routledge.

Marcuse, Herbert. [1945] 1998. "Some Remarks on Aragon: Art and Politics in the Totalitarian Era," in Douglas Kellner (Ed.). Herbert Marcuse, *Technology War, and Fascism*, Volume 1, *Collected Papers of Herbert Marcuse*. New York and London: Routledge.

Marcuse, Herbert. 1978. *The Aesthetic Dimension, Toward a Critique of Marxist Aesthetics*. Boston, MA: Beacon Press.

Marcuse, Herbert. 1972. *Counterrevolution and Revolt*. Boston, MA: Beacon Press.

Marcuse, Herbert. 1969. *An Essay on Liberation*. Boston, MA: Beacon Press.

Marcuse, Herbert. [1955] 1966. *Eros and Civilization: A Philosophical Inquiry into Freud*. Boston, MA: Beacon Press.

Marcuse, Herbert. 1964. *One-Dimensional Man, Studies in the Ideology of Advanced Industrial Society*. Boston, MA: Beacon Press.

Marcuse, Herbert. [1958] 1961. *Soviet Marxism, A Critical Analysis*. New York: Vintage.

Marx, Karl. [1844] 1970. "Pariser Manuskripte 1844," in *Karl Marx Texte zu Methode und Praxis II,* Ernesto Grassi (Hsg.) Reinbek bei Hamburg: Rowohlt Taschenbuch Verlag.

Miles, Malcolm. 2017. "Herbert Marcuse and the *Promesse du Bonheur:* Politics and Literature in Dark Times," *Cultural Politics* (2017) 13 (1): 34-47.

Miles, Malcolm. 2016. "Eco-aesthetic Dimensions: Herbert Marcuse, Ecology and Art," *Cogent Arts & Humanities*, Volume 3, Issue 1.

Oluo, Ijeoma. 2020. *MEDIOCRE: The Dangerous Legacy of White Male America*. New York: Seal Press/Hachette Book Group.

10

EarthCommonWealth Agenda

Racial Equality, Gender Equality, Liberation of Labor, Restoration of Nature, Leisure, Abundance and Peace

> Material force can only be overthrown by material force;
> but theory itself becomes a material force
> when it is seized by the masses. ...
> Theory is only realized in a people
> so far as it fulfills the needs of the people.
> —Karl Marx, [1844] *Critique of Hegel's Philosophy of Right*

> [The] established system preserves itself only through
> the global destruction of resources, of nature,
> of human life, and the *objective* conditions
> for making an end to it prevail.
> —Herbert Marcuse, *Counterrevolution and Revolt* (1972, 7)

The global capitalist system is poisoning and depleting the resources of our material environment *not* meeting the needs of the people. The objective conditions for making an end to it prevail. In today's environmental crisis we are up against the combined power of the global fossil fuel industry and the world's biggest military, that of the U.S., as these are responsible for the lion's share of the world's climate emergency. A politics of neofascism is increasingly contorting our political lives. But today illusions about capitalist democracy have significantly eroded as authoritarian policies have become more apparent during a massive intensification of economic inequality around the globe. So too is the legitimacy of the use of military/police force since the massive Black Lives Matter movement of 2020 and the decades-long debacles of war and waste in Iraq and Afghanistan. A legitimation crisis in the U.S. has been developing persistently over the last decades, by fits and starts: Vietnam protests, Nixon and Watergate; Reagan and the Iran-Contra scandal; Colin Powell's 2003 perfidious address to the United Nations regarding the weapons of mass destruction in Iraq which served as a purported rationale for invasion; the 2014 Senate Report on CIA torture practices. All of these have severely damaged the standing of the U.S. in the world.

Peace as a challenge in empires of exploitation and race

As I write this in June 2022 the world is also confronted with Russia's intensifying war against Ukraine. This is unfolding with pronounced brutality against civilians. Nothing can legitimate it. Confronted with localized warfare and the possibility of even greater global conflagration, visceral revulsion drives the world to condemn and oppose this invasion. A global anti-war movement is being vigorously organized and extended, calling for an immediate ceasefire, the removal of Russian troops, and a renunciation by both Russia and NATO forces of the use of nuclear weaponry.

Russia's war has not emerged from nothing. University of Chicago international relations scholar, John Mearsheimer, has stressed that the U.S. has provoked this crisis by pushing to expand NATO eastward (Chotiner 2022). The situation looks similar to conditions leading up to World War I when rival empires (Lenin [1916] 1963) whose oligarchs were heavily invested in arms industries were enriching themselves and militarizing the economic conflicts over expanded markets and sources of raw materials. In an abbreviated overview of such conflicts from then to now, let me begin here with a recognition of the internationalist workers' movement at the time which was being divided by a rising tide of nationalisms. Today we realize these nationalisms as socially-constructed ethnic identities played up by chauvinists and then pitted against one another to get the masses behind each empire's militarism. Anderson (1983) emphasizes that these nationalisms are constituted largely as "imagined communities."

Prior to World War I in the U.S., the radical press had been highly energized responding to the 19th Century tradition of militant labor activism: the Great Railroad Strike of 1877, the Chicago Haymarket uprising of 1886, and the Pullman Strike of 1894. When this labor movement came additionally to oppose the First World War, the federal government fatally undercut the extensive reach of the most widely read socialist weekly in the U.S., the *Appeal to Reason*. The anti-war message was stigmatized and then suppressed when the paper was denied use of the U.S. postal service to reach its subscribers under the Espionage and Sedition Acts of 1918. Anti-war leader Eugene Victor Debs of the Socialist Party of America was sentenced to a ten-year jail term for organizing opposition to the war.

In Europe, Marxists were divided about whether the labor force would automatically rise up against capital in an almost mechanistic manner or whether even decisive socialist leadership could mobilize a revolutionary anti-war movement. Mass support for World War I led on the one hand to a sense of demoralization on the Left; on the other hand, after the war, there was a renewed international socialist movement against imperial militarism. In 1918 the U.S. deployed an expeditionary force of approximately 7000 soldiers to Russia itself—ostensibly to subdue the Germans there—but actually, these were used to drive out Bolshevik forces (Murray [1955] 1964, 41-43). The Socialist revolution nonetheless overthrew the war-making Russian czar in 1919. At home, the U.S. federal and local police forces suppressed the budding revolutionary movement by arresting radicals and deporting those with Eastern and Southern European backgrounds (Poles and Italians especially) in the 1919 Palmer Raids (Murray [1955] 1964). At the same time in Germany a revolutionary uprising of soldiers and striking workers, with whom Marcuse empathized, sought to establish self-governing socialist republics in Berlin and Munich. The conservatively Marxist Social Democrats (SPD) entered into a deal with the German military: if the SPD would tacitly accept the murders of radical communists, Rosa Luxemburg and Karl Liebknecht, the military would permit the SPD to come to power. Once the revolutionaries were eliminated, however, the military sold out the SPD to the Nazis (Shirer 1960, 83-89; Marcuse [1967] 1970, 102-103).

World War II showed the strength of the Soviet Union as a bulwark against fascism. Herbert Marcuse's 1947 post-war analysis of the recently defeated Nazi government of Germany saw the future as a continuing conflict between neofascism and socialism (Marcuse [1947] 1998). He saw the West as neofascist. His *Soviet Marxism* (1958) depicted Soviet philosophy and politics as expressions of an untenable bureaucratism, technological rationality, restrictive aesthetic realism, etc.; it had lost its fundamental emancipatory impulse. The socialism of the USSR was thus seen as spurious. Marcuse also did something quite unique and unexpected, which set him apart from Cold War-fueled political writing at the time: having sharply and objectively criticized culture and politics in the Soviet Union, he fearlessly risked censure in the U.S. in explaining that *both* the Soviet and Western forms of political rationality had in common the prevalence of technical over humanistic elements in the development of the relations and forces of production. Marcuse did not back away from making profound criticisms of U.S. culture that led him to be branded as anti-American. This was a major departure from the much more cautious politics of the Horkheimer inner circle of Frankfurt School theorists as well as from the conventional wisdom in the U.S. academic sphere. Marcuse felt confident enough to develop an adamantly critical perspective on the U.S. With the 1964 publication of *OneDimensional Man* Marcuse consolidated his key and most characteristic arguments to the effect that U.S. society and culture (different as they were from the USSR) were politically, economically, and intellectually, *unfree*.

After World War II, American *oligarchs* (however much the conventional wisdom has avoided this term even in speaking of Lundberg's super-rich "60 Families" [1937] or the Forbes List of America's 50 wealthiest families[1]) embarked on an anti-USSR campaign and outspent them on military expansion. Some Marxist scholars, like Martin Nicolaus, saw this as the period of the *Restoration of Capitalism in the USSR* (1975). Massive U.S. military outlays continued, and in 1989 the *legitimation crisis* in the Eastern Bloc countries and the USSR led to their non-violent structural transformation, with the transfer of property and power from their quasi-socialist state trappings to financial/industrial oligarchs. Under Boris Yeltsin the new Russian Federation lost any ability to oppose today's neofascism; in fact, Russia now seems to relish the idea of being an imperial power once again.

The U.S. has continued to waste its abundance on military spending: Vietnam, Panama, Grenada, Afghanistan, and Iraq. Yet its wars have also lost their legitimation. They have been widely recognized as fifty years of U.S. aggression involving torture and the gratuitous killing of civilians. Professor Samuel Moyn at Yale and Italian Marxist Domenico Losurdo have criticized the "humanitarian" pretexts of the 21st Century U.S. warmakers, such as the ostensible protection against terrorism and for human rights, civil and gender rights. This has allowed "American war itself to be rehabilitated after Vietnam as legitimate or even progressive" (Moyn

---

1 Forbes, "America's Richest Families: The List" 2020 Ranking https://www.forbes.com/familieslist

2021, 223; Losurdo 2021, 953). The false testimony publicly presented at the U.N. on Iraqi weapons of mass destruction demonstrated that such intelligence and pretexts are routinely fixed, doctored, and loaded. Such was also the case in the Vietnam War's manufactured Gulf of Tonkin crisis and attendant official lies (Marciano 2016, 129).

U.S. military arrogance, unleashed after September 11, came home to roost: soldiers had a record high rate of suicide while serving in Iraq and Afghanistan, one a day during June 2010.[2] Though the U.S. military denies that its suicide rates are higher than a non-military population of the same age and gender demographics, suicide by active-duty soldiers and veterans has been deadlier than combat for the U.S.—twenty a day in the six-year period from 2013-2019.[3] Former President Barack Obama was presented with the Noble Prize for Peace at the start of his term, but by the end, he was infamous for having ordered a military surge in Afghanistan, including intensely stepped-up drone strikes with his personal approval of "kill lists."[4] Much of the world looks at the U.S. military and its unconditionally supportive Democratic and Republican policymakers today (e.g. Clinton and Albright; Bush, Cheney, Rumsfeld) as aggressive warmakers. Even U.S. drone operators today report having "soul fatigue" expressed in PTSD, drug abuse, and divorce, as well as suicide. This, according to a *New York Times* article of April 15, 2022 by Dave Philipps entitled "The Unseen Scars of Those Who Kill Via Remote Control." Reporting on several representative drone operators (from a total of 2300) it was learned that these individuals often accumulate dozens upon dozens of long-distance strikes with Hellfire missiles launched from MQ-9 Reaper drones. Ostensibly targeting enemy terrorists carefully—in missions from 2015 in Iraq and from 2019 and 2020 in Syria and Afghanistan—operators reported that these strikes were increasingly "ordered up on the fly, hitting schools, markets and large groups of women and children."[5]

Will today's Ukraine war go nuclear? According to radical essayist Arundhati Roy, writing years prior to the current conflict: "Nuclear

---

2 *The European Union Times*, July 17, 2010. https://www.eutimes.net/2010/07/us-soldiers-suicide-at-record-high-in-iraq-and-afghanistan/
3 "Suicide Has Been Deadlier than Combat for the Military" *The New York Times*, November 1, 2019. https://www.nytimes.com/2019/11/01/opinion/military-suicides.html
4 Jo Becker and Scott Shane, "Secret 'Kill List' Proves a Test of Obama's Principles and Will," *The New York Times*, May 29, 2012. https://www.nytimes.com/2012/05/29/world/obamas-leadershipin-war-on-al-qaeda.html?searchResultPosition=2
5 https://www.nytimes.com/2022/04/15/us/drones-airstrikes-ptsd.html?searchResultPosition=3

weapons pervade our thinking. Control our behavior. Inform our dreams .... They are the ultimate colonizer. Whiter than any white man that has ever lived. The very heart of whiteness" (Roy [1999] 2019, 6). We might take this as a clear recognition of the likelihood of a nuclear escalation of imperial military interests and options.

Moritz Rudolph, editor of Germany's *Philosophie Magazin* reminds us of the warning against atomic catastrophe issued July 5, 1955 by Bertrand Russell and Albert Einstein.[6] In its essentials it reads:

> ...We are speaking on this occasion, not as members of this or that nation, continent, or creed, but as human beings, members of the species Man, whose continued existence is in doubt...
>
> ...We shall try to say no single word which should appeal to one group rather than to another. All, equally, are in peril, and, if the peril is understood, there is hope that they may collectively avert it.
>
> ...the question we have to ask ourselves is: what steps can be taken to prevent a military contest of which the issue must be disastrous to all parties?
>
> **Resolution**: "In view of the fact that in any future world war nuclear weapons will certainly be employed, and that such weapons threaten the continued existence of mankind, we urge the governments of the world to realize, and to acknowledge publicly, that their purpose cannot be furthered by a world war, and we urge them, consequently, to find peaceful means for the settlement of all matters of dispute between them."

Russell and Einstein wrote this almost seventy years ago. The U.S. had used its atomic might against "non-white" Japanese civilian populations and might well be seen in this regard as having acted as an Empire of Race every bit as much as was the former British Empire. Russia now sees neofascism in reactionary racist U.S. politics and rightly regards NATO expansion as a threat (Bernie Sanders in Nichols 2022).

In 2022 the International Marxist Humanist Association joined forces with several other groups seeking to end the war in Ukraine promulgating an "Internationalist Manifesto Against the War."[7]

---

6 Moritz Rudolph, "Denkanstöße: Hinter den Nachrichten" April 27, 2022. https://www.philo-mag.de/ For the full text of the Russell-Einstein Manifesto, see https //www.atomicheritage.org/key-documents/russell-einstein-manifesto
7 Published by the International Marxist Humanist Organization https://imhojournal.org/articles/internationalist-manifesto-against-the-war/

The criminal war launched by Russian imperialism against Ukraine is the most serious threat to world peace since the end of the Cold War. It brings the world closer to a global conflagration than at any time since Mikhail Gorbachev's peace initiatives. The main culprit for this dangerous evolution is U.S. imperialism, which took advantage of the fall of the Soviet Union in order to consolidate its global military network, expand its presence in various parts of the world and launch invasion wars in Afghanistan and Iraq....

We therefore stand indivisibly for the following demands:

- Immediate and unconditional withdrawal of Russian troops from Ukraine;
- Support for the Ukrainian resistance and its right to get the weapons it needs for its defense from whatever source available;
- Support for the Russian antiwar movement;
- Russia should be forced to pay reparations for what it has inflicted on Ukraine;
- No to any increases in military expenditure—we pledge to launch, as soon as this war ends, a new campaign for global disarmament, the dissolution of all imperialist military alliances and an alternative architecture of international security based on the rule of law;
- Open doors in all countries to all refugees fleeing wars in any part of the world.

In spite of these and other peace efforts, political uncertainty in the U.S. and around the world is mounting. Establishment media in the U.S. promote the military defense of Ukraine categorically and establishment politicians are funding the war effort fully. The U.S. fossil fuel industry sees war in Ukraine as enhancing its profits, as global sanctions against Russia reduce its ability to supply the world's oil and natural gas. Chris Hedges, writing several years prior to the Ukraine war, made the case that global crises have already given our precarious situation a *revolutionary moment*. "In this moment a political, economic, or natural disaster—in short, a crisis—will ignite unrest, lead to instability, and see the state carry out draconian forms of repression to maintain 'order.' This is what lies ahead" (Hedges, 2015, 2). He concludes: "I do not know if the new revolutionary wave and the rebels produced by it will succeed. But I do know without these rebels we are doomed" (Hedges 2015, 20).

Legitimation crises: Opportunities for new beginnings

The U.S. empire is in decline. A steep loss of the customarily unquestioned legitimacy of established power has occurred among a key element of younger people around the globe who see that the U.S. has lost its moral authority in foreign policy as well as in terms of neocapitalist economic crises. The American Pageant version of history writing has also lost its legitimacy. So too, the rhetoric of globalization has lost its gloss as inequalities have surged separating the 1% from the rest of us world-wide. The language of the Republicans and Democrats is insufficient given contemporary crises: impending climate catastrophe, ongoing militarized policing, the aftermath of wars fought and lives lost with no genuine justification, not to mention extrajudicial imprisonment and torture at black sites. The U.S. Supreme Court has lost even its frayed appearance of fairness through sets of ugly hearings and politicized appointments. Its legitimacy has been further put into question by the unwanted revelation that it is intending to strike down *Roe v Wade* eliminating the constitutional right to abortion (see "Leak Intensifies View that Court is Too Political" *The New York Times*, May 5, 2022, page 1).

The concept of "legitimation crisis" was developed by Jürgen Habermas describing how "contradictions can directly threaten system integration and thus endanger social integration" ([1973] 1992, 68). Herbert Marcuse emphasized this encroaching disillusionment in his *Paris Lectures*—in 1974! These presentations focused on the emancipatory potential of these flagging of operational values for radical opposition to global capitalism:

> There is evidence that more and more people no longer believe in, and no longer act in accordance with, what can be called the operational values on which the continued existence of the capitalist system depends. If people no longer adhere to the operational values which keep the system going, then the decline has set in. (Marcuse [1974] 2015, 52)

Legitimation crises in the United States are being addressed by the Republicans and Democrats in sharply different ways. On the one hand, the Alt-Right and their many Republican supporters in government wish to mobilize mass resentment against the so-called "deep state," thus their January 6th 2021 attack on the Capitol. On the other hand, corporate Democrats and many even on the liberal Left, have been attempting to offset the U.S. crises of legitimation during the 2016-2020 Trump era with a build-up of NATO strength against Russia (Kuzmarov and Marciano 2018; Mearsheimer in Chotiner 2022) supported by a frayed anticommunist credo. Now this line of thinking is also being burnished and refurbished to rationalize a zealous war against Russia for Ukraine with a new McCarthyism that will try to silence U.S. antiwar dissent.

Beyond these desperate endeavors of establishment U.S. politicians, German philosophy professor and ecologist, Ulrich Ruschig, writing on Marcuse's views of nature (discussed in chapter 7 above) points to the student strikes, *Fridays for Future* protests, and the militance of the climate activism of Greta Thunberg, from whom we get a clearly radical expression of the current legitimation crisis: "You are failing us, but the young people are starting to understand your betrayal.... [A]nd all you can talk about is money and fairy tales of eternal economic growth. How dare you!" (Thunberg in Ruschig 2020, 94). Similarly, after 17 of his classmates were killed at his school in Parkland, Florida, David Hogg became a student activist who founded the #NeverAgain gun control movement and led a massive national March for Our Lives rally in March 2018. "At every turn our institutions are failing us, and we are paying the price.... But rather than becoming cynical or retreating from these challenges, we fight back" (Hogg in Volpe 2022, xiii).

Since 2000, progressive forces are following the lead of engaged youth like those above and are addressing issues not tackled by establishment politicians and thus breaking with the status quo: economic inequality; racial and environmental injustice; gun violence, school shootings, hate speech, sexual assault. This has been extensively documented by John Della Volpe (2022) a Harvard expert in survey research also currently advising the Biden administration. His volume *Fight: How Gen Z is Channeling their Fear and Passion to Save America* represents his own perspective, not that of either Harvard or Biden. He has analyzed vast polling evidence demonstrating what he calls "the fighting spirit of

Generation Z" that indicates a "once-in-a-generation" attitudinal shift (Volpe 7). In his estimation this is a conscious rejection of conventional patriotic Americanism: "They've decided to fight their own war against injustice and inequality here at home" (Volpe 13). This fight has included: the Occupy movement, the Women's March in the aftermath of the 2016 election of Trump ("the largest single-day march up to that point in U.S. history" Volpe 28), and the Black Lives Matter uprising ("the largest protest in our nation's history. Nothing comes close" Volpe 88). At the same time, he points out that massive youth protests have been occurring in the Sudan, Hong Kong, France, India, Brazil, Columbia, Ecuador, and Germany (Volpe 147-149). The "ethos of the generation" is "worried about everyone on the planet" (Volpe 151).

Volpe asks where this massive youth movement will lead us. Survey data shows that a majority of Generation Z does *not* support capitalism. But supporters of capitalism still outnumber supporters of socialism (Volpe 47). There is also a marginal youth backlash supporting white supremacist and chauvinist movements, the "man against the establishment" paradigm (Volpe 100). Some of these participated in the January 6, 2021 attack at the Capitol. Still, "Gen Zers are also aware that youth involvement nearly anointed Bernie Sanders as the leader of the Democratic Party" (Volpe 12). This disenchantment with politics-as-usual does have enormous emancipatory potential.

Given today's workforce discontent and destabilization, it is no wonder that an openness to socialist alternatives is definitely taking hold among younger people. An opinion piece in *The New York Times*, (Goldberg 2017) carried the heading "No Wonder Millennials Hate Capitalism." Millennials are the "older cousins" of Generation Z (Volpe 2). The piece concludes that the "rotten morality" behind today's intensifying inequalities is more apparent than ever, hence radicalizing young people. This reflects the steady growth among the youth of what Marcuse called the "New Sensibility"—new needs, generated under capitalism, but which capitalism cannot fulfill, for gender equality, ecological economics, and anti-racism.

As Daniel R. Wildcat has attested, the global capitalist system is flirting with catastrophe, and it has been for a while: "Humankind is poised through our actions to create the first planetary catastrophe of human genesis in the history of our cosmos" (Wildcat 2009, 46). It is global capitalism as a dying *system*, not simply monstrous individuals (though there be many) now laying waste to the earth. This earth, from whose material sources—soils, minerals, waterways, and air—we are made and from whom our other-than-human "relatives" have arisen. Circumstances demand that we use our utmost ingenuity *(indi*genuity—Wildcat, 80) to prepare, with nature as an ally, counteroffensive measures against it. A catastrophe of global proportions is possible, yet it is *not* inevitable. While the objective productive forces have ripened such that the global economy can be seen as pregnant with abundance and freedom, the subjective element matters. Without a resolute understanding of our ecological materialism and the ontology of commonwealth, there will be no sufficient practice of negation, and there will be no sufficient transformation. Having come to grips with the imperial past of the U.S., we see that our multi-racial, multi-cultural, and intercultural commonalities must be combined with workforce rebellion as "subverting forces" (Marcuse 1969, 49).

The great refusal as a *collective project*

Marcuse argued that the Sixties' spirit of rebelliousness against the Vietnam War and American consumerism and environmental destruction expressed a visceral repugnance at the totality of the efficiently functioning social order of its advanced industrial society. The Great Refusal "is the protest against unnecessary repression; the struggle for the ultimate form of freedom, 'to live without anxiety'" ([1955] 1966, 149). It is the "refusal with which the opposition confronts the existing society ...it envisages a new culture which fulfills the humanistic promises betrayed by the old culture" 1969, 10). It "takes a variety of forms" (1969, vii) for liberation, particularly in *la contestation permanente* of the 1968 French student movement, but also of the guerrilla forces in Latin America, and the revolutions "being defended and driven forward" while struggling to "eschew the bureaucratic administration of socialism" in Vietnam and Cuba and China (1969, viii-ix). As a collective project, it constitutes a multidimensional expression of negation against systems of domination.

"The way we live is the problem" says indigenous writer Daniel R. Wildcat (2009, 78), whom the reader has come to know in earlier chapters. U.S. militarism and U.S.-led global capitalism are hostile to nature and humanity in general. Subverting forces are called upon now to negate and transcend the way we live while standing on moral high ground. An indigenous and humanist ethics, rooted in labor's latent countervailing, counteroffensive, and collective power, can meet the challenge of building a new world system today. This requires strategic alliances and cross-cultural solidarity, a movement in which *system negation* has the force/power of a new general interest. Seeing that our destinies *are* all interconnected we must also see Marcuse's Great Refusal as a collective project that can bring radicals together powerfully today.

Marcuse is a revolutionary ally, not only because he elucidates the obscenities of global inequality, domination, alienation, ecological crisis, and war, but more importantly because his writing evokes a strategy of solidarity among subaltern groups across traditional barriers of culture. Collective actions must be undertaken that go beyond blaming solitary politicians or that focus only on individuals as the unit of analysis.

On the question of the agents of change, many radical groups internationally already recognize that commodified existence and economic want are not natural, but rather engineered under capitalism. Large swaths or working men and women around the globe have rising expectations and are aware of the need to prioritize human needs over private accumulation. Significant portions of commodified social life need to be rethought and reconstructed. This volume has argued that human essentials need to be met independently of any requirement of an individual payment to procure necessities and consistent with the principles of ubuntu and commonwealth.

How do we deal with the material power of the 1%, the owners and managers of the world's largest income-producing properties: international banks and financial institutions, landowners and developers, the agribusiness oligopoly, timber interests, the corporate media? The coercive power of the CIA, and the FBI, is real, yet the money-is-speech U.S. Supreme Court incurred much damage to its reputation during the confirmation hearings of two notorious male justices, Clarence Thomas (in 1991) and Brett Kavanaugh (in 2018). Their toxic masculinity was excused as natural and expected; their sexual harassment and victim shaming was denied. Recently a white masculinist assault was launched against a new nominee to the Supreme Court, Judge Ketanji Brown Jackson, a black woman, by the Republican party's most toxic Senators and future presidential candidates, Ted Cruz and Josh Hawley accusing her of an allegiance to "woke" racialized education.[8] "A snarling pack of white male

---

8 Jonathan Weisman and Jazmine Ulloa, "Judging a Judge on Race and Crime, G.O.P. Plays to Base and Fringe" *The New York Times*, March 22, 2022. https://www.nytimes.com/2022/03/22/ us/politics/ketanji-brown-jackson-race.html?action=click&module=RelatedLinks&pgtype=Article

Republicans ripping apart a poised, brainy Black woman ..." as Maureen Dowd put it, comparing the treatment of Ketanji Brown Jackson to that of Anita Hill before a Senate Judiciary Committee.[9] This was galling, appalling and repulsive, and representative of the counterrevolutionary values and practice of the prevailing dominator power in the U.S. discussed in chapter 1.

We must intervene in the generative systems that are the engines of inequality in the economy, politics, and culture. We need to apply an ecological materialist analysis to the internally conflicted economic and political systems wreaking havoc today, and (in terms of a unity of theory and practice) assess how we might best utilize the real but latent powers of labor to begin to establish realistic methods and goals for an EarthCommonWealth Alternative. The classic contributions to power structure research by C. Wright Mills ([1956] 2000), G. William Domhoff ([1967] 2022), and Michael Parenti ([2002] 2011) have much to offer in terms of explanation. The task now, however, is how to *dismantle* and replace these structures. This is necessary to attain goals of global disarmament and demilitarization with the dismantling of nuclear arms.

Douglas Dowd, whose work I have frequently relied upon in discussing imperial America, has asked: "As the rich and powerful go about their dirty work, what should we be doing?" (Dowd 2015, 90) and he suggested that, for one thing, a campaign should be waged as a left within the Democratic Party, and beyond it in the streets, focusing on six major issues: "the economy, inequality, big business, taxes, wars, and the environment. The 'six' interact and are interdependent; to rid ourselves of what's harmful in any one of them, all must become substantially undone in ways to serve all, instead of a few" (Dowd 2015, 92). Ijeoma Oluo valorizes "Ocasio-Cortez, Pressley, Tlaib, and Omar—The Most Dangerous Women in Congress" (Olou 2020, 208). These women of color and some as members of the Muslim faith deserved to win election to the U.S. House of Representatives and did so even during the Trump era.

Nothing outraged the congressional Republicans more, however, than the Green New Deal as propounded in the U.S. by Alexandria Ocasio-Cortez with the support of many others, among them Ed Markey, and Bernie Sanders. This is about the climate crisis—and much more: higher education for all; affordable housing; high-quality health care;

---

9 Maureen Dowd, "Real Justice: Justice Jackson" *The New York Times,* March 27, 2022, SR9.

clean manufacturing with the creation of union jobs; support for family farming, and repair damages to native lands. Marcusean speakers at the biannual conference of the International Herbert Marcuse Society in Santa Barbara in 2019 advocated for this is a necessary part of a radical electoral strategy. It tries to tame a bestial and destructive capitalist oligarchy: zero CO_2 emissions in ten years, "all power clean power," no to fossil fuels; no to nuclear power; clean up the earth; restore nature. More than simply a strategy to move the Democratic party to the left, if implemented, it would constitute a transformational /transitional program away from oligarchic capitalism—toward a democratic socialism. The public is to receive ownership stakes when the public invests in renewable sources of power and "jobs." The U.S. would be a much better place if it were more like Finland or Switzerland.

Still, to be substantial and fully sustainable radical ecosocialist policies must do more than "tax the rich." The fuller Marcusean perspective, the Great Refusal, our common project of refusal, emphasizes revolutionary policies must ultimately enable us to: expropriate the expropriators and abolish the foundation of rentier income in property ownership; forgive working families' debt; redistribute property/land; eliminate universal commodity dependency through the decommodification /socialization of the economy "one sector at a time" (Peter Marcuse 2015). The decommodification of production overall supplies a socialist alternative with its core economic and ecological viability. For Marcuse "the issue is not the purification of the existing society but its replacement" (Marcuse [1972] 2005, 175). The purpose of Marcuse's Marxist critical theorizing is to grasp intellectually and to grasp politically the reality of an ecosocialist future though this is now blocked by political-economic circumstances. The EarthCommonWealth Project aims at building a revolutionary program for a new mode of partnership wealth ownership and partnership culture.

Authentic ecology flows into a militant struggle for a socialist politics which must attack the system at its roots, both in the process of production and in the mutilated consciousness of individuals" (Marcuse [1972] 2005, 176). A further criterion that Marcuse sees as crucial is repeated in essay after essay: "The goal of radical change today is the emergence of human beings who are physically and mentally incapable of inventing another Auschwitz. (Marcuse [1979] 2011)

How can we make a future Auschwitz impossible? Police states around the globe are *increasing* in number: Myanmar, Kazakhstan, Belarus, Russia. The U.S. is also in reality an incipient/covert/latent police state. We have seen the U.S.A. support dictatorships—after Auschwitz—in Iran, Guatemala, Vietnam, Indonesia, and Chile. In a 2021-22 series of African coups military leaders have toppled the governments of Mali, Chad, Guinea, Sudan and Burkina Faso. "[M]ore than 114 million people now ruled by soldiers who have illegally seized power" (Mclean 2022). These has been a long history of imperial interventions in Africa and these coups would seem to serve the neocolonial goals of keeping Africa poor and dependent. According to Nick Turse, "Since 2008, U.S.-trained officers have attempted at least nine coups (and succeeded in at least eight) across five West African countries, including Burkina Faso (three times), Guinea, Mali (three times), Mauritania, and the Gambia" (Turse 2022). Black Lives Matter has educated the nation and it has in large measure undermined the legitimacy of police state solutions.

Revolutionary ecological liberation requires counteroffensive tactics that move the struggle forward. Elizabeth Martínez documents dozens of protest actions in pursuit of social justice for women and minorities in *De Colores Means All of Us* ([1998] 2017). She poses the crucial question: Where Is the Moral High Ground?" and her response rings true: "Remember Something Ancient, Imagine Something New" (Martínez 248). Like Vine Deloria, Jr. and Daniel R. Wildcat (as well as Graeber and Wengrow—and Engels) she advises us to remember the *natural way* or *indigenismo*. This can provide the foundation for the *democratic* and *revolutionary* new worldview that should inspire all of us today (Martínez 249).

> Indigenismo can be the soil in which to grow a revolutionary project that will meet basic human needs like health care, full employment, decent housing and education. It can draw the outline of a new kind of society, based on communal goals, cooperation and the respect for [the earth and] all life …(Martínez 251).

Martínez's indigenous-inspired approach is an outcome of her critical social theory and educational philosophy, not any romanticism. She reminds us, too, that *even a thoroughly secular philosophy* can recognize that organizing for social justice requires respect for others' spiritual needs. As she emphasizes, *indigenismo* is consistent with the goals of decolonization, seeking a linkage within minority communities and among them. It refuses to mirror society's individualism and egoism. It is pro-active for the long term with a vision of an egalitarian and free society for the future, rather than primarily engaged in defensive struggles.

The work of Aldo Leopold, as well as Engels, retains a noteworthy value today with regard to the growing recognition in anthropology and history for the *indigenous critique of Euro-American life*. Today's activists in such groups as Pachamama Alliance, the Sunrise Movement, and Extinction Rebellion are examples of "subverting forces" trying to operate as they should on the moral high ground. The indigenous perspective is on guard against corruptions of power, characteristically using ridicule to check an individual's arrogance, male chauvinism, or any *group's* self-aggrandizement or attempt at leadership by command.

The 26th annual U.N. Climate Change Conference of the Parties (COP26) took place in Glasgow, October-November, 2021. Brad Plumer and Lisa Friedman (2021) have reported that negotiators from 197 countries participated: 105 agreed to cut emissions of methane, 130 to stop deforestation. But progress was disappointing even to U.N. Secretary-General, Antonio Guterres. He concluded, "Recent climate action announcements might give the impression that we are on track to turn things around. This is an illusion" (Guterres, in Plumer and Friedman 2021). Instead, there was much lip service to admirable goals and much self-promotional greenwashing, but otherwise few substantive changes or accomplishments. Ramped-up production of electronic vehicles, for example, was promoted rather than investments into public transportation infrastructure. Electronic batteries for these vehicles are reliant on open-pit cobalt mining in the Democratic Republic of the Congo. "[T]he quest for Congo's cobalt has demonstrated how the clean energy revolution, meant to save the planet from perilously warming temperatures in an age of enlightened selfinterest is caught in a familiar cycle of exploitation, greed, and gamesmanship that often puts narrow national aspirations above all else . . ." (Searcy, et. al 2021). Clean energy from sun, wind, hydro, or geo-thermal is absolutely necessary for a sustainable and pollution-free future, but in itself, without changed relations and goals of production overall, it is not sufficient. Profitable over-*production* is the intrinsic destructive force in capitalism, and super-*accumulation* drives it (more on this below).

At COP26 demonstrators numbering in the tens of thousands marched and focused on their key demands: care deeply, act collectively, and support people over profits. According to an activist leader, Leon Dulce, to make a difference we need to focus our discussion on "...the non-negotiables of the exploited, dispossessed and oppressed peoples of the Global South... People and Planet must be put first over Profit ... polluter and plunderer countries and economies must pay ...if we are to win back this world from corporate capture and imperialist domination" (Dulce 2021). Reparations were however not on the table at Glasgow and would seem to require not simply a heavy tax upon the rich but also their large-scale expropriation. Furthermore, the systemic inertia of global capitalist nations must be identified theoretically and politically opposed strategically. Profitable overproduction and profitable waste, derived from the fetishism of exchange values over use values within the privately-owned system of production, account for the self-serving corporate and governmental inaction.

After the disappointing results of the COP26 Climate Crisis conference, grassroots activists have taken up a campaign to make *ecocide* a crime, analogous to genocide via the International Criminal Court (Killean 2021). This movement traces its origins to the devastation to forests, biodiversity, and human beings caused by the U.S. employment of Agent Orange in carpet bombing during the Vietnam War. Corporate and governmental impunity with regard to their programs involving massive for-profit environmental destruction is to be abolished. Today's business owners and managers are to be held accountable for ongoing devastation. This prosecution could occur as a parallel to Beth Macy's account in *Dopesick: Dealers, Doctors and the Drug Company that Addicted America* of the legal case against the Sackler family for untold Oxycontin deaths. How to accomplish recompense, restitution, reparation, or restoration?

In the 1970s Marcuse tied a charge of ecocide to his Vietnam war criticism. "U.S. bombs are meant to prevent the people of North Vietnam from undertaking the economic and social rehabilitation of the land" (Marcuse [1972] 2005, 174). For Marcuse the U.S. program of ecocide was also genocide against the Vietnamese people in so far as it attacked "the sources and resources of life itself." He is sickened by the fact that it seemed that for the U.S.

> ...it was no longer enough to do away with people living now; life must be denied to those who are not even born yet by burning

and poisoning the Earth, defoliating the forests, blowing up the dikes. This bloody insanity will not alter the ultimate course of the war, but it is a very clear expression of where contemporary capitalism is at: the cruel waste of productive resources in the imperialist homeland goes hand in hand with the cruel waste of destructive forces and consumption of commodities of death manufactured by the war industry." (Marcuse [1972] 2005, 173)

"Ecocide is an essential legacy of war" (Marciano 2016, 146). Dropping more tonnage in Southeast Asia than the U.S. had used in all of World War II, became part of a strategy, which Marcuse recognized as a "vital aspect of the [U.S. political war makers' and arms makers'] counterrevolution" (Marcuse [1972] 2005, 173). As I have repeatedly stressed, the U.S. military is the largest single source of greenhouse gasses. In December 2021, U.S. Congress passed its annual military spending bill costing $778 billion and providing a bipartisan $25 billion more in Pentagon funding than requested by U.S. President Joe Biden and nearly $38 billion more than the last such bill of former President Donald Trump's tenure. We must stop the wasted abundance that this military spending represents.

Super-accumulation is one of the chief characteristics of today's capitalist arms manufacturers and the nation's largest banks that use financial and engineering cleverness to fashion investment strategies in accordance with its obsession with short-term market/profit advantage. The growth in income of society's upper *echelons of privilege* is dramatically out of proportion to the reductions in income experienced by nearly everyone else throughout the society. The income, wealth, and power of the most parasitic elements of the U.S. economy and military have grown excessively relative to the system's total output. Meanwhile, components of the system's productive forces (e.g. infrastructure, labor force skills, the global ecosystem) are being down-sized and under-reproduced. The "surplus" population stigmatized, suffocated, crushed.

U.S. foreign investment has left its economy de-industrialized: U.S. corporations invest capital abroad, hiring lower-cost labor internationally, and disinvest domestically, shifting production, employment and fixed capital investment largely to Asia. The U.S. thus became trade-dependent for most manufactures, except, as Hudson emphasizes, for arms-making, still a key source of domestically acquired superprofits. Super-accumulation is built upon racism and the globalized "race to the bottom" for cheapened labor.

What we are seeing today is the beginning of the end of a decaying system, whose productive base is not being reproduced. In the current period overappropriation is achieved primarily when reproduction resources are shifted from the middle class—the American system's vaunted citizenry—toward the financial sector and the society's "1 percent." The *mode of privilege* of the elite *is* being reproduced. The *mode of governance*, i.e. the state, *is* being reproduced. Neoliberal right-wing elites nonetheless wish to absorb for themselves greater amounts of the surplus that has traditionally gone to the liberal state. Intensifying accumulation also requires that the imperative of exploitation becomes more and more predatory. Beyond the super-exploitation of labor, the predatory logic leads to the financial abuse of even large-scale institutional investors and millions of individual middle-class home buyers. Predatory profits come *not* from value production, but from the transfer/extraction of wealth from pension funds and the sale of commercial and residential mortgages of little worth to unsuspecting investors, consistent with the venerable exercise of imperial power. Manic capitalism's obsession with its commodity fetish was not able to control itself, leading to Wall Street's 2008 house of cards collapse.

The system is under duress. Continuing allegiances to crumbling structures of power will be seen as fatally misguided because they entail real material loss and suffering; they can and will swiftly shift. Our duty over the long haul is to replace global capitalism's self-destructive tendencies with intercultural labor force activism and humanism—to create laboring humanity's self-governing cosmopolitan EarthCommonWealth. Marcuse emphasizes that despite the violence of domination and this destructive institutional context, an emancipatory "radical character structure" emerges from advanced industrial society in which subversive needs come to supersede the repressive compensatory needs of the established order: "the potential forces of social change are there" (Marcuse [1979] 2011, 209-210). Revolutionary materialism *does* include a vision of intercultural solidarity against the resurgent politics of white supremacy, oligarchic wealth idolization, profitable waste, as well as the toxic masculinity characteristic of authoritarian populism.

Angela Davis in *Freedom is a Constant Struggle* (2016) urges women and men to build mass movements for systemic change. She stresses the intersectionality of struggles such that "When we see police repressing protests in Ferguson we have to think about the Israeli police and the Israeli army repressing protests in occupied Palestine" (Davis 2016, 45). We have to prioritize a demand for a society without the kind of policing we are experiencing today. She calls for "political alliances that will move us in the direction of transnational solidarities" (Davis 2016, 139). In her latest volume she connects, for example, struggles against racist police murder in Ferguson, Missouri, and the movement for the liberation of Palestine in the Middle East. They are linked in multiple ways, even in terms of the tear gas cannisters used against protesters in both places. Critical social theory thus builds towards *transnational transformation*.

Collaboration around a radical agenda recognizing the basic economic and political needs of diverse subaltern communities is essential. System negation must become a new general interest. Predatory political forces must be counteracted today, and this is best accomplished through the global abolition of rentier income. Marcuse's critical Marxism has been supplemented in this volume with discussions of core ethical insights from African philosophical sources, indigenous American philosophy, wildlife ecology, feminist anthropology, and critical realism. Challenging and changing the system of global capitalism may well be the hardest human undertaking ever, yet it is within our power and expresses our highest and finest species needs in common, a desire for a future that is reclaimed and dignified. EarthCommonWealth is attainable given a collective Great Refusal and activist engagement.

"Destroy patriarchy, not the planet"

Marcuse's emphasis on the emancipatory power of the women's movement has been discussed at length in chapters 4 and 5 above. Let us here, approaching our conclusion, take up once more Riane Eisler's anthropological account of partnership power versus dominator power. "Why do we hunt and persecute each other? Why is our world so full of man's infamous inhumanity to man—and to woman?" (Eisler 1987 xiii). For Eisler, dominator power rests on misogyny and misguided masculinity. For dominator power, morality rests upon obedience to male authority, not knowledge, empathy, or cooperation. Dominator power ranks "man over woman, race over race, religion over religion, nation over nation, [and] man over nature" (Eisler 2000, 4). Partnership ethics looks toward a "more democratic and egalitarian family and social structure, gender equity, a low level of institutionalized violence and abuse ..., and a system of belief, stories, and values that supports and validates this kind of structure as normal and right" (Eisler 2000, 5). Our capacities to love and create make us fully human. Dominator power alienates us from our full humanity.

For the longest stretch of human history humans have lived in partnership societies. Since Comte, sociologists have sought to study human history as a whole. Anthropologists now stress that social development has occurred, but is not always in accord with steady social evolutionary progress (Graeber and Wengrow 2021). Sudden fundamental changes, including regressions, and what Gerda Lerner has called *The Creation of Patriarchy* (1986) punctuated both the equilibrium and any improvement. Dominator cultures increasingly stressed the power to take lives, whereas partnership cultures centered the power to give life. Eisler writes seriously and critically about political economy in *The Real Wealth of Nations* (2007). She asks questions about ownership and income, like Who Owns America? She discusses the power structure research of G. William Domhoff ([1967] 2022). Her "new economics" stresses what I have previously called an *ecology of care*. Our essential work is "caring for people and for nature" (Eisler 2007, 3). In her estimation, this understanding of care is gaining ground in terms of a proper recognition of its economic importance. Capitalism's obsession with production for profit (its fetishizing of exchange values over use values in meeting human needs) is the foundation that for centuries now has warped our social fabric with its lack of caring: people are handled according to business standards instead of being cared for as sensuous living labor in our own right. Tender attention is afforded to the needs and demands of large-scale industrial and commercial concerns for short-term profitability; these displace humane and caring considerations almost entirely—both for humans and the planet. Eisler warns that we are at a tipping point and "We need a caring revolution" (Eisler 2007, 24)

The revolutionary progeny of Prometheus / Persephone

The women's movement has had an immense impact since its third wave emergence in the U.S. during the 1970s. According to my colleague, Tamara Agha-Jaffar, "Only feminism makes explicit the connections between systemic violence against women, against people of color, and against the planet" (AghaJaffar 2002, 102). Marcuse gives the women's movement tremendous credit for its contributions to what he called the "New Sensibility" represented by the "Children of Prometheus." Let's be clear at the outset that we're not interested in whether Prometheus or Persephone had children: we're talking about *all the children of tomorrow*, who need to understand something from both of these figures and "who must learn to live in more environmentally conscious, equitable, and peaceful ways" (Eisler 2000, xiii). For Marcuse, the new sensibility "is emerging today in the women's movement against patriarchal domination, which came of age socially only under capitalism; in the protests against the nuclear power industry and the destruction of nature as an ecological space that cut across all fixed class boundaries; and in the student movement, which despite being declared dead, still lives on in struggles against the degradation of teaching and learning into activities that reproduce the system" (Marcuse [1979] 2011). Marcuse was impressed by the steady growth among young people of *new needs*, generated under capitalism, but which capitalism cannot fulfill, *for gender equality, ecological economics, anti-racism,* and *peace*. For Marcuse the new sensibility is characterized by an ethics of partnership, racial and gender equality, satisfaction from work, earth admiration, and ecological responsibility. The new sensibility reaches for the radical as opposed to the merely rudimentary goals of socialism (1972, 5).

As Tamara Agha-Jaffar interprets the meaning of the classical Persephone myth, it teaches women that they can move beyond victimization and assume responsibility for their own healing and transformation towards empowerment and autonomy. The story of Persephone is one of the rape of an innocent young girl by the god of the underworld, but it shows how even female victimization can be turned into something constructive that can strengthen and empower other women and produce new life (Agha-Jaffar 2002, 54, 119). The empowered progeny of Persephone may be seen as an allegory for nature's own resilience after abuse. No cosmic plan, but ontological grounds for human maturation, partnership and peace with sexuality lifted into the Eros of commonwealth, with Earth as Ally.

Prometheus was punished by Zeus for giving fire [and by extension all other technologies of production] to the human race. His concern for improving humanity's material condition is sometimes misread as a commitment to an all-out productivism, such as that which characterizes a profit-addicted industrial capitalism. Marcuse's *Eros and Civilization* (1955) had unfavourably contrasted the performance principle with the sensuous and aesthetic pleasure principle. The former was signified by the figure of the striving Prometheus; the latter was epitomized by Orpheus and Narcissus. By 1979 Marcuse finds that the *children* of Prometheus have experienced the transvaluation of values that have rejected the unquestioning acceptance of the operational norms of capitalism and the existence of the human body as an instrument of production. These children of Prometheus view technology as a means of liberation from the struggle for existence, part of the "apparatus of freedom" in a post-capitalist future. Their New Sensibility, it bears repeating, constitutes an oppositional philosophy and politics: "[Changed] needs are present, here and now. They permeate the lives of individuals …. First the need for drastically reducing socially necessary alienated labor and replacing it with creative work. Second, the need for autonomous free time instead of directed leisure. Third, the need for an end of role playing [i.e., inauthentic conformity]. Fourth, the need for receptivity, tranquility and abounding joy, instead of the constant noise of production …. The specter which haunts advanced industrial society today is the obsolescence of full-time alienation" (Marcuse [1979] 2011, 211).

> The "children of Prometheus" are not "clueless:" those who rule the economy and politics, who decide what constitutes progress, continue to do so. They are not much interested in a long-term view: the others, who cannot bear this kind of progress, are constituting themselves almost spontaneously into an opposition in new kinds of ways, for the most part outside of and against the established political parties and class organizations. This is a protest from all classes of society, motivated by a deep, visceral, and intellectual inability to comply, by a will to rescue whatever humanity, joy, and autonomy may still be rescued: a revolt of the lifeinstincts against the socially organized death-instinct. (Marcuse [1979] 2011, 224).

All of this has "caused, mainly among the young people, a radical transformation of needs and values which may prove to be incompatible with the capitalist system, its hierarchy, priorities, morality, symbols (the counter-culture, ecology)" (Marcuse [1975] 2015, 304-307).

Daniel R. Wildcat's indigenous realism, calling also for an indigenized ecosocialism, is clear that "[c]ulture must not be primarily conceived as something humans use to control, mediate, and re-engineer nature to fit our human-scale notion of life on this planet. Rather, culture should be understood as expressions of how humans integrate their lives into the landscapes and ecosystems of the earth's biosphere" (Wildcat 2009, 31). He emphasizes that technology need not be rejected if it promotes an indigenous way of living stressing communal possession and respect of the land. The ultimate value of technology is measured by an enhancement of community, communication, and culture (Wildcat 2009, 90, 128).

Marcuse likewise stresses in his culminating philosophical statement "Children of Prometheus" that human civilization cannot be sustained if the value framework of capitalism continues to guide our destiny. The salient message his essay offers is that only through a radical reconfiguration of technology and society—one that cultivates and supports life and health instead of serving to prolong the reign of exchange value and the unencumbered flow of commodities across the global landscape—can civilization escape the trajectory that capitalist development has set humanity upon.

Learning from the ecofeminists

I have discussed women's issues largely in only general terms under what I have inadequately termed "women's inequality," as if this phrase covered all forms of women's oppression. My analysis stressed the need for "partnership power" and "gylany" as these notions are developed in the work of Riane Eisler and Tamara Agha-Jaffar. These perspectives go beyond "catching up" to males in the existing society. Still, the ecofeminist views of Vandana Shiva, Maria Mies, Ariel Sallah, and Silvia Federici have unpacked more fully what I intended when writing about women's justice and equality, but failed to make explicit. I have, for example, criticized humanity's long history of patriarchy, especially capitalist patriarchy, but needed to have detailed what this has meant in terms of the particulars of the multi-dimensional oppression of women today:

- toxic male violence against women through rape, female feticide, spouse abuse, sexual assault, sex tourism, child pornography
- systemic economic exploitation and exclusion and devaluation of women's labor; endless unpaid work; male worker's power over unwaged labor of wife and children; abuse of immigrant women in workforce
- feminization of poverty; damage to families and children; prostitution; alcoholism
- control over women's bodies; no right to decide how many children to have and to care for; criminalization of abortion
- minoritized populations enduring disproportionate rates of maternal mortality and infant mortality

Ecofeminist authors furnish a critique of these multiple forms of injury and damage to women's lives and a significant critique of science in service of destruction of nature, i.e. a critique of the arms' industries and militarism as well as the industrialization of agriculture, with a call for science to become partisan against the oppression of women and nature. Marcuse's support for the women's movement is thoroughly consistent with issues more adequately unfolded in the literature of the ecofeminists (Salleh 2017; Mies and Shiva 2021; Federici. 2020) .

The educative power of struggle

Herbert Marcuse's initial cultural impact in the U.S. was connected closely to the intellectual and political, campus-based turmoil of the 1960s, and was related to his theoretical influence on the global radical student movement and to his addressing key educational issues involved. Marcuse's reputation in the U.S. and in Europe was that of a spokesperson for radical university reform and for the militant new left's analysis of (and resistance to) the foreign and domestic policies of the U.S. government. Marcuse examined, for example, the questions of science and research in service to the "logic of domination" embedded within advanced industrial society (Marcuse 1964, 144). He also addressed the almost infinite facets of alienation and domination in everyday life, i.e., at school, on the job, and in recreational activities, where these were thought to be regulated by a "total administration" (Marcuse 1964, 7). He combatted institutional racism with his critique of pure tolerance (Reitz 2009a) and stressed the emancipatory potential of a renascent sensuality under the guidance of the most rational and legitimate goals of art (Marcuse 1969). A new form of liberal arts education could act against one-dimensionality and cultural alienation, re-humanizing political life (Reitz 2009b). At the same time, education needed to become activist. Students and teachers needed to "become partisan against oppression, militarization, brutalization" (Marcuse [1968] 2009, 38). There needed to be a key unity in education of critical thought and radical action; the need for the movements of change must be made evident in systems of schooling "preparing the ground for a better, more humane society" (Marcuse [1968] 2009, 37).

Critical educators and students needed to continue to take risks and struggle to infuse the curriculum with analysis of the "critical, radical movements and theories in history, literature, philosophy" (Marcuse [1968] 2009, 37). Because humanity is a multicultural species, the curriculum must afford a world-historical, international, and multicultural perspective that examines the pivotal social struggles that have led to the emergence of key standards of criticism in ethics, in logic, in the worlds of art, physical science, production and technology. These standards constitute the *criteria* of judgment which intelligence requires. Catalyst groups within higher education institutions have quite remarkably moved educational theory and practice forward in recent decades, especially the anti-racist and anti-sexist movements for multicultural education reform.

Richard Kahn (2009), professor of educational philosophy at Antioch, was among the first critical educationists to elaborate Herbert Marcuse's value to ecopedagogy and radical environmentalist activism. Kahn was closely attuned to the rise of ecomilitancy of such groups as the Earth Liberation Front and the Animal Liberation Front, often advocating direct action against the military, corporations, and the state, including destruction of property. Kahn viewed such radical activism as primarily of educative value, and argues against construing such direct action as ecoterrorism, as the corporate media and mainstream politicians often do. Kahn points out that, if in Marcuse's estimation violence may be legitimately used against fascism, so too the use of violence to damage corporate property may legitimately be used against corporations that exploit and destroy the environment. He also holds that such activism is short-sighted and deficient in that it lacks theoretical coherence in terms of both radical political philosophy and educative practice. Indigenous protest, on the other hand, grounded in the conservation of resources, as with the 2016 Water Protectors of the Standing Rock Sioux, defies corporate power with the cultural affirmation (through music, dance, poetry and prayer) of nature as ally in human life. This did *not* keep the protesters safe from the violence of militarized police serving the interests of the Dakota Access Pipeline. Still the pipeline was shut down for the foreseeable future in 2020.[10]

Peter McLaren's eminent series of writings in critical educational theory (1997; 2000; 2007; 2015a; 2015b) has called for a pedagogy of revolution and revolutionary multiculturalism—that is, teaching the truth about ending class exploitation, racism, gender inequality, empire, and war. In 2007 he and his co-author Nathalia Jaramillo sharply criticized

---

10 Breanna Draxler, "Water Protectors Celebrate as Dakota Access Pipeline Ordered to Shut Down" *Democracy Now!* July 8, 2020. https://www.yesmagazine.org/video/dakota-accesspipe-line-shut-down

the rising tide of U.S. belligerence and its manipulation of the public mind with real and imagined threats in the service of a militarist patriotism. In *Pedagogy and Praxis in the Age of Empire* (2007) they trace the root causes of our contemporary crises to competition among "petrolarchs" for control of the world's oil and natural gas reserves which is producing a time of permanent war in pursuit of global hegemony.

McLaren's subsequent *Pedagogy of Insurrection* (2015b) highlights the importance of a critique of political economy to educational theory and practice. Its leading section, "Solving the Problem of Inequality: The Market Is Not a Sustainable or Livable Community," begins with the foundational recognition that "[s]chools in the main reflect the inequality found in the structure of capitalist society" (2015b, 19). He makes clear: "the market is not a community. It is only possible to realize your humanity if you are educated in an authentic community.... Critical educators assume the position that equality is both a precondition and outcome for establishing community, and a community is a precondition for deep democracy" (2015b, 21, 23).

> Revolutionary critical educators question capitalist concepts—such as wage labor and value production—alongside their students in order to consider alternative ways of subsisting and learning in the world so as to continually transform it along the arc of social and economic justice.... As such, critical pedagogy calls for a movement that is anti-capitalist, anti-imperialist, anti-racist, anti-sexist, anti-heterosexist and pro-democratic. (McLaren 2015b, 35)

In this work McLaren also rethinks the formation of critical consciousness (i.e. theory formation) and its relationship to radical practice. In a fashion that I take to be a Copernican revolution reversing conventional thinking on the matter, he writes:

> Critical consciousness is not the root of commitment to revolutionary struggle but rather the product of such a commitment. An individual does not have to be critically self-conscious and well-versed in the theories of the Frankfurt School or the writings of liberation theologians in order to feel the obligation to help the poor and the dispossessed. In fact, it is in the very act of struggling along-side the oppressed that individuals become critically conscious and aware and motivated to help others. Praxis begins with practice. (McLaren 2015b, 29-30)

This *educative* power of struggle is illustrated in a high-profile showdown between students and administrators over institutional racism and related conflicts at "Mizzou," the University of Missouri, Columbia, in 2015. Here *theoretical deficiencies* on the part of the top administration, especially their lack of familiarity with features of the multicultural educational reform movement, led to swift disaster for the system President, Timothy Wolfe. After a semester of student protests—against cost-cutting measures (proposals to eliminate the University of Missouri Press and fighting the drastic cuts in health care and other benefits for graduate teaching assistants); against administrative decisions to eliminate the privileges of Planned Parenthood doctors at the university hospital; against administrative cultural insensitivity to issues arising from bigotry on campus; and against the university's passivity regarding lethal racism in law enforcement at nearby Ferguson, Missouri,—system President Wolfe (one of the new corporate kind of university CEOs with no academic background) was cell-phone-videoed responding ineffectually when challenged directly by black students to define *systematic oppression*. When he said this was a matter of the *perceptions* of discrimination held by the black students, the protesters were aghast, and regarded his response as dismissive victim-blaming. When the video went viral, the struggle widened dramatically with black members of the university's Division 1 football team announcing that they would strike until Wolfe resigned or was removed from office. A key economic pressure point had been found. The coach and concerned faculty supported the student strikers, and system President Wolfe and campus chancellor, R. Bowen Loftin, resigned seemingly unassailable positions of power in a matter of days.

The social movements of our age have been its civilizing forces. BLM [Black Lives Matter], with whom the Mizzou students were allied, has effectively educated the nation about the real nature of undemocratic governance (in municipalities and higher education institutions), and the cavalier use of racist deadly force (on and off the campus). The organized social struggles against racism, sexism, poverty, war, and imperialism, have educated wide swaths of this country's population outside traditional classrooms about alienation and oppression, power and empowerment.

Thus, McLaren's critical perspective resonates with my own work, especially as he regards the crises of political economy and the ecology. McLaren's *Pedagogy of Insurrection* takes a visionary turn breaking new ground with his emphasis on several key new themes arising from radical struggles around the world. *First,* the concept of *planetary comunalidad* and the *revolutionary eco-pedagogy* are commensurate with it. McLaren is one of the rarest of critical theorists of education: he has engaged with pedagogical issues developed in the Global South. McLaren contends "*Comunalidad* is a Oaxacan concept that serves as a type of cosmovision, and it deals with 'the complex intertwining of history, morality, spirituality, kinship and communal practices' [derived from] '[t]he concept of reciprocity …that requires the other or others to make …equivalent response[s], and it is meant to be a permanent relation and inclusive of all members of the community'" (McLaren 2015b, 328). McLaren subsequently generalizes lessons for contemporary critical pedagogy:

> Critical educators, who have addressed for decades and with firm commitment topics of race, class, gender, sexuality, disability and other social justice issues are now casting their eyes to the antagonism between capitalism and nature to ask themselves how we can rationally regulate the human metabolic relation with nature. In our struggle for a 'transformed economy founded on the nonmonetary values of social justice and ecological balance' we don't follow a productivist socialism or capitalist market ecology. We emphasize use value, not exchange value and 'a liberation from the alienating economic 'laws' of the growth-oriented capitalist system.' …. [Vandana] Shiva's general principle of 'earth democracy' is congruent with the idea that the foundations of the means of production in land, seed, water and so on, need to be kept in perpetuity by an arranged social commons. (McLaren 2015b, 301, 316)

Secondly, McLaren's long-standing appreciation for the political praxis of Che Guevara and Fidel Castro animates his earlier writing (McLaren 2000) and continues in this volume with a lionization of *"Comrade Chávez."* McLaren's evaluation of the early successes of Hugo Chávez as president of Venezuela (unambiguously elected and reelected in 1998, 2000, 2006) offers an understanding of strategic lessons, even if the later leadership of Chávez and that of his successor Nicolás Maduro have been the subject of much controversy and opposition given the economic turmoil, in part self-inflicted, post-2013 in Venezuela.[11] "Chavezmo" was and is a vital 21st

---

11 Michael Hudson (2022, 14) notes that several U.S-sponsored coups against Nicolás Maduro

Century revolutionary resurgence, part of the "pink tide" including the rise of Evo Morales in Bolivia and Raphael Correro in Ecuador (in some ways similar to the *indigenismo* noted by Wildcat and Martínez as well as Oaxacan *comunalidad)* that resonated deeply with the political needs of South America's impoverished peoples and their resistance to the material suffering of decades of oppression. Chávez gave a voice to the Venezuelan masses and spent heavily on social-needs-oriented programs. Though Venezuela's immense oil resources had been nominally nationalized in 1976, they remained under the control of foreign interests through Venezuelan proxies. Chávez challenged this arrangement in an assertion of Venezuelan sovereignty. Opposition to Chávez and Maduro in Venezuela, with the U.S. in the global forefront, formally recognized the U.S.friendly politician Juan Guaidó over Maduro. This is reminiscent of the U.S.instigated opposition and overthrow of Iran's President Mossadegh after his nationalization of the Iranian oil fields in 1953 as well as the overthrow of Salvador Allende in Chile in 1973. In terms of educational philosophy and policy, "Chávez was not about to let the business sector set the priorities for public education and thereby colonize the commons with the ideas of the transnational capitalist class in which the knowledge most valued is that which is the most exploitable in a capitalist economy, and where knowledge becomes fragmented, instrumentalized and narrowly specialized ...." (McLaren 2015b, 171).

Thirdly, McLaren roundly criticizes *guns in the service of capital*— "The idea that guns preserve democracy constitutes an unconscionable and egregious swindle of benevolence that is unfathomable in the face of continuous bloodshed" (McLaren 2015b, 355). "Regardless of rhetoric, guns are mass-produced to kill ...." (McLaren 2015b, 357). "[G]uns form part of the broader militaryindustrial complex that encompasses our military, the prison system, the law enforcement industry, the border patrol industry, weapons manufacturing corporations, marketing strategists, training schools and gun safety and crime prevention programs" (McLaren 2015b, 357). "We see the interests of the elite capitalist class too clearly in the failure to restrict guns even after such atrocious events as the recent massacre at Sandy Hook Elementary in Newtown, Connecticut" (McLaren 2015b, 358). Commercialized gun violence figures into

---

failed, and Britain seized Venezuela's gold reserves "holding them for whomever U.S. officials might decide should be the official leader of that country;" this meant that Venezuela could not pay for food, medicine, or other needed imports.

Marcuse's critique of repressive desublimation and toxic masculinity. Ultimately, it is corporate capitalism, heavily invested in and dependent on arms industry profits, that must be wholly expropriated and become a public entity! Marcuse's vision of revolutionary ecological liberation would include such expropriation of expropriators in the new system of ownership and democratic ecosocialist governance.

Fourthly, McLaren echoes Marcuse's Great Refusal emphasizing *the praxis of negation*—"We do not want to fit into this destructive society of commodified, monetized relations of capitalism. We refuse to live within relations of subordination wrought by capital with its ever-increasing rate of exploitation. We will not let capital define and redefine us according to its need to maintain its rate of profit" (McLaren 2015b, 341).

Lastly, McLaren eulogizes *"Comrade Jesus"*—linking his own work to that of Cornel West and Chris Hedges, both radical socialist Christians. "I do not suddenly mention this [the teachings of Jesus] out of some otherworldly penchant, but for a concern for the here and the now. The majority of American citizens are Christians of some denomination or other, and it is important to point out as an incontrovertible fact that the message of Jesus in the Gospels is focused on the liberation of the poor from captivity and oppression" (McLaren 2015b, 103).

When religion is a lifeline with a moral imperative of revolt

McLaren leads us on an expedition into dialectics of Christianity and Marxism and on into new philosophical terrain (McLaren and Jandrić 2020). He explores the relevance and meaning of liberation theology within the context of revolutionary critical pedagogy and ecosocialist activism. McLaren is both a Marxist educator and a Catholic convert who refuses to glorify the church. He reviews the past century's history of U.S. exploitation of Central and South America, through dictators and death squads, including the execution of religious leaders who had pledged themselves to the preferential option for the poor. Liberation movements found their ethical ground in solidarity with workers' families in the countryside. Catholicism was finding common moral ground with Marxism. McLaren interprets Jesus as a communist, "the intervening Absolute" delinking us from the alienation of everyday conformity to oppressive reality such that "we are able to seize the torch of liberation" (McLaren 2015b, 105). All of this is a risky move for McLaren, but it is intellectually and politically warranted as well as strategic. Radicals must respect the activism of religiously motivated opponents of capitalist oppression. In a phrase attributed to Ernesto Che Guevarra, "If you tremble with indignation at every injustice then you are a comrade of mine."

McLaren's discussion with Jandrić reviews the 2004 dialogue between the secular critical theorist, Jürgen Habermas, and Joseph Cardinal Ratzinger, a critic of liberation theology. Habermas's thesis here (and again in his 2019 *Auch eine Geschichte der Philosophie [And Moreover a History of Philosophy]*) is that religion is still a part of the non-religious philosophical search for what he calls "postmetaphysical" and "postsecular" truth and justice. Habermas asks: how shall we understand the discourse about belief and knowledge in a secular humanist epoch? The unexpected dialectical outcome is an ostensible *integration* of the secular and the religious! As he sees it, an enduring ethical thread can account for the persistence of religion in a non-religious age. Habermas detects this thread in the conviction that all religions and philosophy gravitate toward a transcendental ethical truth, something like Kant's categorical imperative: partnership ethics of empathy and cooperation, the Golden Rule. Habermas sees this happen most vividly in the Axial Age of Socrates, Laozi, Kongfuzi, Buddha, and Jesus (Habermas 2019, 177-460). In class-divided societies, the claim of any ruling group that it is protecting the common good ultimately loses its legitimation. Yet it is the criterion of the common good which persists as the universal political/ethical ground for emancipatory change. McLaren concludes: "By translating the contents of pre-political religious symbols into secular-rational ones, and vice versa, we can create epistemic/moral foundations for shared, solidaristic post-secular cognitive dispositions" (McLaren and Jandrić 2020, 100). "Both Jesus and Marx maintained a commitment to the poor and the powerless" (McLaren and Jandrić 2020, 101). McLaren emphasizes that even given such unifying insights one must uphold the separation of church and state. He sees Habermas as unfolding a critical pedagogy and attempting "a reciprocal/complementary learning process" (McLaren and Jandrić 2020, 101), which he regards as requiring shared multicultural understanding and religious reflexivity. As one who respects the ethical common ground I can find with religion, though a free-thinker myself, I rate this new intellectually integrative work of McLaren's as of the greatest consequence. I agree with McLaren's and Habermas's perspective on religion's capacity to generate the deepest, most comprehensive levels of love, learning, and leadership. McLaren has long championed revolutionary multicultural education reform to develop antiracist sensibilities and a common ethical/political clarity and a "global ethics of solidarity" (McLaren and Jandrić 2020, 115).

Given the context of political conflict that has surrounded the practical impact of liberation theology, not all historical developments have led to sublation and advance to higher levels. By 2008 the U.S. State Department and the Vatican under Joseph Cardinal Ratzinger, having become Pope Benedict, were at war with those in El Salvador preaching and practicing the preferential option for the poor.

McLaren states explicitly that "I agree with Herbert Marcuse ([1969] 2011) when he wrote in 'The Role of Religion in a Changing Society' that no evaluation of that role can be made without meeting Marx's criticism of religion" (McLaren and Jandrić 2020, 103). At the same time, McLaren posits the existence of a God as a utopian force guiding human history—ensuring that "injustice and exploitation will disappear once and for all" (McLaren and Jandrić 2020, 104). In this assessment, he follows the eschatological thinking of liberation theologists Leonardo Boff and José Porfirio Miranda. McLaren emphasizes that liberation theology as represented by "Miranda (1974, 1980), makes a convincing case that the Bible condemns the exploitation suffered by the poor at the hands of the rich and creates an identity between the rich and the unjust... The poor are blessed because the coming of the Kingdom in the fullness of history will put an end—in the concrete sociological sense—to their poverty and suffering" (McLaren and Jandrić, 106-107).

McLaren also links the liberation theology of Miranda and Boff to philosophical and social *struggle*. Miranda and Boff see conflict and contradiction as propelling an eschatological force. In their liberation theology: "Jesus came to revolutionize the social structure of religion not to occupy a throne …. Rebellion against religion is mandatory for anyone who wants to bring justice into the world" (McLaren and Jandrić 2020, 105). McLaren also holds that Boff in particular sees the foundations of ethics in commonwealth labor, which is my own non-theistic, non-eschatological Marxist ethical position. It is grounded in a philosophy of partnership labor and an egalitarian commonwealth; thus, despite differences, it intersects with liberation theology in the discussion of what it means to be human. Leonardo Boff refers to human agency as spirit, as conscious vitality structured around a vital center. McLaren holds this *spirit* to be grounded in (and a sublation of) the "ontology of *labor*" developed by Marx and Marcuse, which is part of the "vital energy of the cosmos groaning to be liberated...." (McLaren and Jandrić, 234).

In order to understand and to do "what is necessary to remain a viable species on the face of a foundering planet, ... we need not believe that the cosmos is infused with God and Word, or follow the teachings of the patron saint of ecology, Saint Francis" (McLaren and Jandrić, 234). Instead, we may echo the humanism Kant: "Act so as to further the evolution of a humanly favorable dynamic equilibrium in the biosphere" (Erwin László in McLaren and Jandrić 2020, 241). Or we may follow the humanist lead of Marx, which Marcuse describes as accepting "the need for religion as long as mental and physical oppression prevail and no effective forces striving for change of these conditions are operating" (Marcuse [1969] 2011, 183). Thinking of the Euthyphro, to my mind, it is not religion as such, that carries the authentic philosophical power here but the ethical realism embedded in religion when grounded in mutual respect, cooperation, and the reciprocity of commonwealth labor.

Marcuse, Marx, and McLaren agree that the progressive critical elements of religion must be made complete; they must be made into reality. We must use "all possible means of protest" in the "indictment of what those who rule our lives are doing with this country ..." (Marcuse [1969] 2011, 187). For Marcuse religion as indictment can contribute to the Great Refusal:

> [W]e live in a profoundly immoral and profoundly inhuman society behind the veil of a free democratic process and behind the veil of prosperity. Behind the veil of prosperity, waste, destruction, and war, the brutalization of entire populations, and poverty and misery are not only abroad but within our national frontiers—and all this in a historical period in which the resources for the liberation of all men would be available if they would be rationally used in the interests of man and not only certain vested interests. Now, against this society you see today the global rebellion of the youth, together with the liberation movements of the oppressed people in the Third World, and in the Black liberation movement. (Marcuse [1969] 2011, 185)

The affinity of radical socialist Christians Chris Hedges and Cornel

West with McLaren and Marcuse is clear in their shared emphasis on the moral imperative of revolt. Chris Hedges' *Wages of Rebellion* (2015) begins with an epigram from Marcuse's "Repressive Tolerance" essay heralding Marcuse's call to militant resistance to both the rhetoric and the politics of racialized destruction and suppression. Hedges valorizes the Black prophetic tradition in this regard, epitomized by Cornel West. "This tradition, which stretches back to Sojourner Truth and Frederick Douglass, has consistently named and damned the cruelty of imperialism and white supremacy. It has been our most astute critique of empire. The Black prophetic tradition expressed radical truths with a clarity and moral force that have eluded most other critics of American capitalism… The Black freedom movement puts pressure on the American empire in the name of integrity, decency, honesty and virtue." (Hedges 2015, 113-114).

McLaren's Christian ethic of liberation, his Marxist humanism, and his critique of predatory capitalism are clearly congenial to central elements of Marcuse's philosophy. McLaren's critique of U.S. militarism, the surveillance state, Terror War, and especially gun violence, resonates also with the larger work of Marcusean scholars, Douglas Kellner (2003, 2008) and Langman and Lundskow (2017). McLaren's ecosocialist and ecopedogical advocacy has likewise come to undergird the EarthCommonWealth perspective developed in this volume.

In conclusion:
The struggle for EarthCommonWealth: Workforce rebellion as resource with strategic power

Human life around the globe is being threatened by brute force and subtle despoilation with destruction. Looking back, there is Auschwitz, Guernica, Wounded Knee, My Lai, Birmingham, Kent State, Attica … Love Canal, Deepwater Horizon, Standing Rock, Flint … and now Kyiv and Mariupol, Buffalo and Uvalde.

Regressive political forces must be countered today and this is best accomplished through radical collaboration around an agenda recognizing the basic economic and political needs of diverse subaltern communities. System negation must become a new general interest. This volume has extended Herbert Marcuse's critical Marxism with Peter McLaren's analysis of today's predatory stage of capitalism and the *educative* power of struggle. It has discussed core ethical insights from African philosophical sources, indigenous American philosophy, and radical Christian and feminist philosophy. Humanity's first teachings on ethics are to be found in ancient African proverbs. These subsequently served also as a critique of colonialism and neocolonialism. Long suppressed indigenous American sources supply a philosophical and political critique of Eurocentric economic and cultural values. They also offer an understanding of humanity's place in nature, and the leadership of women, and attest to modes of cooperative and egalitarian forms of community. Feminist anthropology furnishes an historical context for understanding the origins of patriarchy and how to move beyond dominator power to new forms of partnership power. Core commonalities have been highlighted pivoting around partnership, reciprocity, benevolence, and consecrated (commonweal) works within the world's major wisdom traditions including Daoism, Confucianism, Hinduism, Buddhism, Judaism, Christianity, and Islam. Intercultural ethical insights contribute *not* primarily to a politics of difference, but rather to a universally humanist politics of solidarity and hope.

Today the 1% is armed with its own theory; the 99% is not. A fundamentally different outlook is necessary. The main problem, as I see it, is to develop an incisive vision for humanity as sensuous living labor. I have developed in this volume a *labor theory of ethics*, an ethical realism grounded on the mutual respect, cooperation, and reciprocity of *commonwealth labor*. Likewise, labor (as the labor force) is a strategic resource with material momentum and political power. This labor may be withheld when necessary and may also liberate itself from the constraints of exploitation. It can shape the world anew.

The radically socialist logic of commonwealth production, ownership, and stewardship bring to fruition, within the realm of necessity, an intercultural architecture of equality, disalienation, freedom, abundance, ecological unity, and balance. I have attempted to address our current crisis in economic theorizing and in sociological theory more generally. Marcuse has offered us insight into the potentials and latent powers of an incipient radical opposition through the united front activism of catalyst groups representing labor, anti-racism, feminism, gay rights, critical pedagogy, ecology, and peace. Reality holds the promise of an egalitarian political-economy through which we may govern ourselves in terms of our fullest potential and with integrity towards the planet through our ecosocialist and humanist alternative, EarthCommonWealth.

EarthCommonWealth envisions the displacement and transcendence of capitalist oligarchy as such, not simply its most ugly and destructive components. This is a green economic alternative because its ecological vision sees all living things and their non-living earthly surroundings as a global community capable of a dignified, deliberate coexistence. The ecological work of Aldo Leopold also comes into play here. Understanding the earth in global ecological terms Leopold saw it is not merely soil and rock; it is a biotic pyramid, a fountain of energy flowing through a circuit of land, minerals, air, water, plants, and animals including the human species. He proposed a dialectical and materialist "land ethic" as a call to conservation and cooperation, in which the individual's rights to private property in land are contrasted unfavorably with historical patterns of communal ownership.

The latent emancipatory power of labor is axial to the Great Refusal Project. The "New Social Movements" around the globe at the start of the 21st Century learned to ally crucially with labor—as with nature. The militant anti-globalization action in Seattle 1999 against corporate capitalism, the World Trade Organization, and other international financial institutions, united "teamsters and turtles." This meant that activist elements of organized labor in the U.S. and elsewhere in the world engaged with environmental organizations, in a massive confrontation with the paramilitary police power that protected the representatives of global capital as they consolidated their payroll-slashing and earth-bashing investment strategies, through outsourcing and the "race to the bottom." In 2001, a similar confrontation occurred in Genoa, Italy. This was one of the most enormous demonstrations against global finance capital Europe had seen in years. The 2011 and 2012 anti-austerity uprisings in Athens, Rome, Madrid, and elsewhere were equally spectacular and militant. So too the massive student protests against tuition increases in Montreal, Quebec, during March, May, and August 2012. These struggles echo the worker-student protests in Paris 1968, and the new forms of radical political-economic thinking emergent from the now regular meetings of the World Social Forum in Porto Alegre, Brazil and elsewhere. Then there were also the left populist movements of SYRIZA in Greece, Podemos in Spain, and the 2016 Bernie Sanders campaign in the United States in which he nearly took the lead of the Democratic party.

Today, Generation Z-ers are demonstrating for racial equality, women's equality, LGBTQ protections, the restoration of the natural environment, meaningful work and leisure, economic security, gun control, and world peace, as Volpe (2021) has indicated in *Fight*.

> It's not American Zoomers driving this change, or Swedish, or French, or Nigerian Zoomers—It's just Zoomers. From 2011 to 2019, the number of general strikes, anti-government demonstrations and riots around the world increased by more than 200 percent. (Volpe 2021, 134).
>
> In France, 2020 was another year for protests and civil disobedience. The year began with tens of thousands of union members, public sector employees, "yellow vest" demonstrators, lawyers, rail workers, and students protesting government plans for pension reform. (Volpe 2021, 147).

It is hoped that the ecosocialist EarthCommonWealth *Project* will appeal to the energies of those engaged in a wide range of contemporary social justice struggles including ecosocialism and all those just mentioned above: antiracism, the women's movement, LGBTQ rights, and antiwar forces. As the *dialectical counterpart* of what I have elaborated as Marcuse's Great Refusal *Project*, the EarthCommonWealth Project is keyed to *the promesse du bonheur commun*—outlining what our common struggle is *for*, as well as what we are struggling against.

The EarthCommonWealth Project is searching for a new system of ecological production, egalitarian distribution, shared ownership, and democratized governance having its foundation in the ethics of partnership productivity with an ecosocialist and humanist commitment to living our lives on the planet consistent with the most honorable and aesthetic forms of human social and political fulfillment.

We face the objective circumstance of survival. Yet this is also a crucial opportunity for a new political and economic beginning. This volume has made the case for building a universal human community on the foundation of the satisfaction of universal human needs. *EarthCommonWealth* is a vision of an ecosocialist *system-alternative* calling for the elimination the capitalist economy's core fetish of exchange value, which is also *the* prerequisite for a restoration of nature and the human material condition. The attainment of *EarthCommonWealth*, as an intercultural labor force humanism, is necessary and *feasible*: it is the instinctual and gravitational center holding social life together despite flare ups and explosions caused by the massive forces of careening corporate capitalism. The EarthCommonWealth Project outlined here strives to be programmatic for a New Global Left and the 21st Century's Revolution—against the wastefulness and destruction of monopoly capitalism—and for racial equality, gender equality, and the restoration of nature, liberation of labor, leisure, abundance, and peace.

Works cited

Agha-Jaffar, Tamara. 2002. *Demeter and Persephone: Lessons from a Myth*. London: McFarland & Co.

Agyeman, Edmund Akwasi. 2021. In Francis B. Nyamnjoh, Patrick U. Nwosu, and Hassan M. Yosimbom (eds). *Being and Becoming African as a Permanent Work in Progress: Inspiration from Chinua Achebe's Proverbs*. Bamenda, Cameroon: Langaa Research & Publishing Common Initiative Group.

Anderson, Benedict. 1983. *Imagined Communities: Reflections on the Origin and Spread of Nationalism*. London: Verso.

Chotiner, Isaac. 2022. "Why Mearsheimer Blames the U.S. for the Crisis in Ukraine," *The New Yorker*. March 1.

Dean Jodi. 2015. "The Communist Horizon" in Charles Reitz (ed.) *Crisis & Commonwealth: Marcuse, Marx, McLaren*. Lanham, MD: Lexington Books.

Davis, Angela. 2016. *Freedom Is a Constant Struggle: Ferguson, Palestine, and the Foundations of a Movement*. Chicago: Haymarket Books.

Domhoff, G. William. [1967] 2022. *Who Rules America? The Corporate Rich, White Nationalist Republicans, Inclusionary Democrats in the 2020s*. New York: Routledge.

Dowd, Douglas. 2015. "U.S. Capitalism and Militarism in Crisis: Our Political Work Today," in Charles Reitz (ed.) *Crisis and Commonwealth: Marcuse, Marx, McLaren*. Lanham, MD: Lexington Books.

Dulce, Leon. 2021. *'People's Struggles and Priorities on the Road to COP26'* webinar by the Southern People's Action on COP26 last October 22, 2021. https://progressive.international/wire/2021-11-05-the-global-souths-red-lines-for-cop26/en

Eisler, Riane. 2007. *The Real Wealth of Nations: Creating a Caring Economics*. San Francisco: BK Publishing.

Eisler, Riane. 1987. *The Chalice and the Blade*. New York: HarperCollins.

Federici, Silvia. 2020. *Revolution at Point Zero: Housework, Reproduction, and Feminist Struggle*. Oakland, CA: PM Press.

Gilman-Opalsky, Richard. 2020. *The Communism of Love: An Inquiry into the Poverty of Exchange Value*. Chico, CA: AK Press.

Goldberg, Michelle. 2017. "No Wonder Millennials Hate Capitalism." *The New York Times*. December 4, 2017.

Graeber, David and David Wengrow. 2021.*The Dawn of Everything: A New History of Humanity*. New York: Ferrar, Straus and Giroux.

Greider, William. 1998. *One World Ready or Not: The Manic Logic of Global Capitalism*. New York: Simon & Schuster.

Habermas, Jürgen. 2019. *Auch eine Geschichte der Philosophie*, Band 1. Frankfurt: Suhrkamp.

Habermas, Jürgen. [1973] 1992. *Legitimation Crisis*. Cambridge, UK: Polity Press. Hedges, Chris. 2015. *Wages of Rebellion: The Moral Imperative of Revolt*. New York: Nation Books.
Hudson, Michael. 2022. *Destiny of Civilization: Finance Capitalism, Industrial Capitalism or Socialism*. Dresden: ISLET Verlag.
Hudson, Michael. [1972] 2021. *SUPERImperialism: The Economic Strategy of American Empire*. Dresden: ISLET Verlag.
Kahn, Richard V. 2009. "For a Marcusean Ecopedagogy" in Douglas Kellner, K. Daniel Cho, Tyson E. Lewis, and Clayton Pierce (Eds.). *Marcuse's Challenge to Education*. Lanham, MD: Rowman & Littlefield.
Kahn, Richard V. 2010. *Critical Pedagogy, Ecoliteracy, and Planetary Crisis*. Bern: Peter Lang.
Kellner, Douglas. 2008. *Guys and Guns Amok: Domestic Terrorism and School Shootings from the Oklahoma City Bombing to the Virginia Tech Massacre*. Boulder, CO: Paradigm Publishers.
Kellner, Douglas. 2003. *From 9/11 to Terror War: The Dangers of the Bush Legacy*. Lanham, MD: Rowman & Littlefield.
Killean, Rachel. 2021. "Why it's time to make ecocide a crime, for the sake of its victims," December 8. *The Conversation Phys.org* https://phys.org/earth-news/
Kozol, Jonathon. 1991. *Savage Inequalities: Children in America's Schools*. New York: Crown/Random House.
Kuzmarov, Jeremy and John Marciano. 2018. *The Russians Are Coming—Again*. New York: Monthly Review Press.
Langman, Lauren and George Lundskow. 2017. *God, Guns, Gold, and Glory: American Character and its Discontents*. Chicago: Haymarket Books.
Lenin, V.I. [1916] 1963. *Imperialism, the Highest Stage of Capitalism*. Lenin's *Selected Works*, Volume One, Moscow: Progress Publishers.
Leopold, Aldo. [1949] 1966. *A Sand County Almanac*. New York: Oxford University Press.
Leopold, Aldo. [1942] 1991. "The Role of Wildlife in Liberal Education" in Susan L. Flader and J. Baird Callicott (Eds.). *The River of the Mother of God and Other Essays* by Aldo Leopold. Madison, WI: University of Wisconsin Press.
Leopold, Aldo. [1953] 1993. *Round River*. New York: Oxford University Press.
Leopold, Aldo. [1953] 1966. "The Land Ethic," in *A Sand County Almanac*. New York: Oxford University Press.
Lerner, Gerda. 1986. *The Creation of Patriarchy*. New York: Oxford University Press.
Losurdo, Domenico. 2021. *Nietzsche, The Aristocratic Rebel*. Chicago: Haymarket Books.
Lundberg, Ferdinand. [1937] 2007. *America's 60 Families*. New York: The Vanguard Press.
Lundberg, Ferdinand. 1973. *The Rich and the Super Rich*. New York: Bantam.
Macy, Beth. 2019. *Dopesick: Dealers, Doctors and the Drug Company that Addicted America*. New York: Little, Brown and Company, Back Bay Books.
Marciano, John. 2016. *The American War in Vietnam*. New York: Monthly Review Press.
Marcuse, Herbert. [1975] 2015. "Why Talk on Socialism?" in Charles Reitz (Ed.). *Crisis and Commonwealth: Marcuse, Marx, McLaren*. Lanham, MD: Lexington Books.
Marcuse, Herbert. [1974] 2015. *Paris Lectures at Vincennes University, 1974*. Edited by Peter-Erwin Jansen and Charles Reitz. Philadelphia, PA: International Herbert Marcuse Society.
Marcuse, Herbert. [1979] 2014. "The Reification of the Proletariat," in Herbert Marcuse, *Collected Papers of Herbert Marcuse*. Volume 6, *Marxism, Revolution, and Utopia*. Edited by Douglas Kellner and Clayton Pierce. New York and London: Routledge.

Marcuse, Herbert. [1979] 2011. "The Children of Prometheus," in *Philosophy, Psychoanalysis and Emancipation, The Collected Papers of Herbert Marcuse*, Volume 5. edited by Douglas Kellner and Clayton Pierce. London and New York: Routledge, Translated by Charles Reitz.

Marcuse, Herbert. [1969] 2011. "The Role of Religion in a Changing Society," in *Philosophy, Psychoanalysis and Emancipation, The Collected Papers of Herbert Marcuse*, Volume 5, edited by Douglas Kellner and Clayton Pierce. London and New York: Routledge.

Marcuse, Herbert. [1968] 2009. "Lecture on Education, Brooklyn College. 1968," in Douglas Kellner, K. Daniel Cho, Tyson E. Lewis, and Clayton Pierce (Eds.). *Marcuse's Challenge to Education*. Lanham, MD: Rowman & Littlefield.

Marcuse, Herbert. [1972] 2005. "Ecology and Revolution," in Douglas Kellner (Ed.) Herbert Marcuse, *Collected Papers of Herbert Marcuse*. Volume 3, *The New Left and the 1960s*. New York and London: Routledge.

Marcuse, Herbert. [1947] 1998. "33 Theses toward the Military Defeat of HitlerFascism," in Douglas Kellner (Ed.) Herbert Marcuse, *Collected Papers of Herbert Marcuse*. Volume 1, *Technology, War, and Fascism*. New York: Routledge.

Marcuse, Herbert. [1964] 1991. *One-Dimensional Man, Studies in the Ideology of Advanced Industrial Society*. Boston, MA: Beacon Press.

Marcuse, Herbert. [1955] 1966. *Eros and Civilization*. Boston, MA: Beacon Press.

Marcuse, Herbert. [1933] 1973. "On the Philosophical Foundation of the Concept of Labor in Economics," *Telos*, No. 16, Summer.

Marcuse, Herbert. [1967] 1970. "The Problem of Violence and the Radical Opposition," in Herbert Marcuse, *Five Lectures: Psychoanalysis, Politics, and Utopia*. Boston, MA: Beacon Press.

Marcuse, Herbert. 1969. *An Essay on Liberation*. Boston, MA: Beacon Press. Marcuse, Herbert. [1958] 1961. *Soviet Marxism, A Critical Analysis*. New York: Vintage.

Marcuse, Peter. 2015. "Socialism One Sector at a Time," in Charles Reitz (Ed.). *Crisis and Commonwealth*. Lanham, MD: Lexington Books.

Martínez, Elizabeth. 2017. *De Colores Means All of Us*. London: Verso.

Marx, Karl. [1844] 1974. "Introduction to *Contribution to the Critique of Hegel's Philosophy of Right*." *Early Writings*. Edited by T.B. Bottomore. New York: McGraw-Hill.

McLaren, Peter and Petar Jandrić. 2020, *Postdigital Dialogues on Critical Pedagogy, Liberation Theology, and Information Technology*. London and New York: Bloomsbury Academic.

McLaren, Peter. [2013] 2015a. "Revolutionary Critical Pedagogy for a Socialist Society, A Manifesto" in Charles Reitz (Ed.). *Crisis and Commonwealth*. Lanham, MD: Lexington Books.

McLaren, Peter. 2015b. *Pedagogy of Insurrection*. New York and Bern: Peter Lang Publishing.

McLaren, Peter. 2005. *Capitalists & Conquerors: A Critical Pedagogy Against Empire*. Lanham, MD: Roman & Littlefield.

McLaren, Peter and Nathallia Jaramillo. 2007. *Pedagogy and Praxis in the Age of Empire: Towards a New Humanism*. Rotterdam: Sense Publishers.

McLaren, Peter. 2000. *Che Guevara, Paulo Freire, and the Pedagogy of Revolution*. Lanham, Boulder, New York, and Oxford: Rowman & Littlefield.

McLaren, Peter. 1997. *Revolutionary Multiculturalism: Pedagogies of Dissent for the New Millennium*. Boulder, CO: Westview Press, a Division of HarperCollins.

McLaren, Peter. 1995. *Critical Pedagogy and Predatory Culture*. London and New York: Routledge.

Mclean, Ruth. 2022. "Five African Countries. Six Coups. Why Now?" *The New York Times*, January 31.
Mies, Maria and Vandana Shiva. [1993] 2021. *Ecofeminism*. London: Zed Books.
Mills, C. Wright. [1956] 2000. *The Power Elite*. New York: Oxford University Press.Murray, Robert K. [1955] 1964. *Red Scare: A Study in National Hysteria 1919-1920*. New York: McGraw-Hill.
Moyn, Samuel. 2021. *Humane: How the United States Abandoned Peace and Reinvented War*. New York: Ferrar, Straus, and Giroux.
National Commission on the Causes of the Financial and Economic Crisis in the United States. 2011. *The Financial Crisis Inquiry Report*. New York: Public Affairs/Perseus Books.
Nichols, John. 2022. "Bernie Sanders's Smart Take on NATO, Ukraine, and Diplomatic Options," *The Nation*, February 15.
Nicolaus, Martin. 1975. *Restauration of Capitalism in the USSR*. Chicago: Liberator Press.
Oluo, Ijeoma. 2020. *MEDIOCRE: The Dangerous Legacy of White Male America*. New York: Seal Press/Hachette Book Group.
Parenti, Michael. [2002] 2011. *Democracy for the Few*. Boston: Wadsworth.
Plumer, Brad and Lisa Friedman, "Climate Talks Bring Promises, Slim on Details," *The New York Times*, November 9, 2021, A1.
Reitz, Charles and Stephen Spartan. [2013] 2015. "The Political Economy of Predation and Counterrevolution: Recalling Marcuse on the Radical Goals of Socialism," in Charles Reitz (ed). *Crisis and Commonwealth: Marcuse, Marx, McLaren*. Lanham, MD: Lexington Books.
Reitz, Charles. 2009a. "Herbert Marcuse and the New Culture Wars," in Douglas Kellner, K. Daniel Cho, Tyson E. Lewis, and Clayton Pierce (Eds.). *Marcuse's Challenge to Education*. Lanham, MD: Rowman & Littlefield.
Reitz, Charles. 2009b. "Herbert Marcuse and the Humanities: Emancipatory Education and Predatory Culture," in Douglas Kellner, K. Daniel Cho, Tyson E. Lewis, and Clayton Pierce (Eds.). *Marcuse's Challenge to Education*. Lanham, MD: Rowman & Littlefield.
Robinson, Kim Stanley. 2020. *The Ministry for the Future*. New York: Orbit/Hachette Book Group.
Roy, Arundhati. [1999] 2019. *My Seditious Heart: Collected Non-fiction*. Chicago: Haymarket Books.Ruschig, Ulrich. 2020. *Die Befreiung der Natur: Zum Verhältnis von Natur und Freiheit bei Herbert Marcuse*. Köln: PapyRossa Verlag.
Salleh, Ariel. [1997] 2017. *Ecofeminism as Politics: Nature, Marx, and the Postmodern*. London: Zed Books.
Searcy, Dionne, Michael Forscythe, Eric Lipton. 2021. "Power Struggle over Cobalt Rattles the Clean Energy Revolution" *The New York Times*, November 21, 2021. A1, A14-A17.
Sekyi-Otu, Ato. 2019. *Left Universalism, Africancentric Essays*. New York: Routledge. Sernau, Scott. 2006. *Worlds Apart: Social Inequalities in a New Century*. Thousand Oaks CA, London, New Delhi: Pine Forge Press.
Shirer, William L. 1960. *The Rise and Fall of the Third Reich*. Greenwich, CT: Fawcett.
Spartan, Stephen. 2016. "Surplus Over-Appropriation and Reproduction Crisis of the Roman Empire" in Charles Reitz (ed.) *Reflections on Science and the Human Material Condition*. Kansas City: Kindle Direct Publishing.
Street, Paul. 2021. "Beyond the Stench: Reflections on Violence, Fascism, and Revolution" *CounterPunch*, December 3. https://www.counterpunch.org/2021/ 12/03/beyond-the-stench-reflections-on-violence-fascism-and-revolution/

sTurse, Nick. 2022. "Another U.S.-Trained Soldier Stages a Coup in West Africa." *The Intercept*, January 26. https://theintercept.com/2022/01/26/burkina-fasocoup-us-military/

Volpe, John Della. 2022. *Fight: How Gen Z is Channeling their Fear and Passion to Save America*. New York: St. Martin's Press.

Wildcat, Daniel R. 2009. *Red Alert! Saving the Planet with Indigenous Knowledge*. Golden, CO: Fulcrum Publishers.

Woolfson, Charles. 1982. *The Labor Theory of Culture: A Re-examination of Engels's Theory of Human Origins*. London: Routledge and Kegan Paul.

System Change Will Not Be Negotiated

Nnimmo Bassey

We frequently hear calls for system change, at public mobilisations, in conference halls and even in negotiation halls. The calls come as slogans, they come in anger and they come as a strong rebuke to the systemic scaffold on which our pains, our exploitation and the denial of our voices and rights are hung. The necessity of system change is inescapable. The present system is dependent on the extreme exploitation and enslavement of nature and labour, built around an inherently unjust core. We are in the dying days of a civilisation driven by fossil fuels. This end is not coming merely because of the recorded and predicted severe species extinction, or by peak oil. It is, rather, being heralded by a looming climate catastrophe and by the reawakening of social forces realising that slavery persists as long as the enslaved is unaware of his state.

As Oilwatch International highlights, there are:

> similarities in the current pattern of resource exploitation in countries of the Global South, and in affected peoples in the rest of the world, which reflects historical legacy of disempowerment of peoples, plunder of natural resources and destruction of environment, and [Oilwatch] considers the recognition of the right of peoples to self-determination and cultural integrity as primary in the resolution of environmental problems.

Our urgent task is to reclaim the future, and this will not be attainable if the current system persists.

Green Capitalism

Green was once a colour. In today's system, it has turned into a silencing code that lulls us into accepting that Nature cannot be protected unless financial value is placed on her. The Rio + 20 summit served as a platform for the elevation of the concept of Green Economy as a major plank for global environmental governance, especially with regard to climate change. Green

Economy permits the financialization of everything, through a plethora of instruments such as those intended to reduce emissions from deforestation and forest degradation (REDD, REDD plus), emissions trading schemes (ETS), clean development mechanisms (CDM) and the like.

Green economy is a neo-liberal idea that hoists the financialization of Nature and carbon offsetting as ideal tools for nature protection. It has been cooked up to entrench current capitalist production modes and power relations where might is right. Poor, vulnerable and cash-strapped nations that contribute little or nothing to global warming see the trickles that drop into their empty bowls from market mechanisms, while their citizens are displaced from their territories, forced to bear a disproportionate burden of real climate actions. With climate change neatly 'boxed' as a matter of means of handling carbon emissions, the world conveniently ignores the root cause of the crises—the origins of those emissions. This entrenched situation is neo-colonial and imperialist. It upturns every notion of justice, including the common but differentiated responsibilities anchor of pre-2011 climate negotiations.

A just climate regime ought not to scratch for funds to tackle the emergencies already throwing up climate refugees. A clear solution for climate finance can be found in the Peoples Agreement. The Agreement demands that countries cut their emissions by at least 50% at source between 2013 and 2017, without recourse to offsets and other carbon trading schemes. It also demands that developed countries commit 6% of their GDP to finance adaptation and mitigation needs. The payment of climate debt is not seen as a mere demand for reparations, but as a means of decolonising the atmospheric space and redistributing what meagre space or carbon budget is left. It is a means towards obligating humans to take actions to restore disrupted natural cycles of Nature. Climate change negotiations offer us a clear lens to see that market environmentalism approaches are merely means of escape from responsibility and measureable action. A look at the Paris Agreement reached at COP21 reveals that the major cause of global warming—fossil fuels utilisation in production and transportation—is not recognised in the process of tackling global warming.

The notion that carbon emitted anywhere can be offset by carbon absorbed anywhere else has given rise to the concept of net emissions. This is offering polluting nations the ultimate escape hatch through which to retain their levels of pollution and consumption, while grabbing lands, forests and waters elsewhere to compensate. It is now well known that at least 80% of currently known fossil fuels reserves must be left untapped and unburned to keep temperature increases to below 2°C. What's troubling is that not only is this not being discussed at climate negotiations, but that new reserves are being sought, and extraction methods are being intensified. A clear throwback to fiddling while the city burns.

The fact that fossil fuels are not renewable does not deter the fossil addicts. In order to remove the cloud of dust (and doubt) over fossil fixations, the industry came up with the term clean coal, and the notions that carbon pollution can be tackled through carbon capture and storage or sequestration, or through geo-engineering. These unproven technologies are all ways of resisting the need for change and ensuring business as usual. The best possible outcome would be to postpone the evil day and build an uncertain future for the coming generation. Unfortunately, that day cannot be postponed much longer.

Centrality of Nature

The call for system change is a call to a common-sense path that would secure the survival of the human race. It is also a call for humans to recognise themselves as just one of the species on planet earth. Studies and observations have shown that species stand better chances of survival when they cooperate, live and work in solidarity rather than in competition; when they build bridges and not walls—give up some space and allow others to breathe. The Earth speaks. The sky speaks. The trees speak. All of Nature speaks. Communication is a vital tool for survival. Take for example the umbrella thorn acacias, a tree in the African savannah, which communicate via their thorns in order to avoid having their leaves being eaten up by the savanna animals. Researchers found that when giraffes start to eat the leaves of umbrella thorn acacias, the trees release some toxic substances (water soluble, carbon based compounds known as 'tannins') that offend the taste buds of the giraffes. This is a direct defence line to even the giraffes that appear immune to the 'devil thorns'.

The researchers noticed that the giraffes would then skip the next umbrella thorn acacia trees, and move by about 100 metres before resuming their dinner elsewhere. Why did they move over such a distance before resuming their feast? This is the explanation according to Wohlleben (2016):

> The acacia trees that were being eaten gave off warning gas (specifically, ethylene) that signalled to neighbouring trees of the same species that a crisis was at hand. Right away, all the forewarned trees also pumped toxins into their leaves to prepare themselves. The giraffes were wise to this game, therefore, moved farther away to a part of the savannah where they could find trees that were oblivious to what was going on.

Trees communicate by a variety of other ways, including through their root systems, affirming metaphorically that indeed, it takes roots to weather the storm.

Re-Source Democracy

We speak of the gifts of Nature as re-sources. Yes, re-sources, intentionally hyphenated because we are speaking not of commodities, but of the vital need for humans to return to the source, to reconnect to Nature and, to think of the source before lifting the chisel, hammer, shovel, drill or rig. Re-source democracy is a call for the recognition of the rights of Nature, including her right to regenerate and maintain her cycles. It is built on a clear understanding of the uses and intrinsic values of the gifts of Nature. Re-source democracy demands the interrogation of the meaning of progress and development, to help us draw the line between what we can accept or reject in our environment. Navdanya further gives clarity to this idea:

> We need a new paradigm to respond to the fragmentation caused by various forms of fundamentalism. We need a new movement, which allows us to move from the dominant and pervasive culture of violence, destruction and death to a culture of non-violence, creative peace and life ... the Earth democracy movement ... provides an alternative worldview in which humans are embedded in the Earth Family, ... connected to each other through love, compassion, not hatred and violence and (in which); ecological responsibility and economic justice replaces greed, consumerism and competition as objectives of human life.

Convergence of Movements

System change will be birthed by a convergence of movements. It will be a matter for all. We have to continually remind ourselves that our lives and realities are formed by a web of relationships, issues and realities; that we require diversity of approaches to effectively confront and overcome them—with diversity of movements coalescing around common organising principles. For example, in the case of ecological resurgence, movements can come together using the Precautionary Principle as a pivot. Another basic impulse will be the recognition of the leadership of communities of peoples, especially indigenous women, on the frontlines of ecological defense and system change struggles.

System Change Will Not Be Negotiated

The present fossil-based civilization is running out of gas and its terminal point is imminent—whether planned or not. Our task is to hasten the demise of this destructive system, in which unjust relations are seen as opportunities for amassing profit. This is the time for drastic actions to bring about ecological health for all our communities and relatives on planet Earth. It is time to change the narrative that we can measure well-being by aggregating gross domestic product. The struggles of First Nation brothers and sisters in North America, the Ogoni in Nigeria's Niger Delta, the Yasunidos of Ecuador and many others show that the battle can be tough and abrasive. But we have no options.

Industrial growth societies have been built on the platforms of gross injustice. And those who benefit from the unjust, disruptive and unsustainable system—the handful of men that have more financial means than billions of men and women—will not listen to logical needs for system change. They have heard it over and over again. It is a system where the poor, no matter how wise, cannot sit at the official negotiation tables. It is a system that believes that, with the right financial means, one can make a dash for safety to another planet if apocalypse happens. History will judge the present generation very harshly if a transition is not made to a Life-Sustaining Society—a society in which humans and the environment are linked, not ranked. This society will come about only if we stand together with Earth Protectors and denounce the criminalisation of dissent and the constriction of democratic space that is fast becoming the norm. It is time to speak up and let a thousand solutions bloom. It is no time to be silent.

System change will come about when the power of We the People becomes a rallying call and a pivot of action. We the People can redefine energy and own our clean, localised, energy generation and production systems. We the People can reclaim our streams, creeks and rivers and deny industry their privatisation and use as sewers. As the saying goes: freedom is not something that is given, it is taken. System change will not be negotiated. Change will come as fists burst through the cracks in the pavements just like saplings spring from hardened soils.

About the author

Charles Reitz: Retired Co-Director of Campus Intercultural Center and Director of Multicultural Education; Professor Emeritus of Philosophy and Social Science, Kansas City Kansas Community College.

His previous books include:

Art, Alienation, and the Humanities: A Critical Engagement with Herbert Marcuse (State University of New York Press 2000)

Crisis and Commonwealth: Marcuse, Marx, McLaren (Lexington Books 2013)

Philosophy & Critical Pedagogy: Insurrection & Commonwealth (Peter Lang Publishing 2016)

Ecology and Revolution: Herbert Marcuse and the Challenge of a New World System Today (Routledge 2019)

Index

Absher, Brandon, 75
Achebe, Chinua, 94–95
Addams, Jane, 2
Adorno, Theodor W., xvi, 17, 68–70, 74, 150
Aesthetic Dimension, The (Marcuse, Herbert), 65, 185, 190
Africacentric universalism, 97
African proverbs, 48, 93–95, 122, 189, 229
    authentic leadership, 95
    collective labor, 95
    communitarian ethos, 94
    human existence, 93
    societal cohesion, 95
    universalizability, 95
Agha-Jaffar, Tamara, 156, 214–215, 217
Agyeman, Edmund Akwasi, 92–95
Alperovitz, Gar, 105
Al Qaeda terror network, 7
alt-right, 20, 36–38, 202
American empire decline
    de-industrialized *rentier* economy, 9
    domestic labor force, 9
    financial imperialism, 8
    income inequalities, 10
    socialism, 10
    socio-economic and political inequality, 9
    welfare/warfare economy, 8
American Pageant mythology, 2–3
anarchism, Philosophical, 58-60
Anderson, Kevin B., 165
androcracy, 155
Animal Liberation Front, 219
anti-authoritarianism, 59
antifascism (antifa)
    Marxism, 59
    and Marxist-anarchist dialectic, 58–60

Thoughts on the Defense of Gracchus Babeuf, 58
antiguerrilla campaign, Guatemala, 7
antisemitism, 1, 32
Appeal to Reason, 195
Apple, Michael, 160
Aquinas, 177
Arbenz, 5
Ardebili, Morteza, 148
Arendt, Hannah, 47, 50, 188
Aristotle, 69, 81, 103, 106, 126–127, 129, 149, 177
Armah, Ayi Kwei, 98
arts of subsistence, 115
austerity budgeting, 174
authoritarianism, 34
Axial Age, 99–102, 225
Azenabor, Godwin, 93, 122

Bahro, Rudolf, 119
Bakunin, Mikhail, 59
Baldwin, James, 95
banality of evil, 50, 118
Banda, Kamauzu, 94
Barrett, Amy Coney, 41
Battle of Seattle, 39
Baudelaire, Charles, 185
Bedford, David, 71
Behemoth (Neumann, Franz), 32
bellwether effect, 95
Benjamin, Walter, xv, 35, 44–45
Bernal, Dolores Delgado, 54
Bernal, J.D., 74–75
Bevins, Vincent, 5–6, 9, 23
Bhaskar, Roy, 74, 77, 136, 147–154
Biden, Joe, 22, 44, 83, 202, 211
bin Laden, Osama, 7
biotic pyramid, 84, 138, 230
Black Bloc, 39
Black Lives Matter (BLM) movement, 41, 194, 203, 208, 220
Boff, Leonardo, 226

Bonobo and the Atheist: In Search of Humanism Among the Primates, The (deWaal, Frans), 146
Bookchin, Murray, 59
Bose, Nirmal Kumar, 126
bourgeois democracy, 34
Boyte, Harry C., 177
Brue, Stanley L., 171
Buddha, 100, 126–127, 177, 225
Buddhism, 26, 99–100, 125–126, 229
Butler, Smedley, 5

CAFOs. *See* confined animal feed operations (CAFOs)
Calderon, Dolores, 54
capital-labor antagonism
　extractive investors, 160
　inequalities, income and wealth, 161
　life chances, 163
　neoliberalism, 160
　polarization, pattern, 162
　racial inequality, 164
　wealth decline, minority families, 161
　wealth distribution, U.S. households, 162
Capital (Marx, Karl), 80, 112, 118, 120, 151, 162, 176
capital valorization crisis
　austerity budgeting, 174
　commercial and residential properties, overbuilding, 175
　commodity-dependency, 177–178
　commodity fetishism, 178–179
　commonwealth of freedom, 177
　decommodification, services, 179
　fast capitalism, 174
　neoliberal and neoconservative policies, 176
　new sensibility, 181
　wage-labor, 178
Capitol, attack on, 202–203
Castro, Fidel, 222
Castro, Javier Sethness, 16, 46, 58

categorical imperative, Kant, xvi, 93, 98, 122, 127–128, 225
Catholicism, 224
20th century U.S. world order
　anti-communist assassinations, 5
　conflict, East and West, 5
　global McCarthyism, 5
　Jakarta Method, 6
　9-11 terror attacks, 7
Chaat Smith, Paul, 140–141
Chalice and the Blade, The (Eisler, Riane), 144
Chaney, James, 45
Chase-Dunn, Christopher, 58
Chauvin, Derek, 94
Chávez, Hugo, 222–223
Chavezmo, 222
Che Guevarra, Ernesto, 225
Cheney, Dick, 36
Cheney, Lynn, 36
Cheney, Tom, 71
Chicago Haymarket uprising of 1886, 195
chief virtue and vice, 81, 103, 127
Childe, V. Gordon, 146–147
Chinweizu, 94
Churchill, Winston, 5
climate catastrophe, 71, 142, 201, 237
climate change, 17, 45, 83, 159, 209, 237–238
Collected Papers of Herbert Marcuse, The (Marcuse), 16
Columbus, 3, 141
commercialized nature, 67–69
commodity fetishism, 178–179
commonwealth. *See also* EarthCommonWealth
　aesthetics, life, 190
　African partnership cultures, 189
　African social organization, 92
　Africa's earliest proverbs, 93–96
　communism, 191
　definition, 92
　ecosocialism, 191
　false (imperial) universalism, 97–99
　intercultural ethical commonalities, 99–102

intercultural labor solidarity, 103–106
new sensibility, 190
promesse du bonheur commun, 188–193
public work for public good, 189
relativism, 96
sensuous living labor, 189–190
ubuntu and utu, 92, 93, 98, 106
universalization of resistance, 192
Commonwealth (Hardt and Negri), 104
commonwealth of freedom, 177
communism
  Indonesia, 5
  perfected, 191
  raw, 191
Comte, 171
comunalidad, 202–203
confined animal feed operations (CAFOs), 159
Conrad, Joseph, 94
Cooperative Commonwealth (Gronlund, Laurence), 103
Cornforth, Maurice, 75
Cornu, Auguste, 74
corporate capitalism, against, xvii, 16, 32, 47, 77–80, 84, 103, 224, 230, 232
counter-consciousness, 119
Counterrevolution and Revolt (Marcuse, Herbert), xvi, xviii, 8, 22, 35–36, 38, 69, 98, 194
Creation of Patriarchy, The (Lerner, Gerda), 156, 214
Crenshaw, Kimberle Williams, 54
critical consciousness, xvii, 119, 220
critical political economy
  capitalism, 160–161
  capital-labor antagonism, 160–164
  income flow to capital, calculation, 172
  inequality and capital valorization crisis, 173–182
  labor theory of value, 166–173
  production process, 168
  wealth accumulation and workforce remuneration, 164–166
critical race theory, 1–2, 36
critical realism
  human existence, 148
  truth of positivism, 152
critical social theory, 17, 38, 47, 60, 103, 149–150, 181, 208, 213
critical theory of labor, 95, 111
Critique of Pure Reason (Kant, Immanuel), 128
Crow, Jim, 4, 50
Cruz, Ted, 205
cultural Marxism, 36

Daoism, 99, 122, 229
Das Kapital (Marx), 10
Davis, Angela, 51–52, 55, 212
Dawn of Everything: A New History of Humanity, The (Graeber and Wengrow), 143
Days of Destruction, Days of Revolt (Hedges, Chris), 78
Dean, Jodi, 170
Death and Transfiguration (Strauss), 134
death squads, 7, 224
Debs, Eugene Victor, 196
Declaration of the Rights of Man, 185
De Colores Means All of Us (Martinez, Elízabeth), 208
de Las Casas, Bartolomé, 3
Delgado, Richard, 54
Deloria, Vine Jr., 140–141, 208
Democritus, 137
de Montesinos, Antonio, 3
Descartes' theory of human personhood, 92
de Waal, Frans, 48, 110, 121, 146, 153, 165
Dewey, John, 72–77, 136
dialectical humanism, 123–125
Dialectic of Enlightenment (Horkheimer and Adorno), xvi, 17, 68–69, 74–77,
Dobb, Maurice, 74–75

Domhoff, G. William, 23, 206, 214
dominator power, 78, 135, 144, 180, 206, 213–214, 229
Dopesick: Dealers, Doctors and the Drug Company that Addicted America (Macy, Beth), 210
Douglas, Frederick, 228
Dowd, Douglas, 2, 6, 8–9, 37, 77, 81, 161
Dowd, Maureen, 50, 206
Dreon, Roberta, 76, 190
drone strikes, 7, 198
Dulce, Leon, 210
Dunbar-Ortiz, Roxanne, 1–2, 104
Durkheim, 149

EarthCommonWealth, 96, 104-105, 138, 142, 182, 192
  counteroffensive, 26
  educative power of struggle, 218–224
  great refusal, collective project, 204–213
  legitimation crises, 201–204
  living labor and, 27–29
  patriarchy, 213–214
  peace, exploitation and race, 195–201
  relativism, 96
  religion, 224–228
  revolutionary progeny, Prometheus/Persephone, 214–217
  workforce rebellion, 228–232
EarthCommonWealth Alternative/Agenda, 192–236
  advanced industrial society, 83
  decommodification/socialization, economy, 85
  ecosocialism, 85
  Great Refusal, 86
  green economic alternative, 84
  restoration, abused nature, 84
Earth Liberation Front, 219
Ebert, Friedrich, 57
ecocide, 210–211
ecological materialism. *See also*: dialectics of nature, historical materialism
  America still undiscovered, 141–142
  biotic pyramid, 138
  ethical relationship to land, 137–140
  Everything You Know About Indians Is Wrong, 140–142
  human origins, history, 143–147
  Leopold, Aldo, 137–140
  materialist dialectic, 136
  naturalism and critical realism, 147–152
  nature, history, 136–137
  practice of conservation, 140
  secular reverence, 152–156
  world and human societies, 135
Ecology and Revolution (Marcuse), 17
Ecology and the Critique of Modern Society (Marcuse), 17
ecology of care, 126–127, 156
Ecology & Revolution (Reitz, Charles), 84
ecosocialism, xv, 26, 29, 49, 85, 142, 156, 191–193, 216, 231
ecosocialist world system
  capitalism, 18–19
  destructiveness, society, 18
  environmentalist essays, Marcuse, 17
  nature, domination, 17
  radical philosophy, 19
Edel, Abraham, 74–75
educative power of struggle, 219–223
  BLM, 221
  Chavezmo, 222
  Comrade Jesus, 224
  critical consciousness, 220
  evolutionary eco-pedagogy, 222
  guns and democracy, 223
  institutional racism, 218, 221
  multicultural education reform, 219, 221
  planetary *comunalidad*, 222
  praxis of negation, 224
  radical activism, 219
  revolutionary multiculturalism, 219
  systematic oppression, 221

Einstein, Albert, 199
Eisenhower, 5
Eisler, Riane, 121, 144–145, 147, 153, 155–156, 213–214, 217
Emerson, Ralph Waldo, 69–72
Empathic Civilization: The Race to Global Consciousness in a World in Crisis, The (Rifkin, Jeremy), 49
empathy, 49, 80, 110–111, 116, 123, 189, 213, 225
Empire (Hardt and Negri), 104
Engels, Friedrich, 70, 74, 99, 111–115, 120, 134–137, 139, 143, 146–147, 209
Engels's theory of human origins, 111
Environmental Protection Agency, 81
equality of Black lives, 15, 78
Eros. *See also promesse du bonheur commun*
    aesthetic dimension, 185
    and beauty, 184
    political, 77–80, 110, 185–186, 191, 197
Eros and Civilization (Marcuse, Herbert), 38, 46, 56, 78, 184, 190, 215
Eros and Revolution: The Critical Philosophy of Herbert Marcuse (Castro, Javier Sethness), 16
Essay Concerning the True Original Extent and End of Civil Government, An (Locke, John), 164
Essay on Liberation, An (Marcuse, Herbert), 35, 38, 42, 86, 187
Euthyphro (Plato), 97, 227
everyday fascism, U.S., 55–56
Everything You Know About Indians Is Wrong (Chaat Smith, Paul), 140–141
evolutionary eco-pedagogy, 222
existentialism, 47, 73, 75
Experience and Nature (Dewey, John), 72, 136
Extinction Rebellion, 78, 209

Fall of the U.S. Idol, The, 10
false (imperial) universalism, 48
    Africacentric universalism, 97
    communism, 98–99
    historical materialism, 98
    left universalism, 97, 99
family and community well-being, 81
Fanon, Frantz, 94, 97
Farber, Marvin, 73–75
Farr, Arnold L., 15, 164
fascism. *See also* neofascism, xviii, 16, 21–24, 32–36, 51–53
    authoritarian mentality, 33
    bourgeois democracy, 34
    definition, 34
    everyday fascism, U.S., 55–56
    genesis, 33
Feenberg, Andrew, 15
Feinstein, Andrew, 82
Feuerbach, Ludwig, 116, 118, 129
Feuerbach thesis, tenth, 129
Fight: How Gen Z is Channeling their Fear and Passion to Save America (Volpe, John Della), 202
Floyd, George, 15, 23, 44, 55, 78, 84
Franklin, Benjamin, 118–119
Freedom is a Constant Struggle (Davis, Angela), 52, 212
freedom of speech, 21, 50, 54
free speech fallacy
    hate speech, opposition to, 21
    pure tolerance, doctrine, 20–21
    racism, 20–21
Freud, 56, 190
Fridays for Future protests, 202
Friedman, Lisa, 209
Fromm, Erich, 32, 47
Fry, Douglas P., 121, 144–145, 147
Fuh, Divine, 94
Fuzi, Kong, 123, 126

Gattungswesen, 48, 80, 117, 153, 155, 177
Gilder, George, 163
Gimbutas, Maria, 48, 144
Gingrich, Newt, 2, 36
global burning, 142

global McCarthyism, 5
Global Police State, The (Robinson, William I.), 44
God, Guns, Gold, and Glory: American Character and its Discontents (Langman and Lundskow), 1
Goethe, 68, 70
Goldhagen, Daniel, 32
Goodman, Amy, 56
Goodman, Andrew, 45
Gorbachev, Mikhail, 200
Graeber, David, 4, 143, 145–147
Grandin, Greg, 9
Great Railroad Strike of 1877, 195
Great Refusal, 66, 68, 86, 180
    commodified social life, 205
    COP26 Climate Crisis conference210
    decommodification/socialization, economy, 207
    ecocide, 210–211
    indigenismo, 208
    neoliberal right-wing elites, 212
    new general interest, 25, 46, 194, 205, 228
    subverting forces, 204, 209
    super-accumulation, 209, 211
    transnational transformation, 213
    white masculinist assault, 205
Greeley, Horace, 165
Greene, Felix, 9, 23
Green New Deal, 206
Greenwood, Robin, 169
Greider, William, 176
Gronlund, Laurence, 103
group marriage, 113
gun terror, 53–55
Guterres, Antonio, 209
Gyekye, Kwame, 93–94, 122
Gyekye's communitarianism, 94
gylany, 155, 217

Habermas, Jürgen, 72, 99, 150, 200, 225
Haldane, J.B.S., 74
Hannah-Jones, Nikole, 1, 3
Harcourt, Bernard E., 23
Hardt, Michael, 103–104
Harre, Rom, 77
Hartwig, Merwyn, 148–149
Harvey, David, 39
Haskell Indian Nations University, 141
hate speech, 20–21, 23, 34, 40, 50, 53–55, 67, 202
Hawley, Josh, 205
Hedges, Chris, 78, 200, 224, 227–228
Hegel, xvii, 94, 101, 116, 118, 120, 122, 129, 135, 179
Heidegger, Martin, 94, 101, 116, 118, 120, 122, 129, 135, 179, 194
Heraclitus, 100, 137
Hidden Life of Trees: What They Feel, How They Communicate— Discoveries from a Secret World, The (Wohlleben, Peter), 133
Hilferding, Rudolf, 75
Hill, Anita, 42, 51, 206
Hinduism, 26, 125–126
Historical Fate of Bourgeois Democracy, The (Marcuse, Herbert), 34
historical materialism, xvii, 73–74, 98, 116, 134, 137, 145, 147, 154
Hitler's Willing Executioners (Goldhagen, Daniel), 32
Hobbes, 69, 146
Hogg, David, 202
Horkheimer, Max, xvi, 17, 32–33, 68–70, 74, 150, 197
How Fascism Works; The Politics of Us and Them (Stanley, Jason), 33
Hudson, Michael, 8–9, 211, 222
human-heartedness, 123
Human Nature and Conduct (Dewey, John), 72, 136
human origins, history
    cooperation, 27, 48, 84, 96, 106, 111, 116, 120, 135, 145
    mine and thine statement, 143
    Original Affluent Society, The, 145
    postmodernism, 145, 147
    primitive communism, 146
Humboldt, Alexander, 137, 139
Husserl, 73

identity politics, 48
Igloliorte, Heather, 127
Immerwahr, Daniel, 9
imperial America
   de jure apartheid, 4
   overseas empire-building, 4
   racial segregation, 4
   trade and investment, 5
imperial presidency, 6, 8
indigenismo, 208, 223
indigenous realism, 141, 216
Inequality and the Global Economic Crisis (Dowd, Douglas), 161
Ingraham, Christopher, 162
institutional racism, 218, 221
intercultural ethical commonalities
   Axial Age, 99–102
   monoculturalism, 102
   moral unity, 99
   socialism, 101
   social power, 102
intercultural labor solidarity
   commons, 104
   commonwealth, 103–106
   Cooperative Commonwealth, 103–104
   humanity, 103–104, 106
   socialist humanism and labor humanism, 104
International Herbert Marcuse Society, 149, 207
Internationalist Manifesto Against War, 198
Inuit Qaujimajatuqangit, 127
Inusah, Hissein, 95

Jackson, Ketanji Brown, 205–206
Jakarta Method, 6
Jansen, Peter-Erwin, 16, 32, 34
Jaramillo, Nathalia, 219
Jaspers, Karl, 47, 92, 99–102
Jesus, 127, 224–226
Judaism, 99, 125–127, 229

Kahn, Richard, 219
Kangussu, Imaculada, 184, 188
Kant, Immanuel, xvii, 93, 122, 127–128, 163, 177, 190, 225, 227

Kantian enlightenment humanism
   categorical imperative, 127–128
   enlightenment autonomy and freedom, 128
   moral reasoning, 129
   oikonomia, 130
   tenth Feuerbach thesis, 129
   universal cosmopolitan state, 128
Kari, Nancy, 177
karma, doctrine, 125
Kavanaugh, Brett, 41–42, 205
Kellner, Douglas, 15–16, 32, 34, 72, 117, 119, 166, 228
Kennedy, Robert F., 6, 55
Khaldun, Ibn, 126
Khasnabish, Alex, 71
Kirsch, Robert, 15
Kisubi, Alfred T., 93, 122
Kondiaronk, the Wyandot, 143
Kongfuzi, 100, 102
Korten, David, 160
Ku Klux Klan, 40
Kuznick, Peter, 4–6, 9

La Bohème (Verdi), 134
labor and EarthCommonWealth, 27–28, 80, 84, 231
   global capitalist crisis, 29
   partnership, 28
   radical ecosocialism, 29
   social productivity, 28
   supply-side economic theory, 28
labor force, society, 9, 25, 68, 79, 82, 103–104, 117, 231
Labor Theory of Culture, The (Woolfson, Charles), 27, 111, 120, 146
labor theory of ethics
   Africa and China, 121–123
   Aristotle and ecology of care, 126–127
   Buddhism, 126
   commonwealth labor, ecology, 113
   Engels's theory, 111–112
   enlightenment and consecrated labor, 125–126
   hand to brain development, 112

Hinduism, 125–126
human beings and nature, 120–121
Iroquois households, 114
Judaism, 125
Kantian enlightenment humanism, 127–130
moral reasoning, 129
original affluent society, 115–120
Plato and dialectical humanism, 123–125
production, communal labor, 112
social behavior, primates, 110
labor theory of value
capital-labor split, 171
GDP, 171
income flow to capital, calculation, 172
income inequality, manufacturing sector, 169
production process, 167–168
propertied and non-propertied populations, relationships, 167
property and power relationships, business system, 170
la contestation permanente, 1968
French student movement, 204
Lahontan, Baron, 4, 143
Laibman, David, 58
Lamas, Andrew, 15
land ethics, 84, 104–105, 138, 140, 142, 230
Langman, Lauren, 1, 4, 42, 186, 228
Laozi, 127, 225
Lepore, Jill, 1, 3–4
Lawrence, Charles, 54
Leakey, Richard, 121, 153, 165–166
Lebensraum, 50
left individualism, 96–97
left universalism, 97, 99
legitimation crises
new sensibility, 203
operational values flagging, 201
planetary catastrophe, 203
student strikes, 202
subverting forces, 204
U.S. empire, decline, 201
youth protests, 203
Lehmann, Nicholas, 40
Lenin, V.I., 34, 74
Leopold, Aldo, 84, 94, 99, 104–105, 137–140, 209, 230
Lerner, Gerda, 156, 214
lethal liberties, 53–55
Lettau, Reinhard, 55
Leucippus, 137
liberation
of labor, xvii, 15, 17, 25, 60, 88, 98, 103, 105, 166, 188
of nature, 17, 70
theology, 224–226
Liebknecht, Karl, 57, 196
Lincoln, Abraham, 119
Listen Marxist! (Bookchin, Murray), 59
Locke, John, 119, 165–167, 169, 185, 207
Logic, The Theory of Inquiry (Dewey, John), 72
Losurdo, Domenico, 97, 185, 197
Luce, Henry, 5
Lukács, Georg, 74–75, 135
Lundskow, George, 1, 4, 42, 186, 228
Luxemburg, Rosa, 57, 196

Macionis, John C., 163
Macy, Beth, 210
Maduro, Nicolás, 222–223
Maley, Terry, 15, 34
Man Makes Himself (Childe, V. Gordon), 146
1844 Manuscripts (Marx), 80, 116, 153
Marciano, John, 3, 9
Marcuse, Herbert, xv–xviii, 1–12, 15–29, 32–60, 65–88, 92–106, 110–130, 133–156, 159–182, 184–232, 237–242
Marcuse renaissance, 2020s
ecosocialist world system, 17–19
free speech fallacy, 20–21
imperial America and neofascist counterrevolution, 21–24

labor and EarthCommonWealth, 27–29
socialism, radical goals, 24–27
Markey, Ed, 206
Martinez, Elízabeth, 208, 223
Martin Luther King, Jr, 55, 187
Marx, Karl, xv, xvii, xviii, 10, 28, 36, 38, 47–48, 59, 73–74, 79–80, 86, 96, 98–99, 105, 112–113, 116–120, 122, 129, 134–136, 149–151, 153–155, 159, 162, 164–165, 167, 169–171, 176–177, 179, 188, 190–191, 225–227
Marxism, 11, 36, 38, 46, 58–59, 67, 105, 134, 137, 145, 150, 196, 213, 224, 228
Marxist Social Democrats (SPD), 57, 196
Matsuda, Mari, 54
May Day, 67–69
Mayer, Jane, 41
McCarthyism, 5–6, 202
McConnell, Campbell R., 171
McGill, V.J., 74
McLaren, Peter, xv, xviii, 49, 160, 181, 219–228
Mearsheimer, John, 195
Mediocre (Oluo, Ijeoma), 50
Mellaart, James, 144
Melman, Seymour, 82
Meno (Plato), 93, 124
metaReality, 149, 152–156
militarized nature, 67–69
military budget, U.S., 82
Mill, J.S., 50
Mills, C. Wright, 206
Mills, Charles, 164
Miranda, Jose Porfirio, 226
modern materialism, 72–73
money-is-speech U.S. Supreme Court, 23, 38, 205
monoculturalism, 102
monopoly capitalism, 9, 11, 29, 232
Morgan, Lewis Henry, 113–114, 143
Morgenson, Gretchen, 169–170
Mossadegh, 5, 223
Mother Earth, 69–72, 142

Moyn, Samuel, 8, 197
Mũgo, Mîcere Gîthae, 92
Muir, John, 137
myth of nothingness, 75

Nagy, Sandor, 58
National Security Act, 1947, 6
naturalism, 72–74, 76–77, 122, 126, 136, 147–152, 184
nature, history, 134
nature as ally
  commercialized nature, 67–69
  common menace, 83–86
  Dewey, John, 73
  Dialectic of Enlightenment vs. Philosophy for the Future, 74–77
  EarthCommonWealth alternative, 83–86
  Emerson, Ralph Waldo, 69–72
  family and community well-being, 81
  global burning, 142
  political Eros, 77–80
  revolutionary ecological liberation and women's equality, 86–88
  U.S. militarism and U.S.-led global capitalism, 82–83
Negri, Antonio, 103–104
neofascism
  antifa, Charlottesville, 56–58
  destructive tendency, society, 56
  premature anti-fascism, 57
  radical struggle, centrality, 51–52
  repressive desublimation, 56
  Russia, 197
  33 Theses (Marcuse, Herbert), 32
neofascist counterrevolution, imperial America
  interpersonal force, 22
  militarized weaponry, municipal policing, 23
  racial and gender-biased capitalism, 22
  torture and prisoner abuse, U.S. military, 23

neofascist culture wars
  alt-right, 36–38
  counterrevolution, 36–38
  hate crimes, Asian-Americans, 37
  liberal democracies, 36
  politics of resentment, 37
  U.S. military interventions, 37
neoliberal and rentier politics, 177
neoliberal ideology, 39
#NeverAgain gun control movement, 202
New German Mentality, The (Marcuse, Herbert), 33
new sensibility, 181, 190, 203, 214–216
  emancipatory violence, 45
  oppositional philosophy and politics, 43
  oppressive establishment violence, 45
  Orphic Marxism, 46
  police violence, 45
  repressive violence, 45
  state-sponsored violence, 44
  structural violence and injustice, 45
  transvaluation of values, 43
Newton, Huey, 55
New Yorker, The, 41
New York Times, The, 38, 44, 50, 52, 77–78, 161–163, 169, 174–176, 180, 198, 201, 203, 205–206
New York Times' 1619 Project, 1, 36
Nicolaus, Martin, 197
Nietzsche, Friedrich, 129
Nkrumah, Kwame, 94
Noble Prize for Peace, 198
Not a Nation of Immigrants (Dunbar-Ortiz, Roxanne), 2
Nwosu, Patrick U., 92–93, 95
Nyamnjoh, Francis B., 92–93
Nyerere, Julius, 94, 98

Obama, Barack, 8, 198
Ocasio-Cortez, Alexandria, 206
Occupy movement, 39, 203
Odysseus' slave girls, 139

oikonomia, 130
Oluo, Ijeoma, 50–51, 188, 206
One-Dimensional Man (Marcuse, Herbert), 16, 35, 38, 47, 71, 75, 80, 98, 119, 149–150, 160, 185
On the Philosophical Foundation of the Concept of Labor in Economics (Marcuse), 115
ontology of labor, 117–118, 227
Original Affluent Society, The, 145
  arts of livelihood, 115
  humanity, tool-making animal, 119
  labor and leisure, 116–119
  partnership customs and behaviors, 120
  stone age economics, 115
Origin and Goal of History, The (Jaspers, Karl), 99
Origin of the Family, Private Property and the State (Engels, Friedrich), 113, 146
Orphic Marxism, 46
over-appropriation crisis. *See* capital valorization crisis
Overstory, The (Powers, Richard), 133

Pachamama Alliance, 209
Palmer Raids, (1919), 196
Pané, Ramón, 3
Parenti, Michael, 119, 206
Paris Lectures (Marcuse, Herbert), 12, 25, 35, 67, 192, 201
Paris Manuscripts of 1844 (Marx, Karl), 190–191
partnership cultures, 122, 189, 214
patriarchy, 2, 180, 213–214, 217, 229
peace, challenged by exploitation and racism
  anti-war messages stigmatized, 195
  conflict, neofascism and socialism, 196
  Internationalist Manifesto Against the War, 199
  legitimation crisis, 197
  NATO build-up, 195
  nuclear weapons, 199

Russia war against Ukraine, 195
SPD, 196
suicide rate, soldiers, 198
Ukraine war, 198–199
Pedagogy and Praxis in the Age of Empire (Jaramillo and McLaren), 220
Pedagogy of Insurrection (McLaren, Peter), 220–221
pedagogy of revolution and revolutionary multiculturalism, 219
Pentagon Capitalism (Melman, Seymour), 82
Permanent War Economy (Melman, Seymour), 82
Phenomenology (Hegel), 101
Philipps, Dave, 198
philosophical anarchism, 59, 147
Philosophie Magazin, 199
Philosophy and Phenomenological Research, journal, 73
Philosophy for the Future: The Quest of Modern Materialism, 74
Piketty, Thomas, 10, 163, 171
planetary *comunalidad*, 222
Plato, xvii, 40, 59, 69, 93, 97, 100, 102, 106, 123–125
Plumer, Brad, 209
police state
    Battle of Seattle, 39
    Black Bloc, 39
    BLM movement, 39
    economic inequalities, 42
    justice, stronger parties, 40
    neoliberal ideology, 39
    Occupy movement, 39
    racial justice, 41
    racism, in higher education, 40
    systematic police brutality, 39
political correctness, 36, 50
political Eros
    business priorities, social affairs, 77
    corporate globalization, 77
    Covid-19 crisis, 79
    lower-wage labor force, society, 79
    militarized white supremacist kill squads, 78
    sensuous living labor, 80
polluted nature, 67–68
Possibility of Naturalism, The (Bhaskar, Roy), 136, 151
Powell, Colin, 195
Powers, Richard, 133
Preamble to the Constitution of Ecuador, 2008, 71
predatory culture, 160
predatory finance, 160
promesse du bonheur commun
    commonwealth past and promise, 188–193
    communal gratification, 186
    Eros and beauty, 184
    erotic and political interconnection, 184
    sensual love, 184
    Stendhal syndrome, 185
    surplus repression, 186
    transvaluation of values, 187
Prometheus/Persephone progeny, 214–217
Pullman Strike of 1894, 195

racial entitlement, 41
racial segregation, *Plessy v. Ferguson*, 4
radical humanism
    egalitarian intercultural cohabitation, Earth, 48
    empathy, 49
    existentialism, 47
    identity politics, 48
    needy and caring view, human nature, 48
    racist scapegoating, 50
    white masculine superiority, 51
radical revolution of values, 187
radical struggle, centrality, 51–52
Raleigh, Walter, 3
Rand, Ayn, 129
Ratzinger, Joseph Cardinal, 225–226
Rawls, John, 163–164
Reagan, Ronald, 7, 36–37, 195
real estate development trusts (REITs), 175
Realist Theory of Science, A (Bhaskar, Roy), 151

Reality and Its Depths (Bhaskar and Savita), 149, 151
Real Wealth of Nations, The (Eisler, Riane), 214
Reason and Revolution (Marcuse, Herbert), 38, 116
Red Alert!: Saving the Planet with Indigenous Knowledge (Wildcat, Daniel R.), 71, 141
Rehnquist, William, 41
rehumanization, 103, 166, 181
Reich, Wilhelm, 32
Reign of Terror, A, 7, 38
REITs. *See* real estate development trusts (REITs)
relativism, 48, 96, 149
religion
    Black prophetic tradition, 228
    Catholicism, 224
    Common moral ground, 99–103, 204, 229
    commonwealth labor, 227
    God existence, 226
    Great Refusal, 227
    Habermas's thesis, 225
    humanism Kant, 227
    liberation theology, 224–226
    post-secular cognitive dispositions, 225
    rebellion, 227
Renaissance of Herbert Marcuse: A Study on Present Interest in Marcuse's Interdisciplinary Critical Theory (Visic, Maroji), 15
Rentiers' Regime, The, 176
repressive desublimation, 56, 224
Repressive Tolerance (Marcuse, Herbert), 16, 18–19, 21, 51–53, 228
repressive violence, 45
Republic (Plato), 97, 123–124
Restoration of Capitalism in the USSR (Nicolaus, Martin), 197
revolution and revolutionary multiculturalism, pedagogy, 219
revolutionary ecological liberation, 26, 60, 67–68, 86–88, 208, 224
    empowered progeny, Persephone, 215
    indigenous realism, 216
    new sensibility, 214–216
    Prometheus, 214–217
    technology, value, 217
    women's movement, 214–215
Rifkin, Jeremy, 48–49
Riis, Jacob, 2
Rise of Neoliberal Philosophy, The (Absher, Brandon), 75
Robinson, William I., 9, 23
Romero, Oscar, 7
Roosevelt, Teddy, 4–5
Rousseau, 59, 69–70, 126, 145–146
Roy, Arundhati, 198
Rudolph, Moritz, 199
Ruschig, Ulrich, 17, 159–160, 202
Russell, Bertrand, 127, 199

Sacco, Joe, 78
Saez, Emmanuel, 163
Sahlins, Marshall, 115, 120, 145, 147
Sanders, Bernie, 83, 203, 206, 230
Sandy Hook Elementary massacre, 223
Sartre, Jean-Paul, 47, 75
Sayers, Sean, 47, 73, 75
Scalia, Antonin, 23, 36, 40–41
Scharfstein, David, 169
Schiller, xvi, 26, 70, 190
Schwerner, Michael, 45
science and technology, 75, 88
Seal, Bobby, 55
Segbifia, Michael, 95
Sekyi-Otu, Ato, 96–99
Sen, 6
Senghor, Leopold, 94, 98
sensuous living labor, 49, 80, 87–88, 99, 103–104, 106, 110, 116–117, 120–121, 154, 166, 177–178, 181, 188–189, 214, 229
    authentic freedom, 178
    being human, 154
    and EarthCommonWealth, 27–29
    promesse du boneur commun, 106

Sethness Castro, Javier, 16, 46, 53, 58–59
Shook, John R., 76
Siddhartha, Gotama, 126
Simmons, Michael L. Jr., 73, 75, 136
Singh, Savita, 148–152, 154
Sleeter, Christine, 54
Smith, Adam, 28, 112, 164–166, 169
Smith, David N., 75
socialism, 8, 82
    decommodification of production, 25
    EarthCommonWealth Counteroffensive, 26
    emancipatory universalization, resistance, 25
    human labor, 26
    minimum standards, 25
    system negation, 25
social science, public education, 72
Socrates, 100, 123–124, 126–127
Soledad Brothers, 55
Sorgestruktur (Heidegger), 110
Souillac, Geneviève, 121, 144–145, 147
Soviet Marxism (Marcuse, Herbert), 196
Spartan, Stephen, 19, 159–182
Spirit and Structure of German Fascism (Brady, Robert), 32
Standing Rock Sioux, 140, 219
Stefancic, Jean, 54
Stendhal syndrome, 185
Stern, Bernard, 74
Stiglitz, Joseph E., 163, 169, 176
Stirner, Max, 129
Stone, Oliver, 4–6, 9, 23
Stone Age Economics (Sahlins, Marshall), 115
Struik, Dirk, 74
subprime mortgages, 175
subverting forces, 204, 209
Sunrise Movement, 78, 209
SuperImperialism: The Economic Strategy of American Empire (Hudson, Michael), 8
Surak, Sarah, 15
surplus consciousness, 119

Taíno of Haiti, 3
Tauber, Zvi, 119
9-11 terror attacks, 7
Terror War, 7, 15, 23, 38, 228
Thales, 100, 137
Thanatos, death instinct, 184
33 Theses (Marcuse, Herbert), 32, 53
Thomas, Clarence, 41, 205
Thoreau, Henry David, 137
Thoughts on the Defense of Gracchus Babeuf (Marcuse, Herbert), 58
Thunberg, Greta, 78, 202
Time for Socialism (Piketty, Thomas), 10
tolerance complicity, 52–53
transnational transformation, 213
Truman, 5
Trump, Donald, 1–2, 8, 15, 21–22, 33, 36–37, 40–41, 44, 53, 78–79, 81, 83, 202–203, 206, 211
Truth, Sojourner, 228
Turse, Nick, 208

Über allen Gipfeln ist Ruh (Goethe), 68
ubuntu, 85, 92–93, 98, 106, 122, 177, 189, 205
U.N. Climate Change Conference of the Parties, 26th annual (COP26), 209
undocumented immigrants, 78
United Front Against Fascism, 55, 192
Unite the Right demonstration, 56
universal cosmopolitan state, 128
universal humanism
    African cultures, 122–123
    China, 122
    Daoism, 122
    reciprocity, 122
University of Buffalo, 72, 136
University of Lagos, 93, 122
University of Wisconsin, 137
Untold History of the United States (Kuznick, Peter), 4
UN Universal Declaration, 128
U.S. militarism and U.S.-led global capitalism

annual military spending, 83
arms trade, 82
capitalism, wasted abundance, 82
military budget, 82
wasteful war production, 83
U.S. world order and global capitalism, decline of
American empire, 8–11
American Pageant mythology, 2–3
20th century, 5–8
historical record, 1
immigrants, 2
imperial America, 3–5
self-righteous global power, 1
waste and destruction, 11–12
U.S.A. Patriot Act, 38–39
utu, 92–93

Veblen, Thorstein, 81
vernacular Kantianism, 96
Vietnam War, 6, 34, 187, 198, 204, 210
Vincennes University, Paris, 11, 35, 67
Vine, David, 9, 23
Visic, Maroji, 15
Volpe, John Della, 202
von Lasaux, Ernst, 100
von Strauss, Viktor, 100
Voter Rights Act, 41

Wages of Rebellion (Hedges, Chris), 228
Washington Post, The, 36, 38, 65, 162
wasted abundance, xvii, 17, 27, 47, 68, 81–82, 84, 211

wealth accumulation and workforce remuneration, 164–166
Weatherford, Jack, 143
welfare/warfare economy, 8
Wengrow, David, 4, 143, 145–147, 208
West, Cornel, 57, 224, 227–228
Whitehead, 75
Who Rules the Universities (Smith, David N.), 75
Wildcat, Daniel R., 71, 76, 141–142, 155, 203–204, 208, 216, 223
Wilson, John K., 54
Winter, Rainer, 23
Wiredu, Kwasi, 93, 122
Wittgenstein, 75, 104
Wohlleben, Peter, 133, 239
Wolfe, Timothy, 221
Wolff, Edward N., 162
women's equality, 15, 25, 60, 86–88, 98, 105
Women's March, 2016, 203
Woolfson, Charles, 27, 111–112, 120, 146
Wyandot, 4, 143–144

Yeltsin, Boris, 197
Yosimbom, Hassan M., 92–93
Yu, Pauline, 103

Zinn, Howard, 1, 3
zoon politikon, 126, 149, 177
Zulu principle, ubuntu, 92

Related Titles from Daraja Press

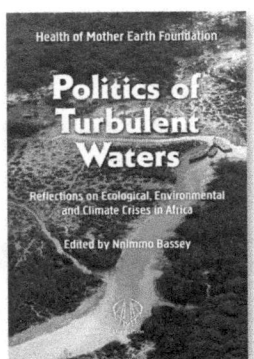

Politics of Turbulent Waters
Edited by Nnimmo Bassey
ISBN 9781990263750

Homestead, Homeland, Home: Critical Reflections
Ato Sekyi-Otu
ISBN 9781990263545

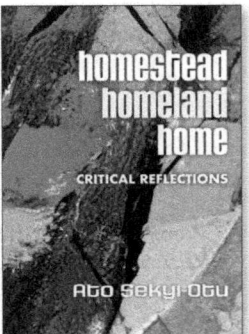

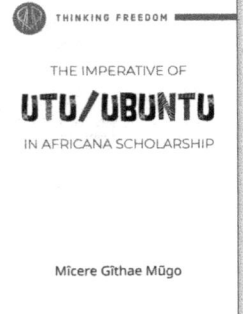

The imperative of UTU/UBUNTU in Africana scholarship
Mĩcere Gĩthae Mũgo
ISBN 9781990263248

Abolitionist Agroecology
Maywa Montenegro de Wit
ISBN 9781990263040

Moving Beyond Capitalist Agriculture
Pandemic Research for the People
ISBN 978-988832975

Order from **darajapress.com** or **zandpress.com**

www.ingramcontent.com/pod-product-compliance
Lightning Source LLC
Chambersburg PA
CBHW060833190426
43197CB00039B/2574